Acts of Interpretation

E. TALBOT DONALDSON

Photograph by Aneta Sperber

Acts of Interpretation

THE TEXT IN ITS CONTEXTS

700–1600

ESSAYS ON

MEDIEVAL AND RENAISSANCE LITERATURE

IN HONOR OF

E. TALBOT DONALDSON

EDITED BY

Mary J. Carruthers

AND

Elizabeth D. Kirk

PILGRIM BOOKS   NORMAN, OKLAHOMA

Copyright © 1982 by Pilgrim Books,
P.O. Box 2399, Norman, Oklahoma 73070

Library of Congress Cataloging in Publication Data

Main entry under title:

Acts of interpretation.

   Includes index.
   1. English literature – Middle English, 1100–1500 – History and
criticism – Addresses, essays, lectures.   2. English literature – Early
modern, 1500–1700 – History and criticism – Addresses, essays, lectures.   3. Donaldson, Ethelbert Talbot.
I. Donaldson, Ethelbert Talbot.   II. Carruthers, Mary.
III. Kirk, Elizabeth D.
PR251.A3 1982   820′.9   82-13148
ISBN: 0-937644-60-X

Contents

CONTENTS

Preface

"As Myn Auctour Seyde, So Seye I"

OME YEARS AGO, E. Talbot Donaldson articulated his own critical creed, with that characteristic humor and wit which he has surely learned from his favorite poet. Likening critical faculties to well-trained dogs, he wrote, "In order to read well one has to put oneself into the impossible position of having all one's wits and faculties about one, ready to spring into activity at the first summons; yet, like hunting dogs, they must not spring before they are summoned; and only those summoned must spring; and the summons must come from the poem."

The essays in this volume display a wide range of interests and methods. It may appear paradoxical to assert that they also have a common point of departure, yet all do: the emphasis on reading the text as the impetus and goal of literary scholarship, which E. Talbot Donaldson has embodied for us, whether as teacher, editor, critic, or colleague. His career has spanned a period of tremendous growth in medieval studies, defined (though never by him) through most of his professional life as leading in two antithetical directions. One, engendered by the New Criticism, emphasized close reading of the text itself; the other, calling itself Historical, placed a radical emphasis upon social and intellectual contexts of the period. E. Talbot Donaldson's particular genius for reading what his authors wrote sometimes looked like an instinct unrelated to historical discipline, but it depended upon an encyclopedic knowledge of the period and the language, matched with unwavering respect for the text itself. In all that he has written or said, his knowledge has enriched rather than replaced his sympathy for the text. Donaldson has worn his immense learning with ease and wit; he is the only practicing medievalist capable of writing comfortably essays without footnotes. His manner expresses his own profound conviction that the task of the critic and scholar is to illuminate the text and that understanding context is a means to interpretation, not its graveyard. "'Humankind,'" he has written, quoting T. S. Eliot, "'cannot bear very much reality,' and I believe that great poetic art offers something very close to an ultimate reality."

These essays are offered by E. Talbot Donaldson's students and colleagues as an expression of our own realization, as we have turned to the diverse areas of scholarly expertise embodied in the organization of this volume, that central to our endeavors has been the insistence he has so gracefully articulated that whatever we do must start and end with the text in front of us. None of these essays treats such activities as source study, philology, editing, and historical investigation as invitations to "salubrious vacations from the awful business of facing a poem directly." They also express our belief in practice that the fashionable polarization which developed between reading the text and studying its surroundings was ultimately false, though it continues to produce a searching debate. The critic must finally say with Chaucer, "As myn auctour seyde, so seye I," a simple statement of a great complexity which captures the essence of the Donaldsonian method.

The editors would like to express their particular thanks to the members of our editorial board, who have labored with us during every stage of this volume: John Pope, Robert Hanning, and Alice Miskimin. We also want to thank Marie Borroff, Alfred David, and George Kane for their help at crucial stages of this project; Aneta Sperber, who made the photograph which appears as the frontispiece; and all those who contributed material for "Speaking of Donaldson." We are saddened by the death of Elizabeth Salter and grateful to Derek Pearsall for help in preparation of her manuscript for press. We thank Paul Strohm, Chair of the Department of English, and especially Kenneth R. R. Gros Louis, Vice-President of Indiana University, Bloomington, for the enthusiastic encouragement they have given to this volume to honor one of their university's Distinguished Professors. For making its appearance possible, we are most grateful to Paul Ruggiers, and a number of supporters whose names appear in our *tabula gratulatoria*, including the English Graduate Union of Columbia University; the

Master and Fellows of Saybrook College of Yale University; and the particularly generous support of Indiana University.

MARY J. CARRUTHERS
ELIZABETH D. KIRK

Holderness, New Hampshire
September 3, 1981

Acts of Interpretation

Part One THE PROBLEM OF INTERPRETATION

Sir Gawain and the Red Herring:
The Perils of Interpretation[1]

ROBERT W. HANNING
Columbia University

"Inference and Guesswork: What else is interpretation?"
I. A. Richards, *The Philosophy of Rhetoric*

ESPITE THE CONSIDERABLE ATTENTION lavished on *Sir Gawain and the Green Knight* by its present-day scholarly admirers, it continues to resist satisfactory, comprehensive interpretation of its hero and his adventures. This essay seeks to explain this recalcitrancy as in good part the result of a paradox at the poem's center: *Sir Gawain* argues that we can understand human experience only in the context of civilization's processes and values yet demonstrates that civilization chronically disguises the significance of its most characteristic manifestations, thereby eluding precise evaluation of its meaning and worth. As a result of this paradox the difficulty, or perhaps impossibility, of interpretation becomes not only a hallmark but a main theme of the poem.

To document in detail how *Sir Gawain* involves both its characters and its audience in the perils of interpretation would require far more space than is here available. In these brief remarks, offered as a token of admiration for the shrewd interpreter of complex texts whom this volume honors, I will confine myself to examining some instances of the poem's justly famous descriptive art, chosen because they represent for

[1] This essay forms part of a longer study devoted to the theme of interpretation in *Sir Gawain*. My ideas about the poem have taken shape in the course of teaching it to undergraduate and graduate students at Columbia University since 1962. I acknowledge with pleasure a debt to many more scholars than those mentioned in the following notes, and to present and former students who have explored the poem with me, including Vicki Armet, Joyce Leana, Linda Georgianna, Robert Stein, John Thoms, Arnold Graber, and Chuck Henry. Sandra Pierson Prior read an earlier version of the essay and made astute suggestions for improving it.

the poet a readily accessible yet symbolically charged aspect of civiliza-tion: its penchant for *decoration*. By decoration I intend the embellish-ment of almost any human activity or artifact so as to render it aesthet-ically pleasing. Society's decorative impulse wholly or partly conceals primary levels of experience or meaning beneath an artfully applied sur-face, be it of paint, rhetoric, game, or ritual. The effect of decoration is frequently to leave undefined, or to obscure, the relationship between the ornamental surface and the underlying "raw material" it embel-lishes. If we are to understand the function of decoration as an attri-bute of civilization, we must therefore attempt to analyze, not simply enjoy, its effect: attempt, that is, to decide whether it improves, disguises, complicates, or subverts the reality that lies beneath it. In short, we must interpret.

Yet the very ambiguity that invites, nay requires, interpretation of the civilized processes of embellishment contrives to thwart interpreta-tion. Our frustration as would-be exegetes of *Sir Gawain*'s highly decorated images epitomizes our difficulties with the poem as a whole, just as the images epitomize the poet's comprehensive vision of the am-biguities inherent in the civilization—at once courtly, Christian, chival-ric, and heroic—that his verse depicts. And in our frustration we are also thrown into affective contact with Gawain himself, whose experi-ence of living in this world, like ours of reading about it, embodies both the necessity and the perils of interpretation.

Several major descriptive passages in the first two fits of *Sir Gawain* explore the relationship between civilization and individual endeavor from various points of view, thereby setting the stage for the crucial events of the last two fits, in which Gawain incorrectly interprets the relative importance, danger, and above all the interconnectedness of the trials he must undergo amid the comforts of civilization (his bed-chamber in Bertilak's castle) and the wilds of nature (the Green Chapel). Each of the ecphrases I have chosen to examine serves as a focus for issues raised in the surrounding narrative context. The first— the description of Bertilak's castle (lines 763–802)[2]—offers initially an

---

[2] All references to and quotations from *Sir Gawain* in this essay utilize the edition by J. R. R. Tolkien and E. V. Gordon (Oxford, 1925; reprint, 1955). The description of Bertilak's castle has been discussed insightfully by Alain Renoir, "The Progressive Magnification: An Instance of

external, almost visionary perspective on civilization, born of needs that arise when the protagonist finds himself in temporary isolation outside its physical and spiritual structures. Gawain's vividly depicted deprivation in the wilderness prompts our preliminary, wholly positive response to the distant prospect of Bertilak's castle; however, as the description unfolds, its image of civilization becomes increasingly complicated, and our interpretive certainty clouded with ambiguity.

It is Christmas Eve, and Gawain, who has endured a lonely, embattled existence far from the haunts of mankind since leaving Arthur's court on All Souls' Day, deeply feels the need to arrive at an outpost of civilization, "sum herber ther heȝly [he] myȝt here masse" (line 755) in celebration of "that syre, that on that self nyȝt / Of a burde watȝ borne oure baret to quelle" (lines 751–52). We, the audience, have a lively sense of other, more worldly comforts society could offer at this point, with the haunting image still fresh in our minds of Gawain, half dead with the cold, attempting to sleep in his armor while high over his head a falling stream turns to icicles.[3] The superb evocation of Gawain's sorry physical and spiritual circumstances—he cries for his sins as much as for the cruel weather[4]—endows his first glimpse of the far-off castle with the force of a salvific revelation, a beatific vision (lines 763–72):

Psychological Description in *Sir Gawain and the Green Knight*," *MSpr* 54 (1960):249–50. In all my discussions of descriptive technique I have also profited from Marie Borroff, *Sir Gawain and the Green Knight: A Stylistic and Metrical Study* (New Haven, 1962), especially chap. 4, "The Criticism of Style"; and Larry Benson, *Art and Tradition in Sir Gawain and the Green Knight* (New Brunswick, N.J., 1965), chap. 4, "Narrative and Descriptive Techniques." See also W. A. Davenport, *The Art of the Gawain-Poet* (London, 1978), pp. 149–50, on the effect of the castle description and its resemblance to ecphrases in other medieval works.

[3] See Renoir, "Progressive Magnification," p. 248, on this striking passage. The text reads: "Ner slayn wyth the slete he sleped in his yrnes / Mo nyȝteȝ then innoghe in naked rokkeȝ, / Ther as claterande fro the crest the colde borne renneȝ, / And henged heȝe ouer his hede in hard iisse-ikkles" (lines 729–32). Of special note is the way the last word of line 732 stops the motion of the line abruptly, even as the cold freezes fast the falling drops of water over the knight's head. The image of Gawain asleep in his "yrnes" anticipates and contrasts with his being "happed" in the enfolding comforts of society at Bertilak's castle, while the suspended animation of the falling water constitutes a prolepsis of the Green Knight's ax descending on the knight's neck, yet twice stopping short, at the Green Chapel in fit 4.

[4] See lines 759–62: "He rode in his prayere, / And cryed for his mysdede, / He sayned hym in sythes sere, / And sayde 'Cros Kryst me spede!'" On the implications of this passage for our interpretation of the pentangle Gawain wears on his shield, see below.

Nade he sayned hymself, segge, bot thrye,
Er he watȝ war in the wod of a won in a mote,
Abof a launde, on a lawe, loken under boȝeȝ. . .
A castel the comlokest that euer knyȝt aȝte, . . .
As hit schemered and schon thurȝ the schyre okeȝ.

The impression that the castle has been conjured up by the force of
Gawain's need and faith is bolstered by the text's quibble on its location, "pyched on a *prayere*" (line 768; meadow/prayer; emphasis mine).

As Gawain rides closer, the castle's emblematic force modulates from
civilization-as-vision to society-as-fortress (lines 781–84):

The bryge watȝ breme upbrayde,
The ȝateȝ were stoken faste,
The walleȝ were wel arayed,
Hit dut no wyndeȝ blaste.

The walls, well made of "harde hewen ston," reach deep into the moat
and up to a "ful huge heȝt" (lines 788–89); they, and the raised draw-
bridge, are Gawain's protective "yrens" (line 729) reproduced on a
larger, more effective scale.

Having depicted the castle as the architectural embodiment first of
Christian desire, then of heroic determination, the description now
takes a final, problematic turn. The upper stories, in keeping with late-
medieval castle design, are so highly decorated that the whole structure once again loses its substantiality, not, however, by reverting to
its status as a shimmering, beckoning quasi-mirage but rather by denying its previously ascertained solidity and masquerading instead as a
mere ornament, or mock castle (lines 795–802):

Towres telded bytwene, trochet ful thik,
Fayre fylyoleȝ that fyȝed, and ferlyly long,
With coruon coprounes craftyly sleȝe.
Chalkwhyt chymnees ther ches he innoȝe
Vpon bastel roueȝ, that blenked ful quyte;
So mony pynakle payntet watȝ poudred ayquere,
Among the castel carneleȝ clambred so thik,
That pared out of papure purely hit semed.[5]

---

[5] Edward Wilson, *The Gawain-Poet* (Leiden, 1976), p. 123, says of this passage: "The very
visibilia of the court support the impression of an exaggerated love of courtly 'sleȝtez.'" He antici-

The phrase used by the poet to characterize this embellishment of hard, unyielding stone, against its very nature—"craftyly sleȝe" (line 797), which might well be rendered "artfully artful"—can stand as a definition of the decorative impulse underlying (or, in this case, literally crowning) the admirable works of civilization. But how are we to reconcile such an impulse with the imperatives of a heroic code? Put iconographically, how are we to interpret the discrepancy between the emblems—civilization as fortress, civilization as deceptive *objet d'art*—embodied respectively in the lower and upper parts of the same castle? Do the *fylyoleȝ*, *coprouneȝ*, *pynakleȝ*, and *carneleȝ* above represent a subversion and diminution of the strength below; that is, are they signs of decadence and warnings of deceits that lie within the castle walls?[6] Or are they a strategic disguising of fortitude beneath the mask of airy gracefulness? The embellishment of bare stone by cultivated art may represent the real triumph of civilization, its ability to transform the world it finds in nature by the *sleȝe* application of imagination and ingenuity. But its *trompe l'oeil* insubstantiality may also constitute a parody or trivialization of Gawain's intensely idealistic vision of civilization as a "herber" for the Christian knight, a nurturing haven that restores contact between struggling humanity and redemptive divinity.

In short, the threefold, serial description of Bertilak's castle, a poetic triumph in its own right, serves to focus our attention on the many perspectives civilization offers to an outside observer. But the unmediated juxtaposition of the perspectives introduces the problem of interpretation into the description without offering grounds for a solution. The castle's decorative component focuses our interpretive difficulties, for its refined aesthetic appeal is much more resistant to straightforward positive or negative evaluation than are the unequivocally spiritual or heroic sentiments evoked by the other segments of the

pates my attention to the castle's artfulness of decoration but interprets it differently (see note 6 below). The castle's appearance of being cut out of paper connects the description with the decorative "sotelety," or paper ornaments, that embellish the food served at Belshazzar's feast in *Cleanness*, lines 1407–1408. See the notes to both passages in Malcolm Andrew and Ronald Waldron, eds., *The Poems of the Pearl Manuscript* (Berkeley, Calif., 1979), pp. 168, 238.

6 Wilson, *The Gawain-Poet*, pp. 122–24, passes a negative judgment on the "sleȝe" aspects of Bertilak's court, as revealed in this passage and in others discussed below. In so doing, I believe he disregards the ambiguities carefully built into these and so many other segments of the text and thus misinterprets the poem in interpreting it too definitively.

description. Further reflection reveals that this problem of evaluating a decorated structure underlies the ambiguous relationship, throughout the early part of *Sir Gawain*, between courtly civilization, with its artful strategies of language and behavior, and other, less-embellished modes of action.

Several descriptive passages antecedent to Bertilak's castle highlight this same interpretive dilemma but place it within a context of Britain's heroic past and Arthurian present. The first twenty-four lines of the poem establish the heroic rhythms of British history after the founding of the nation by Felix Brutus, a vassal of Aeneas (lines 21–22):

> Bolde bredden therinne, baret that lofden,
> In mony turned tyme tene that wroȝten.

Then, at line 25, with the introduction of Arthur, a new atmosphere enters the young tale (lines 25–26):

> Bot of alle that here bult of Bretaygne kynges
> Ay watȝ Arthur the hendest, as I haf herde telle.

The word "hendest," used to describe Arthur, belongs to a courtly rather than a heroic vocabulary. In addition, as soon as Arthur is the subject, the narrator makes his own presence felt as an intermediary between audience and matter and proceeds to emphasize that he is recounting a story he has heard "in toun" (lines 30–32):

> If ȝe wyl lysten this laye bot on littel quile,
> I schal telle hit astit, as I in toun herde, with tonge....

The objective narrative tone of the first twenty-five lines, appropriate to epics and history, gives way to a more subjective, conversational style common to romances from the twelfth century onward, with a narrator who reminds us that we are hearing a traditional story of an "outtrage awenture of Arthures wondereȝ" (line 29) – by implication, an old but not necessarily a veracious account.

The shifting of narrative tone and vocabulary after twenty-four lines prepares us for the poem's central theme of transformation by embellishment. The poet, through his narrator, shows us history – for so the Brutus legend was still widely regarded in his day – turning into literature, that is, into expression still governed by traditional forms, but more hospitable to the decorative use of imagination in its portrayal of adventures. A cognate image for the change within Arthur's court is the Christmas game, which transforms the "baret" of old into nonlethal conflicts where, though there are losers and winners, no one seems really to be hurt (lines 69–70):

> Ladies laȝed ful loude, thoȝ thay lost haden,
> And he that wan watȝ not wrothe, that may ȝe wel trawe.

The "blysse and blunder" (line 18) which the first stanza of the poem tells us alternated throughout the heroic past has now been metamorphosed into contests marked only by "blysse."

The poet's depiction of Arthur's court repeatedly reminds us that civilization is above all a process of additive decoration and embellishment: the dinner table groans under the dishes piled upon it (lines 121–29); Guinevere, at the center of the dais, is so surrounded and decked out with fine fabrics and jewels that she seems transformed from a person into an elegant courtly artifact (lines 74–78):

> ..Guenore, ful gay, graythed in the myddes,
> Dressed on the dere des, dubbed al aboute,
> Smal sendal bisides, a selure hir ouer
> Of tryed tolouse, of tars tapites innoghe,
> That were enbrawded and beten wyth the best gemmes....

The contrast between this world and the Britain of the first stanzas seems fundamental: instead of heroes, fighting on through generations of "turned tyme," we see at Camelot a new, young civilization—a "fayre folk in her first age"—with a king who is "childgered" (lines 54, 86, 87–89):

> His lif liked hym lyȝt, he louied the lasse
> Auther to longe lye or to longe sytte,
> So bisied him his ȝonge blod and his brayne wylde.

The poem carefully refrains from passing unequivocal judgment on Arthur's restlessness, just as it avoids overtly characterizing the youthful exuberance and game playing of the court as the product of either idealism, thoughtless inexperience, or morally dubious escapism. Certainly, in the world over which Arthur and his richly ornamented queen preside, aesthetic norms have attained parity with, if not supremacy over, heroic ones: the king's vow not to eat before hearing a marvel (lines 90–99) can be equally satisfied by a real (that is, dangerous) adventure or by a story about one, while the difference between winning and losing, so crucial on a battlefield, is effaced by the court's elegant laughter at its own domesticated conflict, the Christmas game. Whether this Arthurian modification of traditional British values constitutes the triumph or failure of civilization is a question the text prompts us to ask but prevents us from answering.[7]

Before the Green Knight bursts in on Camelot's New Year's feast, the issues which we have seen raised in the ambiguous description of Bertilak's castle are already present in the poem, though not focused as sharply within a single ecphrasis. We see the castle, with Gawain, from outside and from a position of need, whereas we experience Arthur's court from within, at a moment of social harmony and fulfillment. The entrance of the Green Knight unexpectedly sets up a contrast between a single intruder and the world on which he intrudes. The disruptive, threatening appearance of the newcomer promises an adversary relationship between him and the court and seems to set the stage for a clarification of our ambivalent feelings about the latter. Ultimately, however, the Green Knight, despite his apparent function as a touchstone with which to judge Arthurian civilization, creates as many interpretive puzzles as he solves.

He arrives explosively (lines 134–37):

> For unethe wat3...the fyrst cource in the court kyndely serued,
> Ther hales in at the halle dor an aghlich mayster,
> On the most on the molde on mesure hyghe....

The intrusion of this great creature on the court's celebration inevitably reminds the modern reader familiar with medieval literature of Grendel's equally unexpected, death-dealing entrance into Heorot in

---

[7] See John M. Ganim, "Disorientation, Style, and Consciousness in *Sir Gawain and the Green Knight*," *PMLA* 91 (1976):378–80, for an excellent discussion of the change of tone in the poem after line 24 and of our uncertain reaction to Arthur's court. Cf. Davenport's nuanced reading of the court, *The Art of the Gawain-Poet*, pp. 145–46, and the more judgmental positions taken by Benson, *Art and Tradition*, pp. 214–18, and (opposed to Benson's) by J. A. Burrow, *A Reading of Sir Gawain and the Green Knight* (New York, 1966), pp. 4–10. Wilson's brief comment, *The Gawain-Poet*, p. 118, suggests that his view of the ambiguities inherent in the poet's presentation of Arthur and Camelot is close to my own.

Beowulf. We may safely assume an analogous response by the poem's original audience, especially on discovering that the inviting guest is "oueral enker-grene" (line 150). Yet even here certainty of response is undercut by a rather awkward narratorial attempt to evaluate the Green Knight that serves only to highlight the difficulties attendant upon all efforts at interpretation in this poem (lines 139–41):

> And hys lyndes and hys lymes so longe and so grete,
> Half etayn in erde I hope that he were,
> Bot mon most I algate mynn hym to bene.

A more convincing representation of essential uncertainty in the face of a strange phenomenon one could not ask.

As the description of the Green Knight unfolds, ambiguities multiply in direct proportion to the increasing element of decoration. The visitor is "the myriest" man "that my3t ride" (line 142); his upper body is "sturne," yet "his wombe and his wast were worthily smale" (line 144), an attribute more appropriate for a courtier than for a monster.[8] He and his clothes are green, a color suggestive of nature, and perhaps of the devil, but the clothes are elegant and rich, full of decoration congenial to Arthur's world, however alien he who wears them. The green of the apparel, moreover, is everywhere entwined with gems and above all with gold: "gay gaudi of grene, the golde ay inmyddes" (line 167). In other words, if the Green Knight's basic appearance invites us (as I believe it does) to interpret him as a nature figure—a vital, amoral force invading the artificial court world to challenge its innocence of raw, untrammeled reality—subsequent details steadily undermine this neat opposition of nature versus civilization and complicate our interpretation. For example, the Green Knight's clothes are "enbrauded abof, wyth bryddes and fly3es" (line 166). Are artful pictures of birds and butterflies emblems of nature, or of the imitative, decorative art of civilization that remakes nature in its own image? The golden spurs, enameled bridle trappings, and intricate embellishment of the horse's

---

[8] The best discussion of the Green Knight's appearance, and of his participation in divergent traditions that complicate our judgment of him, is Benson's, in *Art and Tradition*, pp. 58–59. Note how even the phrase "aghlich mayster" (line 136) disorients us: the adjective would seem to require as its noun "monstre," not the nonaversive "mayster"; as it stands, the phrase pulls us toward opposite assessments with equal force, creating critical ambivalence.

mane add to our uncertainty; describing the latter, the poem speaks of (lines 187–90):

> The mane of that mayn hors...
> Wel cresped and cemmed, wyth knottes ful mony
> Folden in wyth fildore aboute the fayre grene,
> Ay a herle of the here, an other of golde....

We have here not simply the embellishment of nature but an inter-twining of the natural and the artful so thorough as to be inseparable. In summing up the appearance of horse and rider, the narrator, as con-fused as we are, marvels that they have such a color (lines 235–36):

> As growe grene as the gres and grener hit semed,
> Then grene aumayl on golde glowande bry3ter.

Is this not, *mutatis mutandis*, exactly the impression Bertilak's castle makes on us with its intertwining of elements of strength ("hard hewen walls") and decoration ("pynnacles...pared out of papure")? Is the Green Knight elementally opposed to Arthur's court, or, despite his uncourtly behavior, is he an emblem of its own dialectic of inter-twined, opposing components: of nature shaped into civilized forms, like the Green Knight's long green hair, which has been artfully cut so that it falls about his torso like "a kynges capados" (line 186)?

The Green Knight's sudden appearance forces the court, like the nar-rator and his audience, into an interpretive posture, and its response to the intruder becomes in turn the subject of further evaluation by the narrator. "Vch mon had meruayle," the narrator tells us, at this turn of events; they had seen strange sights, but never one like this one, "forthi for fantoum and fayry3e the folk there hit demed" (lines 233, 240; the narrator himself, we recall, had tentatively reached the con-trary conclusion that the Green Knight is human). After accusing the court of being afraid ("ar3e," line 241) to answer the newcomer's re-quest to speak with the man in charge at Camelot, the narrator quickly retreats into uncertainty (lines 246–47):

> I deme it not al for doute,
> But sum for cortaysye.

Both courtiers and narrator can only "deme"; no certainty is allowed them on which to base an interpretation.

The Green Knight's challenge to the distinctively Arthurian version of civilization and the court's response to him keep the theme of uncertain judgment before us. When he describes as a "Christmas gomen" his desire to trade axe strokes with a member of the court (lines 283–300), we cannot but regard as highly dubious this ludic embellishment of apparently homicidal activity. On the other hand, when unanimous reticence greets his proposal, we share the visitor's skepticism about the "renoun" of Arthur's company of knights, and with him wonder to what extent the court's exalted reputation is a misleading embellishment of a less noble reality (lines 309–14):

> "What, is this Arthureȝ hous," quoth the hathel thenne,
> "That al the rous rennes of thurȝ ryalmes so mony?
> Where is now your sourquydrye and your conquestes,
> Your gryndellayk and your greme, and your grete wordes?
> Now is the reuel and the renoun of the Rounde Table
> Ouerwalt wyth a worde of on wyȝes speche. . . .[9]

Finally Gawain accepts the challenge, but in a speech of extreme self-deprecation which seems as much a rhetorical exercise in false modesty —a verbal counterpart of courtly games and ornaments—as an accurate assessment of true worth.

After the Green Knight has received his blow, retrieved his head,[10] and galloped off, the court, having involuntarily assumed the role of his audience, now passes judgment on the extraordinary performance it has been forced to behold (this procedure reverses the intruder's exercise of judgment on the court and its "renoun" and returns to the situation in which civilization, secure in its highly ornamental patterns of behavior, must assess the significance of an individual not included in or accounted for by those patterns). Such is the equivocal nature of the interpretation offered by the "inner audience," however, that the poem's external audience is in turn coerced into interpreting its fictional counterpart.

[9] On the importance of the theme of reputation in the poem see Wilson, *The Gawain-Poet*, pp. 125-28; Benson, *Art and Tradition*, pp. 207-48.

[10] There is a suggestion in the text (lines 427-28) that even the grisly beheading has been transformed, perhaps unconsciously, into a momentary game resembling football: "The fayre hede fro the halce hit to the erthe, / That fele hit foyned wyth here fete, there hit forth roled."

Arthur pronounces the whole episode yet another Christmas game, and counsels Guinevere (lines 470–73):

> "Dere dame, to-day demay yow neuer;
> Wel bycommes such craft vpon Christmasse,
> Laykyng of enterludeȝ, to laȝe and to syng,
> Among thise kynde caroles of knyȝteȝ and ladyeȝ."

But he adds (lines 474–75):

> "Neuer the lece to my mete I may me wel dres,
> For I haf sen a selly, I may not forsake."

The poet admits that "Arthur the hende kyng at hert hade wonder," even though "he let no semblaunt be sene," hiding his amazement behind a decorative screen of "cortayse speche" (lines 467–69). Arthur offers his wife and court the best possible interpretation of the Green Knight's advent, leaving us to decide whether his strategy illustrates civilization's admirable ability to assimilate and domesticate life's mysteries and threats or reflects a base wish to avoid facing harsh realities by disguising and trivializing them with the help of convenient holiday language.

Early in fit 2, the poem offers a very different instance of how society brings its decorative (which are also its interpretive) powers to bear on an individual, this time one of its own, whom it seeks to protect and honor, not to explain away. The occasion is the description of Gawain's preparation for his journey to the Green Chapel, ten months after his first encounter with the Green Knight. The process of arming Gawain (lines 566ff.) is additive, each new layer complicating our understanding of the ceremony as a whole. First, a suit of fine armor covers the knight, representing and physically supporting his heroic endeavor. The armor in turn has been embellished with gold, gems, fine fabrics, and rich embroidery[11] indicative of the courtly refinement that

---

[11] The word "gold" runs through the description like a leitmotif: see lines 569, 577, 587, 591, 598, 600, 603, 620; at line 633, Gawain is said to be known "as golde pured." His helmet cover (lines 609–14) is encrusted with gems and embroidered with images of birds, this last a touch recalling the Green Knight's similarly embellished clothing (lines 165–66). The descriptions suggest that Gawain and his adversary are similar in many ways, with the main difference that only the Green Knight balances the gold of his costume with an equally strong element of green. On the poem's color symbolism see William Goldhurst, "The Green and the Gold: The Major Theme of *Gawain and the Green Knight*," CE 20 (1958):61–65.

decorates heroism at Arthur's court, even as pinnacles and crockets decorate Bertilak's strong-walled castle. Finally the shield with its painted pentangle (lines 619–65) stands for the conjunction, in a protective network, of society's palpable gifts (what we today would call its technology, embodied in Gawain's armor plate) and the knight's purely personal qualities. The narrator's interpretation of the pentangle is meant to demonstrate how various systems of virtue harmoniously coexist and interact as an "endeles knot" (line 630) within Gawain. He possesses keen physical senses, religious devotion (represented as well by the portrait of Mary on the inner surface of the shield), and the more courtly attributes of "fraunchyse, fela3schyp, clannes, cortayse, pyte" (lines 652–54). The poem says that these latter virtues are "happed" (line 655), or fastened on Gawain more than on any other knight; the choice of verb suggests that they, like his armor and shield, have been placed over him by civilization as a saving embellishment of his native abilities.

Although the process of arming Gawain, highlighted by the interpretation of the pentangle, seems at first reading unambiguously favorable to both the knight and the court he has undertaken to represent, it becomes more problematic when examined within the narrative and descriptive context. Although Gawain takes up the Green Knight's challenge on behalf of the whole court, to save its reputation, and with the approval of the court's counselors (lines 362–65), when the time comes for him to leave the court to seek the Green Chapel, courtiers who care for him not only mourn his departure to seek certain death (though hiding their grief, in civilized fashion, beneath the decoration of "merthe" and "iape3," lines 541–42) but express regret that the king allowed Gawain to accept the challenge in the first place (lines 682–83):

> "Who knew euer any kyng such counsel to take
> As kny3te3 in cauelacioun3 on Crystmasse gomne3!"

As they see it now, they are losing "a lowande leder of lede3" (line 679) because of excessive pride (line 681) and addiction to game playing. Are we to regard this retreat by the courtiers from their earlier approval of Gawain's endeavor as political prudence or effete cowardice? And how does the courtiers' pessimism about Gawain's survival square with the optimism expressed in the pentangle he has just been given?

A further complicating factor in our assessment of Gawain's protection by the pentangle involves the description offered by the poet, at the beginning of fit 2, of the passing of the seasons in their ordained, inevitable cycle. The point of this evocation of nature's rhythms is to remind us that Gawain, however splendid his existence at Arthur's court, cannot prevent the coming of his moment of truth with the Green Knight. The cycle of the seasons, like the reference at an analogous point in fit 1 to the alternation of "blysse and blunder" in Britain's history, argues for the inevitability of things and by implication against the efficacy of individual heroism or civilization's transforming power. Against this "hevy" message of human helplessness the court, in arming and embellishing Gawain, sets the contrasting image of the pentangle—a stylization of the seasonal cycle into a scheme of interlocking virtues that gives Gawain control over his physical and spiritual fate and testifies to civilization's vision of control over nature and destiny.

Once Gawain leaves Camelot and ventures into the wilderness, his literal and moral armor protect him well enough from the attacks of bulls, bears, and giants but less effectively from the harsh weather, as we have seen; nor can they dispel his lonely misery and evident need for civilization. Above all, that Gawain cries for his sins and prays, "Cros Kryst me spede!" (line 762), raises a fundamental question: given humanity's fallen state—even though redeemed by Christ's sacrifice— to what extent can the pentangle's schema of perfection be applied even to a great knight like Gawain? Is the pentangle an objective description of Gawain's virtue, or is it rather placed on the shield (*pace* the narrator) as an ideal toward which he must aspire but which (as the poem will ultimately show us) he can never attain? Eventually, Gawain's desire to survive his second encounter with the Green Knight subverts all higher considerations, and his failures of courtesy, loyalty, and heroism in the latter part of the poem (however seriously or lightly we interpret them) raise the possibility that the network of virtues portrayed schematically on the shield is merely a misleading disguise, "happed" on Gawain as an artful cover for the human imperfection beneath. If one sees the pentangle as a wishful embellishment of Gawain's life-and-death mission—a moralizing exegesis unsupported by the facts – it becomes yet another blind alley for the exegete, one more instance of the perils of interpretation in the poem.

The events immediately following Gawain's arrival before Bertilak's thrice-described castle announce clearly that the incipient relationship between the lonely, questing knight and the accomplished, festive society which receives him for the Christmas season will be built on a foundation of acts of embellishment and interpretation, with the former both inducing and thwarting the latter, in keeping with the poem's basic paradox. When Gawain enters the castle, he is led to a chamber to be dressed with rich robes, surrounded by cushions, and covered with a mantle embroidered without and furred within (lines 862–81). So "happed" (line 864; the same verb is used in line 655 to describe the attachment of the pentangular virtues to Gawain), he becomes another emblem of all the ways in which the resources and artfulness of civilization decorate the objects, animate and inanimate, on which they are lavished. But the process of embellishment is reciprocal. Once the inhabitants of the castle discover that their guest is the famous Gawain, one of the heroes of the Round Table (lines 901–907), Bertilak articulates the court's sense that it is adorned, however temporarily, by such a visitor in its midst: he thanks Gawain for having so arrived (lines 1033–34; emphasis mine)

> As to honour his hous on that hyʒe tyde,
> And *enbelyse* his burʒ with his bele chere.

The court's judgment of its own good fortune reflects its judgment of Gawain's worth, but the nature of the interpretation they place upon him creates new problems for us in our attempt to understand both the hero and his newfound society. The interpretive frame of reference alters quickly, disconcertingly in this scene. As soon as the knight arrives at the castle and begs admittance (lines 811–12), he who was so alone and pitiful in the forest a moment before, and so in need of Christ's comfort, becomes himself the object of a welcome ceremony almost fit for the Messiah (lines 817–19):

> Thay let doun the grete draʒt and derely out ʒeden,
> And kneled doun on her knes vpon the colde erthe
> To welcum this ilk wyʒ as worthy hom thoʒt. . . .

The tableau, on a Christmas Eve, is too reminiscent of the adoration of the shepherds or Magi to be accidental. The Messiah motif recurs more problematically once Gawain identifies himself (lines 906–27):

> And hit watȝ Wawen hymself that in that won sytteȝ,
> Comen to that Krystmasse, as cas hym then lymped. . . .
> Alle prys and prowes and pured thewes
> Apendes to hys persoun, and praysed is euer;
> Byfore alle men vpon molde his mensk is the most.
> Vch segge ful softly sayde to his fere:
> "Now schal we semlych se sleȝteȝ of theweȝ
> And the teccheles termes of talkyng noble,
> Wich spede is in speche vnspurd may we lerne,
> Syn we haf fonged that fyne fader of nurture.
> God hatȝ geuen vus hys grace godly for sothe,
> That such a gest as Gawan graunteȝ vus to haue,
> When burneȝ blythe of his burthe schal sytte and synge.
>> In menyng of manereȝ mere
>> This burne now schal vus bryng,
>> I hope that may hym here
>> Schal lerne of luf-talkyng."

Even the ambiguous antecedent of the pronoun "his" in line 922 manages to suggest an equation (or confusion) of Gawain and Christ.

But thanks to the intertwining of Christian atmosphere and courtly sentiments in this passage, the "Christlike" Gawain appears simultane-ously as the "fader of nurture," an exemplary spirit of high civilization excelling in "sleȝteȝ of theweȝ" and especially in the language of dalli-ance, or "luf-talkyng." The exegesis of the pentangle on Gawain's shield earlier in this fit, as an emblem of diverse virtue or value systems synthesized in the knight, seems here to be transformed into an act of interpretation wrought on the man – or rather on his reputation, which has preceded him from the Arthurian center of civilization to this wilderness-locked, provincial court. Since, however, we have seen nothing in the poem thus far to corroborate the court's assessment of Gawain's skill in courtly-love conversation, and since the Green Knight has already raised at Camelot the question whether reputation constitutes a true reflection or false ornamentation of reality,[12] we dare

---

[12] See above and note 9; cf. lines 258–64, 309–15.

not too readily accept the judgment here being passed on the honored guest. We have seen Gawain's heroic virtue and lonely isolation in the forest, seen him as well cry for his sins. Does the praise he now receives as an ideal courtier, and the subtler suggestion of Messiahlike qualities about him, constitute a graceful compliment by society, an accurate assessment of his worth from the perspective of a refined civilization, or a confusion of heroic essence and courtly decoration by the courtiers who greet him—or, even worse, a trivialization of Christmas solemnity (by applying its attributes to a chance visitor) that skirts close to blasphemy?

It lies beyond the scope of this essay to show how the elusive genius of civilization underlies and prompts Gawain's crucial misinterpretations, faulty judgments, and suspect behavior in fits 3 and 4.[13] Instead I will close my discussion by adducing one last description of superb ambiguity in fit 2 that effectively symbolizes the poem, the civilization it describes, and the perils of interpretation with which it confronts its hero and its reader. Since Gawain has arrived at Bertilak's castle on Christmas Eve, a day of fasting and penance decreed by the church to prepare for the morrow's great feast, he is served fish rather than meat that evening when he sits down to his first meal. But what fish! (lines 891–93):

> Summe baken in bred, summe brad on the glede3,
> Summe sothen, summe in sewe sauered with spyces
> And ay sawes so sle3e that the segge lyked.

A meal intended to symbolize mortification of the imperfect flesh has been transformed into an image of civilization's power to decorate and embellish, to change a fast into a feast. The secret is literally in the embellishment, in the "sle3e" sauces that make the penitential fish appealing to Gawain. We have seen this key term used to describe the

---

[13] See Burrow, *A Reading of Sir Gawain*, pp. 71–159; A. C. Spearing, *The Gawain Poet: A Critical Study* (Cambridge, 1970), pp. 191–219, "The Testing of Gawain"; pp. 219–36, "The Verdict on Gawain's Performance." Spearing is fully aware of the poem's ambiguities and the poet's refusal to choose between possible interpretations, but he believes that we can and should make such choices. Davenport, *The Art of the Gawain-Poet*, pp. 180ff., also recognizes the techniques "whereby not only is the hero continually caught off guard, but also the reader is cleverly confused and challenged to read the situation truly" (p. 188). In the end Davenport too makes interpretive choices, thus violating what I take to be the poem's point.

decorations atop Bertilak's castle (line 797) and the refined manners Bertilak's courtiers expect to find in Gawain (line 916); in these in-stances the term signifies artfulness, the peculiar mark of civilization in its remaking of nature and experience. But in fit 3, when Bertilak's wife offers Gawain the green girdle, she says its power will so protect him that "he myȝt not be slayn for sliȝt upon erthe" (line 1854), while Gawain, accepting the gift, thinks that "myȝt he haf slypped to be unslayn, the sleȝt were noble" (line 1858). Here the kind of ingenuity we call trickery or deceit seems best to render "sliȝt/sleȝt," the nominal form of "sleȝe." Now, with respect to the sauced fish, which of these two possible meanings is more appropriate? Or is this the place in the poem, as I believe it is, where the two registers of significance inherent in "sleȝe" coexist most equally, making of the fish in its embellished state the *Gawain* poet's supreme emblem of the civilization that nur-tures, elects, deceives, tempts, and (to some extent) defeats the best knight of the Arthurian world?

The saucing of the fish recapitulates the "happing" of Gawain that immediately precedes his meal; the decorative world of Arthur's court, as essentialized by Guinevere on the dais surrounded by tapestries, jewels, and fine food; the embellishment of Bertilak's castle with a forest of decorative pinnacles that deny its solidity. But is the intent here also to subvert the penitential meaning of the day by so disguising its culinary symbol? Gawain "ful hendely" (line 895) calls the repast a feast, and is immediately answered (lines 896–98):

> "As hende,
> This penaunce now ȝe take,
> And eft hit schal amende."

In the atmosphere of "merthe" that reigns at this point (line 900), it is very difficult to evaluate the meaning of this exchange between guest and hosts; Gawain's judgment of his meal may be sincere or politely hyperbolic, while the courtiers' reference to penance may be an ironic boast about their re-creation of a "fast day" as a feast, by serving the prescribed fish, but transformed through saucy embellishment.[14]

[14] On the penitential fish and its ambiguous sauce see Burrow, *A Reading of Sir Gawain*, p. 57; Wilson, *The Gawain-Poet*, p. 124, observes of the meal, "Such devotion to luxury and the 'sleȝe,' when it is coupled with deliberate indifference to the spirit, if not the letter, of a religious obser-vance, is disturbing." Perhaps even this formulation is too strict.

By the end of the poem we may also look back to the sauced fish as an emblem of how Bertilak's court disguises its testing of Gawain beneath its courtly language, entertainments, games, and overall nurture. Beneath civilization's decorative surface there waits the Green Knight's penitential axe (line 2392), could the knight but know it. From another point of view the artfulness of the cooks in saucing Gawain's fish can stand adequately for the artfulness of the poet embellishing his poem with emblems, false leads, and ambiguities that make it at once a feast for the eye and ear and a treacherous wilderness (or penitential experience) for the would-be interpreter. Indeed, I have come, after many years of struggling with *Sir Gawain*, to think of that Christmas Eve fish as, finally, an emblem of all the red herrings the *Gawain* poet places athwart our trail through his imagined world, thereby guaranteeing that, by its ending, we will be thoroughly chastened exegetes and will recognize in Gawain's fall and failings as a knight, a Christian, and a human being an instructive analogue to our own imperfections as critics.

"Synne Horrible":
The Pardoner's Exegesis of His Tale,
and Chaucer's

H. MARSHALL LEICESTER, JR.
University of California, Santa Cruz

I

O MY MIND the Canterbury tale that responds best to patristic or Augustinian forms of analysis is the Pardoner's. Such studies as that of R. P. Miller, showing the relevance to the tale of the tradition of the scriptural eunuch and the sin of presumption, or those of B. F. Huppé and Lee W. Patterson, demonstrating the even greater importance of the complementary sin of despair, are genuinely helpful in elucidating a narrative so patently, though at times so puzzlingly, allegorical.[1] At the same time, as everyone knows, the tale is one of the most fully dramatized, the most "fitted to its teller" of any in the Canterbury collection. It has appealed to dramatically inclined critics from Kittredge on as an example of what is freshest and most untraditional in Chaucer's art. It would be disingenuous of me to attempt to conceal my own bias in favor of the latter kind of criticism, but I think there is something to be gained from attending carefully to the typological elements of the tale, because they are instructive about Chaucer's own attitude toward exegetical methods.

While no one can really deny, since Robertson's studies, that Chaucer uses these methods—at least sometimes—there has been a considerable reluctance by a great many critics to allow the implications that patristically influenced commentators tend to draw from this

[1] Robert P. Miller, "Chaucer's Pardoner, the Scriptural Eunuch, and the Pardoner's Tale," *Speculum* 30 (1955):180–99; Bernard F. Huppé, *A Reading of the* Canterbury Tales, rev. ed. (Albany: State University of New York Press, 1967), pp. 209–20; Lee W. Patterson, "Chaucerian Confession: Penitential Literature and the Pardoner," *Medievalia et Humanistica*, n.s. 7 (1976):153–73.

fact. I take E. T. Donaldson's comment, published seven years after the appearance of Robertson's "Doctrine of Charity in Medieval Literary Gardens" and five years before *A Preface to Chaucer*, as typical of a dissatisfaction that has continued unabated, despite the increasing number of detailed, and often attractive, demonstrations of the presence of typological elements in the poet's work:

> . . .in my criticism I have been reluctant to invoke historical data from outside the poem to explain what is in it. . . . I have therefore eschewed the historical approach used both by the great Chaucerians of the earlier part of this century and by those scholars who have recently been reading Chaucer primarily as an exponent of medieval Christianity. The fact that the difference between what these two historical approaches have attained is absolute—if Chaucer means what the older Chaucerians thought he meant he cannot possibly mean what these newer Chaucerians think he means—has encouraged me to rely on the poems as the principal source of their meaning.[2]

Perhaps one reason for critical hesitation has been the rather illiberal tone of much patristic criticism, tending to insist as it does that most really interesting human activities are, from a medieval perspective, no more or less than sins. To object to this tone is to risk dismissal as a historically conditioned sentimentalist, but I think that what really lies behind the objection is the feeling that if the exegetical critics are right our ancestors were, in their well-documented distrust of poetry, an impossibly reductive lot, unable to distinguish clearly between a daisy of the field and the Virgin Mary, and (perhaps rightly) preferred to see the latter whenever they encountered the former.

Still, in *The Pardoner's Tale*, these so-called historical elements are stubbornly present. It helps a lot to know something about a tradition of interpretation based on the idea that, while men make words stand for things, God can make things themselves stand for other things,[3] in

---

[2] E. T. Donaldson, *Chaucer's Poetry: An Anthology for the Modern Reader*, 2d ed. (New York: Ronald Press, 1975; orig. ed., 1958), p. vi. See D. W. Robertson, Jr., "The Doctrine of Charity in Medieval Literary Gardens: A Topical Approach Through Symbolism and Allegory," *Speculum* 26 (1951):24–49; *A Preface to Chaucer: Studies in Medieval Perspectives* (Princeton, N.J.: Princeton University Press, 1962). Robertson's articles on exegetical criticism and related topics are now collected in his *Essays in Medieval Culture* (Princeton, N.J.: Princeton University Press, 1980).

[3] The *locus classicus* for this idea is Augustine's *De doctrina christiana*, bk. 1. My formulation here follows Aquinas's elegant summary, *Summa theologia* I, 1.1.10, *resp.*

dealing with what is being communicated by a passage like the follow-ing (lines 350–65):

> Thanne have I in latoun a sholder-boon
> Which that was of an hooly Jewes sheep.
> 'Goode men,' I seye, 'taak of my wordes keep;
> If that this boon be wasshe in any welle,
> If cow, or calf, or sheep, or oxe swelle
> That any worm hath ete, or worm ystonge,
> Taak water of that welle and wassh his tonge,
> And it is hool anon; and forthermoore,
> Of pokkes and of scabbe, and every soore
> Shal every sheep be hool that of this welle
> Drynketh a draughte. Taak kep eek what I telle:
> If that the good-man that the beestes oweth
> Wol every wyke, er that the cok hym croweth,
> Fastynge, drynken of this welle a draughte,
> As thilke hooly Jew oure eldres taughte,
> His beestes and his stoor shal multiplie.[4]

At the literal level this specimen of the Pardoner's "gaude" is a blatant appeal to the cupidity, or at any rate to the decidedly secular interests, of his "lewed" audience. The bone is a kind of snake oil. Yet the imag-ery the Pardoner uses about and around the supposed relic—sheep, holy Jews, devouring worms, life-giving wells—seems insistently to imply much more. I do not think it is forcing the passage at all to see in it a persistent typological edge characteristic of his style. The funda-mental link the passage takes advantage of is the equation between sheep and Christian souls, the helpless beasts endangered by the worm that dieth not, whom the Good Shepherd has in care. Accordingly, the ancient holy Jew takes on associations with Jacob, perhaps (via the well), and almost certainly with the promise made to Abraham echoed in the last line quoted (Gen. 22.16–18). This in turn implies a complex and sophisticated series of interpretations of that promise, originally applied literally to and by the children of Israel under the Old Law, but since figurally fulfilled at a spiritual level under the New Law in the care of Christ for his flock. This fulfillment is presently embodied in the

---

[4] Quotations from Chaucer are taken from *The Works of Geoffrey Chaucer*, ed. F. N. Robinson, 2d ed. (Boston: Houghton, 1957).

Pardoner's own profession and act, the salvation of souls by the mercy of Christ, mediated through the *plenitudo potestatis* of the papacy and the agency of the man before us. I am being deliberately impressionistic rather than "textueel" here, because what I want to establish is not a particular exegesis but that a spiritual level of meaning is being deliberately and consciously put in play by the speaker behind and around the literal offer of worldly "heele" and enrichment. It seems to me that the passage is overloaded in the direction of this kind of spiritual significance. There is something gratuitous not about the reading itself but about the Pardoner's insistence on packing it in in the very act of mocking and debasing it with his pitch. It is one thing to announce that you are a fraud and that you intend, though unrepentant, to expose your own fraudulent arts. It is another thing to load those arts themselves with a set of under meanings that exhibit so complex an awareness of the truth you are abusing. The Pardoner seems to be saying not only "look how I deceive the ignorant" but also "look at what an important matter I deceive them about." Whatever his motives for this, it is at least clear that the effect is achieved by a deliberate forcing of mundane and particular matters into a general and spiritual framework while at the same time refusing to let go of the literal level, so that we see both significances at the same time and are unsure to which one to assign priority. I think most readers will agree that much of the power of *The Pardoner's Tale* as a whole derives from a consistent application of this method to the materials of the story. A good deal of the eeriness of the Pardoner's central exemplum, for example, comes from the fact that it reverses the invariable order of causes found in all of its analogues, from *The Arabian Nights* to *The Treasure of the Sierra Madre*. In those stories the gold always comes first, and the point is to show that in looking for gold men find death. But in *The Pardoner's Tale* we *begin* with a search for death and find the gold later. The Pardoner's version thrusts the spiritual implications of the quest into the situation at the outset and juxtaposes them sharply to the extreme, childlike literal-mindedness of the three rioters, who treat death like a bully from the next town.

I intend to argue that such a failure or refusal to distinguish carefully and consistently between literal and spiritual levels of meaning and discourse is at the center of *The Pardoner's Tale*, the single most impor-

tant determinant of the tale's meaning, and that the source of this effect is the consciousness of the Pardoner himself. The Pardoner is, I
will further argue, the first exegetical critic of his own tale, obsessed
with the spiritual meanings he sees beneath the surface of everyday
life. He feels the burden of these meanings himself and attempts, as we
shall see, to impose them on others. The Pardoner has long been recognized as the most self-conscious of the Canterbury pilgrims. Part of
that self-consciousness involves an awareness of his own condition,
and by this I do not mean simply that he attempts to hide his physical
eunuchry, since I am not at all sure that he does. The Pardoner's conduct of his tale indicates that among the things he knows about himself
and is concerned to make others see are the things R. P. Miller knows
about him: that he is the *eunuchus non dei*, the embodiment of the *vetus
homo*, the Old Man whose body is the body of this death, and guilty of
the sin against the Holy Ghost.

II

From the very beginning there is something conspicuous and aggressive about the Pardoner's failure to conceal his various evils and deficiencies, well before he "confesses" some of them in his tale. The
general narrator, the Host, and the "gentils" all see through him at
once, and it seems likely that they can do so because the Pardoner
makes it easy for them. A. C. Spearing has pointed to the obvious
fakery of his authorizing bulls from popes and cardinals, and Kellogg
and Haselmeyer report that the abuse of carrying *false* relics is "so rare
that no contemporary manual even discusses it."[5] Since the relics themselves—pillowcases and pigs' bones—convince no one, we have the impression that this particular Pardoner goes out of his way to stage his
abuses and make them even more blatant than those of most of his
historically attested compeers. The same is true of his physical and
sexual peculiarities. I take it that such things as his immediate echoing
of the Host's "manly" oath "by Seint Ronyan" and his announced pref-
erence for jolly wenches in every town though babies starve for it have

---

[5] A. C. Spearing, *The Pardoner's Prologue and Tale* (Cambridge: Cambridge University Press,
1965), p. 7; Alfred L. Kellogg and Louis A. Haselmeyer, "Chaucer's Satire of the Pardoner," in
Alfred L. Kellogg, *Chaucer, Langland, Arthur* (New Brunswick, N.J.: Rutgers University Press,
1972), p. 228&n.

in common the tactic of calling attention to his oddity by deliberately shamming exaggerated virility. This is a form of camp, in which the hypermasculinity is as fully in quotes as the mock demonism of what Patterson calls his "gross and deliberate parody of sinfulness" (p. 162). The Pardoner's manner *courts* an interpretation that his confession simply confirms and heightens, and what interests me most is that the consistent drift of the interpretation he suggests is theological in character. His prologue continually circles back to typologically charged images like the dove sitting on a barn of line 397, or more direct comparisons such as "I wol noon of the apostles countrefete" (line 447). Although the performance here may be interpreted as a joke, the humor derives from the disproportion between the ultimate issues that are constantly being raised and the cheap faker who raises them—and it is the Pardoner himself who keeps pointing up the discrepancy.

Nor is it clear, even at this early stage, that the Pardoner is only joking. He seems obscurely troubled that his performances can "'maken oother folk to twynne / From avarice, and soore to repente'" (lines 430–31), and, as Patterson has pointed out (p. 164), he insists somewhat too strongly that he does it only for the money. His oddly serious warning about the dangers of false preaching (lines 407–22) reveals how the act has a complexity for him that belies his insistence that he himself preaches only for gain and "al by rote." If we try to deduce the motives that his own sermon reveals in its unfolding, these more serious aspects of the Pardoner's self-presentation—what he wants us to see about himself and the world—begin to come clearer.

The sermon provides an intense, almost hallucinatory vision of a world dominated and consumed by sin, in which gluttony "Maketh that est and west and north and south, / In erthe, in eir, in water, men to swynke / To gete a glotoun deyntee mete and drynke" (lines 518–20). The feeling that sin is everywhere, and everywhere having its effect on the world, is heightened by the tendency to assimilate the effects of all sins to each individual sin, and to combine sins together (lines 591–94):

> Hasard is verray mooder of lesynges,
> And of deceite, and cursed forswerynges,
> Blaspheme of Crist, manslaughtre, and wast also
> Of catel and of tyme. . . .

Such passages in isolation might simply be considered exaggeration appropriate to any preacher striving to move his hearers to repentance.
But the Pardoner's way of exaggerating is more complicated. It is one
thing to say, as both the Parson (*ParsT* 818) and the Pardoner do, that
the world was corrupted by gluttony, or to say that original sin contained all other sins in itself potentially. It is quite another thing to say
that the original sin was gluttony (lines 508–11). A standard theological point is turned around here by deliberately overliteralizing the
spiritual interrelation of all sins to one another, in keeping with the
general tendency of the sermon to treat matter rather than spirit as the
root of all evil: "O wombe! O bely! O stynkyng cod, / Fulfilled of dong
and of corrupcioun!" (lines 534–35).

It is clear enough that the Pardoner hates his body and the flesh in
general. He consistently and gratuitously forces details that express
disgust at the corruption of the physical, from his description of his reli-
quaries "ycrammed ful of cloutes and of bones" (line 348) to the sheep
that need healing, "Of pokkes and of scabbe, and every soore" (line
358) to the brilliant way we are brought too close to the drunkard:
"sour is thy breeth, *foul artow to embrace*" (line 552). Especially in the
description of gluttony, but also elsewhere in the sermon, the Pardoner
moves well beyond mere asceticism to an obsessive insistence on the
brutal and ugly condition of the flesh, and especially of its *burden*, the
sheer labor of keeping this death-bound and filthy bag alive: "How
greet labour and cost is thee to fynde!" (line 537). This kind of thing
gives a peculiarly literal (and powerful) emphasis to the frequent and
quite orthodox refrain that sin is a living death and that the sinner "Is
deed, whil that he lyveth in tho vices" (line 548, cf. lines 533, 558).

I do not think, however, that this sense of physical corruption,
weakness, and impotence is at the root of the Pardoner's character and
problem, any more than I think that he wishes to conceal his own
physical impotence. It should be noted that the ascription of the Fall to
gluttony is funny, and deliberately so. It gets its effect from taking the
stock rant of "Corrupt was al this world for glotonye" (line 504) and
treating it as if it were literally true, and the Pardoner's qualifying
asides ("it is no drede," "as I rede") show that he knows this, that he is
parodying a certain sort of preaching at the same time that he is doing
it. Such parodying of sermon styles is satirical, a mocking condemna-

tion of the inadequacy of literal forms and institutions to contain or even define the reality of sin, and the Pardoner does it throughout his sermon (lines 639–47):

Bihoold and se that in the firste table
Of heighe Goddes heestes honurable,
Hou that the seconde heeste of hym is this:
"Take nat my name in ydel or amys."
Lo, rather he forbedeth swich sweryng
Than homycide or many a cursed thyng;
I seye that, as by ordre, thus it stondeth;
This knoweth, that his heestes understondeth,
How that the seconde heeste of God is that.

This passage makes fun of a style of thinking and moralizing whose literalness renders it preposterous. It pursues classification, labeling, and external order at the expense of clear ethical priorities and gives us an image of the preacher as a demented scholastic. A complementary figure is Stilboun, the "wys embassadour," who is himself a moralist and a preacher but also a Johnny One-note who can only nag over and over that his principals "Shul nat allyen yow with hasardours" (line 618, cf. lines 613, 616). I think the Pardoner means these various examples, and the entire sermon, as comments on the kind of preaching, theology, and pastoral care that goes on in the church he represents. Even the snake-oil pitch to the "lewed peple" with which I began uses its typological elements to juxtapose and contrast what pardoning ought to be doing with what it actually does. We are so used to thinking of the Pardoner as an *embodiment* of the notorious abuses of the fourteenth-century church that we tend not to consider that he has *attitudes* toward them. But his parodic presentation of doctrinal classification, moral exhortation, and religious institutions like the cult of relics and pardoning itself consistently suggests his contempt for the available instruments of salvation as they are used in the real life of the all-too-corporeal *corpus mysticum* around him. He is in fact a *proponent* of the older historical view of the tale as a satire on the corruption of the church. The satire is the Pardoner's, and his own best example is himself.

This last is important. One of the striking rhetorical features of the entire sermon is the way it keeps associating all the sins it describes

with the Pardoner—showing that he is guilty of them. The most striking instances of this tendency are the passages where the Pardoner
demonstrates his experienced familiarity with the sins he purports to
condemn, as in the description of the drunken dice game (lines 651–55)
that Donaldson calls "so knowingly graphic as to exceed the limits of
art" (*Chaucer's Poetry*, p. 1093), or the discussion of abuses of the wine
trade and the difficulty of getting an honest drink (lines 562–72).
There is nothing concealed or private about the Pardoner's complicity
in these vices; rather, he brings himself forward as an instance of them,
and this reflexive element gives a particular bite and appropriateness to
the concentration in the sermon on the increased sinfulness and conse-
quentiality of sin in high places. "A capitayn sholde lyve in sobrenesse"
(line 582), but this one does not, as he shows. Given the context, who
else can the Pardoner be talking about here? "Redeth the Bible, and
fynde it expresly / Of wyn-yevyng to hem that han justise" (line 587),
or (lines 595–98):

> It is repreeve and contrarie of honour
> For to ben holde a commune hasardour.
> And ever the hyer he is of estaat,
> The moore is he yholden desolaat.

All these images are in effect types and figures of the Pardoner himself,
and he in turn is a type and figure of everything about the church—its
institutions, its preaching, its corrupt ministers—that fails to come to
grips with the reality of sin in the world. That reality is, as I have
already suggested, very real to the Pardoner. He portrays the wretchedness and misery of the human condition with immediacy and insight.
He demonstrates how traditional patterns of classification, description,
and exhortation fail to catch or contain the more intimate and existential presence of sin, death, and the burden of the flesh which he sees in
others and feels in himself. He has nothing but contempt, and this in a
deeper sense than we have yet examined, for the consolations of religion, but he takes very seriously the things they are intended to con-
sole. On the one hand there is the horror of life; on the other there is
the church that fails to address or ameliorate that horror—a dead letter, and one that kills. Caught between them and embodying them
both is the Pardoner (lines 530–33):

Ther walken manye of whiche yow toold have I—
I seye it now wepyng, with pitous voys—
That they been enemys of Cristes croys,
Of whiche the ende is deeth

The emphasis in the sermon section of the tale divides fairly evenly between these two perspectives (though both are always present), on either side of our most immediate and least hyper-rhetorical view of him, the passage on the wine of Fish Street and Cheapside. Before that he tends primarily to develop his heightened view of life's ugliness and the universality of sin. After it he concentrates more on the self-condemning mockery of the forms of religious ministry. This division points to and helps explain the development of the Pardoner's consciousness in the tale, the way something *happens* to him here. What happens is that, as he manipulates the conventional materials of the sermon to reflect his own obsessions, he becomes more conscious of himself and more aware of both his power and his powerlessness. The power derives from the way he makes himself into a symbol, generalizes his own sinful and death-bound condition to the world around him. He makes the extent and the seriousness of what he stands for (what he *makes* himself stand for) more explicit as he dramatizes the evil God cannot or will not eliminate. His own presumption, for that is what it is, has the power of making a wasteland of the world. His powerlessness derives from the fact that what he symbolizes (what he *makes* himself symbolize) is emptiness and privation. His despair, for that is what it is, makes his inability to save others or himself the most salient fact of existence.

Cupiditas, of course, means far more than avarice. In the deep Christian and Augustinian sense in which it is the contrary of *caritas*, it refers to a consuming desire for that which one is lacking—it means *wanting* in both senses, or rather, wanting in a particular way. Privation itself is a fundamental fact of the human condition. Saint Augustine images it as the state of a pilgrim far from the blessedness of his home (*De doctrina* 1.4.4). Given this basic lack, two responses are possible. To use (*utor*) the things of this world as a way to get beyond them to God is, paradoxically, to grant them their independence, to open up the possibility of using them in charity, of cherishing them (*De doctrina* 1.33.37). The enjoyment (*fruor*) of the world and others which is *cupiditas* only looks like enjoying them for their own sakes—it really means wanting to enjoy them for oneself, to engulf them and make them the instruments of one's own will. In traditional terms, despair *is* presumption: to say that God cannot forgive you is to place limits on His power and mercy, to usurp a judgment that belongs to Him. In its largest sense *cupiditas* is the desire to do this, and its inevitable frustration produces the hatred of God, self, and others that the Pardoner displays. This is the condition that the Pardoner suffers and wills. It is the condition that he half conceals or avoids in the Prologue and that he *embodies* in the sermon. The extent to which his despair breaks loose in the sermon is indicated by the notorious fact that he forgets at the end of it that he has not yet told us how many rioters there are. I interpret this as a sign of the extent to which he has become caught up in the sermon, lost control of the form of his tale in the act of dramatizing his condition, the universality of that condition, and its effects in the world. It is this heightened consciousness that he carries into the exemplum he is at last ready to tell.

III

The exemplum itself is not well fitted to express the Pardoner's view of things. It is hard to imagine that any exemplum would be, since the form itself is an example of the institutionalized literalism he despises. The traditional form of the Pardoner's exemplum argues the proposition "If you are avaricious you will die" in the most literal, and therefore unbelievable, way. It presents a clarified picture of the operations of divine justice that both the Pardoner's experience and his very existence utterly deny. The exemplum is precisely one of those worthless forms of spiritual teaching, too far removed from the reality of life and sin, that the Pardoner mocks in his sermon. This is one reason he modifies the early parts of the exemplum in the way he does, in an attempt to get the letter of the story to express something about spirit, and the well-attested oddness of the resulting effect shows the inaptness of the form to the purpose.

The peculiarities of the Pardoner's telling are gathered around and focus on the Old Man. The first part of the tale is, in fact, designed to prepare a context for him, and that is why it brings death into the foreground. It has become fairly commonplace by now to see the three rioters and the Old Man as aspects of the Pardoner, and I agree with this notion in general.[6] The problem remains, however, of situating this division in the consciousness of the Pardoner himself, of seeing how he uses it and what he uses it to say. The feeling of miasma in the opening scene arises, as I have previously suggested, from the semi-allegorical treatment of an ordinary tavern scene in such a way as to stress its spiritual overtones (lines 670–84; emphasis mine):

> "Sire," quod this boy, "it nedeth never-a-deel;
> It was me toold er ye cam heer two houres.
> He was, pardee, *an old felawe of youres;*
> And sodeynly he was yslayn to-nyght,
> Fordronke, as he sat on his bench upright.
> Ther came a privee theef men clepeth Deeth,
> That *in this contree* al the peple sleeth,
> And with his spere he smoot his herte atwo,
> And went his way withouten wordes mo.
> He hath a thousand slayn this pestilence.
> And, maister, *er ye come in his presence,*
> *Me thynketh that it were necessarie*
> *For to be war of swich an adversarie.*
> *Beth redy for to meete him everemoore;*
> Thus taughte me my dame; I sey namoore."

The italicized phrases outline points at which the Pardoner's sophisticated typological consciousness imposes on the innocent one of the youth. Because of what is at issue, "felawe" points to the fellowship of all men in sin and before death, "this contree" moves toward "this world," and the final warning urges the need for a different kind of readiness and preparation from what the boy seems to have in mind. And who is "my dame"? Nature? The church? The child speaks more than he knows.

At one level these characters are an image of the Pardoner's audience, of the "lewed peple" who live in ignorant literal-mindedness in a world that is more charged with spiritual significance and consequence

---

[6] See, e.g., Donald R. Howard, *The Idea of the Canterbury Tales* (Berkeley: University of California Press, 1976), pp. 357–58; Edward I. Condren, "The Pardoner's Bid for Existence," *Viator* 41 (1973):200.

than they can imagine. They treat reality as if it were an exemplum and respond to the offense against human integrity, self-sufficiency, and community that death is ("Er that he dide a man a dishonour," line 691), as to an external threat, an isolated event, something merely physical. It has also become common of late to point out that the rioters' quest is a blasphemous parody of Christ's sacrifice, which slew spiritual death for the faithful once and for all.[7] This is true, and it is another instance of the typological processing that the Pardoner goes out of his way to give the tale. But it also seems to me that he regards this aspect of the rioters with a certain ambivalence, even sympathy. There is something attractive in the youthful idealism that so confidently forms a band of brothers to slay death. The rioters do not seem really evil in the early parts of the tale; they are too innocent for that. A student of mine once compared them to fraternity boys, as much for their trivial dissipation as for their idealism, and the Pardoner's earliest characterization of their lives is not "sin" but "folye" (line 464). I think he is momentarily attracted to their quest because it does correspond to something in him, and was once his own. What once must have been a desire to do "Cristes hooly werk," to slay death and save souls by offering them Christ's pardon, is nostalgically revived in the rioter's quest and at the same time placed as naïve and overconfident folly. The rioters, as once perhaps the Pardoner, have no idea what they are up against.

What they are up against is the Old Man, the truth of the experience of the *vetus homo* as that experience is embodied in the consciousness of the Pardoner. He is what their quest leads to, and what they might become if they did not live in an exemplum. The Pardoner uses the Old Man as a spokesman for this sophisticated despair. The Old Man's desire to exchange age for youth (lines 720–26) points to the Pardoner's envy of the innocence of the rioters and of his "lewed" congregation and suggests that what he wants to be rid of is not physical decay but consciousness. Although he sounds suicidal (lines 727–33), the Old Man is not so in the ordinary sense. Because he feels himself eternal, physical death is beside the point. What he wants is to be

---

[7] E.g., Eric W. Stockton, "The Deadliest Sin in the *Pardoner's Tale*," *TSL* 6 (1961):47; Janet Adelman, "'That We May Leere Som Wit,'" in Dewey R. Faulkner, ed., *Twentieth Century Interpretations of* The Pardoner's Tale (Englewood Cliffs, N.J.: Prentice-Hall, 1973), p. 97.

swallowed up, to become nothing, to escape from the restless *con-sciousness* of his privation, his *cupiditas*. This is that sickness unto death of which Kierkegaard speaks, "everlastingly to die, to die and yet not to die, to die the death."[8]

To wish to exchange one's chest for a hair shirt (lines 734–38) is, in effect and typologically, to wish to be able to pay money for the gift of repentance, to wish that the literal version of pardoning were the true one. Besides demonstrating decisively that avarice is not at issue here, this indicates that the Pardoner understands that his situation is willed. He would have to repent to get any relief, and he *will* not, though he knows this is the source of his wretchedness. He also knows what this makes him (lines 739–47):

> "But, sires, to yow it is no curteisye
> To speken to an old man vileynye,
> But he trespasse in word, or elles in dede.
> In Hooly Writ ye may yourself wel rede:
> 'Agayns an oold man, hoor upon his heed,
> Ye sholde arise;' wherfore I yeve yow reed,
> Ne dooth unto an oold man noon harm now,
> Namoore than that ye wolde men dide to yow
> In age, if that ye so longe abyde."

This passage, like the rest of the Old Man's speech, is the place in the tale where the Pardoner most clearly expresses his self-pity. But his language also shows that he understands his condition spiritually and exegetically, that he *interprets himself* in traditional terms as the *vetus homo*. This makes the self-pity begin to shade over into the self-hatred that is its complement. The Pardoner's voicing of the unambiguous passage from Leviticus makes it move toward self-condemnation—from "respect your elders" to "rise up against an Old Man." This is espe-cially clear if the speech is taken where it belongs, outside the tale and in relation to the Pardoner, who goes so far out of his way to show how he trespasses in word and deed.

The encounter with the Old Man is the place in the tale where the Pardoner most openly discloses his own condition. It is the place where we feel the least sense of the detachment of his voice from the

[8] Søren Kierkegaard, *Fear and Trembling and The Sickness unto Death*, trans. Walter Lowrie (Garden City, N.Y.: Doubleday Anchor, 1953), p. 151.

surface of the story, the least irony and manipulation. It is the point at which he completes the process of putting himself into his tale, and the apparent result is that he has nowhere to go. The Old Man can point the way to death, but as soon as he does so he vanishes from the story "thider as I have to go" (line 749). The rioters cannot hear what the Old Man has to tell them, that physical death is only a figure for the spiritual, for something that is eternally within them and in which they live without knowing it. They can only enact the literal and mechanical poetic justice of an exemplum about avarice—or so it seems. Although there is some truth to the idea that the tale becomes more narrow and limited and loses much of its atmosphere of mystery after the departure of the Old Man, it seems to me that his pointing finger remains to haunt the tale in the "signes and othere circum-stances" the Pardoner imposes on the simple exemplum plot.

On the one hand he traces the psychological progress of the rioters. Their idealism quickly flips over into its contrary and generates a world of cynicism and suspicion in which "Men wolde seyn that we were theves stronge, / And for oure owene tresor doon us honge" (lines 789–90), and every man's hand is against every other's. This suggests the basic sense of the world that generated the idealism, the impulse to kill death, in the first place, and so identifies the underlying protodespair of the rioters. This is seen most clearly in the youngest, whose decision to murder his fellows is presented as an accession of self-consciousness. Like his companions he begins with a heightened awareness of the beauty of the world ("thise floryns newe and bryghte," line 839, cf. lines 773–74) that distracts him from brother-hood and the quest for death. This quickly shades into *cupiditas*, the desire to possess the object beheld for himself, in order to complete an existence suddenly perceived as lacking (lines 841–44):

> "O Lord!" quod he, "if so were that I myghte
> Have al this tresor to myself allone,
> Ther is no man that lyveth under the trone
> Of God that sholde lyve so murye as I!"

The account of how the fiend suggested to him that he should buy poison is theologically careful, not for the sake of the theological point but in order to point up a shift from external temptation to an inner motion of the will that discovers the preexisting depravity of the soul: "For-why the feend foond hym in swich lyvynge / That he hadde leve him to sorwe brynge" (lines 847–48). By the time the youngest rioter gets to the apothecary, his imagery has begun to resonate with that despairing sense of wasting away that is the Pardoner's own: "And fayn he wolde wreke hym, if he myghte, / On vermyn that destroyed hym by nyghte" (line 858). The Pardoner seems to try to bring the rioters up to the point at which they might begin to discover the *vetus homo* or outcast old Adam in themselves and so begin to share the con-sciousness of the Old Man.

At the same time the Pardoner plays with the imagery and structure of the tale so as to suggest in a different way what is "really" going on. His typological imagination seizes on certain details of the story in order to allude to the spiritual plot of the tale that its literal unfolding obscures. The "breed and wyn" (line 797) that ultimately kill the rioters, whatever precise interpretation be put on them, are surely an example of a deliberate introduction of sacramental imagery. Similarly, the apothecary's description of the poison has the by now familiar overloaded quality of physical details forced onto a spiritual plane (lines 859–64):

> The pothecarie answerde, "And thou shalt have
> A thyng that, also God my soule save,
> In al this world ther is no creature,
> That eten or dronken hath of this confiture
> Noght but the montance of a corn of whete,
> That he ne shal his lif anon forlete."

The reference, I take it, is to John 12.24: "Truly, truly, I say to you, unless a grain of wheat falls into the earth and dies it remains alone; but if it dies it bears much fruit. He who loves his life loses it, and he who hates his life in this world will keep it for eternal life." The stan-dard commentaries identify the grain as the Eucharist by which the faithful soul ought to live and spiritual fruit to arise. Similarly, the "large botelles thre" (line 871, cf. line 877) which the youngest rioter fills with his poisoned wine refer to the saying of Jesus: "And no one puts new wine into old wineskins; if he does the wine will burst the skins and the wine is lost and so are the skins; but new wine is for fresh skins" (Mark 2.22; cf. Matt. 9.17, Luke 5.37). Jerome takes this as referring to the transition from the Old Law to the New. Until a man is reborn and puts aside the *vetus homo*, he cannot contain the new wine of the Gospel precepts. The *Glossa ordinaria*, following Bede, reads the wine as the Holy Spirit that transformed the apostles from old to new men but whose spiritual precepts destroy the scribes and Pharisees of the Old Law and the proud generally.[9] Since in the story it is evident that the rioters must be the old bottles that are burst, the pattern of typological action in the tale seems clear and consistent: the New Law of Salvation, the Eucharist as the sacrifice of Christ, is poison to these *veteres homines*. This or something like it is the Pardoner's exegesis of the tale. The peculiarity of this exegesis—it is hardly usual to present the instruments of Christ's mercy as poison—reflects the Pardoner's own experience of the promise of salvation and his more spiritual sense of himself as the Old Man. At the literal level, as it applies to the rioters, the justice of the tale has a certain Old Testament savagery, but how much worse to alienate oneself from a loving and merciful God who lays down His own life for man's sins. It is this that makes what poisons the rioters literally a spiritual poison to the Pardoner: it heightens his sense of what he has cut himself off from.

IV

What is striking about all this psychological and theological sophistication, however, is how little effect it finally has on the exemplum. If in the course of his tale the Pardoner has embodied his sense of himself and the world and put his "venym under hewe of holynesse" into literal bottles of poisoned wine—spirituality under hue of venom as it were—that embodiment remains eccentric, sporadic, and largely veiled, more deeply felt by the Pardoner than argued in the story. The large-scale patterns of spiritual reference that critics have detected in the tale are all there, more or less, and they are there because the Pardoner puts them there, but they remain largely implicit and structural,

---

[9] For the bread and wine and other eucharistic symbolism in the tale, see Robert E. Nichols, Jr., "The Pardoner's Ale and Cake," *PMLA* 82 (1967):498–504. For John 12.24–25, see *Glossa ordinaria*, P.L. 114, col. 402, and Aquinas, *Catena aurea*, ad loc. For the synoptic passages see *Glossa ordinaria*, ibid., col. 188; Bede, *In Marci Evangelium Expositio*, P.L. 92, col. 152; Jerome, *Commentaria in Evangelium S. Matthaei*, P.L. 26, cols. 57–58.

carried by typological allusions to be caught only by the learned. Indeed, the very fact that the Pardoner makes the tale *more* typological as he proceeds shows his increasing sense that he cannot get it to say what he wants more directly. One feels that he is trying to make the story bear more weight than it comfortably can, to push its symbolic significance too far.

It seems likely that the Pardoner feels the same way, for when he comes to what should be the rhetorical high point of the exemplum, the description of the death agonies of the rioters, he tosses it away with a "What nedeth it to sermone of it moore?" (line 879) and a coolly toned reference to a medical textbook (lines 889–95). I take the feeling of anticlimax here as an indication of the Pardoner's impatience with the conventional poetic justice of the ending. As it stands, the exemplum does not solve or settle anything he feels to be important. The rioters are gone, but sin, death, and the Pardoner remain (lines 895–903):

> O cursed synne of alle cursednesse!
> O traytours homycide, O wikkednesse!
> O glotonye, luxurie, and hasardrye!
> Thou blasphemour of Crist with vileynye
> And othes grete, of usage and of pride!
> Allas! mankynde, how may it bitide
> That to thy creatour, which that the wroghte,
> And with his precious herte-blood thee boghte,
> Thou art so fals and so unkynde, allas?

It is notable that this moralization of the exemplum, for all its appropriately heightened rhetorical tone, does not arise directly from the events of the tale and only arrives at the "right" moral ("ware yow fro the synne of avarice!" line 905) after several lines of impassioned condemnation of "mankynde" for the same old tavern vices. These vices are generally appropriate to the occasion in the sense that the rioters are guilty of them, but their introduction here breaks the continuity and focus of the conclusion of the tale, and it is difficult to know what to make of the intensity with which they are denounced after the flat tone of the account of the rioters' demise. It is as if the Pardoner were looking for something on which to vent strong feelings and casting about for a pretext. What the passage does accomplish is a return of the image of a world pervaded by sin generated by the sermon section of the tale. Juxtaposed to this image, more directly and immediately than ever before, is the Pardoner's self-presentation, which bitterly and cynically compares his mercenary activity (on which he harps) with what it is supposed to pardon (lines 904–15).

Throughout the tale it has been the Pardoner's explicit project to make an example of himself, to unmask and explain his practices. In the course of the telling, as I have tried to show, his *attitude* toward himself and his profession, his self-hatred and self-condemnation, coupled as always with his hatred and contempt of others, has emerged with increasing clarity and intensity, at least for him. His self-presentation throughout the tale constantly stresses his culpability, and as the tale proceeds, he seems to take this with increasing seriousness, to regard himself as truly exemplary and symbolic of the evil, corruption, and sinfulness of the world—finally, perhaps, as a type of the Antichrist. I have been at pains to show that what exegetical criticism detects in the tale and makes an external doctrinal structure that contains and explains a Pardoner unaware of it is in fact the Pardoner's interpretation of himself, consciously undertaken and offered by him to the pilgrims. It is only when the action of the tale is understood in this way that the epilogue begins to make sense.

By the end of the story the Pardoner seems dominated by his tale: he rejects it at a literal level but remains racked by the heightened and frustrated consciousness of himself that the experience of telling it generates in him. This leads him to force the issues of sin and spirit, the issue of himself, beyond the tale itself into the real world of the pilgrimage. The real moral the Pardoner has come to draw from the real exemplum of the tale, himself, emerges as he completes that exemplum (lines 915–18):

> . . . And lo, sires, thus I preche.
> And Jhesu Crist, that is oure soules leche,
> So graunte yow his pardoun to receyve,
> For that is best; I wol yow nat deceyve.

These famous lines represent not a "paroxysm of agonized sincerity" suddenly arrived at but a simple and direct statement of half of what the Pardoner has been saying all along. They take their full energy here only from the presentation of the other half which immediately follows.

"What you need is Christ's pardon—what you get is mine" (lines 919–45):

> But, sires, o word forgat I in my tale:
> I have relikes and pardoun in my male,
> As faire as any man in Engelond,
> Which were me yeven by the popes hond.
> If any of yow wole, of devocion,
> Offren, and han myn absolucion,
> Com forth anon, and kneleth heere adoun,
> And mekely receyveth my pardoun;
> Or elles taketh pardoun as ye wende,
> Al newe and fressh at every miles ende,
> So that ye offren, alwey newe and newe,
> Nobles or pens, whiche that be goode and trewe.
> It is an honour to everich that is heer
> That ye mowe have a suffisant pardoneer
> T'assoile yow, in contree as ye ryde,
> For aventures whiche that may bityde.
> Paraventure ther may fallen oon or two
> Doun of his hors, and breke his nekke atwo.
> Looke which a seuretee is it to yow alle
> That I am in youre felaweshipe yfalle,
> That may assoille yow, bothe moore and lasse,
> Whan that the soule shal fro the body passe.
> I rede that oure Hoost heere shal bigynne,
> For he is moost envoluped in synne.
> Com forth, sire Hoost, and offre first anon,
> And thou shalt kisse the relikes everychon,
> Ye, for a grote! Unbokele anon thy purs.

When these lines are read in context, it is hard to match them any-where in Chaucer for sheer venom. There is direct venom against the pilgrims, to be sure—"Paraventure ther may fallen oon or two" sounds like a wish—but most of his contempt for them arises from their failure to see and respond to what the Pardoner here says he is. The passage recapitulates in concentrated form all the aggressive methods of drama-tized self-condemnation the Pardoner has used throughout the tale—his conspicuous avarice, his ridiculous bulls, his rag-and-bone "relics," even the hints of perverse sexuality in the obscene invitation of "unbokele anon thy purs"—and tries to ram them down the pilgrims' throats. It does so, moreover, in such a way as to give greatest stress to the symbolic significance of these offered insults. Over and over the speech says: "I am what the pope licenses, what the church supplies for your spiritual needs. I am the instrument of Christ's mercy, the representative of the Holy Ghost among you. I am what you kneel to, whose relics you kiss. I am that *cupiditas* which is the root of evils, the Old Adam, the obscenity of the *eunuchus non dei* that invites to fruitless generation. See what I make of the instruments of salvation. What do *you* make of a church that licenses me, of a world in which I am possible, of a God that allows me to exist?" This too is what the Pardoner has been saying all along. As an instance of what Kierkegaard (p. 207) calls the demoniac form of despair, the Pardoner posits himself as a malignant *objection* to God and his creation. He presents himself as a proof against the goodness of existence and wills his own misery and evil as a protest against God; he forces into the open what was before only implicit in his self-dramatization, trying to *make* the pilgrims see it. This, finally, is what lies behind the Pardoner's typologizing of himself. His consistent practice is to convert the literal, the everyday, the phenomenal, to a sign for spirit. This is his idealism, in the technical sense, and it accounts for the feeling his tale notoriously gives of a world in which the power of the word over reality is nearly total. Having made these transformations, he then insists that the spiritual meaning of an old man, a bottle, or a pardoner is what these things *are* and how they must be treated. This insistence is, in another sense, his literalism, his delusion. But this again is an expression of his own spiritual state, his presumption and despair. The Pardoner's greatest self-condemnation is his moment of greatest pride, the moment when he attempts to force upon the pilgrims his own symbolic, typological vision of himself. What he *wants* here is to get them to take this vision for reality.

What he gets, however, is a set of responses that measures his excess and places it in a world at once more real and more ordinary than the one he has constructed in the course of telling his tale. The Host's answer to the Pardoner's final speech contains touches that seem to recognize the latter's spiritual perspective and perhaps testify to its immediate rhetorical and emotional power: "Nay, nay!" quod he, "thanne have I Cristes curs!" (line 946). But I think that what makes the already angry Pardoner even angrier – and silences him – is not that the Host "reveals" a sexual defect the Pardoner has been at pains to suggest and exploit but that Harry Bailly responds to a spiritual attack with a merely literal one. The Host's answer is not directed to the *eunuchus non dei*, only to a gelding. His response shows that he has missed the point of the Pardoner's self-presentation. His brutal literalism cuts through the tissue of spiritual allusion and moral self-dramatization in the Pardoner's final speech, reducing the Pardoner, his relics, and his "coillons," if he has them, to mere matter, and matter which is not even blasphemous, only insulting. The Host's explosion begins to restore a perspective which has been largely lost in the course of the tale's development when the Pardoner's voice is the only one before us – the perspective of the ordinary world.

There is a mood that sometimes comes on interpreters of *The Pardoner's Tale* in which the histrionics, pervasive irony, and symbolic pretension of the tale, the way it reaches for deep and ultimate meanings, seem open to skepticism: "Isn't it, after all, just a piece of entertainment? Isn't the end just a joke, isn't the Pardoner just a fund-raiser?"[10] This way of viewing the tale is valuable because it pinpoints the distinction the tale as a whole makes between the Pardoner's idea of himself – the way he presents himself – and a more detached and balanced view. This is the view taken by the end of the poem, and associated with the community of the pilgrims, society. Harry Bailly may not know exactly what the Pardoner is doing, but he can tell that it is more than a joke, and at first he responds in kind to its aggressive violence, what he rightly calls its anger: he can feel that the Pardoner is imposing something on him. After his initial outburst, however, the Host begins to put the situation in perspective. He is obviously a little shaken by his own reaction, the extent to which he has been drawn in to the Pardoner's mood, and begins to back off: "I wol no lenger pleye / With thee, ne with noon oother angry man" (lines 958–59). At this point other social forces intervene to break the mood further and to contain it, as the Knight, observing that "al the peple lough" (line 961),

---

[10] See John Halverson's levelheaded and persuasive summary of this strand in the criticism in "Chaucer's Pardoner and the Progress of Criticism," *ChauR* 4 (1970):191.

urges a reconciliation: "'as we diden, lat us laughe and pleye.' / Anon they kiste, and ryden forth hir weye" (lines 967–68).

The conclusion of the tale frames the Pardoner's performance as a social gaffe, a joke in bad taste that has gotten out of hand. It does so by showing us how society closes ranks to repair the breach in decorum, the violation of the tale-telling contract the Pardoner has committed. The kiss of peace at the end is, of course, hollow, a mere social form that lets things move forward smoothly. It allows the group to pretend that nothing untoward has happened and leaves the Pardoner in frustrated possession of his unhappy consciousness. This may well increase our sympathy for him, but the group is nonetheless correct in its assessment of the situation, for the most effective criticism of the Pardoner's presumption is precisely that it is presumptuous in an ordinary sense. It is preposterous that any man should carry the symbolic weight the Pardoner gives himself. If he takes all our sins on his shoulders by committing them, scapegoats himself like Christ in order to dramatize the pervasive presence of spirit in ordinary life, this is likely to make us reflect that Christ did not do this out of self-hatred and that not everyone who climbs upon a cross is Christ or a type of Christ or even a type of Antichrist. Going only on New Testament probabilities, two out of three are likely to be common thieves.

The way the end of the tale is framed so as to bring the Pardoner's typological consciousness into contact with an actuality that contains him and reveals his limitations suggests that, far from being an example of Chaucer's belief in and commitment to typological methods, the tale as a whole represents the poet's *critique* of typology as a way of thinking about the world. We need to make a distinction between typological *methods*, which in Chaucer's practice are simply one set of rhetorical techniques among many and open to anyone who has a use for them, and a typological imagination. Chaucer uses the former occasionally (in fact rather rarely in his own voice in *The Canterbury Tales*), and he has various pilgrims use them for various purposes in their tales. Unlike Dante, however, he does not seem to have the latter. The Pardoner is the one pilgrim who really does seem to have a typological imagination, a mind that habitually views the smallest details of life in the world *sub specie aeternitatis*, and what Chaucer's presentation identifies is the violence this cast of mind does to experience. Because the

Pardoner demands that the world must be more "perfect" in his own terms than it is, he is constrained to see and suffer it "out of alle charitee" as worse than it is, simpler, blacker and less flexible. Chaucer, with his habitual awareness that there is no such thing as disinterested language, sees that even doctrine, as it is encountered in concrete life, did not fall from the sky but is always being used by someone for some end. From this perspective what the poet identifies in *The Pardoner's Tale* is the temptation to pride and the illusion of power that typological thinking encourages. He shows how such think-ing may all too easily forget that it is only God who makes things them-selves into signs for other things at the level of eternal truth. Chaucer's critique of typology identifies it as a potentially defective form of meta-phor or image making that is too easily led to collapse the necessary distinctions between symbol and referent, literal and spiritual, mind and world. Less abstractly put, Chaucer shows that the Pardoner's tale is a bad *tale* because the Pardoner fails to see and sustain the crucial difference between fiction and reality, between a tale and the world in which it is told, and tries to force something he has made onto the world. The end of the tale shows that the typological imagination, by taking a God's-eye view, can all too easily deceive itself into playing God. This is a form of presumption that does not require divine inter-vention to discover its limitations.

The Pardoner is, as I have already suggested, the first exegetical critic of his own tale. He distorts his own sermon and exemplum by allegorizing and literalizing them beyond what they will bear. There is in this, perhaps, a lesson for much subsequent exegetical criticism, which, like the Pardoner himself, is too frequently docetist in ten-dency. That is, this kind of criticism often tends to imply that doctrine is more important than people, that the living temporal-historical ex-perience of real souls has nothing to say for itself, or, typologically and symbolically put, that Christ could not really have deigned to sully his spirit, his divinity, by incarnating it in a real human person. This view is ultimately as unfair to Saint Augustine and the middle ages as it is to Chaucer. It can become a form of historical and critical pride, and it seems to me to be no accident that in its purest form exegetical criti-cism is associated with an attempt to cut off medieval consciousness from our common humanity, to say, for example, that "medieval man" (the generic reference is telling in this context) had no personality because "he" talked about it differently from the way we do.[11] Such a view makes our ancestors simpler and purer, and therefore less human, than we are—or than they were. But I am beginning to sound like the Pardoner myself, and since I do not plan to burn Professor Robertson at the stake, let me say rather that exegetical criticism, if it loses its sense of proportion, can, like the Pardoner, get a little rude.

Chaucer's response, critical as it is of the typological imagination, is not simply a rejection of it but something far more complex and sympathetic. His attitude is not, or not only, that of the pilgrims who dismiss the Pardoner, close ranks, and "ryden forth hir weye"—after all, he wrote the tale. One frequently has the sense in The Canterbury Tales that audiences do not listen, that they do not hear what speakers are saying about themselves in their tales. In part, no doubt, this is a function of Chaucer's recognition of the important difference between real oral performance and the mediated literary imitation of oral telling he provides. No one could get out of a Canterbury tale what is in it by hearing it once, and by presenting the Pardoner's speaking in a written text—in the absence of the Pardoner himself and of the audience that dismissed him—Chaucer gives him more presence as a voice in the work than he apparently achieved on the pilgrimage. The fiction, perhaps, is that only Chaucer really understood the Pardoner and by writing him down gave him the chance to be read and reread—the chance to be heard.

This suggests that it is important to Chaucer that the Pardoner's voice be heard, in all its vividness, intensity, irony, and exegetical power. The reason for this, of course, is that the Pardoner is a considerable part of the poet. His impersonation of the Pardoner gives Chaucer a chance to exercise as well as exorcise his own attraction to the power of the poet's medium, language, over reality, and his fascination with the possibilities of typological symbolism. It also provides him with an opportunity to satirize the abuses of religious language he finds around him. Chaucer's first criticism of such speaking is surely the same as the Pardoner's: that it is too easily used to bolster and justify a corrupt establishment, to cover the ignorance, the lack of intelligence, and the moral obliquity of those who use it. The Pardoner speaks for

[11] D. W. Robertson, Jr., "Introduction," Chaucer's London (New York: Wiley, 1968), pp. 1–11.

the puritan, the utopian, the superior observer of human folly in Chaucer. There is too much truth (and too much fun) in the Pardoner's parody of sermons and exempla to think otherwise. The Pardoner's despair must also sometimes have been Chaucer's, or he could not have portrayed it so vividly. But Chaucer also sees what the Pardoner does not, the presumption of this attitude and the way it demands that God and the world conform to the impossible requirements of a human fantasy. The poet's own practice is counter to the Pardoner's; it consists in disciplining and subordinating his own vision to the portrayal of other consciousnesses, learning to see with the eyes and speak with the voices of others, to let the people, "lered oother lewed," speak for themselves. In *The Pardoner's Tale*, Chaucer both embodies and chastens his own impulse to play God, to judge and condemn his fellows and the world they all inhabit. The result of that chastening and self-discipline shows us Chaucer's difference from the Pardoner, but it also registers the power of the impulse and gives us the Pardoner himself in all his pride and despair, questioning and mocking in a voice of his own that disquiets us yet.

Part Two   THE TRANSMISSION OF THE TEXT

Poet as Reviser:
The Metamorphosis of the Confession
of the Seven Deadly Sins
in *Piers Plowman*

GEORGE H. RUSSELL

University of Melbourne

XPLICATING AND INTERPRETING *Piers Plowman* have often enough since the rediscovery of the poem produced heat rather than light.[1] Amid the often conflicting and irreconcil- able assertions about the poem, the fact of its revision, and, indeed, the general nature of that revision have been received with un- characteristic general agreement. This situation is easily disturbed once questions of motivation, agency, and consequence are raised. But there appears to be a general consensus that the revision of *B* over *A* was successfully controlled and transformed a relatively uncomplicated original into a richer and deeper poem than the one which in its earliest form was brought to a conclusion of bewilderment and frustration, though it was, in the *Visio* at least, sufficiently strong and assured for the revising poet to work with confidence and, as *B* shows, with suc- cess.[2] No such generally favorable view of the *C* revision seems to be current. E. Talbot Donaldson's important study of that version, which

---

[1] The discussion of this part of the poem (*A* 5; *B* 5.1–509; *C* 5.109–200, 6, and 7.1–154) vari- ously features in most accounts of the poem. It is discussed most usefully by Morton W. Bloom- field, *The Seven Deadly Sins* (East Lansing, Mich., 1952), especially pp. 196ff.; R. Tuve, *Allegori- cal Imagery* (Princeton, N.J., 1956), pp. 57ff.; S. Wenzel, "The Seven Deadly Sins: Some Problems of Research," *Speculum* 43 (1968):1–22; and Elizabeth Kirk, *The Dream Thought of Piers Plowman* (New Haven, Conn., 1972), pp. 46ff.

[2] Editions used for this essay are George Kane, *Piers Plowman: The A Version* (London, 1960); George Kane and E. Talbot Donaldson, *Piers Plowman: The B Version* (London, 1975); and Derek Pearsall, *Piers Plowman by William Langland: An Edition of the C-Text* (London, 1978). It should be noted that the *C* references differ significantly from the traditional Skeat references, since Pearsall has printed his text as consisting of Prologue and passus 1–22, not passus 1–23, as with Skeat.

after thirty years remains both the standard account and the most con-vincing reading of the C version, has the look of a defense of the poem in its new form: C has its own virtues derived from a design in many ways sharply different from that of its two predecessors, but not necessarily inferior to and certainly not irreconcilable with them.[3]

Whatever the validity of the judgments made, all serious readings of the poem in its three versions have accepted the importance of the fact of revision. And from the various studies there emerges a sense of the congruence of the A and B versions, judged to result from a successful process of remaking which is not discernible in the transformation of B into C. Notwithstanding their differences of length, A and B seem to offer a sense of common identity and purpose which B and C and, *a for-tiori*, A and C do not.

Whether this is so awaits detailed examination. The subject is un-deniably of great complexity, a condition inherent in the nature of both the process of revision and the quality of the texts used in the process. In plain terms at the outset the first, elementary question is why the revisions were thought desirable or necessary. If A is accepted as a poem that was broken off in uncertainty and possibly confusion, the reason for the first revision, which we know as B, is easily intelligible. Moreover, for any particular part of the poem, especially in the *Visio*, there would have been no intrinsic need for substantial alteration, whatever the inducement to elaboration, for *that* part of the poem might well be satisfactory and allowed to stand without major change. The need, in other words, was inferably first for no more than minor tasks of repair, expansion, and reorganization and then for the grasping of new initiatives and the access of courage and perception needed to carry the task through those later parts of the poem where the first version had seemed to falter.

This is the appearance of the process of revision to B from A. The changes judged to be needed in the *Visio* were evidently not the major ones. A good text was apparently available for the revision, and the process was, it seems, carried through without undue stress and diffi-

---

[3] E. Talbot Donaldson, *Piers Plowman: The C Text and Its Poet* (New Haven, Conn., 1949). There are also, on a smaller scale but more recent, Derek Pearsall's introduction to his edition of C and the introduction supplied by Elizabeth Salter and Pearsall to their edition of selections from the C version in the York Medieval Text Series (London, 1967).

culty. Its essential and substantial product was a complete remaking and massive expansion of the *Vitae*.

The process which produced the transition from *B* to *C* does not seem to have been like that. Here, clearly from the outset, it was a far more radical affair. From the beginning two drives seem to have deter-mined the nature of the revision: a desire to produce a poem different in kind from its predecessors and decisively changed in certain of its directions and a desire to modify and clarify certain theological and political positions adopted in the *B* version.[4] This new poem, more-over, had to be rebuilt from an imperfect available text, requiring not merely voluntary alterations but also those imposed by the need to set right what defective transmission had deformed.[5]

That is, of course, a simplistic representation of a very complex act of creation. It is essentially improbable that the creative artist would con-sciously view or treat his material in this way, but analytical criticism has to begin with some such explanation of the phenomena of revision. And certainly in this case the confluence of the creative and the im-posed, the voluntary and the involuntary needs for revision, often in ways that defy obvious analysis, seems clear: at times the poet must revise because he sees what he finds in his text as a malformation of what he once wrote, at times because his new conception of the poem calls for revision, at yet other times a process of revision imposed upon him by the deficiencies of his text merges, almost insensibly, into a recasting of a long passage which, in other circumstances, he might have let stand. But the processes, in fact, are not necessarily distinct. At any one time a malformation which would of itself demand a correc-tive revision might be the point from which a major recasting of the

[4] No attempt has been made in this essay to advert to the second of these propositions. I have offered some notes on one aspect of the problem in "The Salvation of the Heathen: The Explora-tion of a Theme in *Piers Plowman*," *Journal of the Warburg and Courtauld Institutes*, 29 (1966): 101–16. The most detailed discussion remains that of Donaldson cited in note 3 above. It is worth recalling that this book was written when the question of unity or multiplicity of authorship was a hotly debated one, and that this determines the direction of some, at least, of Donaldson's docu-mentation. As another poet observed: "A ȝere ȝernes ful ȝerne, and ȝeldes neuer lyke, / Ðe forme to þe fynisment foldez ful selden."

[5] The evidence upon which this statement, which is crucial to the following exposition, is based is set out in detail in Kane and Donaldson, *Piers Plowman: The B Version*, pp. 98ff. Certain elements of it are discussed further in G. H. Russell, "Some Aspects of the Revision in *Piers Plowman*," in S. S. Hussey, ed., *Piers Plowman: Critical Approaches* (London, 1965), pp. 27–49.

poem begins. What may begin as simple repair is transformed into major and decisive rewriting. And this reminds us that, at least in the revision of B to C, the process was not necessarily or even probably a completely planned and organized operation and did not necessarily proceed consecutively through the poem. The evidence suggests otherwise. The revision seems to have been selective, sporadic, and local, as the exposition that follows will suggest.

If we consider the relation between A and B in a selected section of a poem now in mid-course, we can hope to see the workings of the process. And, in fact, the version of the "confession" of the Sins, with the sermon context in which it is placed, is remarkably similar in A and B.[6] To generalize at the outset, B's alterations and additions, aside from the important addition of the *figura* of Wrath, seem designed to effect greater intensity and specificity, along with certain changes very broadly characterizable as of political and/or social import. They appear to be part of a process whereby the poem is given a more specific and deeper social involvement, and are possible manifestations of the clearer direction and greater confidence that B has displayed from the beginning.

A brief summary of those changes may be helpful. As the scene opens in B, Reason has replaced Conscience—who has disappeared—as the preacher, and he addresses his advice to the people in the presence of the King, not simply to the people of the Field (B 5.11–12). This new focus is sharpened by insertion of counsel directed explicitly to the King and the Pope at 5.48–51. This and a few minor changes such as the more emphatic advice to parents aside, the introduction of Repentance and the portraits of Pernele Proudheart and Lecher are left largely unaltered. It is only with the description of Envy that the revision begins. Here, B 5.86–125 are in various ways modified, with lines 86–92 alone subjected to heavy revision as against A 5.69–72, clearly in order to emphasize the malignity of Envy and to deepen the horror of the portrait. Wrath now appears among the sins for the first time, and so B 5.135–87 are new. Following this, the portrait of Covetise reproduces with little or no change that of the A version,

---

[6] A good recent account of the transition is given in Kirk, *The Dream Thought of Piers Plowman*. This includes an admirable analysis of the A version and a discussion of the manner in which this was transformed into B.

being, with the small intensifying addition of B 5.192–94, largely
unaltered as far as B 5.229. At this point, which marks the completion
of the A portrait, there is a massive addition, B 5.230–95, which opens
with a grim joke on the nature of restitution and a wry glance at that
kind of pilgrimage which we encountered in the Prologue, followed by
an account of the financial dealings of Covetise, which deepens the
shadows of the portrait as it intensifies the social implications of the sin
and brings Covetise to the brink of suicide. The elaborate portrait of
Glutton is left largely unaltered in its earlier part, with a small but
revoltingly vivid addition, followed soon after by new material at B
5.364–78 which once more involves Repentance and is again designed
to deepen and intensify. In accord with this the opening of the portrait
of Sloth, B 5.385–442, is new, a large insertion again involving Repentance as an interlocutor with the sin and heavy with its social implications. The revision is made *en bloc*, as seems characteristic of the B
revision at this point, with B 5.443–76 remaining largely unaltered
from their A shape. A completes its version of the scene at this point,
but B continues with Repentance's prayer, which places the sins in a
firm theological context of redemptive history and prepares the search
for Truth and the first appearance of Piers, soon to follow. Repentance
and his interventions are, we observe, once again notably emphasized
in this concluding section.

In summary, the B revision over A would appear to be a thorough
but relatively contained operation. Aside from the introduction of
Wrath which occupies B 5.135–87, there are significant alterations of
unquestioned authorial origin only at B 5.11–12, 23, 25, 28, 32–33,
36–40, 41–43, 48–55, 58–59, 86–92, 116, 121–23, 125, 127, 130–87,
192–94, 196, 218, 230–95, *after* 303, 308, 312, 316, 329–30, 337, 340,
351–56, 359, 364–79, 385–441, *after* 466, and 477–509. Of these alterations only ten can be described as large scale; the remainder involve
only small changes which leave the line essentially the same.[7]

By comparison, the magnitude and significance of the second process
of revision from B to C is surprising. This process is different in both
kind and degree from its predecessor and the signs of the difference ap-

[7] The list given excludes cases in which the archetypal text of B departs from that of A, but
demonstrably by corruption. As Kane and Donaldson's introduction makes clear, this occurs in a
large number of cases. In such instances, of course, revision is judged not to be in question.

pear early. There are the massive insertion of the Meed and Mercede passage at C 3.290ff. and the introduction of the "autobiographical" passage at C 5.1–104, which, leading into the sermon and the "confessions" of the sins, supplies a completely new context for both.

As the two versions come together, a pattern of persistent revision begins to emerge. Reason is again the preacher, but Conscience has returned, now in the role of "crocer" to Reason, who is "yreuestede ryht as a pope" and preaches "reuerentliche tofore al þe reume." Conscience, the preacher in A, addressing the people of the Field, who became in B Reason preaching to them in the presence of the King and proffering advice both to him and to the Pope, has now, while retaining the persona of Reason, been given the externals of a spiritual leader with a mission to the King and people both. His sermon is not, however, greatly altered in C. The only changes of substance are at C 5.124–27, 138–39, and after 142, where the revision appears to be spontaneous and not generated by corruption of the original. This pattern of correspondence is broken at line 146, where there appears a large insertion extending to line 179, a passage which in B appeared at 10.298–335, represented in only two manuscripts (RF) for part of its length. This is to be the first of a series of revisions in C different from anything encountered in the AB situation, revisions which result in a substantial recasting of the shape of the poem, specifically in the transfer of material. And this particular case is to the point. Reason's full investiture with the spiritual authority implied by his papal vestments makes it appropriate that he should address himself not simply to the people and their lay moral and social concerns but also, in the special way befitting his position as a spiritual leader, to the clergy, their concerns, and their relationships to one another and to their society.

But the passage holds a further interest. The presumption is that since B 10.298–335 was detached from its original context and transferred to the present one in C it was exposed in a special way to the poet's revising eye. Therefore, the frequent changes made in the passage are important. Many of the lines, while preserving the general tenor of their B counterparts, are heavily revised. And the revision is generated both by detection of error in the B original (as, for example, at C 5.150, 162) and by desire to modify the form and content of that original (as, in a famous instance, at lines 175–77).

Changes of this kind reflect not merely responses to local dissatisfactions of one kind or another but also a determination to remake this part of the poem in a way quite different from that of the first revision. And, as if to confirm this, the lines immediately following the insertion, C 5.180–96 are substantially revised and expanded over the AB version: it is significant that this revision is of a part of the B version where the text is generally accurate and stable. In effect, passus 5 in C has been made new from its "autobiographical" opening to its close. There is really no passus in B corresponding to it, for only its middle lines relate to anything in B.

That the pattern of the C revision is not to be simple or readily predictable would be further made clear from the opening of C 6, the point where the "confessions" begin and Pernele Proudheart makes her appearance. The text of B is reproduced without alteration for the first eleven lines, except for line 4, where the C archetype seems clearly to be scribally corrupt. But from line 11 onward the shape changes. Instead of now introducing Lecher as in AB, the poet gives an intervention by Repentance, followed by a response from Pride (no longer Pernele Proudheart). This passage was transferred here from B 13.275–312α, where it forms part of the Haukyn episode. It is not— and this again is significant confirmation of a process already observed —a mere transfer. The material in its new context has been comprehensively reworked, just as the earlier borrowing in passus 5 had been. The mere bulk is approximately the same, and the original lineaments of the lines are still visible, but the recasting is so complete that only some half-dozen lines are left in the original shape (B 13.282, 283, 293, 307–10). Once more, it would be difficult to argue that the revision here was induced by the unsatisfactory state of the poet's text, since his exemplar here, to judge from C 6.36–37, 42–48, was clearly similar to that preserved in the B manuscripts RF. B 13.282–83, 292–98 are lacking in most B manuscripts but seem clearly original. A more likely inference is that it was his transference of material from another part of the poem for insertion here which prompted him to reconsider and revise it.

Indeed, the revising activity is carried further. A transitional formula from Repentance leads in C to the appearance not of Lecher as in AB but of Envy. Nor is this rearrangement the only change. The B revision had left the portrait of Envy substantially in its A form. Occasional addition and expansion had etched the *figura* more deeply but had left it structurally similar to that of A. C proceeds otherwise. Once more he transfers material from the Haukyn passage, but this time he does not expand; overall he reduces the size of the C portrait by twenty lines.

Detailed comparison shows C beginning by excision. He removes those well-known and well-loved lines of the physical description of Envy (B 5.77–82), offering him to us now not in his intense, repulsive physicality but clothed in allegorical garments, without physical description.[8] Two lines alone survive from the immediate original context. Even so, one of the lines offers an interesting case. B 5.75 is almost certainly archetypally corrupt, reading "*mea culpa*" for A's "cope/coupe" and so offering an unacceptable sense. C 6.64 retains the "*mea culpa*" reading but so alters the shape of the line that the reading becomes both acceptable and effective. And, once more, as if this imposed task of reconstruction had directed his attention to the passage as a whole, C decides to remove original material and supply other lines from a different context.

This process of excision is followed by the importation from B 13.324–41 of C 6.69–85. By contrast with the two earlier importations, these transplanted lines are treated with the greatest respect, and the amount of revision is small. The poet repairs the metrical and sense structures of B 13.325–26; he shortens and tightens B 13.330 and proceeds from this to reshape the immediate context by insertion of C 6.76 and removal of B 13.331–32. The rest of the passage retains its original shape, except for C 6.83–84, where B 13.339–40 appear in a revised form, the latter of the pair at least corrupt and with a defective metrical pattern which he does not allow to stand. As he returns to the original portrait following this insertion, he excludes B 5.89–120; with the rest of the passage he makes no large-scale revision.

---

[8] This process of abandoning lines and passages beloved of critics is judged to be one of the many deadly sins of C.

C 6.86–102 correspond very closely to B 5.121–34.[9] At C 6.94 he re-tains "megre," which on A evidence is unoriginal in B, but he is unwill-ing to accept the shape of B 5.130, where the metrical form is defec-tive. He recasts this line, and, possibly stimulated critically by the ac-tivity, he continues detailed revision to the end of the portrait. The changes, while not substantial, attest his keen and sensitive attention to the text here.

The portrait of Wrath, not found in A, comes next as it does in B. Once more the revising activity of the poet is intense, but once more the pattern of revision is different from that of its predecessor. Here now there is no importation of material, presumably since the sin of wrath scarcely figures in the Haukyn section of B. The amount of detailed alteration is very large, and, unlike the previous passage, this one is expanded, not contracted from the B form. The recasting begins immediately. The opening allegory of B is replaced by a new, matter-of-fact account of the manifestation of the sin of anger throughout the range of society, in the course of which the detail of B is glimpsed only occasionally, as at C 6.120–27, in which elements of B 5.144–52 ap-pear in modified form and an altered context.

But this procedure is not followed throughout the description of Wrath and his actions. The section on the nuns and their quarrels is reproduced very closely as far as line 135 (B 5.160), where the decision to revise a line (not, this time, by the compulsion of detected corrup-tion) carries the revising activity over the lines that follow to the end of the section at line 142, including the omission of B 5.166–68 and its replacement by new material contained in C 6.143–50. This in turn is followed by the section on monks (B 5.169ff.), the first part of which is left largely unaltered, including C 6.155, which appears to be metri-cally defective in B but is allowed to stand. The remaining changes are persistent but confined to detail until the very end of the portrait, where the startlingly introduced first-person pronouns of B are re-

---

[9] A difficult and perhaps indeterminable case is that raised by C 6.89 (B 5.124), where the archetypal AB reading "Diapenidion" is replaced by "derworth drynke." This C reading must be regarded with suspicion. The context does not automatically suggest revision as the ground for the change. Further, "Diapenidion" is in the context both lexically and metrically a difficult reading, and "derworth drynke" has the uncomfortable feel of a scribal gloss. The difficulty is that there is evidence of genuine revision in the immediate context. C 6.91–92 seem to be clearly the product of revision.

placed by those of the third person. And so, after the extensive rewriting of its opening lines, this portrait, in contrast to the one before it, remains closer to its original than does any other so far. The practice of small but clearly original revisions is unquestionably attested, as is the point made by Kane and Donaldson that the process of revision is not, and should not be assumed to be, uniform in its operation.[10]

Now at C 6.170 comes a portrait of Lechery. In AB, it will be recalled, there was a very brief confession by Lecher after that of Pernele. Here we clearly have a calculated revision comparable in scale to that by which the confession of Pernele became the portrait of Pride. The original four lines of AB are retained but heavily modified, and lead, by way of an inserted passage of transition, to lines borrowed from the Haukyn section, B 13.343–51. These are used with only occasional modification as far as C 6.185, where C makes an addition in which the remaining Haukyn lines are discernible, notwithstanding revision. This is the most thoroughly revised of the "confessions," and indeed it is hard to avoid the sense that it might well be a piece of unfinished revision. It is unusually short, and its abrupt ending is quite untypical, lacking any intervention by Repentance.

The B order of the sins is resumed with the introduction of Covetise, whose description, for a change, is close to that in B. Except for insignificant, sometimes indeterminably scribal or authorial, detail, the two versions are parallel. There is evident repair work at C 6.204, 205, 233, and there are what seem to be unoriginal B readings retained at lines 220, 221, and 228. The repair work at line 223 is followed by the now-familiar pattern of detailed modification of the ensuing lines. The general pattern of B 5.230ff. and their progression are retained, but most of the lines up to C 6.252 have received minor modification. In lines 252–57, however, major recasting appears. Once again we see the reviser's activity as unsystematic and irregular, as one would expect of an author returning to review and reshape his creation.

To this material from the earlier version the poet adds C 6.258–85α, which in B stood as 13.358–98α. The shape of this material in its new context is often modified by unmistakeably authorial, persistent atten-

---

[10] Kane and Donaldson, *Piers Plowman: The B Version*, p. 126.

tion to small, even minute, details within individual lines and within the larger sections. Their authorial origin is proclaimed both negatively, by the absence of the characteristically scribal use of inflation, specificity, emphasis, and cliché, and positively, by the evidence of readiness to alter structures, to insert and remove in an intelligent and intelligible fashion which is magisterial in its operation and not dictated by the physical shapes of the contexts. This quality is clear at the conclusion of the passage (C 6.286–93β), transferred from B 13, when Repentance responds to the revelations of Covetise in words that clearly echo, but do not reproduce in detail, B 5.265ff. The transformation of the original material is complete, and, as if to stress the autonomy of the new version, C 6.316ff. are in genesis lines which come in B much later in the passus in the portrait of Sloth (B 5.461ff.); here they are embedded effectively and authoritatively in a new context.

The new portrait of Covetise is, then, the result of detailed and extensive reworking in which existing material is modified with confidence and authority to create a *figura* substantially altered from its predecessor in B. The case of Glutton is quite different. The opening lines of his portrait in the two versions (C 6.350–56, B 5.296–301) are demonstrably close but authorially reworked in detail to the extent that only three of them remain the same in C. That treatment is typical of what follows: in this portrait there is neither importation of material nor large-scale recasting; the difference of C results from persistent attention to the shape and structure of individual lines and takes the form of alterations that suggest close and perceptive reading by a reviser content with the main shape of the portrait but not with its detail.[11] This pattern extends through the greater part of the portrait and leaves B and C in exceptional parallelism. From C 6.419, however, the treatment of B changes. The remainder of the portrait, down to the last three lines, has been subjected to intense and detailed revision that modifies most lines, leaving only two untouched. It alters the whole cast of the passage, in particular by reducing the role of Repentance.

---

[11] Examples of this that might be cited are lines 380–81, 385 and 395 (two lines absent from the B archetype, present here in a slightly altered form, perhaps by imperfect reconstruction), 400 (an archetypal B error preserved), 402, 403, and 406.

The pattern of revision in the early part of the portrait of Sloth is similar to that of Glutton. In the opening twenty lines there is no at-tempt at revision unless, as at C 7.15 (B 5.399) there is manifest B cor-ruption calling for correction. B 5.404 (C 7.20) is archetypally corrupt and the C revision repairs the faulty reading. Perhaps as a consequence of his identification of this corruption and because the need for its repair directed his attention to the detail of the lines, the poet now begins to subject the text to frequent and, on occasion, heavy, de-tailed, but apparently unsystematic, revision. At times, as at C 7.27–29, 53, and 64, there is an apparent response to observed corrup-tion in the text of his original; at others the line is recast without any such evident stimulus, as at C 7.33–34, 38, 41, 49–50, 52.[12] Following C 7.68 the original conclusion of Sloth's confession in B has been replaced by a large insertion from B 13.409–56. This, in its turn, replaces B material which the poet has already used by transferring it to the confession of Covetise (B 5.464–76). From this point the poem moves into the enactment of the pilgrimage, and the "confession" of the sins is complete.

There is probably no other large body of text in the poem in which this revising activity is so intense or in which the poet has dealt so radically and authoritatively with B by relocation of its material, but the processes differ only in degree, not in kind, from those which oper-ated in most of the rest of the poem. And it is proper to speak of pro-cesses, rather than of a process, of revision, for at any point the revis-ing poet may take one of a number of approaches to his material.

The range of possibilities—on occasion necessities—is wide. It ex-tends from readiness to accept, even if by inadvertence, readings which a scrutiny of A or B or AB evidence leads us to consider unoriginal, through revisions of increasing complexity and thorough-ness, to radical recasting and relocation. And, except at one extreme, that is, the unambiguous presence of unoriginality which deforms the context, the poet's response is not predictable. This should not sur-prise: rather, it should be obvious that his motives for undertaking an

---

[12] In the case of the reworked line 53, which seems to be a response to observed corruption in B, one might contrast the following line 54, where an archetypal error in B has been allowed to stand.

extensive revision will have been strong, multiple, and complex. No single motive will cover, far less explain, the detail of the final design of C. In part the process of revision is repair work; in part it is a reworking which remakes the poem, which creates deliberately something different in kind from its predecessor.

Translation from Old English:
"The Garbaging War-Hawk,"
or,
The Literal Materials from Which the Reader Can Re-create the Poem

ERIC STANLEY
University of Oxford

ALBOT DONALDSON'S TRANSLATION of *Beowulf*[1] is highly successful. In introducing it to his readers, he lets us feel that he has been successful not by chance but through the avoidance of pitfalls; he speaks not for valor but for discretion in a translator: "Rather than try to create a new and lesser poem for the reader, it seems better to offer him in prose the literal materials from which he can re-create the poem."[2]

At frequent but irregular intervals scholars and others write about translations of *Beowulf* and how to do it or how not. Donald K. Fry's admirable *Beowulf* bibliography lists nearly thirty items "about trl" up to July, 1967. He published before the appearance of John Crane's "To Thwack or Be Thwacked: An Evaluation of Available Translations and Editions of *Beowulf*" (*CE* 32 [1970]: 321–40). Crane speaks of the Donaldson translation: "Its appeal throughout is always to the upper-level of college student" (p. 327). I do not know whether the translator feels thwacked by that, but I do not feel thwacked as the typical reader; the translation appeals to me, and the upper level of college student is where I belong.

Among the best of such studies is Chauncey Brewster Tinker's book

---

[1] *Beowulf: A New Prose Translation* (New York, 1966).

[2] The words quoted do not occur in the preface to the 1966 edition but are one of the changes made for the republication of the translation in *Beowulf: The Donaldson Translation, Backgrounds and Sources, Criticism,* ed. Joseph F. Tuso (New York, 1975), p. xvi.

on the subject.[3] His own translation is among the best in prose,[4] and it is pleasing to think that he too did well with the actual translation because he was in the process of surveying translators' failures. Yet even Tinker has, in a favorite passage, some words like "must needs" and "the wan raven...shall chatter freely": "Therefore many a spear, cold in the morning, must needs be clasped by the fingers, uplifted in the hand; the sound of the harp shall not waken the warrior, but the wan raven, eager o'er the doomed, shall chatter freely, telling the eagle how he sped at the feast, when with the wolf he plundered the slain."[5]

Every translator has his own recipe for avoiding the mistakes made by others. Prose has fewer pitfalls than verse; to undertake a verse translation requires courage. I have looked at most of the English verse translations of *Beowulf*, and to characterize them a little, I select from each a short and, I hope, typical passage. I think several of the more recent translators come out well, but they are usually the ones who have been least forceful in what they do to the language, and they do not use rhyme. In short, they are the closest to prose.

Michael Alexander's translation of the poem has undergone many changes. The revised version, given first, is an improvement on the earlier version:

> "This mail-shirt travelled far,
> hung from a shoulder that shouldered warriors:
> it shall not jingle again. There's no joy from harp-play,
> glee-wood's gladness, no good hawk
> swings through hall now, no swift horse
> tramps at the threshold. Terrible slaughter
> has carried into darkness many kindreds of mankind."[6]

[3] *The Translations of Beowulf: A Critical Bibliography*, Yale Studies in English, vol. 16 (1903). Edwin Morgan's *Beowulf: A Verse Translation into Modern English* (Aldington, Kent, 1952 [reprinted in paperback, Berkeley, Calif., 1962]) has a particularly valuable discussion of the art of translating the poem. A very good contribution to the subject is made in Adelheid Stiegler's Munich doctoral dissertation, *Studien zur Übersetzung des altenglischen Beowulfepos* (1964).

[4] *Beowulf Translated out of the Old English* (New York, 1902).

[5] For all Old English poems I give the line numbering of *The Anglo-Saxon Poetic Records*, adding for short poems the volume and page number. The quotation from Tinker comes at p. 141, and translates lines 3021b-27.

[6] *Beowulf: A Verse Translation* (Harmondsworth, Middlesex, 1973), p. 122, lines 2260-66.

"This mailshirt travelled far,
hung from a shoulder shouldered warriors;
it shall not jingle again. There's no joy from harp-play,
gleewood's gladness, no good hawk
swings through hall now, no swift horse
tramps at threshold. The threat came:
falling has felled a flowering kingdom."[7]

Kevin Crossley-Holland gives the first version below for the same lines in the course of his complete translation;[8] but the lines of the second version are from his "Literal Gloss"; that is, they are word for word:

"The linked mail may no longer
range far and wide with the warrior,
stand side by side with heroes. Gone is the pleasure
of plucking the harp, no fierce hawk
swoops about the hall, nor does the swift stallion
strike sparks in the courtyard. Cruel death
has claimed hundreds of this human race."

"Nor may ring-mail
alongside war-leader widely journey
heroes beside. Not at all harp's joy,
mirth of song-wood, nor good hawk
through hall swings, the swift steed
fortress-yard beats. Bale-death
many of human races forth on-sent!"

It is obvious, therefore, that Crossley-Holland never confused the literal gloss with the translation. It would have been possible to have regarded such literalism as poetry adopting Anglo-Saxon attitudes, and, as we shall see, several verse translations seem the product of such confusion.

Burton Raffel's translation grows on one.[9] When I first read it and reviewed it,[10] I thought it lacked some of the courage which William Morris had to excess; and so it does, but it seems now that Morris's

---

[7] *The Earliest English Poems: A Bilingual Edition* (Berkeley, 1970), p. 68, the same lines. The last line reproduces the *f* alliteration of the Old English.

[8] *Beowulf* (London, 1968), pp. 97 and 133.

[9] *Beowulf: A New Translation* (New York, 1963).

[10] *Modern Language Review* 59 (1964):253.

courage as displayed in his translation of *Beowulf* is of the kind of which even a little is too much. Raffel's simplicity of diction and syntax is as bearable as good prose:

> "Take these treasures, earth, now that no one
> Living can enjoy them. They were yours, in the beginning;
> Allow them to return. War and terror
> Have swept away my people, shut
> Their eyes to delight and to living, closed
> The door to all gladness. No one is left
> To lift these swords, polish these jeweled
> Cups: no one leads, no one follows. These hammered
> Helmets, worked with gold, will tarnish
> And crack; the hands that should clean and polish them
> Are still forever."[11]

If great poetry were the result, no Anglo-Saxonist would grudge a little freedom in translation. Kenneth Sisam, accurate scholar of Old English that he was, may have done a disservice to his subject by taking too schoolmasterly a view of Ezra Pound's modern interpretation of *The Seafarer*,[12] though perhaps Pound's poem is not great enough to excuse his freedom. I. Seraillier is free in his translation of *Beowulf*, of which the following is a sufficient sample:

> "And many a man shall greet his fellow with gifts
> Over the surging water, the seagulls' way."
> Then Hrothgar, the grey-haired king, giver of treasure,
> Embraced him, clinging to his neck and weeping bitterly
> As if his heart would break.[13]

Edwin Morgan's translation into verse seems to me the most satisfactory of all the attempts to reduce *Beowulf* to Modern English verse. He coins some mild compounds and ventures with some freedom to interpret the poem anew for modern readers:

> All these death swept,
> Years gone, away; and one man remained

[11] P. 93, lines 2247–57.

[12] In Pound's *Personae* (New York, 1926), pp. 64–66; Sisam gave his views on the poem as a translation in the *Times Literary Supplement*, June 25, 1954, p. 409.

[13] *Beowulf the Warrior* (London, 1954), p. 34, lines 1860–74, loosely and with much omission.

From the host of the people, the last wanderer there,
A watchman grieving over friends, to augur
For his own life the same: brief use, brief love
Of long-prized wealth. The barrow of the dead
Stood ready on the plain near the breaking sea,
New-made on the headland, built hard of access;
Into its interior the jewel-guardian took
That cherishable mass of the treasures of men,
Of the beaten gold, and uttered these words:
"Now earth hold fast, since heroes have failed to,
The riches of the race! Was it not from you
That good men once won it? Battle-death, evil
Mortal and terrible has taken every man
Of this folk of mine that has left life and time,
That has gazed its last on feast and gladness.
No one I have to be sword-bearer or burnisher
Of the beaten-gold goblet, the dearly-loved drinking-cup:
That chivalry has slipped away."[14]

Morgan is literal enough for us to know what words of his render each half line of the poem, and good enough for us to feel that some new grace has been given to many ancient lines.

More often, alas, when reading verse renderings of *Beowulf*, one longs for honest, kersie prose. Thus Mary E. Waterhouse's translation is serviceable but far from distinguished verse:

> No lady's custom such
> For maid to practise, peerless though she be,
> That a peace-loving girl exact the life
> Of a good man for a pretended insult;
> But Offa, Hemming's kinsman, dealt with that.[15]

Better, at least to my taste, Gavin Bone avoids excessive ordinariness:

> "With the first in war the corselet cannot walk,
> Nor keep company with a hero. No harp sings on,
> No pleasure of the playing-wood—no good hawk
> Swings down the hall, nor the stallion of pace

---

[14] 1962 ed., p. 61, lines 2236b–54.
[15] *Beowulf in Modern English* (Cambridge, 1949), pp. 67–68, lines 1940b–44.

Beats on the terraced camp. Life-harm has caught
Many a creature out of his dwelling-place!"[16]

Ordinariness combined with antiquarian word lore pulls down D. H.
Crawford's verse:

The warder had slain
one of a few; and so in fell wrath
the feud had been wreaked. 'Tis a mystery where
a mighty earl and brave will come by the destined
end of his life, when no longer he may
with men of his kindred inhabit the mead-hall.
With Beowulf 'twas so, when the warder of the barrow
he sought in mortal strife; he himself knew not
what should constrain him to part with the world.[17]

That a translator of *Beowulf* should have expected anything other
than failure from rhyming fourteeners seems amazing. A. Strong had
the advantage of R. W. Chambers's well-known "*Beowulf* and the
Heroic Age in England" as a foreword to his translation, but otherwise
little can be said of the work to recommend it. The poeticizing language
is further from normal speech than that of most. As poetry it seems a
bad translation, though not inaccurate, so that it may be forgivable to
quote from it the line about the "revel...In the lift at night," unfortunately not to be fully savored by speakers who use "elevator" for "lift":

Ay, surely the lord of the Weders, the monarch fell in war,
Had done with the days of his living, and a wondrous death had dreed.
But erst saw they over against him a being of monstrous breed,
For loathly there on the meadow lay the dragon. The guest of shame
And terror, the fiery serpent, was utterly shent with flame:
Fifty feet was his length as he lay there. Revel oftwhile had he kept
In the lift at night, and thereafter down into his cavern swept,
But now by death was he fettered, and the last of his pleasure and pride
Has he ta'en in his earthy caverns. But there lay there by his side
Beakers and stoups amany, and platters of price thereto,
And many a sword-blade splendid that the rust had eaten through.[18]

---

[16] *Beowulf in Modern Verse* (Oxford, 1945), p. 65, lines 2260b–66.

[17] *Beowulf Translated into English Verse* (London, 1926), p. 116, lines 3060b–68.

[18] Sir Archibald Strong, *Beowulf Translated into Modern English Rhyming Verse* (London,
1925), p. 93, lines 3037–49a.

There is a greater competence in C. Scott Moncrieff's translation of *Beowulf*, in spite of the pinchbeck compounds, and in spite of the difficulty a modern reader has when faced with regular, caesural virgules:

Then swiftly (as I heard) / the son of Weohstan
When this word was spoken / his wounded lord,
War-sickened, obeyed, / went in his ringed byrny,
His braided battle-sark, / under the barrow's roof,
Saw he then in his triumph, / as by the seat he went,
A masterful tribe-thegn, / treasures many,
Glistening gold / on the ground gathered,
Wonders on the walls, / and the Worm's den,
The old twilight-flier's; / flagons stood there,
Far-dead men's vessels, / with none to furbish them,
Husked of their platings.[19]

In some of these verse renderings the wording is too far from modern linguistic reality, and the word order even further, as an attempt is made to recapture a long lost relative freedom.

Modern English can hardly accommodate the Nibelungen stanza:

Diu junge marcgrâvinne   kuste die künige alle drî,
(alsam tet ir muoter).   dâ stuont ouch Hagene bî.
ir vater hiez in küssen;   dô blihte si in an.
er dûhte si sô vohrtlîch   daz siz vil gerne hete lân.[20]

This is the rhythm which W. E. Leonard chose to imitate in his translation of *Beowulf*. Perhaps he was attracted to it by the variation in rhythm permitted especially in the final half line of each stanza, and which in the following last half line he uses well. But the strange compounding and archaisms, as well as the long line which has to be endured till the rhyme word breaks in, make the attempt unsuccessful:

He took the cup from Wealtheow,   a warsman fierce-to-smite;
And then he offered answer,   eager for the fight.
Beowulf made a speech then,   bairn of Ecgtheow he:

---

[19] *Widsith, Beowulf, Finnsburgh, Waldere, Deor* (London, 1921), p. 91, lines 2752–62a.
[20] *Das Nibelungenlied*, ed. H. de Boor (Leipzig, 1949), 27.1665: "The margrave's young daughter kissed all three kings (as did her mother). Hagene too stood close to them. Her father bade her kiss him. She looked at him then: he seemed so terrifying to her that she would very gladly have left it undone."

> "When with my troop of tribesmen, I mounted on the sea,
> And sate me in my sailor-boat, I had this thought in me:
> Either to work for all time thy peoples' will at last,
> Or to fall afighting in grip of Grendel fast
> Firm am I to do my earlman's deed withal,
> Or to dree my end-of-days in this mead-hall."[21]

Although Leonard's rhythms and Anglo-Saxonisms are an amalgam far removed from border balladry, the overall effect of the caesura in the unbalanced long line, enhanced as it is by *bairn* and *dree*, reminds one of the ballads, and *Beowulf* seems to have lost its stateliness in the transformation.

John R. Clark Hall's metrical translation had been preceded by a prose translation, to which he directs those readers "who wish to make a detailed study of the poem."[22] The merit of the translation is perhaps chiefly its use of a verse line reminiscent of Old English. It is easy to find examples of poetic diction in Clark Hall's verse which, for all their artificial revivals, add little other than philological memories – e.g., "doughty, sure, is the chief" (line 369) and "what time his son hangs" (line 2447). Sometimes Clark Hall alters the length of his lines to something shorter; it is not easy to understand why:

> "Moreover the war-dress which bore in the battle
> the bit of the sword-blades, amid the shield-clashings,
> decays with its owner; nor may the ringed byrnie
> go far on its travels along with the chieftains, –
> attendant of heroes. No harp gives out gladness,
> the glee-wood no pastime.
> No good hawk sweeps
> around the hall, nor no swift horse
> the court-yard paws. The bale of death
> has banished hence hosts of our race."[23]

Clark Hall in his verse and in his prose translation made frequent use of "nor" to translate *ne* even when it stands immediately before a verb

---

[21] "Beowulf and the Niebelungen Couplet," *University of Wisconsin Studies in Language and Literature* 2 (1918):151, lines 628b-38. These lines are reprinted with only minor changes in *Beowulf: A New Verse Translation for Fireside and Class Room* (New York, 1923), p. 29.

[22] *Beowulf: A Metrical Translation into Modern English* (Cambridge, 1914), p. vii.

[23] P. 82, lines 2258-66.

("nor may the ringed byrnie"), presumably because "nor" (unlike "not") permits inversion of subject and verb, thus giving something of the feel of Old English word order.

F. B. Gummere's translation is based on two questionable assumptions. The first is the complacent view that his medium is adequate to the task: "No greater mistake exists than to suppose that the rhythm and style of these early English poems cannot be rendered adequately in English speech."[24] Secondly, he thinks that Beowulf is not much of a poem and can be put into an adequate modern poetic form by anyone, who need not be much of a poet for the purpose. Gummere uttered his remark during a controversy with C. G. Child, himself a good prose translator of the poem and a mild critic of Gummere's verse translation.[25] Child gives brief reasons why a verse translation of Beowulf is impossible and goes on to say how Gummere almost achieves the impossible. Gummere, like Drawcansir, goes to the attack in all directions simultaneously and proves his own adequacy by reducing the poet of Beowulf to a stature no more than his own:

But is Beowulf the work of a really great poet? Is it what we now call a really great poem? Is it not rather a precious specimen of a mass of amazingly average and uniform poetry which is great only so far as it is national, racial, epic in the large sense, thinking the thoughts of a new, half-formed civilization, reflecting the life of a keen and conquering folk, and echoing to the clash of battle down long years of warfare on land and sea?[26]

Child's reply to Gummere is more than a debating point: it is central to an understanding of the art of translating poetry, that faithfulness to the original should be aimed at even if it cannot be achieved because of a limited understanding of the original: "A prose translator has his own share of errors to lament, but they are not conscious mistranslations, due to the medium employed."[27] A brief specimen of Gummere's skill as a translator of Beowulf shows why Child may have been restrained in his praise:

[24] The Oldest English Epic (New York, 1909), p. 19.
[25] Child's review appeared in MLN 24 (1909):253-54. For his translation, see p. 97.
[26] MLN 25 (1910):63.
[27] Ibid., p. 157.

Yet here must the hand of the henchman peerless
lave with water his winsome lord,
the king and conqueror covered with blood,
with struggle spent, and unspan his helmet.
Beowulf spake in spite of his hurt,
his mortal wound; full well he knew
his portion now was past and gone
of earthly bliss, and all had fled
of his file of days, and death was near.[28]

The medium employed in translating is at its most grotesque in William Morris's verse translation of the poem, *The Tale of Beowulf*, so much so that if one were asked, Who is the greatest of the translators of *Beowulf*? the answer would echo André Gide's about a better poet, William Morris, *hélas!* The following is, I think, among the less obscure and more successful passages:

Then heard I that swiftly the son of that Weohstan
After this word-say his lord the sore wounded,
Battle-sick there obeyed, and bare forth his ring-net,
His battle-sark woven, in under the burg-roof;
Saw then victory-glad as by the seat went he,
The kindred-thane moody, sun-jewels a many,
Much glistering gold lying down on the ground,
Many wonders on wall, and the den of the Worm,
The old twilight-flier; there were flagons astanding,
The vats of men bygone, of brighteners bereft,
And maim'd of adornment; was many an helm
Rusty and old, and of arm-rings a many
Full cunningly twined‖ All lightly may treasure,
The gold in the ground, every one of mankind
Befool with o'erweening, hide it who will‖[29]

On the whole, however uneasy one may be about Morris's rendering as a specimen of late-nineteenth-century English verse, it is better than

---

[28] *The Oldest English Epic*, pp. 140–41, lines 2720–28.

[29] Colophon: *Here endeth the Story of Beowulf done out of the Old English tongue by William Morris & A. J. Wyatt* (Hammersmith, Middlesex, 1895), p. 96, lines 2752–66. Wyatt provided the prose translation for Morris to versify. Instead of ‖, Morris prints the Kelmscott leaf ornament before and after the proverbial utterance of the last two and a half lines. The cheap reprint (London, 1898) uses full stops instead and has a comma after "battle-sick" in the third line.

all the English verse translations that preceded it, of which the following are typical samples:

> "So to hoar-headed hero 'tis heavily crushing
> To live to see his son as he rideth
> Young on the gallows: then measures he chanteth,
> A song of sorrow, when his son is hanging
> For the raven's delight, and aged and hoary
> He is unable to offer any assistance."[30]

> "I the land-dwellers, my own people,
> Counsellors-in-hall, that have heard say
> That they used to see a pair of such
> Mickle mark-steppers holding the moors,
> Spirits of elsewhere: one of these was,
> As they most certainly might then perceive,
> A woman's form."[31]

H. W. Lumsden arranges his verse in long lines:

> Hopeless of life, but stern and grim, the mighty blade he drew,
> And struck so fiercely at her neck, a stroke so hard and true
> The bone-rings broke, and through her flesh fordoomed sheer
>   went the sword.
> Down on the floor she fell; his handiwork made glad the lord;
> All gory was the glaive.
>   Light stood within, the flame burned sheen,
> Even like as in the firmament heaven's candle shines serene.[32]

Most of the lines could be arranged as ballad meter, though some lines
require a little violence for that:

> All gory was the glaive. Light stood
> within, the flame burned sheen,
> Even like as in the firmament
> heaven's candle shines serene.

The first complete translation into verse is in short lines, reflecting
the hudibrastic manner of printing Anglo-Saxon verse in English books;

[30] J. L. Hall, Beowulf: An Anglo-Saxon Epic Poem (Boston, [1892]), pp. 82–83, lines 2444–49.
[31] J. M. Garnett, Beowulf: An Anglo-Saxon Poem (Boston, 1882), pp. 41–42, lines 1345–51a.
[32] Beowulf: An Old English Poem Translated into Modern Rhymes (London, 1881), p. 49, lines 1565–72a.

it is not in ballad meter, however, but in tail rhyme, reminiscent of Sir Thopas:

> The Prince of Earls yet furthermore,
>   The Kinsmen of Healfdene,
> Twelve Treasures on his Guest did pour,
> Then bade them speed them on their Way,
> In Peace their Friends a Visit pay
>   And quick return again.
> The Scylding Chief, the Monarch high,
> Good in his fair Nobility,
>   Then kiss'd the worthy Thane,
> His Neck in Warmth he did embrace
> While on the grey-hair'd Hero's Face
>   The Tears of Grief are seen.
> Aught was more likely than, (since he
>   Was now infirm and old,)
> That they should more each other see,
>   And Conferences hold.
> So well he lov'd the gentle Thane
> That he in no wise might restrain
>   The tender Bosom-flood;
> But long'd in secret for his Guest
> Fast in his Spirit-bonds possess'd
>   Who warr'd with the Men of Blood.
> Beówulf thence with Gold full proud,
>   Glad with his Treasure-Hoard,
> Along the grassy Meadows trod
> To where his Sea-bound Ship abode,
> And safely still at Anchor rode,
>   As waiting for her Lord.[33]

Early translation of *Beowulf* is a struggle with a difficult text, often beyond accurate comprehension. At worst, a modern reader who has some familiarity with the poem has to look hard at a translation purporting to correspond to something not easily reconciled with it. It is like reading a translation produced by a weak candidate in an examination: one has to look hard to recognize the passage, and, having iden-

---

[33] A. Diedrich Wackerbarth, *Beowulf: An Epic Poem Translated from the Anglo-Saxon into English Verse* (London, 1849), p. 72, lines 1866-83.

tified it, one has to look harder to see which phrase in the translation corresponds to some words of the original and then which words in the original have been left untranslated. Thus the following is intended by William Taylor of Norwich for lines 2724–33a, referred to as coming from the "thirty-seventh saga":

> Thus spake Beowulf:
> My wound will not heal,
> Black is the flesh,
> And I knew that to-day
> The pain would increase.
> From joys of the earth
> I am shut out for ever.
> To-day is fixed,
> And my death is nigh.
> Now, my son, will I hand you
> The harness of war,
> In which I rejoiced
> At the storm of the fight,
> Which my father gave me.
> And with it I give,
> As to the most worthy,
> The whole of my wealth.
> I have govern'd the people
> For fifty winters.[34]

Comparison with the standard achieved by Taylor in that extract will lead the modern reader to judge J. J. Conybeare's work with some respect. He translated extensive extracts of *Beowulf* into graceful blank verse the elegance of which owes little to the original:

> "Chieftain! give place not to presumptuous thought.
> Now is thy prowess in its flower of prime;
> But the day comes, when pain, or slow disease,
> Or the fire's ravening force, or whelming flood,
> Or battle blade, or arrow's deadly flight,
> Or hateful age, or the more sudden stroke
> That dims and quells at once our mortal sight,
> Shall rack thy heart, and bow thee to thy doom;

[34] *Historic Survey of German Poetry* (London, 1828), 1, p. 87.

Conquering the conqueror. So full many a year
Under high heaven did Hrothgar [i.e., *the speaker*] hold this realm.
And spread from land to land his warrior sway.
Right little dreamt I in that hour of pride
That aught might rise beneath yon firmament,
Of power to work me sorrow or annoy."[35]

Henry Wadsworth Longfellow, in a review article in *North American Review* (47 [1838]), made use of Conybeare's translations, one literal into Latin and the other in blank verse, to get back to something closer in feel to Anglo-Saxon verse. Longfellow's translation of lines 189–257 has found its way into the many collections of his verse. Conybeare turns lines 198b–204 into modern blank verse thus (p. 38):

> And soon that noble soldier bad array
> A goodly ship of strength. The hero spoke
> His brave intent, far o'er the sea-bird's path
> To seek the monarch at his hour of need.
>   Full swift address'd them to that enterprise
> His loved associates.

Conybeare skips lines 203–204, but the Latin gives for lines 202–204 (p. 86):

> Istud navigium ei
> Prudentes asseclæ
> Cito instruxerunt,
> Quum iis carus esset.
> Exacuebant animos,
> Omen captabant.

Longfellow turns all this into:

> He bade him a sea-ship,
> a goodly one, prepare.
> Quoth he, the war-king,
> over the swan's road,
> seek he would
> the mighty monarch,
> since he wanted men.

---

[35] *Illustrations of Anglo-Saxon Poetry*, ed. W. D. Conybeare (London, 1826), pp. 60–61, lines 1760b–73.

> For him that journey
> his prudent fellows
> straight made ready,
> those that loved him.
> They excited their souls,
> the omens they beheld.[36]

It is likely enough that Longfellow referred to the Anglo-Saxon original, printed parallel to the Latin in Conybeare.

In verse translation of *Beowulf* we can go back no further. The faults are glaring even in this selection, which was made to bring out some of the better lines rather than the worst. Mild praise is as far as one might wish to go for mildly successful translations. No wonder that many translators thought prose the safer way. The more conscious the trans-lator is of the poetic art of the poem in a language and a form of verse very different from what is available to us in Modern English, the more he shies away from the attempt to imitate that poetic art in our language or to replace it with a different art.

Prose translation is another matter. The literal gloss is for informa-tion only. It must be sufficient to allow the reader to identify the syn-tax for understanding the continuous sense. An inflected language with a freer word-order than Modern English is more convenient for that purpose, Neo-Latin or Modern German, for example. It makes no difference for literal glossing if the piece glossed is prose or verse.

In fact, the first translation into Modern English of any Anglo-Saxon verse was made as a literal gloss without awareness that it was verse: Alfred's verse Prologue to the *Pastoral Care*. The Parkerian edition of Asser included Alfred's prefaces, in prose and verse, to the *Pastoral Care*.[37] The text is that of Parker's manuscript, now Cambridge University Library Manuscript Ii.2.4.[38] In the Parkerian edition the translation is printed interlinearly, and presumably it was to be read word for word with the Old English read word for word:

Ælfred   Kyng wysheth greetyng   *to Wulfsige Bishop*
Ælfred Kyning   hateþ gretung [*margin* alias. gretun (sic)] Wulfsige   Bisceop

---

[36] *North American Review* 47 (1838):104.

[37] Matthew Parker, *Ælfredi Regis Res Gestae* (London, 1574), sigs. Fj–Fij.

[38] For details see N. R. Ker, *Catalogue of Manuscripts Containing Anglo-Saxon* (Oxford, 1957), no. 19.

hys worthy   louely &   frendly,   & thee to know I will, that to me it comth
his worðum luflice 7   freondlice; 7   þe   cyðan   hate; þæt me   com

very   often in   mynde   what manner of wisemen long since were throughout
spiðe [sic] oft on gemynd;   hwylce   witan   geo   wæron geond

the English nation, both of the spirituall   degree as of the temporaltie.
Angelcyn;   ægðer ge godcundra hada   ge woruldcundra.

The verse appears the same way.[39] The heading, however, "Liber loquitur," shows that the translator recognized correctly that this part of the Preface is figurative and therefore poesy as understood in the age of Sidney. I set the end of the poem (lines 8–16) in verse lines:

Bicause he of mankynde   the most   begat
Forþam he mancynnes   mæst gestrinde

to heauen   warde,   of Romaynes   the best
wodera [sic] wearde   Romewarena   betst

man, of courage wealthiest,   of power most free.
manna; mod   weligost   mærða gefrægost.

After that me into english   Ælfred the king
Siððan   me to englisc Alfred cyning

turned   worde eche one,   & me to his writers
awende words gehwilc; 7   me his   writerum

sent   South & North.   To that ende he commaunde them such lyke me
sende; Suð 7 Norð.   Forþam   he   het   him swilcra ma

to bryng after theyr   copy   that he to his bishops
brengan be þære bysyne   þæt he   his biscopum

send them might,   because they to certain of his bishops were nedefull,
sendan meahte; forþam hi   his sume   be þorftan

which the latin   speech   lest   vnderstood.
þa   þe leden spræce læste   cuðon.

The translation is designed to go closely with the Old English, and it is on the whole not unsuccessful. Of course, it is too literal for reading

---

[39] See ASPR 6:1105, p. 110, for the arrangement of the Old English; Dobbie did not use this particular manuscript. In the Parkerian edition it is printed at sig. Fij^vo.

in its own right, away from the original. The habit of interlining a con-tinuous gloss in the printed text of an obscure language goes on, as every schoolboy, every undergraduate, knows. A good example of an interlinear gloss to an Old English poetic book is to be found in Edward Lye's—and then Owen Manning's—copy of F. Junius's edition of *Cæd-monis Monachi Paraphrasis Poetica* (Amsterdam, 1655).[40] The inter-linear gloss by Lye and Manning is into Latin. It underlies their lexico-graphical use of the poems. There is no sense of elegance, not even of continuity. The aim, not well achieved, was merely to get the sense right, word for word.

Prose achieved elegance in translation before verse. Laurence Nowell seems excellent to me, and surprisingly accurate, though the text is easy, "The Voyages of Ohthere and Wulfstan":

The principall purpose of his traueile this way, was to encrease the knowledge and discouerie of these coasts and countreyes, for the more com-moditie of fishing of horsewhales [*margin*: Or, morsses], which haue in their teeth bones of great price and excellencie; whereof he brought some at his returne vnto the king. Their skinnes are also very good to make cables for shippes, and so vsed. This kinde of whale is much lesse in quantitie then other kindes, hauing not in length aboue seuen elles. And as for the common kind of whales, the place of most and best hunting of them is in his owne

---

[40] The volume, now part of MS 823 of the Society of Antiquaries, was donated to the society by Thomas Thorpe (the bookseller) of Bedford Street, London, in January, 1835. The librarian of the society, Mr. John Hopkins, kindly allowed me to consult the book, and I wish to thank him for his help during my visit. I do not know what the connection, if any, is between Thomas Thorpe and Benjamin Thorpe, F.S.A., but the preface to the latter's edition for the Society of Antiquaries of *Cædmon's Metrical Paraphrase* (London, 1832) mentions Lye's translation only as one might through material available to the public (e.g., Thorpe, p. vi, refers to Nichol's *Literary Anecdotes 5* [1812]:403-4), and not as if Thorpe had Lye's copy of Junius's *Cædmon* in front of him. There is other evidence that Lye's Latin translation was not a stage toward Thorpe's. For example, Thorpe would not have put as a speculation (p. 24, line 12) "Lye reads *aswaniað*, which he seems to have copied from Somner" if he had known as a fact from Lye's Junius (p. 9), "Somn. legit *asuaniað*." He knew Lye's (and Manning's) glosses into Latin of the Cædmonian poems only through the *Dictionarium Saxonico- et Gothico-Latinum* (London, 1772), the first dictionary to make systematic use of Junius's edition. Two hands occur in this copy of Junius, Lye's and, infre-quently, Manning's; cf. the Society's *Minute Book* 36 (1830-35):440. That the infrequent hand is Manning's is demonstrable from the agreement between emendations suggested in that hand and readings in the Supplement by Manning to the *Dictionarium* (e.g., p. 24, that *hyge wælmos teah* be emended to *hyge wælm ofteah*, line 980 of *Genesis*, adopted by Thorpe, p. 60, n. *b*, from the *Dic-tionarium*, Supplement, s.v. *hige*; similarly, Thorpe, p. 117; Lye's Junius, p. 43; and *Dictionarium*, Supplement, s.v. *hleor-lora*).

countrey: whereof some be 48. elles of length, and some 50. of which sort he affirmed that he himselfe was one of the sixe, which in the space of 3. dayes killed threescore. He was a man of exceeding wealth in such riches, wherein the wealth of that countrey doth consist. At the same time that he came to the king, he had of his owne breed 600. tame Deere, of that kinde which they call Rane Deere: of the which number 6. were stall Rane Deere, a beast of great value, and marueilously esteemed among the Fynnes, for that with them they catch the wilde Rane Deere. He was among the chiefe men of his countrey one: and yet he had but 20. kine, and 20. swine, and that little which he tilled, he tilled it all with horses. Their principall wealth consisteth in the tribute which the Fynnes pay them, which is all in skinnes of wilde beasts, feathers of birds, whale bones, and cables, and tacklings for shippes made of Whales or Seales skinnes. Euery man payeth according to his abilitie. The richest pay ordinarily 15. cases of Marterns, 5. Rane Deere skinnes, and one Beare, ten bushels of feathers, a coat of a Beares skinne, two cables three-score elles long a piece, the one made of Whales skin, the other of Seales.[41]

That combination of good prose and accuracy, by the standards of its times, is rare. There is not space in this study, which is sketchy even for translations of *Beowulf*, to do much more than quote from this, the first example of Old English prose into good modern prose. Verse into prose, good and bad, is, however, near the center of this study. After the Parkerian beginning with the verse Preface to the *Pastoral Care*, translated word for word, most translation of verse was into Latin. That too lies outside the scope of this study. It did correspond, espe-cially in Hickes's *Thesaurus*, to the best early Anglo-Saxon scholarship and answered the needs of scholars who would have doubted the art of Anglo-Saxon verse, except as rough or half-formed.

Samuel Henshall, one of the most ignorant of those who before the end of the eighteenth century exposed their state of knowledge in print, was significantly aware of the shortcomings of understanding Anglo-Saxon verse and prose by way of Latin glossing. His book on the acquisition of a knowledge of Anglo-Saxon arrogantly proclaims a policy of translating Anglo-Saxon into Modern English not merely

---

[41] Richard Hakluyt, *The Principal Navigations, Voiages, Traffiques and Discoueries of the English Nation*, 2d ed., vol i (London, 1598), p. 42. The extract reprinted here corresponds to p. 18, line 34, to p. 19, line 58 in D. Whitelock's revised edition of *Sweet's Anglo-Saxon Reader* (Oxford, 1967). For the ascription to Nowell see D. S. Brewer, "Sixteenth, Seventeenth and Eighteenth Century References to the Voyage of Ohthere," *Anglia* 71 (1953):208–209.

word for word (the older interlinear glosses had done that) but by seeking the supposed descendants in Modern English of the Anglo-Saxon words and using them in translation root by root: *The Saxon and English Languages Reciprocally Illustrative of Each Other: the Impracticability of Acquiring an Accurate Knowledge of Saxon Literature, through the Medium of Latin Phraseology, Exemplified in the Errors of Hickes, Wilkins, Gibson, and Other Scholars, and a New Mode Suggested of Radically Studying the Saxon and English Languages* (London, 1798). Henshall's method of translation is sufficiently illustrated by quoting his interlinear translation of two pieces of verse, altered by me to correspond to the arrangement of the lines as in modern editions. First, Caedmon's "Hymn":

> *Now we shall hearen heaven's Reach word,*
> Nu we sceolan herigean heofon Rices weard,
>
> *mighty's might; and his mode of thought;*
> mitodes miht; and his mod gethanc;
>
> *worked worlds father; so he worlds give was;*
> weorc wuldor fæder; swa he wuldres geh wæs;
>
> *eke Do-right earth in stilled;*
> ece Drighten ord onstealde;
>
> *he erst shaped elder Barns*
> he erest gescop ælda bearnum
>
> *Heavens to roof holy Shaping;*
> heofon to rofe halig Scyppend.
>
> *then middle earth men's kind world**
> tha middan geard mon cynnes weard
>
> *eke Do-right after tied,*
> ece Drihtne æfter teode,
>
> *free folds from (the) Almighty.*[42]
> firam foldan frea Ælmihtig.

A pleasing footnote goes with the asterisk of the last word of the

---

[42] Henshall, p. 47. The West-Saxon text is (with errors) that of John Smith, *Historiae Ecclesiaticae Gentis Anglorum Libri V, a . . . Baeda* (Cambridge, 1722), p. 597.

antepenult line: "*The omission of a letter here, l, is sometimes not to be much regarded."

Gough, in his copy of Henshall's book (now in the Bodleian Library), in addition to the penciled "What nonsense" in the margin of Cæd-mon's "Hymn," draws attention to the fact that a translation into English was available in Maurice Shelton's *Wotton's Short View of Hickes's Grammatico-Critical and Archeological Treasure* ([London, 1735], p. 19):

Now will we praise the Governour of the Heavenly Kingdom (*or* Heaven,) the Power of the Lord, and the Purpose of his Mind, and the Deeds of the Father of Glory; Who, as he wonderfully existed, hath always remained from the beginning Lord Everlasting. He, after he had fashioned the sacred Firma-ment, made it first for a Covering to the Sons of Men. Then he, the Protector of Mankind, Lord-Eternal, and God Almighty, ordained the Earth for Man's Habitation.

Henshall does no better with a little bit of "The Battle of Brunan-burh"; that he deviates into sense in line 72, "Welch," may be the result of his having used Bishop Edmund Gibson's *Chronicon Sax-onicum* ([Oxford, 1692], p. 114). These are the last lines of the poem:

Nor were there Wail more,
Ne   wærth   wæl   mare,

in this Island,	*ever as yet, (with)*
on this Eiglande,	æfer gyta,

folks	*filled,*	*before*	*this,*
folces	gefylled,	beforan	thissum,

(by) swords edges	*thus they us (that) seeketh book,*
swordes ecgum,	thæs the us secgath bec,

elder oth' wisemen,	*sith-thence Eastern hither,*
ealde uth witan,	siththan eastan hider,

Angles and Saxons,	*up came,*
Engle and Seaxe,	up becomon

o'er (the) briny broad,	*Britain soughten*
ofer brynum brad,	Brytene sohton,

Lance with Smiths,   Welch   overcame,
wlance wig Smithas,   Wealles ofer-comon,

earls   harrowed,   earth they gotten.[43]
eorlas arhwate,   eard   begeatan

Henshall's reviewers had no difficulty demonstrating his incompetence and regarded the work as ignorant and presumptuous in attack-
ing scholars of the standing of Hickes. Richard Gough and Charles
Mayo[44] are detailed and learned in *Gentleman's Magazine* (68 [1798]:
2.861–65). *The Analytical Review* (28 [1798]:2.360–63) is very similar
in tone and substance. The review refers to Horne Tooke in the third
person; nevertheless he was the reviewer, as Henshall's reply in *Anti-
Jacobin* ([1798]:2.579–88) suggests by implication.[45] Henshall, a little
hurt by criticism, denies (pp. 582–83) that he "had been attempting to
give the most intelligible translation."[46] The reviewer of Henshall's
book in *British Critic* (16 [1800–1802]:2.530, 536–37) did not resort to
vituperation:

The author having discovered, what certainly is not very new, that the
English language is derived in a great measure from the Saxon, conceived,
that the best way to illustrate the more ancient dialect, was to place the
modern in immediate opposition with it, as far as might be practicable. There
is good sense in the thought, but nothing very wonderful, nor any thing at all
authorizing the discoverer to insult all those writers who have interpreted the
Saxon language by the Latin.

It might be thought that Henshall's learning was not worth the paper
he had it printed on. He is, however, not insignificant in the history of
translation from Anglo-Saxon verse. George Ellis called on him to provide a rendering of "The Battle of Brunanburh" for the first volume of his
second edition of *Specimens of the Early English Poets* (London, 1801).
Ellis tells us (p. 15), "This celebrated ODE is rendered into English,

---

[43] Henshall, p. 41, lines 65b–73.

[44] According to *DNB*, s.n. Samuel Henshall.

[45] So also *DNB*, loc. cit.

[46] Politics played a role in giving Henshall and his work space in *The Anti-Jacobin Review and Magazine*. See *DNB*, s.nn. John Gifford and William Gifford, as well as John Horne Tooke; reviewers are identified in the British Library copy of the *Anti-Jacobin* (P.P. 3596). John Reeves's review of Henshall's book, in the *Anti-Jacobin* (1798):1.381–87, was favorable but Henshall himself had reviewed for the journal only in the preceding issue, and was a frequent reviewer.

as literally as possible, to show the very great affinity between our present Language and its Saxon forefather, which, it is hoped, will be admitted as an excuse for some occasional obscurity."

An extract will suffice:

> The war screamers,
> Left they behind.
> The hoarse bittern,
> The sallow paddock,
> The swarth raven
> With horned nib,
> And the house-wooding* heron,
> Eating white fish of the brooks;
> The greedy gos-hawk,
> The grey deer,
> And wolf wild.
>   Never was there wail more,
> In this island,
> (Ever since
> By folkes filled)
> Before this
> By sword's edge.
> (Thus they that seek books,
> Elders of the witens,)
> Since that the easterns hither,
> Angles and Saxons,
> Up became. (*arrived*)
> O'er the broad brine (*sea*)
> Britain they sought.
> Smiting with lances,
> The Welch they conquered,
> The earls harrowed,
> The earth gotten. (*the land obtained.*)[47]

A footnote explains "house-wooding": "*That builds his house in the loftiest woods." The second paragraph is, with minor changes, the one Henshall had printed in his own book, as we have seen.

The whole of this poem was also given in Ellis's specimen in a metri-

---

[47] Henshall is named at p. ix as the author; this passage corresponds to lines 59b-73, *Specimens*, 1.29-31.

cal version in imitation of the Rowley poems. It was written by John Hookham Frere when he was still at Eton.[48] The first of the two paragraphs quoted above is turned by Frere thus:

> Leving the crowen, and the tode,
> Hawkes, doggis, and wolves tho;
> Egles, and monie other mo,
> With the ded men for their mede
> On hir corses for to fede.[49]

After poetry of these two kinds, Frere's schoolboy jingles and Henshall's learned ignorance clothed in fustian, prose must have seemed best to writers of good sense.

Sharon Turner does not stoop to name Henshall as the author of an earlier translation which he dismisses as incorrect, before going on to turn his more nearly correct version into some kind of prose, the last few lines of which are:

> The screamers of war
> they left behind,
> the raven to enjoy,
> the dismal kite,
> and the black raven
> with horned beak;
> and the hoarse toad;
> the eagle afterwards
> to feast on the white flesh;
> the greedy battle-hawk,
> and the grey beast,
> the wolf in the wood.
>   Nor had there been a greater slaughter
> in this island
> ever yet
> of people destroyed,
> before this
> by the edge of swords,

---

[48] See *DNB*, s.n.

[49] *Specimens*, 1.34. If Frere did not retouch his poem after he left Eton, he must have used Gibson's edition of the *Chronicle*, both the Latin and the Old English, and not Henshall's "literal" rendering.

(This is what the books tell us
of the old wise men)
since from the East hither
the Angles and the Saxons
came up
over the broad waves,
and sought the Britons.
The illustrious smiths of war!
the Welsh they overcame;
the earls excelling in honor!
and obtained the country.[50]

Among the very best translators from Old English is Anna Gurney, whose life, as recorded by *DNB*, was impressively triumphant, and whose work has received recognition from Norman Garmonsway in an excellent study.[51] When the translation appeared (anonymously),[52] Miss Gurney was less than twenty-four years old. Her translation of "The Battle of Brunanburh" into elegant prose is in marked contrast to the poetic translation by Henshall which Longfellow calls "an attempt at a translation—and, perhaps, the most unsuccessful attempt ever made in any language."[53] Of course, Miss Gurney benefited from Turner's translation, but her good sense made her reject the "hoarse toad" of her predecessors, and she does well to turn the *wlance wig-smiþas* of the penultimate long line freely into "on the anvil of battle":[54]

They left behind them the screamers of war, the birds of prey. The sallow kite, and the black raven with the horny beak, and the hoarse-voiced eagle devouring the white flesh, with the battle-hawk, and the grey beast the wolf of the wood. Never in this island had a greater destruction of men been worked by the edge of the sword, say the books of the Wise Elders, since the Saxons and the Angles came hither from the east—to Britain over the broad sea. Since those glorious Earls, who smote the Welch on the anvil of battle, and obtained their lands.

[50] *The History of the Anglo-Saxons*, 2d ed. (London, 1807), 2.290–91; the poem is not translated in the first edition, vol. 4 (London, 1805), cf. p. 384.

[51] "Anna Gurney: Learned Saxonist," *Essays and Studies*, n.s. 8 (1955):40–57.

[52] *A Literal Translation of the Saxon Chronicle* (Norwich, 1819).

[53] *North American Review* 47 (1838):115.

[54] The passage quoted is at p. 134. Perhaps she did not know the word *wlanc*, which comes only here in the *Chronicle* and which Turner failed to translate correctly at line 341, where he has "wealthy."

Compared with Miss Gurney's prose, James Ingram's translation of the poem is wooden:

> They left behind them
> raw to devour
> the sallow kite,
> the swarthy raven
> with horny nib,
> and the hoarse vultur,
> with the eagle swift
> to consume his prey;
> the greedy gos-hawk,
> and that grey beast
> the wolf of the weald.
> No slaughter yet
> was greater made
> e'er in this island,
> of people slain,
> before this same,
> with the edge of the sword;
> as the books inform us
> of the old historians;
> since hither came
> from the eastern shores
> the Angles and Saxons,
> over the broad sea,
> and Britain sought,—
> fierce battle-smiths,
> o'ercame the Welsh,
> most valiant earls,
> and gained the land.[55]

Ingram produced a more spirited verse translation for the rhythmical addition to the West Saxon genealogy in Textus Roffensis.[56] The original is:

> Se Cerdic wæs, swa ic ær cwæþ, se forma
> þe West-Sexana land mid wige on Wealum geeode.

[55] *The Saxon Chronicle with an English Translation* (London, 1823), pp. 144–45.
[56] N. R. Ker, *Catalogue of Manuscripts Containing Anglo-Saxon* (Oxford, 1957), no. 373A, art. 5; P. Sawyer, *Early English Manuscripts in Facsimile*, vol. 7 (1957), p. 15 and f.8ᵛ.

And his ofspryncg dyde,   swa him gebyrde wæs,
fæste bewerode þæt he ærost gewann.
Eac eacan begeat heora anra gewelhwilc,
symle be ðam cræfte þe heom God lænde.[57]

Ingram, for some reason, turned what he believed to be "three irregular stanzas of Cædmonian metre" into the measure of "John Gilpin":

Cerdic was HE of Saxons first,
    Who won West-Saxon land;
And through the ranks of Britons burst
    With his victorious band.

His offspring, as that race became,
    Whom war and glory led,
Defended and made fast the claim
    Which he so nobly sped.

By that same craft, which God had lent
    To each successive son,
They held, and with increas'd extent,
    The empire he had won.[58]

The Rochester lines play no great part in Anglo-Saxon scholarship; "The Battle of Brunanburh" does. Thomas Warton had written about the poem and translated it chiefly from earlier Latin translations.[59] For the second edition Richard Price translated the poem from Anglo-Saxon direct, not without errors. The end is as follows:

Nor was (there) a greater slaughter,
on this island,
ever yet,
of folk felled,
before this,
by (the) sword's edges,
of that that say to us (in) books,

[57] "The aforementioned Cerdic was, as I have said, the first who gained the land of the West-Saxons by warfare in Britain. And his descendants did as was fitting for them, they firmly defended what he had won in the first place. Moreover each one of them conquered additional territory, always according to the strength which God granted them." The division into lines of verse is doubtful because of the irregularity of the meter.

[58] Ingram, pp. 375–76.

[59] *The History of English Poetry*, vol. 1 (London, 1774), pp. [xxxvii]–[xl].

old historians,
since eastward hither,
Angles and Saxons,
up came,
over (the) broad seas,
Britain sought,
splendid war-smiths,
overcame (the) Welsh,
earls exceeding bold [keen],
obtained (the) earth.[60]

A record of translations of *Beowulf*, which is the primary purpose of this study, has to be strengthened by many infusions of other translations from Anglo-Saxon. There is no end to it. For "The Battle of Brunanburh" I want to confine myself to three more examples, the last of which is Tennyson's. Short extracts are all there is room for.

Edwin Guest's *A History of English Rhythms* (London, 1838) was, very rightly, a highly influential book. His verse translation of "The Battle of Brunanburh" was in long lines; for example:

Left they behind them (the carcase to share)
Him of the sallow coat—the swart raven
With horned nib; and him of the grizzled coat—
The ern white-plumaged behind, his prey to gorge;
The greedy war-hawk, and the grey beast,
The wolf of the weald.[61]

Hallam Tennyson's prose translation is of interest chiefly because his father used it for his verse rendering. These lines are translated thus:

Many a carcase they left behind them, many a sallow skin for the swarthy raven with horny beak to tear; the livid corpse they left behind them for the ern with white-tail to gorge on carrion, for the greedy war-hawk, and for the gray beast, the wolf of the weald.[62]

The debt to Guest is certainly very obvious; perhaps it was inevitable.

Tennyson's versification of his son's prose is also close to Guest. The poem is easily accessible, and I quote no more than the same lines:

[60] Price's *Warton* (London, 1824), 1.xcix–ci.
[61] 2.69, lines 60–65*a*.
[62] *Contemporary Review* 28 (1876):921.

> Many a carcase they left to be carrion,
> Many a livid one, many a sallow-skin –
> Left for the white tail'd eagle to tear it, and
> Left for the horny-nibb'd raven to rend it, and
> Gave to the garbaging war-hawk to gorge it, and
> That gray beast, the wolf of the weald.[63]

I used Tennyson's "garbaging war-hawk" for the title of this paper and contrasted it with E. Talbot Donaldson's modest claim that a good prose translation, though no substitute for the original Old English poetic text, will help the reader to re-create it in his understanding. In the quarter of a century between Henshall and Miss Gurney the foundations were laid for the two kinds of translations from Old English: on the one hand, in Henshall's manner translation into a poeticizing nonlanguage studded with etymological reminders of the words in the original (all of it in varying degrees of accuracy); and on the other, in Miss Gurney's manner for prose as for verse, translation into clear and graceful Modern English. Glossing literalism into short phrases corresponding to the (half-line) units of Anglo-Saxon verse is not easily distinguished from poeticizing literalism. In verse and prose attempts are made to imitate lexical and rhythmic features of the original; only the school of translators who can look to Miss Gurney as their model avoid such devices.

For prose translations of *Beowulf* into Modern English, from the beginning of the nineteenth century onward, I give quotations briefer than those for verse translation, only enough to give some idea of the translator's manner or mannerism. Sharon Turner comes first; he arranges the phrases of his prose as if they were verse:

> Then let him abide
> the judgment of the Lord,
> he whom death taketh.
> I know that, if he can,
> he will subdue the Jute people
> in the battle-hall.
> But from me he shall have
> a dearly-purchased ruin.

---

[63] *Ballads and Other Poems* (London, 1880), p. 177.

94

If death taketh me,
bear me from the bloody slaughter
to my grave,
and think that ye have consumed
a solitary warrior
unlamenting.
Nor need ye long grieve
about the life of my body.
If Hilda takes me away,
send to Higelac
my battle-garments,
the best that my breast wears,
the choicest of my clothes,
the work of foreigners.
Let Fortune go as she chooses.[64]

The archaizing manifests itself chiefly in *ye* and *-eth*.

Ebenezer Henderson's short extracts in translation probably go back to the Latin translation in G. J. Thorkelin's *editio princeps* (Copenhagen, 1815) of *Beowulf*. It is of interest as the first translation of any passages of *Beowulf* into ordinary prose:

In the mean time the royal servant (*the poet,*) commemorated in songs the virtues of such as had fallen in battle—he who retains in his memory all the traditions of past ages. One word produced another, and when joined together, they formed a history of the voyage of Beowulf. It was sagely composed, and easy of interpretation, because the events followed each other in historical order. What he thus masterly composed, he repeated to such as were present. I heard noble deeds set forth in elegant poems; things which had never before been known to the children of men.[65]

J. M. Kemble's translation of *Beowulf* is, of course, well known as a great scholarly achievement. Its influence on the understanding of the poem was immense.[66] It must also have reinforced the feeling that Old

---

[64] *The History of the Anglo-Saxons*, 2d ed. (London, 1807), 2.302. The passage corresponds to lines 440b–55. It is not in the first edition (London, 1805).

[65] *Iceland; or the Journal of a Residence in That Island, During the Years 1814 and 1815* (Edinburgh, 1818), 2.330; lines 867b–77.

[66] See Bruce Dickins, "J. M. Kemble and Old English Scholarship," *Proceedings of the British Academy* 25 (1939):66 (=p. 18 of separate).

English is fittingly rendered by un-English in literal imitation of the original language:

Thus was the bold warrior saying, of evil tidings, he lied not much *either* of fates or words: *the* troop all arose, sadly *and* bubbling with tears they went under *the* promontory of eagles, to behold *the* marvel: *they* found there upon *the* sand, occupying *the* death-bed, him who in earlier times had given them rings, lifeless: then was *his* ending-day gone forth for *the* good *king, so* that *he the* prince of *the* Westerns, perished by a wondrous death.[67]

Benjamin Thorpe's edition of 1855 complete with "a literal transla-tion" has been reprinted as recently as 1962. The quality of the transla-tion may be gauged by a brief specimen:

> Sat then on *the* ness
> *the* bold warrior king.
> while *he* bade farewell
> to *his* hearth-enjoyers,
> *the* Goths' gold-friend:
> his mind was sad,
> wandering and death-bound,
> *the* fate close at hand,
> which the aged *man*
> must greet,
> must seek *his* soul-treasure,
> asunder part
> life from body:
> not then long was
> the prince's life
> wrapt in flesh.[68]

A sober translation goes with T. Arnold's edition of *Beowulf* (Lon-don, 1876), p. 190 (lines 3021b-27):

"For this cause many a spear, cold at morning, shall be grasped by the palms, upheaved in hands; by no means shall the warrior waken the music of the harp, but the dusky raven eager over the fallen shall utter much, say to the eagle, how at the meal he sped, while with the wolf he made rapine among the slain."

---

[67] *A Translation of the Anglo-Saxon Poem of Beowulf* (London, 1837), p. 122, lines 3028-37.

[68] *The Anglo-Saxon Poems of Beowulf, the Scôp or Gleeman's Tale, and the Fight at Finnesburg* (Oxford, 1855), p. 163, lines 2417-24.

John Earle's prose translation has its own ancient-sounding artificiality, but the prose runs easily, without breaking at the end of each Old English verse unit:

So the great-hearted hero rested him; – high in air loomed the edifice, wide-spanning and gold-gleaming: – the stranger slept within, until the black raven announced heaven's glory with a blithe heart. Then came bright light striding over shadow; fiends scampered off. The ethelings were ready dight to fare back to their Leeds; – the magnanimous visitor was minded to take ship, for a voyage far away.[69]

Earle's "Leeds" is, of course, to leodum (line 1804b); he used the word often in Modern English, though OED shows that Lede had long been obsolete.

In the twentieth century prose translations of Beowulf are even more numerous. C. G. Child (London, 1904) introduces "nicked" for heaðo-scearde of the manuscript (line 2829, p. 77, lines 2826b–35):[70]

The dragon with his twisting coils might no longer rule his treasure-hoards, for the edge of the steel, the hard handiwork of hammers, nicked in battle, had taken him hence, so that the far-flier fell to the ground, stilled by his wounds, nigh to his treasure-house; in no wise might he sweep sporting through the air at midnight, make show of himself, proud of his treasure-holdings, for he fell to earth through the handiwork of the leader in battle.

W. Huyshe, Beowulf: An Old English Epic ([London, 1907], p. 167, lines 2694–2702a):

Then, as I have heard, in the need of the people's king, the hero showed unceasing courage, skill, and keenness, as was natural to him; he heeded not the head – albeit the brave man's hand was burned while he helped his kinsman – but he struck the evil beast a little lower down – man-at-arms that he was! – so that the shining and gold-adorned sword plunged in, and the fire began to abate forthwith.

W. W. Lawrence, "The Haunted Mere in Beowulf" (PMLA 27 [1912]:211–12) – "translated in a literal rather than in an imaginative

---

[69] The Deeds of Beowulf, an English Epic of the Eighth Century Done into Modern Prose (Oxford, 1892), p. 59, lines 1799–1806.

[70] I am indebted to John C. Pope for pointing out to me that I was wrong in my earlier assumption that Child's "nicked" translates fornamon (line 2828) instead of the unamended reading.

way"—is a kind of rhythmical prose keeping to the verse lines (lines 1365–76a):

> "There may each of nights a strange marvel be seen,
> fire on the flood. Not so wise is any
> of the children of men as to know about those depths.
> Although the heath-rover, harried by hounds,
> the stag in the pride of his antlers, seek that forest-grove,
> driven thither from afar, sooner will he yield his life,
> his breath on the bank, than plunge in,
> hide his head. That is an uncanny place.
> There the blending of the waters riseth up
> dark to the welkin, when the wind stirreth
> evil weathers, until the air darkles,
> the heavens weep."

E. J. B. Kirtlan, *The Story of Beowulf* ([London, 1913]), p. 190), has a straightforward translation of the passage (lines 3021b–27) which I quoted also from Arnold's translation:

"And many a morning cold shall the spear in the hand-grip be heaved up on high, nor shall there be the sound of harping to awaken the warriors, but the war-raven, eager over the doomed ones, shall say many things to the eagle how it fared with him in eating the carrion while he, with the wolf, plundered the slaughtered."

Generations of undergraduates and others have used R. K. Gordon's translation in the Everyman Library:[71]

"How fared ye on the voyage, dear Beowulf, when on a sudden thou hadst desire to seek combat afar over the salt water, warfare at Heorot? Surely thou hast somewhat mended for Hrothgar, the famous prince, his wide-known sorrow? In my heart's grief for that I was troubled with surgings of sorrow; I put no trust in my loved man's venture; long while I besought thee that thou shouldst have naught to do with the murderous monster, let the South-Danes themselves fight out the struggle with Grendel. I utter thanks to God, that it is granted me to behold thee unscathed."

J. R. Clark Hall's translation of the poem first appeared in 1911 and was widely used. A corrected and revised, completely new edition by

---

[71] *Anglo-Saxon Poetry* (London, 1926; frequently reprinted); I quote from the first edition, *The Song of Beowulf* (King's Treasuries of Literature, 1923), p. 79, lines 1987–98.

C. L. Wrenn came out in 1940. For a very long time (perhaps still today) it was the best translation for the use of serious students, so much so that for many readers it has become the poem itself:[72]

"There was singing and merriment. The patriarch Scylding, who had heard of so many things, told of bygone times; now and again a man brave in battle touched his joyful harp of wood with happy effect. Sometimes he told a true and mournful tale; anon the generous king rehearsed aright a strange adventure; then again after that the veteran battle-chief, trammelled by his age, would make lament over his past youthful days and strength in battle. His heart was moved within him, as he, old in years, brought much of the past to mind."

Penguin Books include *Beowulf* in David Wright's prose translation and, as we have seen, in Michael Alexander's verse translation too.[73] The prose translation (Penguin Classics, Harmondsworth, 1957) is muted in tone, as a short example shows (p. 80, lines 2254b–66):

"Gone are the brave. The tough helmet, overlaid with gold, must be stripped of its golden plates. They sleep who should burnish the casques. Armour that stood up to the battering of swords in conflict, among the thunder of the shields, moulders away like the soldier. Nor shall the corselet travel hither and yon on the back of a hero by the side of fighting-men. There is no sweet sound from the harp, no delight of music, no good hawk swooping through the hall, no swift horse stamping in the castle yard. Death has swept away nearly everything that lives."

L. D. Pearson's translation (Bloomington, Ind., 1965) is a mixture of verse and rhythmic prose. The following extract has both (p. 102, lines 2262b–77):

> "The joy of harp
> Is gone, the gleewood's mirth; no good hawk
> Swings along the hall, no swift horse
> Paws the court. Death-bale has sent on many."
> So, sad-hearted, one bemoaned his sorrow
> For the others' loss; he wandered somber
> Day and night until death's flooding touched his heart.

---

[72] *Beowulf and the Finnesburg Fragment* (London, 1940; I quote from the 1950 printing), p. 127, lines 2105–14.

[73] See above, p. 68, note 6.

An old dawn-spoiler found the joy-hoard standing open, he who flaming hunts out barrows, naked malice-Worm, a fly-by-night embraced by fire; earth-dwellers greatly fear him. His task is seeking hoards in earth and, wise in winters, guarding heathen gold; he shall be no whit the better for it.

Constance B. Hieatt's translation, *Beowulf and Other Old English Poems* (Indianapolis, 1967), is unadorned prose, even for the "Elegy of the Last Survivor" (p. 68, lines 2252b–62a):

"I have no one who can bear a sword or polish a precious drinking cup; the host has gone to another place. The strong helmet adorned with gold must be deprived of its adornment, for those whose duty it was to polish the armor now sleep; likewise the mail, which once endured the bite of iron weapons over clashing shields in battle, now crumbles away as the warriors did; never again can it travel afar with the warriors, side by side with heroes."

Norman Garmonsway's translation, completed by Jacqueline Simpson, in *Beowulf and Its Analogues* (London, 1968), is discreet and successful, in the tradition of Anna Gurney (p. 79, lines 3021b–27):

"Because of this, many a spear, cold in the morning air, shall be grasped and raised in the hand; no sound of harp shall awaken the fighters, but the black raven, eager for doomed men, shall have much to speak of as he tells the eagle how he fared in his feeding, when with the wolf he plundered the slain."

The last translation of *Beowulf* I wish to quote from is Michael Swanton's, designed to go with his text of the poem ([Manchester, 1978], p. 141, lines 2236b–41a), slightly prosy prose, as if ashamed of the possibility of poeticizing:

Death had carried off them all in former times, and the one man remaining of the tried warriors of the people, he who lived there longest, a guardian mourning his friends, expected the same fate as theirs—that only for a little while would he be allowed to enjoy the long-accumulated treasures.

It might seem a fitting tribute to E. Talbot Donaldson to quote now from his translation, as if to crown all. As I have said, I like his translation, but I will not quote from it, not because "'twere prophanation of our joyes" as lovers of *Beowulf* to utter what is well done but because, like several good prose translations, the avoidance of error by tact is high among the reasons for its excellence—"Th'eschewing is only the remedye." For information about the original, literal translation word for word (interlinearly or like an interlinear gloss or literally phrase by phrase) is useful; as W. E. Leonard said, "The very literalness has an indisputable literary effect."[74] Unadorned, muted prose, as far from *Kunstprosa* as it is possible to go, as far from archaism as modernity en-sures, seems best for literary success. The alternative is poetry, but poetry invites comparison with the original. No poet has really suc-ceeded with translating Anglo-Saxon verse; Longfellow, Tennyson, William Morris—they have not done as well as have less famous poets, Edwin Morgan especially. The "literal materials from which the reader can re-create the poem" are as much as a translator can hope to pro-vide; and if he cannot give the reader the material from which to re-create the poem, he can at least help him create an understanding of the poem in good Modern English.

---

[74] "Beowulf and the Niebelungen Couplet," *University of Wisconsin Studies in Language and Literature* 2 (1918):100, with immediate reference to Kemble's translation.

Part Three THE TEXTUAL PLANE

What Comes After Chaucer's *But*:
Adversative Constructions in Spenser

JUDITH H. ANDERSON
Indiana University

HE BEARING OF AN ARTICLE called "Adventures with the Adversative Conjunction in the General Prologue to the *Canterbury Tales*; or, What's Before the *But*?" on the Proem to book 6 of *The Faerie Queene* is unlikely, indirect, and thoroughly illuminating. The article examines how the illogical use of *but* in Chaucer's Prologue indicates the pressures of a mind "made nervous by the complexities of its own discourse, worried by subtle implications dimly perceived but not openly recognized, or harassed by emotional responses to the material it is trying to order." Familiar examples of such subjective usage occur in the portrait of the Prioress: "But, for to speken of her conscience"; in that of the Knight: "His hors were goode, but he was nat gay"; in that of the Wife of Bath: "But she was somdeel deef, and that was scathe."[1] The same article might be seen as final, compelling evidence of the presence of a dramatic persona in *The General Prologue*, though the article's author (to whom this *Festschrift* is dedicated) resolutely avoids making this claim or at least making it explicitly; he does manage to observe, however, that while "Chaucer's narrator in the Prologue is capable of both logical and illogical *buts*...he produces the latter in a majority of two to one—which is one reason why the Prologue is such interesting poetry."[2]

I

Turning from "Adventures with...*But*" to Spenser's sixth Proem, I

---

[1] *Chaucer's Poetry: An Anthology for the Modern Reader*, ed. E. Talbot Donaldson, 2d ed. (New York: Ronald Press, 1975), lines 142, 74, 448. Subsequent references to *The General Prologue* are to this edition.

[2] Quotations are from the first paragraph of Donaldson's article on *But, So meny people longages and tonges*, ed. Michael Benskin and M. L. Samuels (Edinburgh: by the eds., 1981).

found what seemed a curiously familiar phenomenon, the recurrence of logical and illogical *but* no less than eight times in the twenty-seven lines of stanzas 4 to 6. This recurrence, whether conjunctive (five times) or prepositional (three times), is an intensification of Chaucerian practice in *The General Prologue*, and, as if its cumulative effect on the tone of Spenser's Proem were not already unsettling enough, it is further reinforced by other adversative and concessive constructions (*yet*, four times; *though*, twice) and made still more noticeable by equivocal reference and by lexical ambiguity. Doubleness—duality and, indeed, duplicity—is in the warp and woof of these stanzas:

Stanza 4: Amongst them all growes not a fayrer flowre,
    Then is the bloosme of comely courtesie,
    Which *though* it on a lowly stalke doe bowre,
    Yet brancheth forth in braue nobilitie,
    And spreds it selfe through all ciuilitie: (5)
    Of which *though* present age doe plenteous seeme,
    Yet being matcht with plaine Antiquitie,
    Ye will them all *but* fayned showes esteeme,
   Which carry colours faire, that feeble eies misdeeme.

Stanza 5: *But* in the triall of true curtesie,
    Its now so farre from that, which then it was,
    That it indeed is nought *but* forgerie,
    Fashion'd to please the eies of them, that pas,
    Which see not perfect things *but* in a glas: (5)
    Yet is that glasse so gay, that it can blynd
    The wisest sight, to thinke gold that is bras.
    But vertues seat is deepe within the mynd,
   And not in outward shows, *but* inward thoughts defynd.

Stanza 6: *But* where shall I in all Antiquity
    So faire a patterne finde, where may be seene
    The goodly praise of Princely curtesie,
    As in your selfe, O soueraine Lady Queene,
    In whose pure minde, as in a mirrour sheene,   (5)
    It showes, and with her brightnesse doth inflame
    The eyes of all, which thereon fixed beene;
    But meriteth indeede an higher name:
    Yet so from low to high vplifted is your name.[3]

[3] My emphasis. All references to *The Faerie Queene* are to *The Works of Edmund Spenser: A*

Occasionally the syntax of the Proem has provoked a passing comment, but to the best of my knowledge the recurrence of *but* and of other related syntactical constructions, both deployed with increasing subjectivity, has never seemed especially significant to readers of Spenser. Yet the fact of such recurrence is truly remarkable, and this is what Donaldson's article led me to notice.

Where in Chaucer's *General Prologue*, syntax that is illogical in sequence, ambiguous in effect, and subjective in character mainly serves narrative realism, in Spenser's Proem to book 6 it serves a realism that is essentially conceptual. In the *Prologue* it expresses an illogical or ambiguous relation between one aspect of human behavior or appearance and another; in the Proem it expresses a similar relation between an antique ideal, at once mythic and visionary, and the "forgerie" of present time. In both works, however, such syntax also indicates a dynamic, developing process. Whether seemingly a visual and narrational process (Chaucer) or a visionary and self-expressive one (Spenser), it is thus a truly temporal process, whose meaning is accretive, continuing, and incomplete except when grasped and held as a totality. This process, like the syntax that shapes it, embraces qualifications, contrasts and negations, objections, exceptions, and limitations that cannot be rationalized or otherwise eliminated without distortion.

Although I have suggested that the forms of realism served by this process differ in *Prologue* and Proem, I do not want to imply that they exclude one another rigidly. Chaucer's portrait of the Parson focuses at least nominally on a particular parson, but in more sustained and specific terms it also treats the relation of an ideal to present corruption and in this way resembles Spenser's sixth Proem. When Chaucer's realism is most Spenserian in the *Prologue*, however, his procedures are in some respects least Chaucerian: the portrait of the Parson is virtually devoid of the irony of immediate, dramatized observation. Although it is full of satire of the lazy, self-serving parsons not present dramatically on the pilgrimage, it never satirizes the good Parson

---

Variorum Edition, ed. Edwin A. Greenlaw et al., 11 vols. (Baltimore: Johns Hopkins Press, 1932–57); cited as *Var*.

himself nor even has a few well-padded belly laughs at his expense, as happens with the Clerk. Curiously enough, these distinctions have a syntactical corollary. The portrait of the Parson is studded with *buts* (seven of the thirty-seven adversative uses of *but* Donaldson finds in *The General Prologue*), but most of these are basically logical rather than illogical uses; for example, "Ful loth were him to cursen for his tithes, / But rather wolde he yiven, out of doute" (lines 488–89). Compared with most of Chaucer's other portraits, that of the Parson is more of a set piece. While effective satire, it is less a process of perceiving the particular Parson than a rational assessment or disciplined statement of the more general gap between parsonical ideal and parsonical reality.

Coincidentally and somewhat superficially, Spenser's Proem to book 6 might resemble the atypically Chaucerian portrait of the Parson, but Spenser is most truly Chaucerian when his perceptual procedures in this Proem resemble those of the illogical and ambiguous observer of other portraits in *The General Prologue*. Further, they are far more typically Chaucerian than they are at the outset of *The Faerie Queene*. In the first Proem, for example, when Spenser refers to the Queen actually ruling England, his syntax is essentially logical and unambiguous, and his image of her, while iconic, allusive, and laudatory, is, like the brilliance and purity of crystal, atemporal and static. In the sixth Proem, however, the Queen is actually, rather than ideally, realer than in the first, and ambiguous or illogical syntax – the syntax of duplicity, as I shall call it – finally focuses on her person. This last fact makes Spenser's relation in this Proem to the duplicitous Chaucer of double meanings – the Chaucer of irony, ambiguity, and equivocation – more pronounced, despite the characteristic differences in form (narrative as against conceptual realism) between their works that remain firmly present. When Spenser is most Chaucerian in the Proem to book 6, he is thus least Spenserian – if by Spenserian we mean the poet of the Proem to book 1, whose conception of the real Queen, the actual Elizabeth, is ideal and, because less complexly human, poetically less interesting. It should be obvious that I find such a definition of Spenserian too limited and, indeed, too static, accounting as it does for barely half *The Faerie Queene*.

II

The first three stanzas of Spenser's Proem to book 6 do little more than
hint at the distance between an antique ideal and the present forgery
that threatens true vision in stanzas 4 to 6 (cited above). But with explicit recognition of this distance only a few lines away, the third
stanza glances darkly at trouble in implanting "the sacred noursery /
Of vertue" in earth. The poet asks the Muses to reveal to him the
nursery of virtue that has been hidden in their keeping from men "Since
[ever since or because] it at first was by the Gods with paine [painstak-
ingly, painfully, or along with pain] / Planted in earth."[4] When the
nursery of virtue is embedded in earth, its purity–or at least its pain-
lessness–is doubtful, and the origin of its latency–its concealment–is
elusive. Yet whether the nursery of virtue is earthly and embedded or
latent and visionary, an inclusion of alternatives that the ambiguous
syntax of stanza 3 enforces, it was initially derived "From heauenly
seedes" and nourished "with carefull labour" by the Muses "Till it to
ripenesse grew, and forth to honour burst." The diction of this line suggests the burgeoning of a plant, the opening of a flower, latency revealed, potential fulfilled–ripeness, readiness, presence. That the verb
burst, the emphatic final word of the stanza, is potentially both a present and a past form (albeit the past tense in stanza 3) reinforces these
suggestions and prepares for the use of the present tense throughout
the next stanza, perhaps most dramatically in its opening lines:
"Amongst them all [the blossoms in the nursery] growes not a fayrer
flowre, / Then is the bloosme of comely courtesie." Real presence,
after all, occurs in time.

It hardly seems accidental, given the associative process of the
human mind, that specific reference to the "present age" should come
in stanza 4. Here opposition between the present and the past, the
actual and the ideal, becomes open. Now "present age" is contrasted
directly with "plaine Antiquitie," a mythic time and condition continuous with its origins in "the sacred noursery / Of vertue." Explicit
reference to present time entails further syntactical complications,

---

[4] Donald Cheney has noted the ambiguity of the phrasing "with paine / Planted in earth"
(discussion sponsored by the Spenser Society, New York, December, 1978).

specifically a movement from an ambiguity of continuity and inclusion in stanza 3 (earthly and embedded or latent and visionary) to an ambiguity of discontinuity and fragmentation. This movement is progressive in stanza 4. Twice, once on either side of line 5, the stanza's midpoint, the construction "though...Yet" occurs. In the first instance, concession is made to the "lowly stalke" of courtesy's flower, which nevertheless ("Yet") blossoms "in braue nobilitie" and spreads through "all ciuilitie." Thus described, the relation of flower to stalk is less adversative than merely conjunctive and continuous. In the second instance, however, a far more intensely adversative pairing of *though* and *yet* occurs, and the fact that the same construction has already occurred in this stanza makes its recurrence in virtually the same position within the later lines conspicuous. This time concession is not to lowliness but, it would appear, to its opposite, the "present age," seemingly plenteous in courtesy, yet really in an adversative relation to "plaine Antiquitie." This second time, *yet* is a conjunction only in name. Even syntactically the present is "matcht" with the mythic fulfillment of virtue that occupies the first half of the stanza, and it is found wanting:

> Of which [blossom(s) of courtesy: "all," "it"] though
>   present age doe plenteous seeme,
> Yet being matcht with plaine Antiquitie,
> Ye will them all but fayned showes esteeme,
> Which carry colours faire, that feeble eies misdeeme.

The word *all* occurs both in the first line of stanza 4, where it expresses inclusiveness of reference ("Amongst them all growes not a fayrer flowre"), and, as cited just above, in the eighth line, where it participates in duplicity, in the ambiguity of deception. By line 8 earthly reality not only opposes and belies the reality of vision but very nearly obliterates it. The strongest meaning of lines 7 to 9 is that all the blossoms of courtesy in the present age are merely showy pretenses misjudged by the morally insensitive, of whom the present age would appear to consist. Weakly and rather unpersuasively, however, these lines allow a less negative reading. If we take *being* in line 7 to modify *age* rather than *which...them all*, the blossoms might still be considered true, albeit subject to misjudgment; in that case their latency would remain relevant, and their virtuous potential would remain real. Alternatively, it is also conceivable, if unlikely, that *being* modifies *Ye* in line 8 and thereby refers essentially to the failures of perception, the misjudgments, of the poet's present audience. Such misjudgments would imply a measure of human control as well as culpability and conversely at least some possibility of regeneration. The one fact unambiguously clear at the end of stanza 4 is that syntax has become less than tightly logical. Indeed, it has become perplexed and perhaps downright treacherous.

The theme of perception might be regarded as the corollary of illogical syntax and especially of adversative constructions in the stanzas that follow. As we have seen, this theme too is introduced in the closing half of stanza 4 and especially in lines 8 to 9 ("seeme," "showes," "eies misdeeme"). Although the *but* in line 8 is a preposition, it is nonetheless significant as an anticipation of a whole chorus of *buts* in stanza 5, whose keynote it thereby intensifies: "But in the triall of true curtesie, / Its now so far from that, which then it was." This *but*, the first word of the initial line of the stanza, is clearly the adversative conjunction yet is also a dubiously logical use of it. Exactly what the opening of stanza 5 is adverse to is not readily apparent. The opening lines merely heighten the primary meaning of the end of stanza 4: there we read that present courtesy is showy pretense and now that it is so far from what it was "That it indeed is nought but forgerie." In strictly logical terms the conjunction that opens stanza 5 should be *and* rather than *but*, whose illogical presence is made still more conspicuous by the four *buts* that troop after it in the same stanza. The first of these — "nought but forgerie" — is prepositional or probably so, because when perceived for long in the adversative context of stanza 5, it threatens to become a syntactical pun (i.e., nought...but is). As used in the line, this prepositional *but* demonstrates its near identity with the adversative conjunction, a historical likeness that the *OED* more than once remarks.[5]

The adversative conjunction that opens stanza 5 ("But in the triall of true curtesie") is truly logical only if we take it to be in opposition to the less likely but more positive readings of the end of stanza 4, which I detailed above, namely, the possibilities that the latent blossoms of

[5] *OED*, s.v. *But*, headnote and note following examples under A.3; C.I.1.b (b.), 3, 4.

courtesy remain relevant and could be available to an audience deem-
ing rightly. But this logical interpretation seems farfetched at best and
entirely inaccessible to one not reading with pickax and thumbtacks. It
serves mainly to show how much less the poet's syntax responds here
to logic than it expresses something like the pressures of a mind "made
nervous by the complexities of its own discourse, worried by subtle implications dimly perceived but not openly recognized, or harassed by
emotional responses to the material it is trying to order." Further, the
poet's syntax—or, to speak more sensibly, the poet of the sixth Proem
—does so knowingly. His syntax is not itself the butt of its own illogic,
as happens so often when the Chaucerian narrator, the dramatic persona of *The General Prologue*, in perceiving his fellow pilgrims unwittingly expresses the irony and indeed the illogic of being human. Since
irony is a type of ambiguity or double vision, the Chaucerian narrator,
unlike the poet of the sixth Proem, embodies a verbal duplicity he does
not fully recognize or control.

Roughly the central portion of stanza 5, lines 4 to 7, increasingly extends courtesy into a context of opposition, exception, and limitation,
an adversative context in which doubleness and deception, both forms
of disunity, are implicit. Predictably in these lines the theme of true or
false perception becomes more insistent, and the poet's dis-ease, like
the doubleness of his expressions, becomes more pronounced: present
courtesy is nothing but forgery,

> Fashion'd to please the eies of them, that pas,
> Which see not perfect things but in a glas:
> Yet is that glasse so gay, that it can blynd
> The wisest sight, to thinke gold that is bras.

In the first two of these lines, however, the courtesy that is fashioned
to please begins to sound morally more mixed than simply false and
suggests the human condition more than it does the abstraction Falseness. The verb *pas* means either "pass by" or "pass away," and the
preposition *but* (potentially an adversative conjunction: i.e., but see in
a glass) means either "except" or "unless." Thus the faulty sight of the
heedless is not readily distinguished from the only sight of perfection
available in a mortal existence. The clear echo in line 5 of the famed
verse from I Cor. 13.12, "For now we see through a glass darkly,"

strongly enforces both readings. At the same time it enforces the real-ity of the gap that has opened between ideal perfection and the condi-tions of human existence – between virtue visionary and virtue em-bedded, between the fairest flower of courtesy and the feigned show. In the sixth and seventh lines of this stanza it is not surprising to find a flicker of sympathy along with great sadness for the gayness of a glass that dazzles the wisest. As perfection becomes more elusive and un-earthly, it becomes in a sense less real.

"But vertues seat is deepe within the mynd, / And not in outward shows, but inward thoughts defynd": these final lines of stanza 5 redefine and relocate virtue in a seeming effort to save its relevance and vitality, its present reality. They do so logically but very abruptly. The two adversative conjunctions within them testify to the disconti-nuity of "outward shows" and "inward thought," of the mind and the world outside it. If these two realms are related, it is as adversaries. Even the conjunction *and* in line 9 is drawn into the context of opposi-tion, a logical plus thus becoming in point of illogical fact a minus: "And not." Still, at the end of the stanza the interior realm, while limited and again hidden, albeit this time "deepe within the mynd," is humanly real. By suddenly and emphatically reinterpreting the hopeless opposi-tion between the ideal or true and the actual or false as an opposition between inner truth and outer falseness, the poet renders truth, living truth, more exclusively subjective. He thus limits *but* preserves its in-tegrity *and* does so with an abruptness that is more emphatic than con-fident or rhetorically persuasive.

The *but* with which stanza 6 opens may well be the most suspect adversative in the Proem. Having defined virtue as inward in the last two lines of stanza 5 and there having twice asserted the adversative conjunction ("But vertues seat . . . but inward thoughts"), the poet now begins, "But where shall I in all Antiquity / So faire a patterne finde" as in you, "O soueraine Lady Queene"? The reader need only try sub-stituting *and* for this opening *but* to measure the unsettling effect of the poet's echoing all those *buts* in the preceding stanza. *And* would have been immensely more reassuring in tone. Instead, as the line now stands, the initial *but* is openly and insistently adversative.

In stanza 6 the poet introduces the Queen, whose presence in this Proem the earlier Proems have led us to expect, and in this one, as in those earlier, his treatment of her becomes finally the index of the rela-tion of *present* virtue, living truth, to an ideal and visionary Antiquity. In stanzas 6 to 7, which close the sixth Proem, however, this relation-ship bears only a superficial resemblance to that found in the first two Proems of *The Faerie Queene*, and if aligned with the third Proem, it serves to illuminate the poet's uneasiness with the Queen's bright image at an earlier stage of the poem than is generally acknowledged.[6] Largely as a result of the emphatic trio of *buts* in the last two lines of stanza 5 and the first line of stanza 6, the beginning of the latter stanza appears contrived or, to adapt the poet's own words a few lines before, pretentiously "fayned" and excessively showy. *But,* the adversative conjunction between the two stanzas, which is in fact a disjunction, sounds at once forced and uneasy. Scrutinized logically, as perhaps out of politesse or policy it should not be, it suggests that the Queen is somehow adverse to an inward definition of virtue because she is an outward show, a suggestion positively bristling with alarming ambigu-ity. An outward show of true virtue alive in the present age is scarcely credible at this stage of the Proem.

Strictly speaking, of course, ambiguity itself is illogical and by its very presence contributes to the irrationality of the *but* with which stanza 6 opens. As Humphrey Tonkin has noticed, the phrasing of the lines this *but* immediately introduces further ensures that we are unable to be certain whether the location of the virtuous Queen is in Antiquity or in the present: "But where shall I in all Antiquity / So faire a patterne finde . . . As in your selfe"?[7] In other words, we are not

---

[6] In the Proem to book 3, as in earlier Proems, the poem continues to mirror the Queen, and although she is now invited to see herself "In mirrours more then one" (i.e., in Gloriana or Belphoebe), both glasses are essentially virtuous. But in this Proem the present embodiment also begins to vie with the antique image, living Queen with Antiquity. Uneasy nuances cluster around the word "living" (1.8–9; 2.1–2, 6; 3.5–9; 4.1–3). Adversatives (five in stanzas 2–5) begin to sound every bit as subjective as strictly logical. The poem becomes a slightly compromised "colourd" show that shadows the Queen's "glorious pourtraict" and fits "antique praises" to "pre-sent persons," a process of tailoring neither so close nor so natural as the unbroken continuity of bright reflections in Proems 1 and 2. The poem is uneasily differentiated from the "liuing colours" and "right hew" of Sir Walter Ralegh's *Cynthia*. With the reference to Ralegh we are getting closer to the real, historical Elizabeth, whose relation to the Faerie Queene is to become increas-ingly discontinuous.

[7] *Spenser's Courteous Pastoral: Book Six of the "Faerie Queene"* (Oxford: Clarendon Press, 1972), p. 24.

really sure about her location in time and place and hence about her true nature and identity. In view of the poet's nervously studied contrivance in beginning the stanza, scrutiny of his logic seems rather tactless, but failure to scrutinize it is mere complicity. The poet's compliment to the Queen here is courteous in some sense but is also ambiguous—neither wholehearted nor single-minded, probably despite half himself. It is equivocal, and he seems troubled by the real possibility that there may be in it only a flattering show of true courtesy.[8]

In the eleventh canto of Spenser's book 5 an exchange between Artegall, the Knight of Justice, and Burbon, a Knight whose name and story allude to recent French history, provides a relevant gloss on what is happening in stanza 6. Artegall rebukes Burbon for timeserving, and Burbon, for his own part, denies that he is false to truth, claiming that, when necessity constrains, "To temporize is not from truth to swerue, / Ne for aduantage terme to entertaine." Artegall's rejoinder is uncompromising: "Fie on such forgerie...Vnder one hood to shadow faces twaine. / Knights ought be true, and truth is one in all" (stanza 56). Since Burbon's figure openly embodies contemporary, topical reference, Artegall might as well have said "present forgerie" and thereby have anticipated the poet's disillusioned view in the Proem to book 6. In this Proem, Artegall's and Burbon's dissenting voices have been together submerged, rather than silenced or totally separated. It is as if the poet had swallowed both voices, without being himself taken in, of course, by either one. Yet knowingly, as a result of this infolding, the poet's own voice, like his syntax, has become fundamentally more duplicitous.

The rest of stanza 6 confirms the essential duplicity of perception in the Proem but ironically in this way frees the poet truthfully to fashion an alternative to it: perfection needs only truth; imperfection needs fiction. The one need only be found, expressed, and celebrated; the other needs to be bettered and transformed or else escaped. In the first four lines of the stanza the poet has asked where he can find so fair a pat-

---

[8] For recent statements of an opposite view of Proem 6, see Thomas H. Cain, Praise in "The Faerie Queene" (Lincoln, Neb.: University of Nebraska Press, 1978), pp. 155–56; and Daniel Javitch, Poetry and Courtliness in Renaissance England (Princeton, N.J.: Princeton University Press, 1978), pp. 143–44. Trenchant as both these writers are, they read Proem 6 selectively and appear to overlook its syntactical, verbal, and logical complexities.

tern "where may be seene / The goodly praise of Princely curtesie" as in the Queen and has implied visual, tangibly showy associations both through his diction ("faire...patterne...seene") and by directing a rhetorical question with dramatic presence to the Queen. Now, immediately following this direct address to her ("O soueraine Lady Queen"), he suddenly upends the logical assumptions he has invited from the opening word of the stanza ("But") and interiorizes, literally implants, the pattern of courtesy in the Queen's mind: "In whose pure minde, as in a mirrour sheene, / It showes." Evidently queenly virtue is not an "outward show" at all but an inward one and, assisted by a few more carefully planted verbal echoes, an associative thinker can hardly help adding, an "inward thought," as perhaps the virtuous Queen herself is also to be "defynd." I have had occasion earlier to observe that inner virtue is real but in a limited way.

But queenly virtue is not quite so easily implanted or, for that matter, transformed. The "mirrour sheene" (bright, shining, resplendent) is not so readily kept distinct from the "glasse so gay" in the preceding stanza that dazzles the "wisest sight," including the poet's perhaps. Distinguishing mirror from glass is made all the more difficult by the acclaim that follows the assertion "It [presumably the pattern] showes"; namely, "and with her brightnesse doth inflame / The eyes of all, which thereon fixed beene." Although in good Spenserian usage the possessive pronoun *her* means "its" and refers to the pattern, in the present context it cannot avoid suggesting the Queen herself and thereby drawing our gaze outward. It tends to direct our attention from intangible pattern to tangible sovereign. The verb *inflame* does nothing to counter these merely phenomenal or showy suggestions and in conjunction with "The eyes of all" could be taken to reinforce them. Further, the appearance of *but* as the first word in the next line and as the seeming successor to *inflame* momentarily acts to confirm an impression of excess: "doth inflame...But meriteth" something better than inflammation.

The concluding lines of stanza 6—"But meriteth indeede an higher name: / Yet so from low to high vplifted is your name"—extend to the Queen the compliment adversative-concessive. At this point in the Proem *but/yet* is a conspicuous combination, and elliptical syntax in the first of these lines renders it more so. The subject of *meriteth* in line

8 is elusive; I take it to be *patterne*, in which case "an higher name" than "Princely curtesie" is the meaning intended. Since the *but* beginning line 8 is clearly adversative, it requires a point of reference earlier in the stanza that is negatived, limited, or otherwise qualified here, and, once we determine that the referent is not in the inflamed eyes of the lines just preceding, thus canceling our momentary impression that it was to be found there, "Princely curtesie" or "praise [praiseworthiness, virtue] of Princely curtesie" five lines earlier becomes the logical candidate. But in this case the rich rhyme between lines 8 and 9 ("name"/"name") in reality qualifies sharply the Queen's virtuous status. It suggests a division between "an higher name" and "your name" and in fact implies that the comparative referent in line 8 is the Queen's name: "an higher name than yours" is the logical expectation of the syntax in lines 8 to 9, and the seemingly anticlimactic rich rhyme ensures that we attend closely to meaning.[9] Curiously enough, had line 8 begun with *and* rather than with *but*, or had line 9 begun with *and* rather than with *yet*, or had either line ended differently, both lines might have afforded straightforward adulation. As they stand, careful, deliberate, and duplicitous, they fit the larger pattern of stanza and Proem and make editorial tampering unjustified.[10] They forcefully suggest both the real imperfection of the Queen's court and its praiseworthy potential, its ever-unrealized worth:

> Then pardon me, most dreaded Soueraine,
> That from your selfe I doe this vertue bring,
> And to your selfe doe it returne againe.

[9] In the phrase "It showes," *it* could conceivably, although less logically, refer to "praise of Princely curtesie," which is virtually identical with "patterne" in line 2. Since *praise* occurs in a clause subordinate to *patterne* the latter is the logical referent of *It*. In any case, the less likely reading of *praise* as the referent would not alter significantly the preceding discussion, except to make *praise of Princely curtesie* both the subject of *meriteth* and an important part of the object in line 8: "an higher name [than 'praise of Princely curtesie']." If anything, this reading would strengthen the ironical undertones of lines 8 and 9.

[10] *Var.* 6.186: Church suggests that the word *name* means "appellation" in line 8 and "character" in line 9. *Var.* 6.459 notes that four of Spenser's editors or commentators (the earliest in 1758) have emended "name" to "fame" in line 9. Their emendation—interpretative at best and at worst arbitrary—has not been generally accepted. The recent editions of both A. C. Hamilton (*The Faerie Queene* [London: Longman, 1977]) and of Thomas P. Roche, Jr. (*The Faerie Queene* [Harmondsworth, Middlesex: Penguin, 1978]) read *name* in line 9.

In the final stanza of the Proem the Queen and her court are clearly a fiction, idealized and distinct from the present age, a reflection in the "mirrour sheene" and not in the "glasse so gay." This doubling of the kinds of mirrors (or glasses) is itself a duplicity absent from the first two Proems, but it is also one that clarifies and redeems in the present context:

> Right so from you all goodly vertues well
> Into the rest, which round about you ring,
> Faire Lords and Ladies, which about you dwell,
> And doe adorne your Court, where courtesies excell.

Having finally acknowledged the essential duplicity of the Queen, having realized not only poetically but even syntactically in the Proem that she is Una only in vision and dark conceit, the poet can celebrate her truly and faithfully as fiction.

It may be the essential duplicity of human experience—complexity, ambiguity, irony, illogic, deception—that finally brings the major works of Chaucer and Spenser, different as they may be, together. And it may also be the essential duplicity of experience that keeps them apart. Chaucer imitates and ironically appreciates this duplicity; Spenser acknowledges it in the end and perhaps escapes it. Chaucer might be said to embody and in some narratively real sense to externalize it in a dramatic persona; Spenser might be said to internalize it—as he internalizes the voices of Burbon and Artegall and, through an implanted fiction, the virtue of the Queen—and thereby to transform it. But Chaucer's and Spenser's employment of the techniques and devices of duplicity—their deliberate use of illogical syntax and of illogical adversatives in particular—suggests the existence of a linguistic bedrock of comparison that could redefine the character of Chaucer's influence on Spenser and could illuminate what Spenser meant in *The Faerie Queene* by describing Chaucer as the "well of English vndefyled" whose spirit survived in Spenser himself (4.2.32, 34).

The Grain of the Text

DEREK BREWER
Emmanuel College
Cambridge University

I

HE TWENTIETH CENTURY has seen a remarkable series of great scholars and critics of medieval English literature in the United States, and no one has shone more brightly than E. Talbot Donaldson. His special contribution has been the capacity to combine minute scholarly examination of texts in the light of deep philological knowledge with extreme sensitivity to poetry and with powerful general critical ideas. He conveys the whole with sparkling wit and genial wisdom. Following in his footsteps, "I come after, glenynge here and there," "though that my wit be lite" and offer some observations mainly focused on the close detail of Chaucer's text.

II

Chaucer felt very strongly the need for accuracy and precision in rendering his text. He specifically remarks on this need at the end of *Troilus and Criseyde* (5.1793–99) and in the enraged words of his poetic address to Adam his own scribe about the mistakes he makes. Anyone who has any acquaintance with the medieval English manuscripts of Chaucer's poetry knows how well justified was Chaucer's rage. Yet even now, after eloquent essays by Talbot Donaldson and the magisterial work by him and George Kane on the *Piers Plowman* manuscripts, there is still evidence of superstition about the reliability of scribes, and even of their practice of writing final -e. There are still some who prefer a halting meter on the grounds that an editor cannot be sure of fourteenth- or fifteenth-century practice. I propose to show that there is one thing we can be sure of, and that is that even good scribes are unreliable. This is a counsel of hope, not despair. A modern

editor like E. Talbot Donaldson (if any could be!) who has a conspectus of all the manuscripts and a concept of accuracy equal to Chaucer's
own can therefore do much better than any fifteenth-century scribe. I
shall also show that he has good empirical grounds for assuming that
the meter of *Troilus* is regular and that he can legitimately accept or
disregard any scribal use of final -*e* in order to preserve the regular, not
monotonous, basis of Chaucer's meter in that poem. That has implications for Chaucer's practice with final -*e* and his meter in *The Canterbury Tales*, on which E. Talbot Donaldson has written so convincingly,
but I restrict myself to *Troilus*.

In order to check the accuracy of scribes, we need a control. The obvious control is to have the same scribe copy out the same passage
twice under the same conditions and at no great interval of time.
Although we can be fairly sure that certain sections of the text of
Troilus in different manuscripts were copied by the same scribe, we
cannot be *absolutely* sure that he used the same exemplar, though it
seems to me to be likely, and of course time and conditions are unknown. The matter can, however, be put beyond reasonable doubt by
repetitions within the same text by the same scribe. There are a
number of duplicated lines in texts of *The Canterbury Tales*, but the
odd line does not offer much in the way of clear evidence. There is fortunately firmer evidence in Cambridge University Library Manuscript
Gg.IV.27 and Bodleian Rawlinson Poet. 163. Both of these are "good"
manuscripts. In particular Gg.IV.27 is the great Chaucer collection of
the early fifteenth century. It contains important texts not only of
Troilus but also of *The Canterbury Tales*, and of *The Parliament of
Fowls*, while it is the sole witness to the so-called G Prologue to *The
Legend of Good Women*. The scribe obviously had access to authentic
Chaucerian texts. It must be said that he was also eccentric, but even
his eccentricity, for example in spelling, has regularity, and his texts
can be, as in *The Parliament of Fowls*, extremely good.[1] If anything, the
scribe was of superior conscientiousness. This did not prevent him, on
two occasions, from inadvertently copying the same short passage
twice by turning a page and resuming at an earlier stage than he

---

[1] *The Parliament of Foulys* ed. D. S. Brewer (Manchester: Manchester University Press; New
York: Barnes and Noble, 1972), pp. 58–64.

needed. Since the repetitions are contiguous, the break could reasonably be assumed to be only of a day or two at most and might have
been of only an hour or so, when he went off for a meal. The situation
with the Bodleian Manuscript is only a little different.

In Gg.IV.27, lines 1.582-95 are the last lines on folio 21r. The scribe
turned the leaf and accidentally copied them again, canceling them
with a thin red line which leaves them perfectly legible. The same
thing happened at 2.1233-39. There are no major divergences but a
continuous play of slight variation line by line. I give an almost complete list of the first repetition in Gg.IV.27, disregarding only variation
in the use of abbreviations. In the following pairs the first word in each
case comes from the first version on folio 21r, and the second from the
repeated version on folio 21v:

582	pandare/pandaris	rewthe/reuthe
583	ofte/oftyn	
584	qud he/he seyde	euere/eyþer
585	be tweþe/atwixe	
588	Wost/wist	
589	peyne/payne	
592	god/good (Corpus and most other MSS reading glad[d][e])	
593	or/&	
594	loued/louyd	lyf/lyue
595	Hyd/Hyde	

In addition, line 591 has an oblique stroke dividing the line after ry3t in
both versions; line 592 is divided after wo in only the second version;
lines 593, 594, 595 divide the line only in the first version.[2] So much as
an example of the scribe of Gg.IV.27.

The scribe of Rawlinson Poet. 163, described as hand 4 by Root, on
folio 54v gives lines 3.1212-46 following 3.1099 and repeats them
again in the correct position on folio 57r. The page of his exemplar
must have flipped over without at first being noticed soon after he took
over, there having been four scribes engaged on this version (it seems
that all used the same exemplar). I follow the same procedure as above
in making comparisons:

---

[2] Not all these oblique strokes, which are very fine, are observable in the facsimile: *The Poetical Works of Geoffrey Chaucer: a Facsimile of Cambridge University Library MS Gg.IV.27*, with introductions by M. B. Parkes and Richard Beadle, 3 vols. (Cambridge: D. S. Brewer, 1979).

1212 is/ys
1213 *first a/omitted*   In second version *that* is later inserted
1214 muste/mosten   often se/al day see
1215 drynke/drinke &
1216 drynke/drinken   peyne for destresse/peynes & distresse
1218 hathe/hath
1219 also (*other MSS* now)/*om.*   semethe/comethe often
1220 bitternesse/buternesse
1222 Non swyche they felten/Swyche felt they non*ne*   born/borne
1223 bette/bettere
1224 heede/hede
1225 werken/worchen   comythe/comethe
1226 quit/quyte
1227 for/*omitted*
1228 swych ioye wondere/swyche feste hit joye
1230 aboute atre/about atree
1231 wrythe the swete/wrythen ys the
1232 ech/eche
1234 styntethe ferst/stynthe fyrst
1235 she herithe/that she herethe   heerde/herde
1236 hegge/hegges   steryng/sterynge
1237 sykere/*omitted*
1238 creyde/cresseyde
1239 Opened/Opned
1240 saght/sawe
1241 dey must/dien moste   he may/y can
1242 iskapen/ascapen
1243 in/into
1246 Wyth/wythe   late vs neu*er*/vs neu*ere*

Other manuscripts at times also repeat a line or two and occasionally a stanza, but it would be tedious to multiply examples. In any line substitutions, and both omission and insertion, are possible. In Rawlinson Poet. 163 there are omissions in five lines out of thirty-five; that is, 14 percent of lines are metrically defective through omission, though in one of these lines, 1213, the scribe inserted *that* perhaps unconsciously from a sense of the metrical pattern spoiled by the earlier omission of *a*.

There are two lessons here, obvious enough but frequently disregarded. *First, no single word or spelling of any single scribe however "good" he normally seems to be or with however good an exemplar before him, can be trusted.* Second, and conversely, because scribes are variable and were after all intending to copy out accurately and the text is not difficult, the conspectus of all surviving readings of a line and the presence of roughly twenty witnesses *put the modern editor in a position vastly superior to any scribe to reconstruct the author's original text.* It will be apparent that I subscribe in principle to Kane and Donaldson's work on *Piers Plowman,* though I should emphasize that I limit my observations here to the text of *Troilus* alone. The nature of the manuscripts, none a holograph, all relatively close to the author; the extreme likelihood of coincidental variation, of "contamination," of the use of different exemplars for one copy; the sophistication of copies by insertion of leaves all make recension of limited value. For most of the poem one must proceed line by line (like the scribes) and where the variation occurs try to decide which version could have given rise to which other, independent of how good or bad any manuscript generally is. For an edition of *Troilus* it is reasonable to take Corpus Christi College Cambridge Manuscript 61 as copy-text for its fullness, care, regular spelling, and general accuracy, but that text is no more sacrosanct than the irritatingly variable (not to say often incorrect) version of, for example, Bishop Cosin's Library, Durham V.11.13. In this note I necessarily refrain from full discussion of the principles of textual criticism, but the evidence of variation that I have given must surely explode any lingering elements of belief that any individual scribe "knows best" and that the most scholarly thing to do in editing a Middle English manuscript is to print a "good" manuscript with the minimum of emendation. If there are only one or two manuscripts, that might perhaps be the right thing to do, but it cannot be a general rule. The editorial motto should be, "Be bold, be bold, be not too bold."

We may recall Chaucer's lines in *Troilus* as revealing both a concept of accurate transcription and a fear that it may not take place. We may then ask what fifteenth-century scribes actually made of these lines so obviously directed to them. Did they respond? Not in the least. Of the fifteen manuscripts and three printed versions (of Caxton, Wynkyn de Worde, and Thynne, which may count here as equivalent to manuscripts) in which these lines are preserved, one at least, and often more, makes an error in *each* line except the last. Yet the multiplicity of witnesses, the clarity of the poet, and the minor nature of the variations allow a modern editor, though not a medieval scribe, confidently to restore what Chaucer actually wrote.

III

E. Talbot Donaldson has himself long convinced me of the regular metrical basis of Chaucer's five-stress verse. More recently Windeatt has argued for the basic regularity of the verse of *Troilus*.[3] There is still room for an empirical argument, based on the manuscripts, to make assurance double sure, and to reinforce the lesson, long taught and practiced by Donaldson, that an editor needs, in a word, to *edit*.

First, it must be noted that, although no manuscript can be trusted in any single word or spelling, the scribes were not wanton. They were "approximators," in an entirely natural way. They were not *trying* to make mistakes. They were just careless copiers. In a poem of over 8,000 lines in roughly twenty versions, where we therefore have well over 160,000 lines, there is a likelihood of a statistical impression of a meter. It is in fact impossible, in terms of subjective experience, to go through so many lines without realizing that (1) there is an expectation of a regular five-stress iambic line, (2) the speech stress may vary from the basic pattern as a kind of counterpoint without destroying it, (3) scribes frequently destroy the pattern, but in perfectly obvious ways, by omission, obvious substitution, etc., and (4) scribes occasionally "correct" the meter.

Let us first emphasize a point so obvious that it is usually overlooked. The poem is set out in all manuscripts in lines of approximately equal length, beginning usually with a capital letter, put into stanza form, and rhyming. If they were written in contemporary French, Italian, or Latin, all languages known to Chaucer, the presumption would be that they had a regular meter. Why should they not with Chaucer? Rhyme is much less effective when the lines are irregular. Connected with rhyme, but also with meter, is the question of word order. The "natural"—that is to say, the normal—prose or oral sequence of words is constantly disturbed in *Troilus*—the first stanzas are prime examples both over several lines and within a line; but indeed the whole poem is

[3] B. A. Windeatt, "'Most conservatyf the soun': Chaucer's *Troilus* Metre," *Poetica* (Tokyo) 8 (1977):44–60.

crammed with examples. Individual scribes often revert to normal prose order within the line, demonstrably falsely, thus demonstrating the textual error well recognized by the editors of classical texts, called *simplex ordo*.

I propose now, however, to proceed with further empirical observations based on all the manuscripts, not on just one or two, where the absence of significant variation and of any awkwardness or confusion of meaning, allows one to draw some confident conclusions which lead to further implications. There are some lines in *Troilus* which may be regarded as "proving" lines, establishing with objective clarity the norms which subjective experience, not to say common sense, vouches for in many other lines when familiar adjustments have been made. For example, 1.75 is, apart from familiar, minor and totally insignificant spelling variants, one of the rare lines in which every witness agrees, reading, in Corpus 61,

> He caste anon oute of the town to go.

1.173 is another:

> Hire goodly lokyng gladed al the prees.

In the first line no question can be raised whether a final -e, or inflexion of a verb, should or should not be pronounced. There are ten unequivocal syllables, and in the second example the speech rhythm exactly follows the normal "iambic" stress pattern. In this and in another line with minimum variation where spelling variants are insignificant it would be perverse to sound the final -e after r:

> But were he fer or ner I dar sey this.
> [1.451]

Another line in which every witness exactly coincides, indeed with only three trivial spelling variants in all seventeen versions, is 1.482:

> Fro day to day in armes so he spedde.

Here, however, if one wished to be perverse and disregard the history of English sounds, one could argue that *armes* is a single syllable. 1.493 has some interesting variants. Corpus 61 reads:

> If that his lady vnderstood nat this.

There are only two substantive variants, each for *If that*. Harley 2392 substitutes *Whethir*, and Wynkyn de Worde, *Yf I*. They are clearly errors; yet each at least scans.

Consider lines 1.443, 444, 446, 448:

> For lust to hire gan quiken and encresse
> That euery other charge he sette at noughte
> To sen hire goodly loke he gan to presse
> And ay the ner he was the more he brende.

There are very few variants to these lines, and none affecting the meter. The lines occur close together. Their regular rhythm, with a few familiar simple licenses, is incontrovertible.

Among them occurs 1.447:

> For ther by to ben esed wel he wende.

With the rhythm running in our heads and the well-attested custom even centuries later of pronouncing separately the final *-ed* of the past participle, it would require a remarkable deafness to the English language to deny that this line too, with *esed* as a dissyllable, must also scan regularly. Then we may look, in the same stanza, at 1.445:

> Forthi ful ofte his hote fire to cesse.

With the rhythm of the other lines in our heads it is impossible to deny the same rhythm to this line. It merely requires, what E. Talbot Donaldson with his command of historical philology showed long ago to be entirely acceptable, the pronunciation of the final *-e* in *hote*, grammatically required in the weak declension used after the possessive. The meter does not require the final *-e* in *fire* to be pronounced. It would not be historically justified—the accusative case was not a dissyllable. Four manuscripts in fact spell the word without *-e* (as, incidentally, and quite reasonably, does Robinson in his edition; whether an editor should remove such unetymological final *-e*'s from his copy-text if they occur is a pretty question).

It would be possible to select a number of lines where scribal variation is insignificant or easily accounted for and the text unchallengeable, not depending on the pronunciation of final *-e*, which demonstrate unquestionably a ten-syllable five-stress "iambic" line. Once such a line is taken as the hypothetical norm, it is possible to show thousands of other lines in which, either by the pronunciation of ety-mological final -e or verbal inflexions or plural inflexions, and having established where necessary the correct reading by well-tried textual methods, a regular iambic beat modified as needed by natural speech rhythm is incontestably present. This, together with the clinching ef-fect of rhyme, and of the disturbance of normal prose order of words already referred to, is proof of the intended regularity (not monotony) of Chaucer's verse in *Troilus*. With this norm established, it is not then merely circular to emend the text when occasion arises in accordance with the requirements of the meter. No acquaintance with one or two manuscripts or prints and their individually limping meter is sufficient to sustain any argument for the roughness, or indeed the absence, of meter in Chaucer's *Troilus*. A conspectus of all the witnesses makes clear the surpassing sweetness and music, the untiring movement for-ward, simple yet never tedious, subtly not crudely varied, of the five-stress "iambic" meter of the poem. How Chaucer came by it and what it signifies in our cultural history are other questions of great interest not to be attempted here. The fact is certain. It has considerable im-plications for the meter of *The Canterbury Tales* and consequent editorial practice.

Beowulf Comes Home:
Close Reading in Epic Context

EDWARD B. IRVING, JR.
University of Pennsylvania

HEN I FIRST STUDIED *Beowulf* under Robert J. Menner, our graduate class was kept so busy with the philological prob-lems that bulked so large in those days that we never actu-ally had time to read the whole poem. What we omitted was "The Return," or "Beowulf's Report to Hygelac"—that talky inter-lude between the beheading of Grendel's mother and the first sallying forth of the dragon after Beowulf's fifty-year reign (lines 1651–2199). Plainly if you have to cut, you must cut here; it is the least essential part of the poem. But less essential is not the same as unimportant, and this passage has suffered some undeserved neglect.

There are some real questions to ask (and perhaps with luck to answer) about this part of *Beowulf*, particularly about the scene at the Geatish court in which Beowulf tells his uncle King Hygelac of his adventures in Denmark.[1] That this story is so elaborately retold is worthy of notice in a poem otherwise not repetitious but usually com-pact, laconic, and allusive. Why must it be retold? One may argue that the poet here is careful to introduce saved-up new material or that the original audiences for epic poetry never minded retellings like this,[2] but

---

[1] Few critics seem to have discussed this scene at much length. See A. G. Brodeur, *The Art of Beowulf* (Berkeley: University of California Press, 1959), pp. 82–83, who stresses the strong bond between Hygelac and Beowulf; Martin Stevens, "The Structure of *Beowulf*: From Gold-Hoard to Word-Hoard," *MLQ* 39 (1978):219–38, who calls the scene "the high point of the poem" in the context of his argument that it represents "the epic poet's celebration of self" (p. 237); R. Barton Palmer, "In His End Is His Beginning: *Beowulf* 2177–2199 and the Question of Unity," *AnM* 17 (1976):5–21, who sees the final exchange of gifts as a "surrogate coronation" since in it Beowulf moves from being a retainer to being a king. Several articles by Kemp Malone will be cited below. Let me here offer thanks to Donald Howard and Robert Creed for useful criticism of an earlier version of this essay; they are freed of all responsibility for its opinions.

[2] I have so argued, for example, in *Introduction to Beowulf* (Englewood Cliffs, N.J.: Prentice-Hall, 1969), pp. 69–71.

these reasons are not good enough for this poet. Surely the story is not retold out of mere incompetence at condensing narrative material, for we have seen the poet capable of handling more material than this in ten lines when he wants to.

But there are also other problems of structure in this part of the poem. Perhaps the insertion at this point, during Beowulf's walk from his ship to the Geatish hall, of what seems to us the wildly digressive episode concerning Thryth (or Modthryth) and Offa (lines 1931–62) has led modern readers to feel that the poet is not concentrating hard enough on his job. Why is that episode added here? Those who seek to date and place the poem would be delighted if we could be certain that a court poet was here flattering Offa's namesake King Offa of Mercia, who reigned from 757 to 796, but aesthetically the episode might still seem disappointing. At the end of the scene with Hygelac, the so-called "male Cinderella" passage (lines 2183b–89) describing for the only time Beowulf's inglorious youth, when the Geats thought him of no worth as a warrior, has often been criticized as unrelated to anything else and rather crudely stuck in here.[3] In a more general way readers so recently dazzled by the splendors of Hrothgar's Danish court may find the Geatish court provincial, dingy, and decidedly anticlimactic.

The poet has not lost his touch in this part of the poem, but we may have to try harder than usual to make out what he is doing. Let me here suggest a hypothesis that at least purports to connect things under a common heading. Even if not wholly persuasive, it may stimulate further reflection on this section of the poem.

We should first consider Beowulf's last hours in Denmark in order better to understand the circumstances of his return to his native land.[4] A ubiquitous theme here is the love and admiration felt for the Geatish youth by the grateful king Hrothgar, whose famous sermon (lines 1700–84) begins by praising Beowulf highly and continues by warning him of the potential perils of the success foreseen for him. Simultane-

---

[3] For example, by Fr. Klaeber, *Beowulf and the Fight at Finnsburg*, 3d ed. (Boston: D. C. Heath, 1950), note to lines 2183ff.

[4] Alvin A. Lee contrasts Denmark and its brilliant scenes with Geatland, which "is, on the whole, the setting for tales of death, confusion, and social chaos" (*The Guest-Hall of Eden* [New Haven, Conn.: Yale University Press, 1972], p. 177).

ously, Beowulf himself is demonstrating political skills. His returning the sword he borrowed from Unferth to its owner with polite thanks (lines 1807–12) reveals his habitual courtesy, but the act may also imply some sort of political truce between the two nations, since the furious verbal battle earlier between Unferth and Beowulf had had strong nationalistic overtones.[5] Furthermore, the speech that Beowulf addresses to Hrothgar just before leaving (lines 1817–39) is his most political of the entire poem. He makes three earnest promises, each one contingent on a possible need expressed in an if clause: if you need my individual help again, I'll be ready; if enemies attack you, I'll bring a thousand men; if young Prince Hrethric decides to visit the Geatish court, I'll see that he finds friends there. Without tactlessly naming names, Beowulf shows that he is aware of the two threats to Denmark hinted at in the poem: possible attack on the hall by the nearby Heathobards and possible usurpation of the throne from Hrothgar's son(s) by his nephew Hrothulf. Beowulf unhesitatingly pledges not only his own help but the help of his uncle Hygelac, saying, "I know that he will want to stand by me with words and actions, even though he is young."[6]

Hrothgar's response to these promises is rapturous. Only wise God, he exclaims, could have sent such sayings into your spirit![7] He asserts his belief that the Geats, if Hygelac should die, could not have a better candidate for their throne than Beowulf, and he then credits Beowulf with singlehandedly bringing an end to a period of hostility that he says had existed previously between Danes and Geats. His tears flowing as he surmises that he will never see this splendid young man again, Hrothgar kisses and embraces Beowulf. The scene is suffused with unusually intense emotion.

These passages express unrestrained praise, gratitude, and love for Beowulf. His talents are as amply displayed and as highly valued in Denmark as they could well be. Not only his past achievement but his potential for the future are given full attention.

[5] See *Beowulf*, lines 590–606, the end of Beowulf's reply to Unferth.

[6] "Ic on Higelace wat, / Geata dryhten, þeah ðe he geong sy, / folces hyrde, þæt he mec fremman wile / wordum ond weorcum," etc. (lines 1830b–35). The text quoted herein is that of Klaeber's third edition, though without his diacritics, and with a few minor changes in punctuation; translations are mine.

[7] "Þe þa wordcwydas wigtig Drihten / on sefan sende" (lines 1841–42a).

Now this poet, like most other Old English poets, habitually works and thinks in strong contrasts,[8] and so it should not surprise us if Beowulf is being set up by this warm scene with Hrothgar for a some-what cooler reception to follow in Geatland. Warm welcome is no foregone conclusion for a young hero-prophet returning, even with a shipload of tangible honor, to his own country.

Beowulf's ship now moves powerfully toward Geatland, undeterred by wind or wave from reaching its goal. Geatland turns out to be an in-timate place in both space and time. Contrasts with Denmark abound. There are no such rituals of challenge or greeting as there had been in Denmark, and the hall is close to the shore (*sæwealle neah*, line 1924); the travelers have not far to go to find Hygelac (*næs him feor þanon / to gesecanne sinces bryttan*, lines 1921b–22). The king himself is tersely characterized as *Higelac Hrepling*. While *Hrepling* is a simple patronymic, son of Hrethel, the much smaller scale of Geatish history is suggested by it, since it is also an honorific title. For the Geats, Hrethel seems to be their Oldest One, equivalent to the legendary Scyld from whom the Danes take their proud title of Scyldings. The Geats as a group are in fact called *Hreðlingas* in the heroic action of Ravenswood (line 2960).

But our attention is now diverted away from Hygelac to his "very young" queen Hygd, who despite her youth is all a queen should be— specifically, generous in giving rewards to Geatish warriors. In this she is apparently quite unlike the mysterious Thryth, whose youthful violence toward her own subordinates is now described. If Hygd is generous to her subjects, Thryth is pathologically hostile to hers; if Hygelac lives peaceably among his companions (*selfa mid gesiðum*, line 1924), none of the dear companions (*swæsra gesiða*, line 1934) in Thryth's court dare even look in her direction for fear of being sum-marily executed. Is it imaginable that we are to consider Thryth's behavior as normal for a "very young" queen, the aggressive arrogance of the royal brat? Would Hygd's decorous behavior then be seen as remarkable in so young a princess? One would be reluctant to accept such conclusions.

---

[8] For some instances see chap. 1 of my book, *A Reading of* Beowulf (New Haven: Yale University Press, 1968); and T. A. Shippey, *Old English Verse* (London: Hutchinson University Library, 1972), pp. 36–43.

Thryth meets, falls in love with, and marries the great Offa and thereafter gives up her murderous ways; the shrew is self-tamed by her love for him. Perhaps this happy marriage is offered as a model of the marriage of Hygelac and Hygd, and, on the other hand, strange as it may seem to us, the earlier phase of the Thryth story may be presented as an antimodel, a path not taken. If things were the opposite of what they now are at the Geatish court, then a brave young man like Beowulf might now be walking to his death. That is to say, the poet may give us our sense of the stability of Hygelac's royal *ham* by showing us a glimpse of the kind of violence it might well contain but does not. In this light we may see Hygd's youthful behavior as an achievement; similarly, the various smoldering threats to Denmark's stability and the cautionary tales told about bad King Heremod made us value what the Danes struggled to attain and uphold. We might tentatively conclude then that the Thryth episode is chiefly intended to show us both negatively (young bad Thryth) as well as positively (older devoted Thryth and famous great Offa) what a good court Hygelac and Hygd have, young as they are.

The references to their youth are still puzzling. In plot terms, Hygelac must be young enough to lead his people on the fatal expedition to the Continent and young enough to leave then as his heir the child Heardred, not yet old enough to rule unaided.[9] But there may be another good reason: stressing Hygelac's youth is the best way to draw a strong contrast between him and the aged Hrothgar.[10]

In narrative pacing, in any case, the Thryth episode serves as an effective retard, stretching out that short walk from beach to hall and increasing suspense about the encounter of uncle and nephew. Messengers go back and forth; Beowulf approaches the hall where he has heard the king waits; Hygelac waits, having heard that Beowulf has returned alive. The traditional hall-scene is sketched out in a few quick strokes (lines 1977–83a):

[9] See lines 2369–79a, where Beowulf refuses Hygd's offer of the throne to him after Hygelac's death.

[10] Possibly related to this contrast is the notion that the Geats are a "very young" people, without the rich legendary past of the Danes. Kemp Malone refers to a contrast "between a major and a minor power" ("Symbolism in 'Beowulf': Some Suggestions," in *English Studies Today*, 2d ser., ed. G. A. Bonnard [Bern: Francke Verlag, 1961], p. 85).

Gesæt þa wið sylfne se ða sæcce genæs,
mæg wið mæge, syððan mandryhten
þurh hleoðorcwyde holdne gegrette,
meaglum wordum. Meoduscencum hwearf
geond þæt *heal*reced Hæreðes dohtor,
lufode ða leode, liðwæge bær
hæle*ð*um to handa.

[Then he who had survived the fight took his seat opposite (the king) himself, kinsman opposite kinsman, after he had greeted his loyal lord in formal speech, with powerful words. Hæreth's daughter (Hygd) moved all round the hall with mead-cups, loved (i.e., acted out her love for) those people, carried the drinking-cup to the warriors' hands.]

Any more background would distract us from the sharp focus on this encounter of kinsman and kinsman, lord and man. Only Hygd moves here, and the expression *lufode ða leode* seems to carry special emotional intensity. The phrase *gesæt þa wið sylfne . . . / mæg wið mæge* is also powerful. *Wið* in Old English means not so much "in the presence of" as "up against." In *Beowulf*, *wið* is most often used to describe conflict or hostility; that is not the case here, but we could justifiably speak of confrontation.

Now Hygelac makes his only speech of the poem. He is curious to know what adventures these voyaging Sea-Geats have had. While his first phrase, in its plural pronoun, gestures politely toward all the men who went to Denmark, the rest of the speech focuses on Beowulf alone. The speech must be cited in full (lines 1987–98):

"Hu lomp eow on lade, leofa Biowulf,
þa ðu færinga feorr gehogodest
sæcce secean ofer sealt wæter,
hilde to Hiorote? Ac ðu Hroðgare
widcuðne wean wihte gebettest,
mærum ðeodne? Ic ðæs modceare
sorhwylmum seað, siðe ne truwode
leofes mannes; ic ðe lange bæd,
þæt ðu þone wælgæst wihte ne grette,
lete Suð-Dene sylfe geweorðan
guðe wið Grendel. Gode ic þanc secge,
þæs ðe ic ðe gesundne geseon moste."

["How did it turn out for all of you on the journey, dear Beowulf, after you yourself unexpectedly took it in mind to go seek a fight far away over salt water, a battle in Heorot? Did you in any way remedy the widely-known woes of Hrothgar, that famous prince? What anxiety I suffered over it, what surges of sorrow. I had no confidence in your venture, dear man. I begged you over and over not to go near that murderous demon, to let the South-Danes themselves settle their war against Grendel. I say thanks to God that I am permitted to see you safe."]

This speech implies attitudes not wholly consistent with what we might expect from an intelligently affectionate uncle. Hygelac originally regarded (and still regards) Beowulf's trip as ill-advised and unnecessary. His decision to go was sudden (*færinga*) and hence probably ill-considered; he went far away to look for trouble (*feorr, ofer sealt wæter, to Hiorote*) in someone else's country.[11] Hygelac says that he pleaded with his nephew to let the Danes handle their own monster.[12] While Hygelac must concede that his nephew has come back alive, he does not apparently assume that the Geats succeeded in their mission of killing Grendel. His second question could even be given a sarcastic inflection: Did you in any way help old Hrothgar with those problems of his? Hygelac explicitly says he never had any faith in the venture; nothing indicates that he has since changed his mind. It is plain, however, what he is not saying—that I can see at once you have been most successful, and I apologize for not having had more faith in you.

I admit to tilting the speech in one direction, but we must consider the strong possibility that this is in some sense a speech of challenge, one like Unferth's challenge earlier (lines 506–28) in that it demands a prompt heroic response, but of course quite unlike Unferth's speech in not being hostile or malicious, or indeed even consciously a challenge on Hygelac's part. One can view Hygelac as the Anxious Parent, sincerely loving the child Beowulf but not yet ready to see him as mature —still too absorbed in scolding him for risking his life to attend as yet to

---

[11] Although there might be some larger irony in Hygelac's scolding Beowulf for undertaking a rash overseas venture in view of what happens later when Hygelac himself dies in a swashbuckling raid on the Continent, the poet rarely seems to have in mind "long-range" irony of this kind.

[12] There is, of course, inconsistency here with the statement earlier that wise men (*snotere ceorlas*, line 202) among the Geats had urged him on (*hwetton higerofne*) to undertake the fight against Grendel.

the actuality of his achievement. But of course to any child such a parental attitude is itself the greatest challenge.

Supporting evidence for this attitude of Hygelac's (and of the other Geats) exists in the "male Cinderella" passage at the end of this scene (lines 2183b–89):

> Hean wæs lange,
> swa hyne Geata bearn   godne ne tealdon,
> ne hyne on medobence   micles wyrðne
> drihten Wedera   gedon wolde;
> swyðe wendon, þæt he sleac wære,
> æðeling unfrom.   Edwenden cwom
> tireadigum menn   torna gehwylces.

[For a long time he (Beowulf) was humiliated, since the sons of the Geats did not consider him to be good (i.e., brave), nor did the lord of the Weders (probably Hygelac) wish to make him worth much on the mead-bench; they strongly believed that he was lazy, an unaggressive prince. (But) reversal came to the man rich-in-glory for every grief.]

This passage is sometimes taken to mean that Beowulf *was* a lazy, sluggish youth, like young Offa in Saxo Grammaticus,[13] before he suddenly acquired his heroic status, but it says no such thing. It says that the Geats did not reward him because they did not think he was any good as a warrior. Blame for this rests not on Beowulf but on the Geats for being unperceptive.[14]

This passage does, however, fit in well with Hygelac's speech and indeed explains its tone. Hygelac speaks patronizingly because he has had no reason to expect much of his nephew. If the king is to be enlightened about the Danish venture, Beowulf's long speech that follows is anything but otiose, since he must establish solidly his heroic

---

[13] Saxo Grammaticus, *Gesta Danorum*, ed. J. Olrik and H. Raeder (Copenhagen, 1931), 1.113–17.

[14] This view of the episode is close to that of Kemp Malone, "Young Beowulf," *JEGP* 36 (1937):21–23, who sees a quiescent middle stage in Beowulf's career, after his promising early boyhood, a stage when he deliberately refuses to use his strength for trivial ends. "He awaits God's call to high service in a great cause. During this stage he falls out of favor at home; his fellows, and even his lord, knowing as they do the greatness of his strength, cannot understand his refusal to use it in the rough and tumble of everyday life in the hall; they attribute his inactivity to sloth and want of spirit" (p. 23). Malone restated this view in a later article (*Anglia* 69 [1951]:295–300).

credentials. We can then see much of his report as answering charges either explicit or implicit in Hygelac's speech: it is a genuine reply.

Beowulf must first address himself to the devastating charge that his mission was a failure, and to do so he promptly summons witnesses from both the human world and the world of monsters to attest to his victory (lines 2000–2009a):

> "Þæt is undyrne,   dryhten Higelac,
> micel gemeting,   monegum fira,
> hwylc orleghwil   uncer Grendles
> wearð on ðam wange,   þær he worna fela
> Sige-Scyldingum   sorge gefremede,
> yrmðe to aldre;   ic ðæt eall gewræc,
> swa begylpan ne þearf   Grendeles maga
> ænig ofer eorðan   uhthlem þone,
> se ðe lengest leofað   laðan cynnes,
> facne bifongen."

["It is no secret to many men, Lord Hygelac, that great encounter, what sort of combat-time Grendel and I put in on the spot where he had inflicted so many sorrows and long-lasting misery on the Victory Scyldings. I avenged *all* that—so that not one of Grendel's kinfolk anywhere on earth has occasion to boast of that dawn-brawl, not the one who lives the longest of that hated race, clutched by crime."]

Grendel's defeat is by now a victory that extends both in space, as a very public and already famous "meeting" in Denmark, and also in time, never to be forgotten or denied in future by even the longest-lived monster of Cain's race. Beowulf thus asserts his claims roundly and with his usual slightly ironic assurance; there will be time enough later to fill in the details of the fight.

But now Beowulf must cope with a second charge, that he has been foolishly interfering in Danish affairs. One way to answer this is to show that he was not for long an outsider among the Danes, who needed him badly and were helpless on their own. He soon became almost a naturalized Dane; Hrothgar was ready to adopt him as a son. The process of acceptance by the Danes, long in the first telling, is here breathtakingly abbreviated, so that Hygelac must feel that King Hrothgar took one quick look at his young visitor and seated him on the bench with his own sons. Beowulf's immersion in Danish affairs (and, significantly, his detachment from them) is further dramatized by the Ingeld story that follows (lines 2020–69a), where he coolly predicts the probable failure of Hrothgar's attempt to settle an old feud with the neighboring Heathobards by marrying his daughter to their prince. Without explicitly criticizing Hrothgar's judgment, Beowulf reveals himself to be not only understanding of foreigners' problems but wiser than wise old Hrothgar. His involvement in no way dims his icily sharp vision of the durability of resentment and violence. We may imagine Hygelac a little astonished as such acumen.

But there is another, and perhaps better, way for Beowulf to reply to the charge of not minding his own business. When he resumes telling his uncle about Grendel, he quickly reframes this conflict in new terms: it is now Grendel versus the Geats. It is not the Danes but "us" that Grendel comes to the hall to visit that night; it is the Geat Hondscio (here first named), that dear man (*leofes mannes*, line 2080), who is devoured "first of all" (*he fyrmest læg*, line 2077), almost as if the whole feud really began with this action and not with Grendel's first attack on Heorot twelve years earlier; Grendel then becomes Hondscio's *bona*, his legal slayer (*muðbonan*, line 2079; *bona blodigtoð*, line 2082); and thus vengeance by Beowulf has now become an obligation.[15] Later (line 2120) Grendel's mother is said to discover that it was *wighete Wedera*, the enmity of the Geats, that has destroyed her son. Beowulf vividly describes peering into Grendel's *glof*, that mitten foodbag made of dragons' skins by devils' craft. He wanted to put me in that, the hero exclaims, *unsynnige*, innocent Geat that I am, but he could not, once I stood up in anger. Little needs to be added after that (lines 2093–96a):

> To lang ys to reccenne, hu ic ðam leodsceaðan
> yfla gehwylces ondlean forgeald,
> þær ic, þeoden min, þine leode
> weorðode weorcum.

[It is too long to tell how I paid that great marauder his reward for every evil, when, O my lord, I honored your people with deeds.]

What the young hero now hurries toward in his account is the I-thou intensity of his direct and intimate message to his beloved king. Trans-

[15] On the blood feud in Anglo-Saxon England, see Dorothy Whitelock, *The Audience of Beowulf* (Oxford: Clarendon Press, 1951), pp. 13–19.

lation conveys almost none of the rich poetic density of line 2095: its three pronouns, its internal rhyming, its close juxtaposing of *min* and *þine*. The heroic deed was carried out as promised, but what matters is that it was carried out *for* Hygelac and for the Geatish people.

Beowulf now tells of the following day's banquet in Heorot, where he was generously rewarded by Hrothgar. It is easy to see why Hyge- lac should hear about the rewards (they will be presented to him by his nephew in a moment), but we may wonder why the hero devotes ten lines (2105–14) to the vocal entertainment at the banquet (not told of before, unless the scop's tale of Finnsburg comes under this heading), in particular the performances of King Hrothgar himself. We so often study this passage out of context as a precious description of poetic repertory and performance that we may forget that it is also a charac- terization of Hrothgar: the dignity of his strong memory, his deep and varied feelings, his great age. Indeed, this is none other than the emotion-filled old man we saw saying farewell to Beowulf. The focus on Hrothgar continues as Beowulf tells of the helpless pain the king feels that no funeral rites could be performed for his favorite thane (*leofne mannan*, line 2127), Æschere, who was carried off and killed later that night by Grendel's mother. Such frustrated grief is like that felt by old Hrethel in Beowulf's later memorable description (lines 2441–71) of how a father helplessly mourns his dead son. Perhaps Hygelac is here invited to see his own presumed grief for the loss of his man Hondscio as being similar to the grief of Hrothgar for Æschere. Beowulf may be tactfully offering Hrothgar to the young Geatish king as a paradigm of royal decorum and compassionate responsibility.

A slight tension may in fact surround the emotional relationship in this little triangle: the young and brilliant retainer with two "fatherly" lords. Would it be absurd to wonder whether Hygelac might not be a little jealous of the renowned Danish king who saw so much more in the young hero than he did? If so, he is quickly reassured (lines 2131–34):

> Þa se ðeoden mec   ðine life
> healsode hreohmod,   þæt ic on holma geþring
> eorlscipe efnde,   ealdre geneðde,
> mærðo fremede;   he me mede gehet.

[Then the lord (Hrothgar) in his grief of heart implored me by your life to act the warrior's part in the press of waters, to risk my life, earn fame; he promised me reward.]

Consequently when Beowulf plunges into the evil mere, it is a heroic action done not only for the bereaved Hrothgar but also for Hygelac, whom Hrothgar here invokes.[16] All three persons of our triangle (*ðeoden mec ðine*) are mentioned in one line (2131), a tight collocation like the compression for emotional effect commented on earlier in line 2095. We are almost led to feel that Beowulf might not have carried out his deed if Hrothgar had not here invoked Hygelac's name.

The jaunty speed with which Beowulf now tells of the killing of Grendel's mother is characteristic of the hero, but it also shows plainly that the poet is not being needlessly prolix in his retelling of what was a long and complicated action narrative. So condensed is this account in fact that Hygelac would have to be paying the closest attention to be sure what happened. As before, the hero is really hurrying toward the crucial final lines of his speech and toward his final gesture toward Hygelac (lines 2144–51):

> Swa se ðeodkyning þeawum lyfde;
> nealles ic ðam leanum   forloren hæfde,
> mægnes mede,   ac he me maðmas geaf,
> sunu Healfdenes   on minne sylfes dom;
> ða ic ðe, beorncyning,   bringan wylle,
> estum geywan.   Gen is eall æt ðe
> lissa gelong;   ic lyt hafo
> heafodmaga   nefne, Hygelac, ðec.

[This is how that mighty king lived, with good customs. In no way did I lose the rewards, the prizes for my strength; far from it, the son of Healfdene gave me whatever treasures I wished. And those I want to bring to you, O warrior king, to offer them with my good will to you. All joys are still dependent on you. I have few close relatives, Hygelac, except you.]

The extraordinary attention given to Hygelac in these last three

---

[16] In the earlier narrative, in fact, Hrothgar never invokes Hygelac; he mentions him only once, in his final speech, speaking of the possibility of Beowulf succeeding the Geatish king (lines 1845ff.). In Denmark it is Beowulf himself who mentions his uncle often and even seems to "invoke" him at one point (lines 435–36).

sentences (note the repeated pronouns: *ða ic ðe; eall æt ðe; nefne, Hygelac, ðec*) must end any suspicion of even momentarily divided loyalty on Beowulf's part. If the great Danish king did honor him extravagantly, it was only (Beowulf seems to be saying) so that he could pass all these honors on to his own beloved kinsman-king. The gifts represent tangibly the esteem in which the hero has been held – and should be held. They also prove that Beowulf is not lying about his feats in Denmark; wealth like this could never have been acquired any other way. Thus the gifts function as a counterchallenge to Hygelac. By offering them to his uncle, Beowulf is silently asking: Do you know now what to do with them, and with me?

Apparently this Danish wealth is given some kind of further meaning by the identification of its past ownership. What is now brought into the hall for presentation is the war gear of Hrothgar's late brother Heorogar, arms with a presumably illustrious history among the Danes. It is not clear from the poem why Heorogar's son Heoroweard did not receive them, though it is stated that he did not.[17] Even if we can only speculate about the obscure background of Danish dynastic politics, we must surely see the gift as expressing Hrothgar's special affection for Beowulf, perhaps connected with his attempt to "adopt" the young hero. This kind of gift must particularly impress Hygelac.

As in the earlier great banquet at Heorot (lines 1008b–1238), the public nature of the scene is stressed by the poet-speaker's own sudden movement into the foreground as recorder and commentator, as one who has heard of this great event (*hyrde ic þæt. . .*, lines 2163, 2172) and one who makes openly approving didactic statements about Beowulf's (and Hygelac's) behavior (*swa sceal mæg don*, line 2166, "so should a kinsman do").[18] Furthermore, the poet goes on to contrast this meticulously loyal nephew-retainer with others he has heard of: those others (unnamed) who weave treacherous nets of malice and betray

---

[17] Why the treasure might have been diverted from Heoroweard is most fully discussed in R. W. Chambers, *Beowulf: An Introduction*, 3d ed., supplement by C. L. Wrenn (Cambridge: Cambridge University Press, 1959), pp. 29–30, 426–29.

[18] See the discussion in *A Reading of Beowulf*, 130ff. For some interesting views on gift giving in the poem, see Harry Berger, Jr., and H. Marshall Leicester, Jr., "Social Structure as Doom: The Limits of Heroism in *Beowulf*," in *Old English Studies in Honour of John C. Pope*, ed. Robert B. Burlin and Edward B. Irving, Jr. (Toronto: Toronto University Press, 1974), pp. 37–79, esp. 44–50.

their friends, who murder companions, who are unable to control their emotions and their strength. The reader may feel that there is a direct sequence of thought from this passage into the ensuing "Cinderella" lines (2177–84):

> Swa bealdode bearn Ecgðeowes,
> guma guðum cuð, godum dædum,
> dreah æfter dome; nealles druncne slog
> heorðgeneatas; næs him hreoh sefa,
> ac he mancynnes mæste cræfte
> ginfæstan gife, þe him God sealde,
> heold hildedeor. Hean wæs lange,
> swa hyne Geata bearn godne ne tealdon. . . .

[In this way the son of Ecgtheow (Beowulf) made plain his boldness, this man known for battles and great deeds; he eagerly pursued fame. By no means did he slay hearth-comrades who were drunk; his spirit was not ferocious; on the contrary, though battle-brave, he cherished the generous gift God had given him by the greatest strength of any man. For a long time he had been humiliated, since the sons of the Geats did not consider him to be good. . . .]

The connection, if any, would suggest that Beowulf's singular self-control, the total disciplining of his immense native strength, was evident even in his youth. Perhaps it was precisely because he did not throw his weight around the mead hall like the typical heroic bully that the Geats foolishly concluded he was torpid.[19]

If Beowulf offered a counterchallenge to Hygelac by presenting his gifts, the king meets it royally (lines 2190–99), matching gift for gift, placing in his nephew's arms what may be Geatland's most revered relic, the very sword of Hrethel, and giving him such enormous tracts of land that the poet must intervene discreetly to remind us that Hygelac has not given away all the kingdom.

Such a reading of the "Return" passage tries to see the component parts of it as interrelated, and as related to other parts of the poem. The analogy of Unferth's exchange with Beowulf (and of other similar testing scenes in Germanic literature) supports the conclusion that this is one more case where a hero must rise to meet a verbal challenge.

---

[19] Cf. the view of Malone, mentioned in note 14 above. For a memorable picture of a drunken mead-hall braggart, see the poem "Vainglory" in the Exeter Book.

Hygelac's skeptical and patronizing speech compels Beowulf to respond by showing what he has become (or by showing, as we know but the Geats do not, what he has been all along). An audience better attuned to fine points of heroic decorum than we can be would look forward to his speech and would take full pleasure in his proud and public Coming of Age—an archetypal scene rich enough in human fantasies to be played over and over in romance and novel and play and film through the centuries.

It may be objected that such an interpretation is hard on Hygelac, making him seem less than perfect and thus unworthy of Beowulf's devotion. One might reply by arguing that Hygelac, following universal avuncular tradition, is deliberately testing his nephew to observe how he responds to needling; a similar theory has been advanced to account for Unferth's insulting Beowulf. Or one might murmur sagely that, alas, imperfect people do receive unmerited devotion in this world; this is simply realism. Or, in fiercer mood, one might assert that Hygelac is indeed fatally imperfect, however Beowulf may feel about him; he is an impetuous aggressor who will later destroy himself, and perhaps ultimately his kingdom too, by the reckless raid on the Continent, where he meets death at an early age.

But it is likely that all such replies reflect the modern concerns and viewpoints we find it so hard to struggle out of, if we ever can. What was most important to the poet was to display his hero in the most vivid and dramatic way possible, and toward this single end Hygelac is simply being used as straight man. It is the revealed figure of the hero, inseparable from his glory, that here expands to fill the field of our delighted perception.

Part Four THE STYLISTIC AND ICONOGRAPHIC
CONTEXT

An ABC
To the Style of the Prioress

ALFRED DAVID
Indiana University

HE PRIORESS is a "woman of style." She is, as E. Talbot Donaldson shows, a product of Chaucer's style and in particular of his manipulation of the vision, or lack of vision, of the narrator. In some measure she is the creation of syntax —of artful redundancy, ambiguity, and anacoluthon.[1] But, of course, she is also a stylish woman. To every medium—table manners, costume, prayer, storytelling—she brings an artist's touch, lending a certain grace and refinement, some nuance of "fetysnesse" to ordinary objects and everyday routine. Even her physical appearance expresses her style and provides a clue to its origins. She is, as Donaldson puts it, "a romance heroine masquerading as a nun."[2] That is Chaucer's ironic touch, but it reveals also that the romance heroine is the very model of a late-medieval prioress. Not every nun would have been endowed with "eyen greye as glas" and a "mouth ful smal, and therto softe and reed,"[3] but she would have admired these stereotypical romance features as much as Chaucer the pilgrim did. As for a smile "ful symple and coy" she might have copied one from a number of fourteenth-century madonnas. By 1400 the spirit and form of romance have invaded religious art; we may observe them at play in the capitals of Gothic columns, in the margins of the books of hours that wealthy noblemen had made as gifts for their wives, or in the Prioress's rosary.

The rosary with the famous gold brooch works like an icon summing up the Prioress. It is exactly her style and is evidently an expensive and fashionable religious *objet d'art.* "[Rosaries] grew...more varied

[1] E. Talbot Donaldson, "The Masculine Narrator and Four Women of Style," in *Speaking of Chaucer* (New York, 1970), pp. 59–64.

[2] Ibid., p. 48.

[3] Quotations from Chaucer are from F. N. Robinson, ed., *The Works of Geoffrey Chaucer*, 2d ed. (Cambridge, Mass., 1957).

with the course of the century," writes Joan Evans. "In 1372 Queen Jeanne d'Évreux had a rosary of a hundred pearls with ten 'seignaux' of gold; and in 1381 Adam Ledyard, a London jeweller, had in his stock paternoster beads of white and yellow ambers, coral, jet and silver gilt, and aves of jet and blue glass."[4] In the following century ladies would wear their rosaries as necklaces.[5] The Prioress's rosary thus exemplifies not just her own style but the tendency of the age to turn religion into an art.

Eileen Power and Muriel Bowden have demonstrated how Chaucer's Prioress is typical of her kind; her wimple, her lapdogs, her brooch all have their counterparts in such documents as bishops' registers.[6] Style, however, does not yield up its secrets to such direct historical documentation. An oath, a piece of jewelry, a prayer to the Virgin all have style in themselves and are components of a style present in the ensemble of particular traits, actions, and objects. An indirect way of defining style is by analogy, and for the present purpose one of Chaucer's more straightforward early works can serve as an analogue and gloss to the more complex and problematic art of *The Canterbury Tales*. In this essay I wish to draw an analogy between the Prioress's style and that of *An ABC*, Chaucer's alphabetical prayer to the Virgin.

An ABC is a poem that would undoubtedly have appealed just as much to a medieval nun as to a modern one,[7] and, in fact, some of the same images and language found in the early poem are also used in the Prioress's Prologue.[8] Both Chaucer's prayer and that of the Prioress belong to what we might term "conventual style." The early poem exhibits the style purely and simply; in the frame of *The Canterbury Tales* the style is identified with the Prioress and may be compared and contrasted with the styles of other pilgrims. The analogy works in two ways. *An ABC* serves as an introduction to the art of the Prioress; at the same time the Prioress's portrait and the larger framework of *The*

---

[4] Joan Evans, *A History of Jewellery, 1100–1870* (Boston, 1953), p. 50.

[5] Ibid., p. 77.

[6] Eileen Power, *Medieval People* (Boston, 1924), pp. 59–84; Muriel Bowden, *A Commentary on the General Prologue to the* Canterbury Tales (New York, 1948), pp. 92–106.

[7] Sister M. Madeleva, C.S.C., *A Lost Language* (New York, 1951), pp. 11–16.

[8] *ABC*, lines 49, 89–91; *PrT* 467–73. P. M. Kean compares *ABC*, lines 89–91, and *PrT*, lines 467–73, in *Chaucer and the Making of English Poetry* (London, 1972), pp. 194–96.

Canterbury Tales help place the early poem in a social and historical perspective.

Before turning to the style of *An ABC*, I want to comment briefly on two received opinions about it, which I believe to be only partly true and which set up a false expectation of what the poem is like: the notion that it is a very early work, possibly the earliest we have, and the notion that it is a translation. The idea that *An ABC* predates *The Book of the Duchess* stems from a rubric in Speght's second edition of 1602, the first printing of the poem, for which there is no other evidence: "Chaucer's A.B.C. called *La Priere de nostre Dame*: made, as some say, at the request of Blanch, Duchesse of Lancaster, as a praier for her priuat vse, being a woman in her religion very deuout."[9] The poem's ten-syllable line and eight-line stanza, which Chaucer used in *The Monk's Tale* (hence known as "the *Monk's Tale* stanza") and in several ballades, points rather to the period when Chaucer was adapting Boccaccio's *De casibus* tragedies (the future *Monk's Tale*) and translating the life of Saint Cecilia (later to become *The Second Nun's Tale*)— that is, a time when Chaucer was engaged in didactic and religious subjects and was experimenting with the hendecasyllabic line and stanza forms of his Italian sources. *An ABC* has a French source, Deguilleville's *Pèlerinage de la vie humaine*, but Chaucer's prayer sounds very different from the French octosyllabics and the twelve-line stanza Deguilleville builds ingeniously, though monotonously, with just two pairs of rhymes.[10] Chaucer's poem closely imitates the French for the first two or three lines of each stanza and then proceeds with relative freedom. It is certainly not a "translation" in the same sense as *The Romaunt of the Rose*, which is a consistently faithful

---

[9] Viktor Langhans makes a convincing case against Speght's authority in *Untersuchungen zu Chaucer* (Halle, 1918), pp. 302–304, but the idea that the poem is very early persists, and it is always printed first among the short poems. Speght's rubric may be motivated by a desire to link Chaucer to John of Gaunt and his family. In the 1598 edition he printed a fifteenth-century poem, *The Isle of Ladies*, under the title *Chaucers dream*, which he said was about the marriage of John of Gaunt and Blanche of Lancaster and also "shewed Chaucers match with a certaine Gentlewoman, who although shee was a stranger, was notwithstanding so well liked and loued of the Lady Blanch, and her Lord, as Chaucer himselfe also was, that gladly they concluded a marriage betweene them."

[10] W. W. Skeat prints a French text along with *An ABC* in *The Complete Works* (Oxford, 1894), 1.261–71. References to the French are from this edition.

Englishing of the French. Because of the assumptions that *An ABC* is early and that it is a mere translation, the poem is generally regarded as a youthful effusion of religious feeling that has a simple beauty and fervor not found in the original. Reading the poem with such expectations tends to conceal its carefully labored artifice, those "semely" and "fetys" elements that link its style with that of the Prioress.

The most artificial thing about the poem is, of course, the arbitrary structure imposed by the letters of the alphabet. *An ABC* is not one continuous prayer to the Virgin so much as twenty-three separate prayers. Its repetitiousness may make it tedious to the modern reader, but that is, of course, what makes it a prayer. Repetition is the fundamental structural principle in prayer, and so it is in *An ABC*; the poem never goes anywhere because prayer never goes anywhere. The ultimate effect is no different from that of a series of Hail Marys, except that the poem seeks to express its worship in a richly decorated style. Exactly the same effect is achieved in the illuminated books of hours, where the same words are woven into ever-changing patterns of line, color, and imagery. George Pace has shown how the effect of Chaucer's *ABC* in medieval manuscripts is partly visual: the structure leaps to the eye through the illumination of the capitals beginning each stanza.[11] Thus the poem literally imitates those "Kalenderes enlumyned" in praise of the Virgin.

The last lines of the poem take us back to the beginning in the rhyme words *merciable, merci able*:

> Ben to the seed of Adam merciable,
> Bring us to that palais that is bilt
> To penitentes that ben to merci able. Amen.
>
> Almighty and al merciable queene. . . .

In the same way the final lines of *Pearl* and *Sir Gawain and the Green Knight* make a circular closure. We experience something like this effect when Chaucer awakens at the end of *The Book of the Duchess* with the book over which he fell asleep still in his hand. A sense of circularity is something prayer, dream, and romance have in common.

If the poem is constantly saying the same thing and circling around

---

[11] George B. Pace, "The Adorned Initials of Chaucer's *ABC*," *Manuscripta* 23 (1979):88–98.

the same point, however, it is also striving to surprise and please by the elegance and refinement of the language. In *An ABC* Chaucer is playing—one is almost tempted to say trifling—with certain epithets and images. The French poem uses several of the traditional types of the Virgin, for example *de salu porte* ("door of salvation"), *bysson. . .qui ardoit* ("burning bush"), *Temple sainte ou Dieu habite* ("temple of God"), *Fontaine patent* ("open well"). Chaucer retains these but, as Wolfgang Clemen says, "expands the French poet's bald statements into rich, sweeping phrases."[12]

Chaucer tends to turn the abstract typological figures into pictures. The bush burns "with flawmes rede. . .of which ther never a stikke brende."[13] Especially interesting is the transformation in the second stanza of *de salu porte* into "Haven of refuge." John Koch, in a note to his edition, suggests that Chaucer's French text may have read *port* ("harbor") instead of *porte*, but the French manuscripts show no such variant.[14] More likely we are meant to read "Haven" not as an abstract idea but as a concrete image—the safe harbor for the ship of line 16 for which the French text offers no equivalent at all: "Help, lady bright, er that my ship tobreste!" If one were to read the lines out of context, one would naturally assume the "lady bright" to be a courtly mistress who is the guiding light to the ship that represents the lover and his for- tunes. Chaucer uses the Petrarchan conceit in Troilus's song: "Al sterelees withinne a boot am I" (1.416). Analogous to the lady as lode- star to the lover's ship is another type of the Virgin as in a famous lyric:

> Of on that is so fayr and bright,
> *Velud maris stella,*
> Brighter than the dayes light,
> *Parens et puella.*

Chaucer borrows a legal image from the French—the petitioner's shame and confusion have brought an "action" against him (*ABC*, line

[12] Wolfgang Clemen, *Chaucer's Early Poetry*, trans. C. A. M. Sym (New York, 1963), pp. 175–76.

[13] Rosemary Woolf discusses Chaucer's development of "the aesthetic potentiality of the type" in this passage and cites a painting in which "the Virgin and Child appear at the top of a burning rose-bush" (*The English Religious Lyric in the Middle Ages* [Oxford, 1968], p. 286).

[14] John Koch, *Chaucers Kleinere Dichtungen* (Heidelberg, 1928), p. 43.

20; French, line 25) – and develops it in ways that are not in his source. The Virgin becomes our "advocat" who pleads on our behalf "for litel hire" (lines 102–103). Mercy dwells ever at the court, "That cleped is thi bench, O freshe flour" (lines 158–60). "Bench" is the technical term for a court (e.g., King's Bench); but the epithet "freshe flour" evokes another meaning of "bench" or more commonly "bank," as in "a bank of flowers." Ten manuscripts, actually the majority, give exactly that meaning by substituting the preposition *of* for the apostrophe O, thus reading "bench of freshe flour."[15]

In a case like the latter, one cannot really be sure whether there is wordplay or mixed metaphor, but there is unquestionably wordplay in both the French and the English poems. The use of *rime riche* in the French makes some wordplay practically obligatory in every stanza. For example, there is an elaborate play on *mere-amere-mer* ("mother"- "bitter"-"sea") recalling a series of similar puns in the conversation of Tristan and Iseult after they have drunk the potion (lines 73–75):

> Glorieuse vierge mere
> Qui a nul onques amere
> Ne fus en terre ne en mer.[16]

The manipulation of images and the element of verbal wit bear out the contention of Theodor Wolpers that the rhetoric of *An ABC* is modeled on the lover's complaint in courtly verse – an art of elegant flattery and persuasion.[17] Chaucer's legal imagery is apt, for the petitioner presents his "bille" like a skilled lawyer pleading for the mercy of the court.

One other way in which the style of *An ABC* follows both late-fourteenth-century courtly and religious art is in a pervasive emotionalism. A heightened emotional pitch is produced by the clash of opposites: good and evil, innocence and cruelty, the hope of salvation and the fear of damnation. The playwrights exploit such conflicts in the drama, particularly in the opposition between Christ and his crucifiers

---

[15] Five manuscripts substitute *countree* for *court* in the preceding line.

[16] Skeat (*Works*, 1.454) notes the allusion to the traditional derivation of *Maria* from Hebrew *Marah* ("bitterness"), found also in the English.

[17] Theodor Wolpers, "Geschichte der Englischen Marienlyrik im Mittelalter," *Anglia* 69 (1950):29–32.

or the innocents and Herod's soldiers. We see it in painting and poetry in an emphasis on the physical suffering of Christ. Such an art of affec-tive piety seeks to arouse a corresponding emotion in its audience, to move the audience to tears of sympathy and repentance. Weeping thus manifests an appropriate religious and aesthetic sensibility.

One of Chaucer's chief innovations in adapting his French source is to introduce a dramatic opposition between the Virgin and the Devil. In Deguilleville's poem there is only one reference to the Devil in the opening stanza: "Vaincu m'a mon aversaire." The reference may be to the dramatic episode in the narrative that precedes the prayer in which seven highwaymen (the deadly sins) have beaten and overcome the pil-grim. Deguilleville, however, does not dwell in the prayer on the powers of evil who seek to drag down the soul of the suppliant. The poem is rather an extended meditation on the Virgin's great mercy and power to save the pilgrim. If he is threatened, it is by the righteous wrath of the Father against which he asks the Mother to intercede.

Chaucer retains the pilgrim's overwhelming sense of guilt and dread (e.g., lines 52–55), but he also retains something of the allegorical flavor of the narrative of *Le Pèlerinage* where the pilgrim is fleeing hostile forces who seek to destroy him. The "cruel adversaire" ("cruel" is added) of the first stanza is not forgotten. He is Mary's adversary, too: "Thin enemy and myn – ladi tak heede! – / Unto my deth in poynt is me to chace!" (lines 47–48). He is "oure foo" seeking his prey. She is asked for medicine for the wound that "my foo" would "entame" (reopen). The poet urges (lines 84–86):

> Lat not oure alder foo make his bobaunce
> That he hath in his lystes of mischaunce
> Convict that ye bothe have bought so deere.

The image presents Satan as the adversary in a judicial tournament. Although all previous editors gloss "lystes" as "wiles" (there may well be a play on this meaning), Donaldson catches Chaucer's image in his gloss: "arena," that is, where the proud victor might "make his bobaunce."[18]

---

[18] E. T. Donaldson, *Chaucer's Poetry: An Anthology for the Modern Reader*, 2d ed. (New York, 1975), p. 695.

The cumulative effect of these references is to make the Virgin and her enemy competitors for the prize of the suppliant's soul. Although burdened by his own guilt and shame, he is nevertheless threatened by a wicked and powerful foe as damsels in romance are threatened. The Virgin would lose "worship" (in the Malorian sense of "honor") were she to withhold her saving might. The dramatic nature of the poem should not be overstated, but more than any other quality it lends Chaucer's poem a romantic character typical of much of the art of the period. The cult of the Virgin is itself a product of late-medieval art. We cannot picture the Queen of Heaven in other than courtly terms, for she, too, is a woman of style. Since she is the greatest of all romance heroines, it is inevitable that queens, prioresses, and poets should copy her style. Her graciousness, however, requires demonic foils. She is engaged in a perpetual war against the forces of malice from whose clutches she is forever rescuing her devoted followers.

When we turn to the portrait of the Prioress, this analysis of *An ABC* enables us to see that her "curteisie" and her "conscience and tendre herte" are complementary aspects of her style. Her easily flow-ing tears are as much a part of it as her exquisite table manners. Her weeping over a mouse in a trap, dead, or, perhaps worse, not quite dead (note the effect of "if it were deed *or* bledde"), conveys a personal warmth considered to be an excellent thing in a woman. That we should think it to be so is another legacy of the age of romance, and in this respect the Prioress anticipates the heroines of the sentimental novel.

The life of a prioress is like a string of beads or pearls. Madame Eglentyne's endeavor is to make that string shine brightly. The most important part consists in the daily round of offices, which she sings "Entuned in hir nose ful semely." The triumph of her art is found in the description of another daily ritual: eating from her dish and drinking from her cup. The ordinary meal is celebrated as meticulously as the mass: "Ful semely after hir mete she raughte." The recurrence of the phrase "ful semely" (again in "Ful semyly hir wympul pynched was") through the portrait emphasizes an essential element of her style by imitating it.

The portrait has a feeling of constraint, of a talent thwarted by its confinement to the cloister. That is the basis of both the amusement and the sympathy the reader feels for the Prioress. Her tale is under no such restriction and provides a suitable outlet for her talent. Its style answers to that of *An ABC* and surpasses it.

Although it tells a story, the miracle of the little clergeoun is also a prayer and a lyric poem. The narrative is framed by two prayers, the Prologue, which is a prayer to the Virgin, and the closing stanza, a prayer to Saint Hugh of Lincoln, another child martyr. Moreover, several apostrophes break the narrative movement of the tale and sustain the tone of invocation and praise much like the apostrophes to the Virgin throughout *An ABC*: "O martir sowded to virginitee" (line 579); "O grete God, that parfournest thy laude" (line 607). The repetition of the Latin "O Alma redemptoris mater," "Alma redemptoris," "Alma" rings through the tale like a chant. More than any of the other of the tales the Prioress's has a liturgical flavor, not only in echoes of the liturgy but in the dialogue and description.[19]

The words spoken are primarily words of supplication, and the characters are pictured in attitudes of kneeling or prostration. The little clergeoun prays his older companion "Ful often tyme upon his knowes bare" to teach him the Latin of the "Alma." The mother seeks her child through the ghetto crying out upon "Cristes mooder meeke and kynde" and piteously praying every Jew for news of her child. The child is carried in a "greet processioun" to the abbey church, where the bier is placed before the altar. The mother swoons beside it. Mass is celebrated. The abbot conjures the child by the Trinity to tell the cause of his singing. When the child finally dies, the abbot and all the monks fall to the ground, where they lie weeping and praising the Virgin. The narrative thus moves through a series of striking religious tableaux in which the characters are caught for a moment like statues or figures in wax.

The language of *The Prioress's Tale* is more sober than that of *An ABC*. The extravagant wordplay and imagery, which sometimes work awkwardly in the early poem, are absent, but the tale, too, aims at a sensual beauty to express its spiritual meaning. We find the types of the Virgin again in the Prologue: "the white lylye flour," "mooder

---

[19] On the echoes in the tale of the mass for the Feast of the Holy Innocents, see Marie Padgett Hamilton, "Echoes of Childermas in the Tale of the Prioress," *MLR* 34 (1939):1–8.

Mayde," "bussh unbrent, brennynge in Moyses sighte." In the tale she
is "welle of mercy" and "Cristes mooder sweete" (line 656), who speaks
tenderly like a real mother: "My litel child, now wol I fecche thee."
Conversely, the human characters in the story are transformed into
types. The widow sorrowing for her son becomes "This newe Rachel"
(line 627), the type of the *mater dolorosa*. The child becomes one of the
virgin martyrs in the procession of the Lamb and, like the dead child in
Pearl, is transfigured in apocalyptic imagery (lines 609–10):

> This gemme of chastite, this emeraude,
> And eek of martirdom the ruby bright.

The villainous Jews also acquire a typological status as the "cursed
folk of Herodes al newe" (line 574), complementing "This newe
Rachel." The Jews are seen as the people of Satan, "Oure firste foo"
(line 558), who incites them to the murder. They are the antagonists of
the Virgin in the kind of melodramatic opposition we have seen in *An
ABC*. Their turpitude is the stylistic counterpart of the child's innocence and the Virgin's mercy. Their presence is required to give the
tale the emotional character that matches its formalism.

In recent times the flagrant anti-Semitism of the tale has aroused a
critical controversy about the character of the Prioress and the interpretation of her story. Some critics see the tale as a dramatic expression of the Prioress's blind prejudice, which Chaucer is satirizing as
contrary to the true teachings of the Church and the doctrine of charity. Other critics find such a reading completely unhistorical. To think
about the treatment of the Jews in the tale as a question of style,
though it will not resolve the controversy, suggests at least that the
issues are broader than the character of a nun or even conventional
medieval anti-Semitism. To dismiss the anti-Semitism in the tale as
"conventional" is to beg the real question why it should have become
conventional, for the Jews were not always so despised in the Middle
Ages. The persecution of the Jews and the proliferation of legends of
ritual murder that accompanies it begins to accelerate in the course of
the twelfth century and leads finally to the expulsion of the Jews from
France and England in the thirteenth century.[20] A century later
literary anti-Semitism is still flourishing in the drama and in the
miracles of the Virgin. Why should this be?

The stylistic analogies between *An ABC* and the portrait and tale of the Prioress suggest that the answer lies in the emergence of a new religious and literary sensibility that increasingly finds aesthetic satisfaction in religious experience. This sensibility is aroused by emotional contrasts like those between the Devil and the Virgin in *An ABC* and the Jews and the child martyr in *The Prioress's Tale*. Such contrasts are part of a general poetic stylization. *An ABC* heralds a new kind of religious lyric strongly influenced by courtly poetry; its style anticipates the more extravagant aureate style of the next century.

The Canterbury Tales gives us the social and human context in which this kind of literary development takes place. The poem and the Prioress help explain one another. They reveal between them a new and fashionable religiosity that combines gentility with emotion, decorousness with enthusiasm. Still dressed in the forms and symbols of orthodox Christianity, it is a sentimentalized religiosity that worships beauty as a version of truth.

The Canterbury Tales also allows us to contrast this new style with more traditional varieties of religious style and experience, most sharply with the plain, unsentimental style of the Parson. The portrait of the Parson tells us nothing about his appearance or dress. The only object associated with him is his symbolic staff, which expresses him as the Prioress is expressed by her rosary. In his Prologue the Parson rejects all artifice. His typological reference to "Jerusalem celestial," to which he seeks to guide the pilgrims, is literal and unadorned. His long sermon on the seven sins and their remedies seeks to instruct his audience in the way of penitence rather than to move them to tears of repentance. By giving the Parson the last word, Chaucer implies a tacit conservative judgment upon the new style of which he is himself one of the early masters. But it is the demure Prioress who holds the poets and readers after Chaucer under her spell as she already holds the pilgrims:

> Whan seyd was al this miracle, every man
> As sobre was that wonder was to se.

[20] See, for example, Cecil Roth, *History of the Jews in England*, 3d ed. (Oxford, 1964), pp. 18–90 passim; Friedrich Heer, *The Medieval World*, trans. Janet Sondheimer (1961; reprint, New York, Mentor Books, 1963), pp. 309–11.

Pearl's "Maynful Mone":
Crux, Simile, and Structure

MARIE BORROFF
Yale University

T IS TRUE of the memorable poetic image that many lines of meaning converge toward it, and many lines of expressive force correspondingly radiate from it. In this essay I shall trace a number of lines or radii whose center is the rising of the "maynful mone" in *Pearl*, line 1093.

The simile appears at the beginning of the nineteenth, or next-to-last, section of the poem. The two preceding sections have given an account of the Celestial Jerusalem, as seen and described by Saint John in the Book of Revelation. Section 17 tells of the architectural plan of the city and the precious substances of which it is made; section 18 tells how God and the Lamb illuminate it, obviating the need of sun and moon, and how the River of Life flows from the throne of God, with the twelve Trees of Life, bearing their fruit twelve times a year, ranged alongside it. The link word of this latter section is *mone*, and the word makes its farewell appearance in the lines I am concerned with here. The simile of the rising moon introduces the account of the processional within the city, where the dreamer ultimately sees his beloved Pearl. It is thus a transitional image, standing between a phase of the dream that corresponds with scriptural authority and a phase of personal experience, vouchsafed to the dreamer individually as a result of the maiden's intercession. (The poet's account of the processional does contain many details drawn from Revelation, but these materials are freely adapted and rearranged. Briefly, the poet converts the tableaux of the original into a scene of ongoing activity.)[1]

---

[1] The members of the procession are evidently the 144,000 virgins who appear in the company of the Lamb on Mount Sion in Rev. 14.1–5. This event is described to the dreamer by the Pearl maiden in sec. 15, stanzas 3ff., in language which closely follows the biblical source. The account of the activity at the center of the city after the procession has reached it is based in large

I quote eight lines, of which the vehicle and tenor proper of the simile ("as . . . so") take up the first four (lines 1093–1100):[2]

> Ryȝt as þe maynful mone con rys
> Er þenne þe day-glem dryue al doun,
> So sodaynly on a wonder wyse
> I was war of a prosessyoun.
> Þis noble cite of ryche enpryse
> Watȝ sodanly ful wythouten sommoun
> Of such vergyneȝ in þe same gyse
> Þat watȝ my blysful an-vnder croun.

With regard to the compound *day-glem* (literally, "day-gleam") in line 1094, it should be observed that, whereas the modern reader thinks of a "gleam" as something fitful or fugitive, like the vanished "visionary gleam" of the *Intimations Ode, glem* in Middle English could mean "beam or radiance of emitted light," as in *sonne glem* ("sunbeam"). *Day-glem* thus means "light of day."[3] The figurative use of the verb *dryue* with reference to the waning of light at evening has parallels in other passages of Middle English poetry, where it is linked by alliteration with *day* (as here) or *dark*, or both.[4] Line 1094 cannot be translated

---

part on Rev. 5.8ff. There the elders, having harps and vials full of odors, are said to prostrate themselves before the Lamb. The angels around the throne, the four beasts, and the elders join in praise; the Vulgate text adds "et erat numerus eorum millia millium" (5.11; cf. *Pearl*, line 1107, "Hundreth þowsandeȝ I wot þer were"). To this chorus are added the voices of all creatures in heaven, on earth, and under the earth (5.13; cf. *Pearl*, lines 1125–26, "Þe steuen moȝt stryke þurȝ þe vrþe to helle / Þat þe Vertues of heuen of joye endyte").

[2] All citations are to *Pearl*, ed. E. V. Gordon (Oxford, 1953).

[3] MED, s.v. *glēm* n., sense 1(a). *Day-glem* in *Pearl* is cited s.v. sense 1(e) "the light of day or dawn." The compound is erroneously translated "the morning glow, dawn" s.v. *dai* n. sense 13(b), where *Pearl* is the only example given.

[4] MED s.v. *drīven* v. sense 7b (a). Citations include "Quen it [is] dreuyen to þe derke & þe day fynyst" from *Wars of Alexander*, and "Or this dredfull day was drif to nyght, ther was slayn many a doughty knyght" from *The Song of Roland*. A similar idiom may have been used in the original version of line 1999 of *Sir Gawain and the Green Knight*, where the poet tells of the coming of dawn on the day when Sir Gawain must leave the castle. The manuscript reads "Þe day dryuez to þe derk, as Dryȝtyn biddez." The first half line makes perfectly good sense; it is translated "Daylight comes up on the darkness" in Norman Davis's revision of the Tolkien and Gordon edition (1967). But it is possible that the poet wrote "þe derk dryuez to þe day" and that the two words were reversed in accordance with the more usual sequence by a commonsensical or absent-minded scribe.

literally; a reasonably close modern approximation would be "before daylight has wholly died away."

The mighty moon that rises while some daylight still remains on earth is the moon at or near the full, appearing low in the east opposite the sun, which has just set in the west.[5] I feel certain that the poet has the full moon specifically in mind. If so, it is possible that *maynful* in line 1093 was originally two words, *mayn ful*, in which case "þe mayn ful mone" would be "the great full moon" itself.[6] In any case, the moon seen as a circle in the eastern sky is a fit symbol of the celestial realm within which the processional is about to appear. The place of its rising — *oriens* in Latin, "rising" and, by transference, "east" — is traditionally

[5] Peter Comestor, in his discussion of the work of the fourth day in Gen. 1 in the *Historia scholastica*, remarks, with regard to the creation of the moon, that "quod autem luna in plenilunio facta sit ex alia perpenditur translatione, quae habit: *Et luminare minus in inchoatione noctis*. In principio enim noctis non oritur luna nisi panselenos [i.e., 'plenilunar,' the standard Greek term], id est *rotunda*. . . . Inde perpenditur, quod sol factus est mane in oriente, et facto vespere luna facta est in initio noctis, similiter in oriente. Volunt tamen quidam quod mane simul facti sint, sol in oriente, luna in occidente, et sole occidente, luna sub terra rediit ad orientem in inchoatione noctis" (*PL* 198, col. 1061). ("It is considered by another version that the moon was created at the full; [this version] reads 'And the lesser luminary [was made] at the beginning of the night.' For at the beginning of night, the moon rises only when it is full, that is, *round*. . . . Whence it is thought that the sun was made in the morning in the east, and when evening had come, the moon was created at the beginning of the night, likewise in the east. However, some argue that both were made at the same time, the sun in the east, and moon in the west, and by the time the sun was setting in the west, the moon had returned under the earth to the east at the beginning of the night.") I am grateful to Rosemarie Potz McGerr for providing me with this reference.

[6] *Maynful* is clearly one word, separated by a space from *mone*, in the facsimile of the manu-script (ed. I. Gollancz, EETS 162 [Oxford, 1923; reprint, 1971], 54r). But the manuscript is not a holograph, and a scribe could have rewritten an original *mayn ful* as *maynful*. Moreover, word division is sometimes irregular according to modern standards (as one would expect). Without looking for examples, I noted *aldoun* and *wernalle* in lines adjacent to the moon simile; modern editors silently rewrite as *al doun* and *wern alle*. The adjective *mayn* does not appear elsewhere in *Pearl*, or in *Patience* or *Purity*, but it is used four times in *Sir Gawain and the Green Knight*, once with reference to Gawain's horse, and thus with implications of large size as well as strength. *Maynful* is used once in *Purity* in the phrase *maynful gode*, i.e., "almighty God," line 1730 (see Barnet Kottler and Alan M. Markman, *A Concordance to Five Middle English Poems* [Pittsburgh, 1966]). The possibility that the original wording was *mayn ful mone* cannot be ruled out on metrical grounds, since, though sequences of three heavy syllables are exceptional in *Pearl*, they do occur. Examples I have noted include *holtwodeȝ bryȝt* (line 75), where the plural ending *-eȝ* is probably syncopated, *fyldor fyne* (line 106), *cler quyt perle* (line 207), *schorne golde schyr* (line 213), *schyr wod-schaweȝ* (line 284), and *brende golde bryȝt* (line 989). Of these, *cler quyt perle*, with its sequence of two descriptive adjectives plus noun, is closest to *mayn ful mone* in structure.

associated with the advent of Christ.[7] And its circular shape links it with several other exemplars of circularity in the poem, all associated with the kingdom of heaven.

The first and most important of these is, of course, the pearl. Invoked as a terrestrial gem in the opening stanza, in terms that gradually come to suggest a lovely young woman, the pearl is invested with a series of attributes, of which roundness is the third. First, it is pleasing to princes (or to a prince; the Middle English text does not have the apostrophe that would force the phrase to commit itself to one or the other reading in modern English). Second, it is peerless among gems that come "out of oryent" (in view of the symbolic significance of the east in Christian tradition, *oryent* must be counted, along with *prynce* and others, among the bivalent terms in the passage having sacred as well as secular meanings). Third, the pearl is "round"; the attribute is here passed over lightly, merging immediately into the more general one of "rekennes" or "rightness" in "vche aray," every setting.

When the pearl reappears in its symbolic aspect in the parable of the merchant, told by the Pearl maiden in section 13, it is again said to be round. It resembles the kingdom of heaven, "þe reme of heuenesse clere" (line 735), "For hit is wemleȝ, clene and clere, / And endeleȝ rounde, and blyþe of mode" (lines 737–38). Roundness is an attribute of the heavenly kingdom because it is "endless." Here again the reader's sense of the modern value of a Middle English word may blur the meaning of the original. We tend to think of something "endless" as ex-

---

[7] Rabanus Maurus, in the *Allegoriae in sacram scripturam*, begins the entry for *Oriens* as follows: "*Oriens* est Christus, ut in Zacharia: 'Visitavit nos oriens ex [alto],' id est, venit ad nos Christus de coelo" (*PL* 112, col. 1012). The reference is to the words of Zacharias, father of John the Baptist, in Luke 1.78. Cf. the antiphon "O Oriens" in the series of "Antiphonae Majores" or "Great O's" that figure in the liturgy of Advent and were used as source-materials by the author of the Old English "Advent Lyrics." In this antiphon Christ is addressed both as "Oriens," i.e., "rising" or "east," and "Sol," i.e., "sun": "O Oriens, splendor lucis aeternae, et Sol justitiae: / veni, et illumina sedentes in tenebris et umbra mortis" (quoted by Robert B. Burlin in *The Old English Advent: A Typological Commentary* [New Haven, Conn.: Yale University Press, 1968], p. 41). Burlin notes that "'the Orient' figured in several prophetic utterances which were to lend substance to later Messianic and Christian symbolism," and cites, from the Old Testament, Ezek. 43.2, the text of which in the Vulgate is "Et ecce gloria Dei Israel ingrediebatur per viam orientalem"; he also refers to the interpretation of Rabanus Maurus mentioned above. The wording of the "O Oriens" antiphon seems specifically reminiscent of Isa. 9.2: "Populus qui ambulabat in tenebris, Vidit lucem magnam; Habitantibus in regione umbrae mortis, Lux orta est eis."

isting "without cessation." A circle can be traced around and around without stopping, as the planets rotate perpetually and move perpetually in their curved orbits. But *endeleȝ* here means not so much "without an *end*" as "without *ends*"—that is, without termination rightward or leftward in space.[8] Being "end-less" in this sense, the circle contrasts with another figure, the line.

The two figures appear in *Pearl* with complementary symbolic significance. The line takes visible form as the *rawe*, or "row," of laborers in the parable of the vineyard, a detail added by the poet to the account in Matthew. When the time of payment comes, the lord of the vineyard tells his steward to set the workers in a row, in such a way (we infer) that those who began working earliest in the day stand "first," at the head of the line, and those who began latest stand "last," at the foot. The sequence is thus a spatial analogue to the temporal sequence made up of the successive hours of the day; each has a beginning and an end. The lord's decree on the order of payment reverses the expected order of both time and space. The line of laborers is to be read "back" in time, from later to earlier, and "backward" in space, as if, in terms of Western culture, a line of print were to be read from right to left instead of from left to right. Both reversals fulfill the prophecy that precedes the parable in the Gospel (it is the last verse of Chap. 19; the parable follows in 20.1–16): "But many that are first shall be last, and the last shall be first." The prophecy is reiterated at the end of the parable in the final words of the lord to one of those who have "murmured" against his decree: "So the last shall be first, and the first last, for many be called, but few chosen" (I quote the Authorized Version).

Now the prophecy itself admits of two different and complementary interpretations, both of which are found in the patristic commentaries.[9]

---

[8] See *MED* s.v. *ende* n.(1), senses 1 and 14.

[9] Thus the thirty-fourth homily of the series entitled *Opus Imperfectum in Matthaeum*, a work of uncertain authorship attributed in early times to Saint John Chrysostom, first explains the prediction in temporal terms as signifying, *inter alia*, that the Jews, who were called before the Gentiles, are to be saved after them. The homily continues, "Aut ideo primos dicit novissimos futuros, et novissimos primos, non ut novissimi digniores sint quam primi, sed ut coaequentur" (*PG* 56, col. 822). ("Or, he says that the first shall be last and the last shall be first, not because the last are to be more honored than the first, but because they are to be made equal.") Pseudo-Chrysostom goes on to cite Isa. 28.5 and 62.5, where the Lord and the redeemed Jerusalem, respectively, are likened to a crown, and interprets these verses in a way directly relevant to my argument: "Sicut enim in corona, cum sit rotunda, nihil invenies quod videatur esse initium aut

According to one interpretation it signifies reversal: the first and the last will change places. According to the other it signifies equation: the first and the last will be identical. The former interpretation applies to the literal subject matter of the parable, to the line of laborers with its series of positions in space corresponding to a series of points in time. The latter applies to what is signified by the parable, to the reward of eternal life in God's presence symbolized by the perfect roundness of the pearl. All the saved participate equally in this reward, and its value is infinite, literally "beyond compare," unlike earthly rewards, which are measured in terms of a quasi-linear scale of values or degrees ranging from high to low. In the parable the reward is symbolized by the daily penny, given to all who labored in the vineyard regardless of when they came to work. In earthly terms not all can be paid simultaneously; the line is a means of making the process of payment simpler and more orderly. In heaven the blessed have no places relative to one another; all are paid as one. Their relationship is like that of the 360 degrees of a circle, which can be counted off from any arbitrarily chosen point on the circumference.

Roundness, then, is an important symbol in *Pearl*; what it symbolizes is abstraction from the linear or dimensional, two-ended mode of earthly space, time, and value. In addition to the pearl, the poem contains three other emblems of roundness, though the attribute is not predicated of any of them explicitly. The first of these is the crown, which metaphorically signifies the kingly or queenly rank of all who enter the heavenly kingdom. The Pearl maiden is wearing a crown when the dreamer sees her on the other side of the stream; she doffs it to greet him but puts it on again to instruct and correct him. Mary, too, has a crown, as the dreamer knows. Puzzled by the maiden's asser-

---

finis: sic inter sanctos, quantum ad tempus in illo saeculo, nemo novissimus dicitur, nemo primus" (*ibid.*). ("For as in a crown, since it is round, you will find nothing which seems to be the beginning or the end, so among the saints, so far as time in that realm is concerned, no one is called last, no one first.") The two interpretations of the dictum that the first shall be last and the last shall be first are given, with pseudo-Chrysostom as explicitly acknowledged source, by Saint Thomas Aquinas in his interpretation of the parable. See *In Matthaei Evangelium* in the *Catena aurea, Opera omnia*, ed. Fretté (Paris: Vivès, 1876), 16.344, and *Commentarium super Matthaeum*, idem, 19.523. Cf. the *Expositio in Matthaeum* of Saint Paschasius Radbertus, *PL* 120, col. 683. Paschasius adds the image of a revolving wheel. I am grateful to M. Teresa Tavormina for her assistance in this aspect of my research.

tion that she is now a queen in heaven, he wonders if she has displaced the Virgin, and asks (lines 427–28):

> Þe croune fro hyr quo moȝt remwe
> Bot ho hir passed in sum favour?

As the form of his question shows, he is thinking of crowns in terms of earthly scales of merit and rank. The order in terms of which Mary is "empress," as the maiden says, over all those who are kings and queens in heaven is not comparative but organic, mutually corroborative and fulfilling. The relationships among its members are like those among the parts of a living body, as is explained in lines 457ff. in accordance with Saint Paul's simile in I Cor. 12. Finally, all the members of the procession within the celestial Jerusalem are crowned "of þe same fasoun" as the maiden who has appeared to the dreamer, just as all wear "þe blysful perle" even though in the parable there is but a single pearl of great price.

A second emblem of circularity, akin in significance to the crown, is the garland. After awakening from his dream, the narrator bemoans his expulsion from the heavenly kingdom but consoles himself by reflecting that his pearl is safely established there (lines 1185–88):

> If hit be ueray and soth sermoun
> Þat þou so stykeȝ in garlande gay,
> So wel is me in þys doel-doungoun
> Þat þou art to þat Prynseȝ paye.

The fact that the word *garland* in Middle English could mean "coronet" or "crown" (though it clearly has its modern meaning, "wreath of flowers," in line 1186)[10] is additional evidence for the symbolic affiliations I am concerned with here.

Third, there is the penny in the parable. Since it is a daily wage, it was identified by the patristic writers with the "daily bread" asked for in the Lord's Prayer. And this in turn was identified with the communion wafer, likewise round in shape, "shown us every day," as the poet says (line 1210), by the priest at mass.[11]

[10] See *MED* s.v. *gerlŏnd* n., senses 2(a) "a chaplet or coronet of gold, etc." and 2(b) "a crown or headband symbolizing office."

[11] A late Middle English text of interest in this connection is discussed by Laurence Eldredge in "Imagery of Roundness in William Woodford's 'De Sacremento Altaris' and its Possible

Circularity of an abstract sort is exemplified by the plot and design of the poem itself. In its beginning is its end. In the first section the nar-rator lies down on the flower bed where his pearl is buried; his soul leaves that "spot" during the dream, but his body remains there (lines 61–62). In the last section he returns to the point of departure (lines 1171–72):

> Þen wakned I in þat erber wlonk;
> My hede vpon þat hylle watȝ layde.

The *hylle* is the *huyle* or "mound" of line 41, where "perle hit trendeled doun," and the *hyul* of line 1205, over which, as the dreamer says, he received his fateful vision.[12] His gesture, after he awakens, of reaching out in longing—"Þer as my perle to grounde strayd / I raxled"[13]—repeats that described in line 49–"Bifore þat spot my honde I spenned." This circularity in the plot of the poem is found also in its verbal patterning. Each section is linked to the preceding one by the reiteration of rhyme words, and the rhyme word of the last section, which is also that of the first line of the poem, links the end back to the beginning to complete the design.[14]

The simile of the "maynful" (or "mayn ful") "mone" is significant in

---

Relevance to the Middle English 'Pearl' " (*N&Q*, n.s. 25, no. 1 [1978]:3–5). In the *dubia*, or divi-sion, of the treatise which Eldredge edits, Woodford argues that roundness of shape is appropri-ate for the communion wafer because roundness symbolizes perfection, spotlessness, and simplic-ity and because it reflects the shape of the penny paid to the workers in the parable of the vine-yard. According to Robert W. Ackerman ("The *Pearl*-Maiden and the Penny," *RPh* 17 [1964]:615–23), "The association of the daily bread in the Lord's Prayer with the gift of salvation and also the Eucharist is standard in medieval scriptural commentary" (pp. 620–21). Ackerman shows that the daily bread was identified with the penny paid the workers in the parable by Friar Lorens, in his popular late-thirteenth-century didactic treatise *Le Somme des Vices et des Vertues*, which may have been known to Chaucer. Lorens's interpretation is also found in the *Ayenbite of Inwit*, a Middle English translation of the treatise by Dan Michel of Northgate.

[12] *MED*, s.v. *hīl* n., cites only lines 41 and 1205; the etymology given is "prob. OE *hygel* 'hillock.' " *Hylle* in line 1172 is probably a scribal rewriting of an original *huyle/hyul*. However, the word *hill*, from OE *hyll*, overlaps with *hīl* in meaning. See *MED* s.v. *hil(le* n. sense 2(a) "A man-made hill or mound."

[13] "I raxled" is translated as "I stretched myself" in both Gordon's edition and A. C. Cawley, *Pearl, Sir Gawain and the Green Knight*, Everyman's Library, no. 346 (London, 1962). But accord-ing to *OED*, *raxle* v. has the same array of meanings as *rax* v., of which *raxle* is a frequentitive. These include "to extend the hand, etc.; to reach out" (sense 3).

[14] See "Design and Its Significance" in Marie Borroff, Introduction, *Pearl: A New Verse Transla-tion* (New York, 1977), pp. xvi–xix.

that it participates in a symbolic opposition between roundness and
linearity that is thematically important in *Pearl*. But it also conveys a
visual image, and in so doing it bears on the description that follows in
an interesting way. Since we "see" the full moon just before we "see"
the procession within the city, it is as if the moon's circular outline
were superimposed on the city's perimeter—as if the Celestial Jerusalem, for the purposes of this part of the vision, were round rather than
square. The kingdom of heaven *is* round—the maiden has said so in ex-
pounding the attributes of the pearl of great price in section 13. If we
object that the same city cannot be both round and square, we are
thinking, like the dreamer, in terms of spatial dimensions as we experience them on earth. But the rules of geometrical or positional space (as
one might term it) do not apply to the heavenly kingdom as it is
imagined by the *Pearl* poet. For one thing, the river that separates the
dreamer from the maiden is not "real"; it is a spatial symbol of the division between mortality and immortality. In order to "cross" it, we must
change not our position in space but our mode of existence, through
the death of the body. As soon as the dreamer takes the apparent
dimensions of the dream scene literally and rushes down the bank
toward the river, his dream dissolves. Again the maiden appears to
him (and us) to be standing on the opposite bank, within hailing
distance. But she is also discovered in the procession within the city,
and we realize, on consideration, that in a sense she is always there.
Her seeming position in space during the conversation within the
dream symbolizes her divinely vouchsafed role as instructor-
intercessor.[15]

This lack of conformity to the rules of positional space—space as we
know it—is even more striking in the treatment of the procession. From
the moment the dreamer first sees it, it fills the city (lines 1097–1100):

> Þis noble cite of ryche enpryse
> Watȝ sodanly ful wythouten sommoun
> Of such vergyneȝ in þe same gyse
> Þat watȝ my blysful an-vnder croun.

This being the case, it must be moving not through any particular

---

street but through all the streets, approaching the throne from every direction as if by way of the convergent radii of a circle "on golden gate3 þat glent as glasse" (line 1106). This centripetal movement complements the centrifugal movement of the River of Life as the poet describes it in section 18: there it is said to course powerfully "þur3 vche a strete" (line 1059). Again, if the river fills every street, there is no room, in earthly terms, for the procession. And what is true of space must be true also of time: if the procession occupies every part of the city, it is also simultaneously setting out, arriving, and moving at every point between departure and arrival.

I said earlier that the simile of the risen full moon is transitional, linked retrospectively to authoritative revelation and ushering in a personal, though equally valid, phase of the dream vision. It is transitional also in another way. The orbit of the moon, in the Ptolemaic system of astronomy, is the boundary between earthly and heavenly realms.[16] Although the word *sublunary* had not yet entered the language in the *Pearl* poet's time, expressions such as "under (the) moon" and "under the circle of the moon" were conventional designations in Middle English for the realm of earthly existence.[17] Since the moon as seen from earth is variable, perpetually waxing and waning, it was and is a natural emblem of the vicissitudes of mortal fate.[18]

In three of its appearances as link word in section 18 of *Pearl*, *mone* is used in the phrase "an-vnder mone," meaning "on earth." The dreamer says, of the sight of the celestial Jerusalem, that (lines 1081–83)

> An-vnder mone so great merwayle
> No fleschly hert ne my3t endeure,
> As quen I blusched vpon þat bayle,

---

[16] See *MED* s.v. *mōn(e* n. (1), sense 1(b), "the moon as the cosmological divider between the earth and the heavens." Citations for this sense include *The Pricke of Conscience*, line 992, "þe hegher {world} reaches fra þa mon even Til þe heghest of þe sterned heven."

[17] These and other phrases may be found in *MED* under the definition cited in note 16.

[18] Cf. Chaucer's *Clerk's Tale*, E 995, 997–98: "O stormy people! unsad and evere untrewe! / ... / Delitynge evere in rumbul that is newe, / For lyk the moone ay wexe ye and wane!" William Caxton, complaining of the inconsistencies of the English language in a well-known passage in the Prologue to his *Eneydos*, wrote, "For we englysshe men ben borne vnder the domynacyon of the mone, whiche is neuer stedfaste, but euer wauerynge, wexynge one season, and waneth & dyscreaseth another season" (quoted, with modernized punctuation, from *The Prologues and Epilogues of William Caxton*, ed. W. J. B. Crotch [EETS 176, Oxford, 1928; reprint, 1956], p. 108).

and that (lines 1090–92)

> Hade bodyly burne abiden þat bone,
> Þaȝ alle clerkeȝ hym hade in cure,
> His lyf were loste an-vnder mone.

It is his spirit, not his "fleshly heart," that has experienced the vision, as he has told us at the beginning of section 2 (lines 61–62):

> Fro spot my spyryt þer sprang in space:
> My body on balke þer bod in sweuen.

The spirit returns at the end of the dream to rejoin the body un-harmed. (In view of the fact that the poet distinguishes so carefully between sublunary and translunary realms, it would seem that the dreamer's use of the phrase "vnder mone" when he inquires of the maiden where she and her companions dwell is to be taken as yet another sign of his characteristic mode of misapprehension. "As ȝe ar maskeles vnder mone," he says, "your woneȝ schulde be wythouten mote" [lines 923–24]. They are not, of course, "vnder mone," any more than the city of Jerusalem the maiden is talking about is in the land of Judea.)

The moon in *Pearl* faces in two directions, literally and symbolically; it has both positive and negative aspects, a *sensus bonus* and a *sensus malus*. Seen as a circle of radiant white, the full moon can join the pearl it resembles in symbolizing the heavenly kingdom.[19] But the moon is also, by virtue of its astronomical position, associated with the limita-tions and flaws of mortality. Unlike the pearl, it is not only variable but maculate. The poet has singled out this latter characteristic for disap-proval in explaining why it is excluded from the celestial Jerusalem (lines 1069–70):

> The mone may þerof acroche no myȝte;
> To spotty ho is, of body to grym.

But the negative aspects of the moon are canceled out in its final ap-pearance, as the rising full moon of the simile that opens section 19.

---

[19] A quotation from the vernacular encyclopedic poem *Cursor Mundi* in *MED*, s.v. mọ̄n(e n. (1), indicates an association in medieval tradition between the full moon and the Passion: "He [Christ] wald for vus martered bee / þat time when þe moyn wor ful."

Here the moon becomes a wonderfully apt symbol not only of the content of the dreamer's experience but of the manner of its befalling. For wherever his spirit may be during the dream, he himself is an inhabitant of the sublunary realm, and the rising of the full moon is a "sublunary" event in the most exact sense possible: it can be seen only from an earthly vantage point, by one looking up at the heavens.

Strictly speaking, the tenor of the simile is not the city within which the procession is about to materialize but the dreamer's sudden awareness that a procession is in progress: "So sodanly on a wonder wyse / I watȝ war of a prosessyoun." The risen full moon is a sight of which we may indeed "suddenly" become aware. Gaining in brightness as darkness falls, it draws attention to itself in the sky where it has actually been present for some time. So too the procession, though from the dreamer's point of view it "suddenly" fills the city, has in a profounder sense been there all along. Everything in the poem thus far has been preparing him to see it.

Considered as a natural event, the rising of the full moon has an additional and more important dimension of significance. It takes place at the end of the day, at the time in the parable of the vineyard when the laborers have finished their work and are about to be paid. A retrospective glance at the parable as told in *Pearl* reveals that the later passage in fact echoes the earlier one, though in a way that is more likely to attract the attention of the exegete than that of the common reader.

In lines 529ff. the pearl maiden tells of the sending into the vineyard of the last group of laborers at the eleventh hour, called "euensonge" by the poet. This occurs "on oure byfore þe sonne go doun." Then "þe worlde bycome wel broun";

> Þe sunne watȝ doun and hit wex late.
> To take her hyre he made sumoun;
> Þe day watȝ al apassed date.

(The statement that "þe worlde bycom wel broun," I take it, refers to the thickening of dusk before darkness falls rather than to full darkness.[20] In terms of the later passage, the laborers are summoned before

---

[20] See *MED* s.v. *brŏun* adj. sense 1(a) "dark, dull," and cf. sense 1(b) "cheerless, . . .gloomy." The gloss "fuscus, subniger" is cited s.v. sense 1(a) from the fifteenth-century *Promptorium parvulorum*.

daylight has wholly died away.) The stanza describing the events of the eleventh hour and later and the stanza containing the simile of the rising full moon have the same B-rhyme, and the two stanzas share three rhyming words: *doun*, *summoun*, and *boun*. Of these *summoun* especially is an echo with a difference. The members of the procession within the celestial city need not be "summoned," for they have already been both called and chosen.

What the dreamer sees in section 19 is in fact the participation of the blessed in the reward symbolized by the penny in the parable. Unlike the row of laborers, the "lines" formed by those who move through the streets have neither beginning nor end. Nor can anyone in them be thought of as first or last, since the entire group is constantly starting out, arriving, and moving at every intermediate point. The only speci- fied position is that of the Lamb, who leads the way. He is the "head" of which the members of the procession are the body, since his volun- tary self-sacrifice (of which his visible and freshly bleeding wound is the emblem) has made salvation possible and has established the Church through whose sacraments the individual soul attains it. Salva- tion itself, the heavenly reward, is experienced as an eternity of bliss — eternity in the sense not of perpetual duration but of release from linear time.

Remembering that the daily penny was identified not only with salvation but with the daily bread of the Lord's Prayer, which in turn was identified with the communion wafer, we see that the blessed souls are in fact in a state of eternal communion with the divine pres- ence. The penny in the parable is an element in a symbolic representa- tion, but the consecrated communion wafer is real and symbolic at once. It is a part of the earthly experience of the faithful and a foretaste of the life to come. The comparison in line 1115 of the members of the procession to maidens at mass is profoundly in point: the celebration of communion on earth and the celebration within the celestial city are related to each other much as the vehicle and tenor of a metaphor are related: the latter is what the former means.

Following out the lines of meaning that converge on the simile of the "maynful mone" in *Pearl*, we are led into a number of interrelated areas of medieval learning: geometry (more exactly, the branch of geometry now called topology), theology, astronomy, patristic exegesis. The image is to that extent recondite, drawn from books rather than from life. But it is also based on a universal experience, an event that all sorts and conditions of men have witnessed in all ages, and one to which many men, not least the *Pearl* poet, have responded as a sign of the splendor of the created world. It thus typifies the combination of artifice and simplicity, of intellectuality and human emotion, that has perennially attracted and rewarded the attention of the critics of *Pearl*.

Part Five THE INTELLECTUAL CONTEXT

Time, Apocalypse, and the Plot of *Piers Plowman*

MARY J. CARRUTHERS
University of Illinois at Chicago

HE ESSENTIAL PLOT of *Piers Plowman* has already, and accurately, been described as the life of a Christian soul and the events of Christian history from the beginning to the apocalypse, the individual and general plots related through analogy and metaphor.[1] This description understands the word "plot" in its basic and simplest sense as "story." Yet any reader of the poem also knows that the unfolding of this story is exceedingly complex and difficult to follow. After a passus or two one may justly feel like complaining that the poem has "no plot," even though it has a rudimentary story. At this level we distinguish "story" from "plot," because by "plot" we also mean the ways in which the events of the story are related to one another as we read them in temporal sequence.

It is this structural meaning of "plot" to which my title refers. For the purposes of this essay I define "plot" as the organization of events within a narrative. It offers the means by which the poem creates within itself the illusion of temporalness and thus defines the poet's conception of temporal relationships. It also conveys the values which the poet assigns to time and temporality. We think of a well-constructed plot as one in which the causal connections of events are clear and rational. E. M. Forster wrote that "the king died and the queen died" is not a plot, but "the king died and the queen died of grief" is.[2] Critical theorists often think of plot in terms of architecture, demanding that each incident in the story in some way "eventually

---

[1] The most succinct statement is that of E. Talbot Donaldson, *The Norton Anthology of English Literature*, rev. ed. (New York: W. W. Norton, 1968), 1.273–74.

[2] E. M. Forster, *Aspects of the Novel* (London: Edward Arnold, 1927), pp. 82–83.

promot[e] the completion of the whole."[3] As an image "the whole" is essentially spatial not temporal, events striving, as our neoclassical theorists write, toward "temporal synthesis" or "congruence" or "perfect unity of design"—toward a permanence which, like a building or a golden bird, transcends generations and time.[4] Viewed from the assumptions of this aesthetic, "plot" is one thing *Piers* certainly appears not to possess, even though it obviously tells us a kind of story involving some central characters. *Piers* has "no plot" not because nothing happens but because nothing that does happen seems very much to affect anything else that happens. As readers of this poem, we are continually frustrated by wanting connections in the narrative without being able, when we come right down to it, to fit the poem's events into a connected whole.

Piers Plowman is written within the intellectual tradition of Christian eschatology, which values time and temporality differently from neoclassically based aesthetics. The plot of history in this tradition is salvational, and time is not something to be transcended but to be embraced as the medium in which salvation occurs. Apocalypse, in salvational history, is not part of a suprahuman, cosmic process unrelated to time but part of the "order expressed in human choices and enacted in human action and its results."[5] History, in other words, is significant only when understood as the working of divine providence through human lives and wills, through time. The essential life is that of Christ, who lived in a particular time, yet whose life provides the key to the inward significance of all time leading up to it and all time after, including the apocalyptic end. Significance in salvational history is achieved not beyond time but within time, in the temporal repetition of the salvational pattern.

Piers Plowman, like *The Confessions* and *The Divine Comedy*, is a meditation upon faith in the guise of an autobiography. This observa-

---

[3] Arthur Murphy (1762), quoted by R. S. Crane, "The Concept of Plot and the Plot of *Tom Jones*," *Critics and Criticism: Ancient and Modern* (Chicago: University of Chicago Press, 1952), p. 616.

[4] Crane, ibid., uses the phrase "temporal synthesis" (p. 620); "unity of design" is Murphy's phrase, quoted by Crane (p. 616); "congruence" is the word of Frank Kermode, *The Sense of an Ending* (New York: Oxford University Press, 1967), p. 5.

[5] R. A. Markus, *Saeculum: History and Society in the Thought of St. Augustine* (Cambridge: Cambridge University Press, 1970), p. 87.

tion is worth considering in relation to its plot.[6] Because Christian history is concerned with the inward meaning of events, not their political or social aspects, its most successful expression is biography and especially autobiography. An astute historiographer has recently remarked concerning Saint Augustine: "Augustine wrote one true work of Christian history and that was his autobiography, for which he had the supreme advantage of interior knowledge of the events of his own life; autobiography may be the only entirely satisfactory form of Christian history."[7] The purpose of history, for a Christian, is to provide justification for his own expectation of salvation in the unique life of Christ and to confirm his faith. All other achievements of history are incidental to this one. The Gospels and the Acts, as New Testament studies have shown,[8] are confessions of faith first and biographies only secondarily. They are not histories in either the modern or the classical sense; that is, they are neither "scientific" descriptions of events nor a set of moral exempla or "Great Lives."[9] They were written to fulfill the command of Jesus to witness "these things" so that "repentance and remission of sins should be preached in his name among all nations" (Luke 24.47–48). They are intended to confirm faith and to assure the personal salvation of those who understand and believe.

The inner meaning of a Christian's life reveals itself, using the authoritative example of Saint Augustine, in its adherence to a salvational pattern evident in history. Thus autobiography is the perfect medium for a meditation upon the meaning of all history. The battle of souls is fought again within the compass of one soul, and one soul's progress can become the type and mirror of all souls' progress. The logically enigmatic proposition that all is comprehensible only in one is

[6] Judith H. Anderson, *The Growth of a Personal Voice* (New Haven, Conn.: Yale University Press, 1976), has perceptively analyzed the significance of the autobiographical mode in *Piers Plowman*.

[7] Nancy F. Partner, *Serious Entertainments* (Chicago: University of Chicago Press, 1977), p. 229.

[8] Oscar Cullmann, *Christ and Time*, trans. F. V. Filson, rev. ed. (Philadelphia: Westminster Press, 1964), pp. 97–100.

[9] Arnaldo Momigliano, "Pagan and Christian Historiography in the Fourth Century A.D.," *Paganism and Christianity in the Fourth Century* (London: Oxford University Press, 1963), pp. 79–99, is a seminal discussion of the critical differences between pagan and ecclesiastical history before Saint Augustine.

resolved by the life of Christ, for in his life, history, the comprehensive narrative of all time, and biography, the story of one individual, are united.

All Christian biography focuses upon the moment of conversion for that is its crisis. In *Piers* there are a half dozen such moments: the conversion and confession of the king and the folk on the field, embodied in the Seven Deadly Sins; Piers's conversion after Truth's pardon; Conscience's conversion and pilgrimage with Patience; Hawkyn; the conversion of Will during the Tree of Charity episode and his pilgrimage to Jerusalem with Abraham and the Samaritan; Will's turn into Unity-Holychurch and Conscience's concluding pilgrimage after Grace and Piers Plowman. The organization is "modular," rather than linear or circular or even spiral. Each unit shares a similar structure, and some units are embedded within larger manifestations of the same essential pattern. It is the sequence of wandering, conversion, and pilgrimage, the basic story of this poem, modeled upon the pattern which occurs again and again in canonical history (e.g., the Exodus) and describes the essential salvational plot of every Christian soul. Initially prey to the sensual temptations of the flesh, the cares of the body, and the intellectual temptations of vain curiosity, the soul wanders aimlessly and wretchedly. Then at a particular moment of illumination, she becomes aware of the home finally promised to her, and, following this conversion, continues her life as a pilgrim, journeying in time to her sacred goal. The word "conversion" itself implies the design of movement which at some moment climaxes in a radical "turning toward" (*convert-*) and subsequent movement with a new orientation. Conversion re-interprets all that leads up to it. It organizes a life and gives to inchoate wandering a form. It is the moment in which life acquires its governing plot.

This pattern of wandering and pilgrimage accounts for the poet's fascination with beggars and pilgrims. How can you tell the difference between a mere beggar and a true lover of Christ, between "lond-leperis heremytes" (15.213)[10] and genuine pilgrims? The answer is "þoruʒ wil oone" (15.210). When Will starts out, he is a hermit

---

[10] All quotations are taken from George Kane and E. Talbot Donaldson, *The B-Text of Piers Plowman* (London: Athlone Press, 1975).

"vnholy of werkes" (Prol., 3), a roamer in russet (8.1), "in man*e*re of a mendynaunt" (13.3), who has no place in the Church or among his fellow Christians. But, beginning in passus 13 and 14, Will's role as a suspiciously beggarly wanderer changes. He sets out on a pilgrimage with Patience and a converted Conscience, which ends in the contri-tion of Hawkyn. At the beginning of passus 15, Will is still seen as a "fole" and a "lorel," but only because he refuses now to pay attention to outward, worldly considerations such as rank and social class. His foolishness is that of the converted Christian, the fool for God whose wisdom is not of this world. Passus 15–18 confirm Will's conversion and continue his pilgrimage—as the Samaritan tells him, all men have been robbed by outlaws in the world's wilderness except Faith, Hope, Charity, "And þiself now and swiche as suwen oure werkes" (17.104). Will is a pilgrim after Saint Truth, part of the company of the re-deemed. Converted, he awakens to the bells of Easter, the community of his family and neighborhood church, and ends up within Unity-Holychurch, in his dream as in waking life. After it falls, he is a partner in the renewed pilgrimage of Conscience (who is, of course, the dreamer's own conscience). Will's journey through the entire poem is an instance of the pattern of wandering, conversion, and pilgrimage, beggar and fool to pilgrim and God's minstrel (15.209–12):

> Therfore by colour ne by clergie knowe shaltow [hym] neu*e*re,
> Neiþer þoru3 wordes ne werkes, but þoru3 wil oone,
> And þat knoweþ no clerk ne creature on erþe
> But Piers þe Plowman, *Petrus id est christus.*

The design of wandering, conversion, and pilgrimage marks also each narrative subunit. The wandering of the Prologue is followed by Lady Holy Church's injunction to Will, as he falls on his knees before her, to seek Truth. That clear goal is lost in the aimlessness of False and the ambiguities of Lady Meed, until the wavering king is convinced by Reason (4.175ff.) that his law has been corrupted and can be redeemed only by "leaute in lawe" (4.180). Reason, Conscience, and the king all go off to church as a sign of their new conviction. Their conversion leads to the more general conversion of the wandering folk through Reason's preaching, signaled by the confession of the Seven Deadly Sins and Repentance's prayer (at 5.478–505). This conversion in turn produces the folk's resolve to seek Saint Truth. That pilgrimage is lost in mere wandering, ambivalent guideposts, delay, and frustration on Piers's half acre, until Piers's conversion after he receives Truth's pardon (7.122–25):

> "I shal cessen of my sowyng," quod Piers, "& swynke no3t so harde,
> Ne about my [bilyue] so bisy be na moore;
> Of preieres and of penaunce my plou3 shal ben herafter,
> And wepen whan I sholde [werche] þou3 whete breed me faille."

Piers's plowing and sowing henceforth are sacramental, a sign of his changed goal. The pilgrimage is then taken up by Will, at first in hope but then in increasingly frustrated, aimless wandering as he searches for Dowel through most of passus 8–13.

The narrative units instruct by their differences as well as similarities. I do not think it difficult to see in these conversions a change from an emphasis upon law and the state, a worldly and millennial concept of redemption, to a realization that conversion is not a legal but a spiritual matter, that it occurs in individual hearts, that indeed "My kingdom is not of this world," and that one's own life has a part in the general redemptive pattern of history. To call this change, which begins to occur in passus 6–7, an allegorical representation of the change from the Old Law to the New, as I have done, is probably to describe the narrative program too rigidly and academically. One objection raised to a figural reading of the Tearing of the Pardon scene is that the scene does not really change anything. There is no dramatic shift between the world of passus 6 and that of passus 8, no Old and New Law distinction which the text obviously maintains. I admit that this objection is forceful—it made me pause even when I argued most rigorously for a figural reading of this scene. I still believe that the scene is climactic, that it does produce a change in the narrative and introduces a typological perspective on time and history to the poem (in part just because it repeats, with a difference, the pattern of the first conversion episode), but I also think that many medievalists, including myself, have misunderstood the use by Langland of figural, typological plotting in this poem. We have thought too exactly upon the canonical figuralism embodied in the prophetic, revealed relationship of the Old Law to the New Law as constituting the only model for typological understanding, whereas it often must serve a less rigorous, more limited purpose.

One cannot be sure of the absolute, inward significance of any event other than of the limited number recounted in Scripture, whose ultimate content has been divinely revealed.[11] Thus noncanonical and postcanonical events cannot be authoritatively understood; this does not mean, however, that typology has no place in Christian analysis of current events. Rather, its role is heuristic instead of truly prophetic, in the manner in which the Old Testament is authoritatively prophetic of the New. A good example of the noncanonical use of figuralism can be found in this incident from the recent American past. The Reverend Andrew Young has told the story of a black preacher in Selma, Alabama, on the occasion of a march protesting the jailing of the Reverend Martin Luther King. The march route went past a squad of Selma firemen carrying heavy hoses, who, when ordered by their commander to open them on the marchers, refused to turn on the water. As the marchers passed them, the preacher cried out, "Great God Almighty done parted the Red Sea one more time!" This use of typology is, I suspect, much closer to the conception underlying the plot which the reader encounters in *Piers Plowman* than are the elaborated commentaries on biblical events one finds in sources like the *Glossa ordinaria*. The preacher in Selma, seeking a way of signifying the event in which he was participating, did so by relating the Selma firemen to an event in authorized salvational history, the liberation of the Hebrew slaves by God's parting of the Red Sea. To press hard upon authoritative parallels between the two events, as though the biblical

---

[11] See Markus, *Saeculum*, pp. 14–15, where he remarks that, for Augustine, history is understood not as a description of the past but as a statement about past events: "The privileged status of sacred history derives from the privileged status of the biblical authors...rather than from the nature of the events they tell of." Outside these privileged narrations God's revelation provides no clue to the absolute significance of events (pp. 158–59). The interpretation of noncanonical history is not revealed but is still hidden. "Post-canonical prophecy is concerned with 'history' only in the sense that it bears upon the time of its present: on acts, events and things with which the Christian community is faced in its own time and place. It is a summons to decision and to action" (p. 160). This statement characterizes precisely the heuristic use of typology in *Piers* and by the preacher at Selma.

event is in some real way prophetic of the contemporary one, is point-less for the meaning resides in the speaker's converted recognition (and that of his flock) that this event is occurring within a sacred context. God still cares for his people – the guarantee of that lies in the simple fact of pattern, the "rhythm of our world," as Saint Augustine calls it, which the converted and redeemed can perceive. The Selma preacher's comment is not an exegesis but a joyful recognition of success as God saves his people one more time.

The later conversions – of Conscience in passus 13, Hawkyn in 14, and Will in 16–18 – refer back to the earlier ones. Just as the divinely revealed historical process incorporates a progressive revelation cul-minating in the life of Jesus, so these conversion episodes parallel those of the *Visio* but give them a dimension which is interior, mystical, and eschatological rather than legalistic and millennial. For example, Con-science and Reason are paired in passus 4, but the king's conversion comes about through the preaching of Reason, who calls for the estab-lishment of a legally instituted, millennial kingdom. Reason also preaches the sermon calling for general repentance at the beginning of passus 5. Piers's half acre is instituted as a millennial society, based upon legal social contracts between its members. In passus 13 the con-version experience is Conscience's. He bids farewell to Clergy (who, along with Wit and Dame Study, is one of Reason's family) in order to prove more with Patience, that Christlike virtue which Piers adopted at the end of passus 7. Hawkyn is an amalgamation of all the Seven Deadly Sins, but he can knowingly repent and receive shrift from Patience. No societies are established until Grace founds Unity-Holychurch in passus 19 (though it also collapses from within). Will's conversion, undertaken through the agency of Piers in passus 16, pro-duces a mystical, inner conviction similar to that of Piers in 7 and Con-science in 13, one which Will expresses at the end of his vision in 18 in his desire to unite himself with Christ's Crucifixion and Resurrection through the ritual of creeping to the Cross. Through the paralleling of characters, each an image or aspect of Will the narrator, the whole action from passus 8 through 19 can be seen as a single sustained narra-tive of wandering (Will in search of Dowel), conversion (Conscience and Hawkyn), and pilgrimage (first with Patience and then with Piers, the Samaritan, and Faith). The pilgrimage is to Jerusalem; its goal is

Will's vision of the triumph of Jesus,[12] the cognitive heart of this poem, as it is of redemptive history.

In view of the structure I have just described, it is interesting to consider how events are causally related by the narrative. *The Canterbury Tales* begins with a splendidly cosmic "Whan...thanne" construction, which presumes to link all its clauses as part of an interdependent whole. The story also is described as occurring on a particular day in a particular place. By contrast, *Piers Plowman* simply starts with a listing of actions: "I shoop...[I] wente...I was wery...I lay...I slombred ...gan I meten." "I sei3" and "I mete" are common introductions to the events in Will's dream, and the tense in which actions are told varies from the simple, indefinite past to an indefinite narrative present. The sentences describing actions are held together by *and* and *ac* and *thanne*, occasionally interspersed with *til*. Only in the speeches in which Will is instructed by the various faculties of his soul does one get a *forþi*. This pattern holds through the Tree of Charity episode, until the poem begins to narrate the life of Jesus. Until then no effort is made to connect events except as one thing after another, *a and b ac c til e and f*. The causes are hidden to the narrator. Only in passus 18, when Christ appears in glory at the gates of Hell, does the narrative contain such conjunctions as *thus, so, for, but*, and the subordinating constructions, *and but x...y*, or *siþen x...y*. This is a perfect formal narrative expression of what Saint Paul writes in Col. 3.3–4: "...your life is hid with Christ in God. When Christ, who is our life, shall ap-

---

[12] Morton Bloomfield notes that the poem concentrates on the figure of Jesus the conqueror, rather than the more usual late-medieval stress upon the humanity of Jesus (*Piers Plowman as a Fourteenth-Century Apocalypse* [New Brunswick, N.J.: Rutgers University Press, 1961], p. 100), noting that this reflects a very early Christian, New Testament tradition. Commenting on the Primitive Christian understanding of eschatological hope, Cullman (*Christ and Time*) writes that the New Testament "proceeds from the assumption of a decisive battle already victoriously concluded, but which does not yet set an end to military actions as long as the armistice has not yet been signed" (p. 84); this conviction replaces the Jewish messianic expectation set in the future. "It is emphatically not true that the Primitive Christian hope stands or falls with [an] expectation of imminent end," since it rests surely upon an event *which has already occurred*, the triumph of Jesus (pp. 87–88). The most important of the early formulas of faith was "Kyrios Christos," "Christ rules as Lord" (Rom. 10.9), which expresses the victory already gained by Christ's death and resurrection, forming the basis for that "sure expectation of future glory" which is Christian hope (Cullmann, pp. 151–154).

pear, then shall ye also appear with him in glory." Christ's triumph makes apparent the causes previously hidden.

Nor is the exact placement of events in a particular time important in this poem. For example, in the Prologue, Will sees some contemporary clergy who "seruen as seruaunt₃ lordes and ladies, / And in stede of Stywardes sitten and demen" (Prol., 95–95). These present-tense clerics are immediately translated into the scriptural future as Will says (Prol., 98–101):

> drede is at þe laste
> Lest crist in Consistorie acorse ful manye.
> I parceyued of þe power þat Peter hadde to kepe,
> To bynden and vnbynden as þe book telleþ.

One pervasive effect of Langland's constant use of the Bible to comment upon his own times is to enforce the time sense of the poem, in which scriptural history is the significant referent of all events—the present acquires its meaning in relation to that history. It is an expression, I think, of the "time tension" which Christian eschatology produces, the sense of living in a time that is caught between the decisive event in the past (the Resurrection) and a final event in the future. Because Christian hope sees time as "a line upon which every section has its significance in the divine economy, then in the present, on the one hand simple world denial is not possible, but world affirmation is also limited by the line's goal, of which the believer knows and at which the form of this world shall pass away."[13] Langland's use of tenses, his linking of current time to scriptural time both past and future, suggests this time perception, of a present which is in yet not of time.

The essential importance accorded to the life of Jesus, thoroughly New Testament and thoroughly Augustinian as it is, produces an effect upon the temporal proportions of this poem. The life of Jesus, though not the end of time, is its culmination and fulfillment. Once those events occurred, the battle was over, the victory won, even though the Church is still engaged in the activity of spreading the Gospel and witnessing its faith until the Apocalypse, whose hour and

[13] Cullmann, *Christ and Time*, p. 213. See also Markus, *Saeculum*, pp. 53–71 and 178–86; and Jürgen Moltmann, *Theology of Hope*, trans. James Leitch (New York: Harper & Row, 1967), pp. 190–202.

manner of coming are also hidden, shall come. The period of Antichrist begins in the New Testament with Pentecost; the coming of the Holy Spirit itself is a sign of the fullness and end of time. When Peter, directly after the descent of the Paraclete, preaches in Jerusalem, he says: "This is that which was spoken by the prophet Joel; And it shall come to pass in the last days, saith God, I will pour out of my Spirit upon all flesh: and your sons and your daughters shall prophesy, and your young men shall see visions, and your old men shall dream dreams" (Acts 2.16–17). In *Piers* also the Church exists in these last days, besieged by Antichrist and false brethren.[14] Christ came in the fullness of time, he fulfilled canonical history, and his life provides the reference point for all time before and after. From the point of view of literary plot, Christian history refers both its beginning and end to an all-causative, all-significant middle. Because of this, both beginning and end lose importance in relation to the midpoint. It seems to me that *Piers Plowman* mirrors this distinctively Christian economy of time in its own plot. It neither has a decisive beginning nor builds toward a climactic ending.

It is not necessary that the poem begin as it does. In fact, the beginning is a surprise, a reversal of expectations. May mornings and slumber-inducing brooks usually produce a very different sort of dream from the one Will proceeds to have, since his is filled with people in ordinary tasks. But this surprise means very little – the poem does not depend on it, and, in fact, one quickly realizes that the dream beginning is mostly just a narrative convenience. Langland continues through the poem to underscore this by interrupting it with periods of waking which in turn only obscure further the limits between wakefulness and sleep in the poem (most notably at the beginning of C, line 6, when Will meets Conscience and Reason during his waking period). When one gets into the world of the Prologue, no significance is attached to

---

[14] Moltmann comments, "...the loss of eschatology...has always been the condition that makes possible the adaptation of Christianity to its environment.... Christianity in its social form took over the heritage of the ancient state religion. It instilled itself as the 'crown of society' and its 'saving centre,' and lost the disquieting, critical power of its eschatological hope" (pp. 41–42). Markus (*Saeculum*) traces the rejection by Saint Augustine of millennarian hopes for an institutionalized Christian empire (pp. 33–54), concluding that in the second part particularly of *The City of God*, "Rome has been removed from the *Heilsgeschichte*, the Empire is no longer seen as God's chosen instrument for the salvation of men" (p. 54).

the manner or order of introduction of the various folk on the field, nor does Will promise or speculate upon such a significance (again, one might contrast Chaucer's apology in *The General Prologue* for not plac-ing folk "in hir degree / Here in this tale as that they sholde stonde"). When he turns to Lady Holy Church at the beginning of passus 1 to ask "what [may] þis [by]meene?" and her response is advice to save his soul, it is obvious that meaning is conceived in an altogether ultimate fashion, not bound to specific, particular events but embracing all spe-cific, particular events in Christian lives within a pattern of salvation.

The patterned process of Christian time ends, of course, at Apoca-lypse, a moment of extreme crisis. Christian time concludes as all things are transposed radically, an event which is utterly unimagin-able, parallel to the moment of one's own death. Time closes then, and with it so does plot, and indeed all ideas of form and pattern. We imagine the afterlife and the Heavenly City in terms self-evidently fanciful and fictive and cannot imagine at all the act of transposition from this world. That is the moment of seizure, *raptus*, "a l'alta fantasia qui mancò possa." This ending is not the capstone of a building but the rupture which alters the entire structure to something essentially un-knowable. It is radically surprising, not as *peripeteia*, which produces a pleasing sense of *concordia discors*, but as a catastrophe. Eschatological Christianity places a believer like Langland in the radical, though non-revolutionary, position of being in the world but not of it, a pilgrim whose true home lies elsewhere.[15] "He which testifieth these things saith, Surely I come quickly, Amen. Even so, come, Lord Jesus." That cry of Saint John which ends Revelation exactly captures the eschato-logical expectation of ending, and is echoed in Conscience's cry after Grace at the end of *Piers Plowman*.

The eschatological time tension, the perception that one lives in "the

[15] The difference between an eschatological view of history and a revolutionary utopian or millennial view lies in one's attitude toward the *saeculum*; as Markus (*Saeculum*) remarks, "Seen in an eschatological perspective, there can be no existing or possible society in which there is nothing to criticize" (pp. 168–69). Augustine's views, according to Markus, set him finally apart from the tradition of ecclesiastical history in Eusebius and Orosius, who thought that a divinely ordained kingdom on earth is promised (pp. 157–66). Karl Barth succinctly defines the eschato-logical view of society: "It belongs to the very nature of the state that it is not and cannot become the kingdom of God" (Karl Barth, "The Christian Community and the Civil Community," in *Com-munity, State and Church* [New York: Anchor Books, 1960], p. 168).

last days" in a missionary Church besieged within and without by worldly powers, yet determinedly witnesses that which is true in the sure expectation of future glory, accounts for the way in which all the poem's conversions lead only to more conversions, and the very last of all to yet another. Langland's temporality places him in this ancient Christian tradition, sharing more with Saint Paul than with Aquinas or the medieval humanists, for whom, in the task of reconciling Christian with classical thought, Apocalypse shrank in relative importance to fictions of consonance and continuity.[16] From Langland's viewpoint, however, to tie everything up into a consonant whole as the classical canons of art would dictate would be to confirm the fictiveness of such an imposed design. As Frank Kermode has described such fictions, they are "coherent patterns which, by the provision of an end, make possible a satisfying consonance with the origins and with the middle," but they "imagine a significance" which is in constant tension with "reality," and thus must be constantly modified, betraying their fictive natures.[17] But the eschatological plot is no fiction, and it has no imaginable end, because congruence and consonance are not its ultimate values. Its conclusion lies beyond the capabilities of plot and form. The process of history stops unfolding at its midpoint, the triumph of Jesus; there can be no further development or "ending," only the continuing offer and acceptance of salvation. Time as we know it has no end of which we can know—to pretend otherwise is to be untruthful. And *Piers* is a poem devoted to Saint Truth.

The narrative structure produced by such a perception of time is most surprising to any classically derived notions of literary plot. But if we consider plot simply as the means by which temporality (defined as time design) is created in a literary text, then *Piers Plowman* does have

---

[16] The contrast between the Christian Aristotelian thought of Aquinas and the eschatological perspective of the later Augustine is analyzed by Markus, *Saeculum*, pp. 174–78; see also Bloomfield, *Piers Plowman*, pp. 175–78. Robert Adams, "The Nature of Need in *Piers Plowman* XX," *Traditio* 34 (1978):273–301, concludes that passus 19 and 20 represent thhe signs of the last days themselves—to the ones he adduces, I would add the descent of the Holy Spirit in passus 19. In interpreting the apocalypticism of these last passus, one should recall that all days after the life of Christ are "the last days"; see, in addition to Acts 1–2, Cullmann, *Christ and Time*, pp. 81–93.

[17] Kermode, *The Sense of an Ending*, pp. 17, 4; see also pp. 35–64. Perhaps nowhere is the difference between the scholastic-humanist tradition of *The Divine Comedy* and the eschatological tradition of *Piers Plowman* more evident than in this matter of consonant design.

a plot, even though it has no ending (or, for that matter, any deter-
minative beginning). What the poem does is gradually build up within
itself a significant, repeating pattern of movement from wandering to
conversion to pilgrimage, from hurt to reconciliation. That each of its
pilgrimages dissolves into a new wandering is part of the pattern, con-
firming that the design still exists and is still informative. In the search
for Saint Truth which is this poem, plot exactly mirrors the motivation
of Christian history, both general and individual, and in its incorpora-
tion of the repeating salvational pattern becomes itself one of the signs
that point the way to Truth, to be read by those with the ears to hear
and the eyes to see.

The Franklin's Tale:
A Story of Unanswered Questions[1]

MORTON W. BLOOMFIELD
Harvard University

HE MOST EXTRAORDINARY SCENE in *The Franklin's Tale* is that of Dorigen sitting upon the high bank overlooking the sea and complaining over the "grisly rokkes blake" (F 859). She addresses the Creator in a combination of prayer and complaint, "Why han ye wroght this werk unresonable?" (line 872). The cruel rocks do no good; they only destroy ships and their contents. How could a good God who out of love made man in his own image have created such means to destroy him? Then, shifting to the third person from the second and from a direct address to a statement, she plainly expresses her dissatisfaction at theological attempts to explain this mystery and ends in a strong wish that the rocks sink into hell. As Joseph points out, in this vivid scene Dorigen, who has not questioned her husband's wisdom, is ready enough to question God's.[2] This "complaint" against God makes problematic the whole of creation, or rather emphasizes the problematic in creation.

This is the first example in Western literature of which I know where the horrible and frightening aspects of nature lead a spectator to question God's goodness. The innocent wish of Dorigen, made because of her love of her husband, is to lead almost to the breakup of her marriage. Her idealistic love gets her into trouble. She cannot accept this inordinate power of God, and seems fascinated with it, as Chaucer's century was. There is no answer to Dorigen's prayer and to the dilemma she faces. We are left with an unanswered and possibly unanswerable question—but a most fundamental one.

---

[1] Dedicated to my old and dear friend E. Talbot Donaldson, who is "most free" in both the medieval and the modern senses of the word. He is a true scholar, critic, and human being.

[2] *ChauR* 1 (1966):23. All quotations from Chaucer are from F. N. Robinson, ed., *The Works of Geoffrey Chaucer*, 2d ed. (Boston: Houghton Mifflin, 1957).

It is also curious that this address to God with its passionate tones is the only possible obvious violation of the pagan atmosphere, machinery, and accoutrements that dominate and color the tale. The story is laid in pagan times.[3] Phoebus is prayed to; the teller, the Franklin, comments on the magic that it is pagan and "in oure dayes is nat worth a flye" (line 1132), and he speaks of "hethen folk...in thilke dayes" (line 1293). There is such an intensity in the passage, which is an obvious violation of the pagan setting, that we must regard it as of special importance to the tale. Certainly the issue of God's goodness is a question of great importance in any case, but it does seem to have a special bearing on this tale of pagan knights and ladies. It could be that Dorigen is speaking to the god of nature and of natural law, but her language is full of Christian overtones and resonances. Of course, we cannot expect Chaucer, in spite of his relatively sensitive view of history, to have a sense of historical exactitude when dealing with pagan Celts. We cannot criticize the "Christian" view of God that he allows to seep into the story here in Dorigen's soliloquy.

Dorigen raises a basic question of existence, and her raising it provides the whole motivation for the action of the plot. Her hatred of the rocks, so firmly embedded in her mind, leads her to propose half-playfully to her would-be lover, Aurelius, that she will grant his desires if he will take the rocks away. She wants the rocks removed so that her husband will come back safely. She wishes it so much that she is willing to hazard her own love for and loyalty to him to get Arveragus back.

Set against Dorigen's prayer a little further on in the tale is Aurelius's prayer to Apollo (lines 1031–79), which he utters after he returns home from his fruitless plea to Dorigen for love. Like Dorigen, he begs him to remove the rocks by a miracle and cause a flood to cover them for two years so that he may say to his lady, "The rokkes been aweye."

---

[3] See J. S. P. Tatlock, Scene of the Franklin's Tale Revisited, Chaucer Society (London, 1914). On the importance of "trouthe" and the attitude toward God, see M. R. Golding, "The Importance of Keeping 'trouthe' in the Franklin's Tale," MÆ 39 (1970):306–12; and Kenneth Kee, "Illusion and Reality in Chaucer's Franklin's Tale," ESC 1 (1975):1–12. Robert B. Burlin, Chaucerian Fiction (Princeton, N.J.: Princeton University Press, 1977), p. 205, contrasts the two requests of Dorigen and Aurelius, but, although admitting Dorigen's question to be better motivated than Aurelius's, he condemns both as not living up to the highest Christian ideals of patience in adversity. Burlin points out on the same page how frequently both characters refer to God the creator but does not interpret these references in relation to their pagan belief in a creator god.

Apollo has power over Lucina (the Moon), who controls the sea. He, Aurelius suggests, can certainly obtain his desire if he so wishes, or, Aurelius proposes, have the rocks sink down to hell. Like Dorigen, Aurelius gets no answer. His request is, however, specific; hers was merely general and philosophic, no matter how much inspired by her love for her husband. It is not idle speculation. .

The tale also ends on a question asking who is the most generous of the three noble-hearted characters in the tale. Arveragus when he hears the story of his wife's foolish vow decides that his honor demands that she keep it. Aurelius cannot bear the nobility of the husband and finds that his real problem, as Owen has pointed out,[4] is not, as he had thought, the rocks but the character of the husband and wife. He gives up his lawful prize. Then finally the clerk of Orleans whose magic had produced the illusion of the rocks being away displays his generosity by not insisting on his payment from Aurelius. The Franklin ends his tale by saying "which was the moste fre [generous], as thynketh yow?"

The action proper begins and ends with a question—and there are questions throughout. Dempster and Tatlock[5] have proposed as Chaucer's main source the story of Menedon in Boccaccio's *Filocolo*, which is a *questione d'amore*, a love question, such as might have been proposed at a court of love. In Boccaccio, however, we have an answer— from the judge Fiametta, who says that honor is more precious than wealth or a lover's pleasure and places the husband's generosity above that of the other two. In Chaucer we get no answer. In fact, a case can be made for each of the three noble characters. It is a matter not merely of the relative value of honor, love, or money but of how involved in responsibility each of the generous men are. The clerk has done his job properly on a clean contract basis and has had no responsibility for bringing about the problem. Honor and love may rank above money,

---

[4] See Charles A. Owen, Jr., "The Crucial Passages in Five of the *Canterbury Tales*: A Study in Irony and Symbol," in Owen, ed., *Discussions of the Canterbury Tales* (Boston: D. C. Heath, 1961), pp. 80–81 (original in *JEGP* 52 (1953):294–311).

[5] W. F. Bryan and Germaine Dempster, eds., *Sources and Analogues* of Chaucer's *Canterbury Tales* (Chicago, 1941), pp. 377ff. The *Filocolo* tells of a woman who wishes to get rid of an importunate lover because her husband may hear of his wooing and who asks for fruit from a blooming fruit tree in January. The task, unlike that in *The Franklin's Tale*, has no relation to her love for her husband.

but when honor and love are compromised, then we may choose money. The Squire had no right to propose to a married woman anyway. Dorigen had no right to make a rash vow. The husband must support and back his wife regardless. Aurelius and Arveragus are then partly responsible for the dilemma. The clerk is not.

The case for Aurelius is his sufferings. He suffered for the woman and obeyed her every command. He was entitled to his paramour. He was not the first nor the last to approach a married woman with sexual intent. It was not his fault that Dorigen made a silly proposition. He went through fire and water for her sake and deserved his reward. Besides, his act of generosity is the key act in the denouement.

The case for the Knight is the case, as Fiametta saw, for honor. In every class in which I have taught this tale, I have always found supporters for each of these men as the one who is the most "free." It is only right that there be different answers. It too, like the questions to God, is an unanswerable question in any absolute terms.

The sick Aurelius is rescued from the despair brought on by Dorigen's decision—that only if he removed the rocks so that no stone is seen would she give him her favors—by his brother, who takes him to an expert in natural magic at Orleans. This magician shows the brother his powers in *prestigium*, as his type of magic was known.[6]

This scene is vividly presented even to the extent of a discussion between the magician and his servant about when supper was ready. The magician who could produce illusions could not tell when supper was ready, nor could he produce it, but was dependent on his servant. Reality baffles him. Thus when he removes the rocks, he only does so by illusions. The rocks of this world cannot, alas, really be removed but can only seem to be removed.

The next important scene, and perhaps the most puzzling of all the scenes in the tale—certainly the most debated—is the long complaint by Dorigen on hearing that Aurelius has had the rocks removed and that she is now being called upon to deliver herself to him. She is alone,

---

[6] See Roger Bacon's discussion of his method in his *Epistola de secretis operibus artis et naturae et de utilitate magiae*, ed. J. S. Brewer (London, 1859), pp. 534–35. He discusses it in chap. 5, "De experientiis perspectivis artificialibus." For other examples in other romances see William Henry Schofield, "Chaucer's *Franklin's Tale*," PMLA 16 (1901):419n.1; see also A. A. Prins, "Notes on the *Canterbury Tales* (3)," ES 35 (1954):158–62.

her husband having gone out of town for a few days. We then have a complaint to Fortune which runs for some one hundred lines (lines 1355–1456), consisting mainly of a series of exempla. Donald Baker has divided them into three categories: women who committed suicide before being ravished, women who committed suicide after being raped, and women who remained faithful in the face of pressuring temptation.[7] It is her second complaint after her "complaint" to God toward the beginning of the tale.

This scene has puzzled commentators largely because of its inordinate length. It seems to prolong the climax needlessly, and certainly the list of historical characters—all from ancient Greece and Rome, incidentally—is boring to modern sensibilities. Even as a parallel to the earlier "complaint" it seems out of proportion.

It does, however, in spite of its length raise the issue to a height and dramatizes Dorigen's loyalty to her husband. It makes clear—perhaps more than clear—that she is faithful to her husband and is placed in an excruciating dilemma. There is no answer to her question any more than to her plea to God about the rocks.

Another point which must be borne in mind when trying to find a rationale for this long complaint is what one might call the formal variation, the stopping of the narrative action, moving out of time and normal sequentiality in order to develop, explain, or enrich the action. This is an element found in much literature even down to modern times. It is found in Shakespeare's soliloquies and in the extensive interventions of the persona-author in various works of Chaucer, above all in *Troilus and Criseyde*. We find it then both on the character level and on the personal-author level. In this device we have a kind of stopping of the action to allow the presence of another kind of statement which bears on the action but is not itself action. It may be a simple commentary on the action or part of it, a placing of the action in a context which explains it or finally an enrichment, perhaps ironical, perhaps not, of the action or a combination of these. Our example illustrates primarily the second purpose. This does not, of course, explain the length of Dorigen's formal variation, but it provides a rationale for it and many other similar interjections into Chaucerian narrative.

---

[7] "A Crux in Chaucer's *Franklin's Tale*: Dorigen's Complaint," *JEGP* 60 (1961):56–64; see also Harry Berger, Jr., "The F-Fragment of *The Canterbury Tales*: Part II," *ChauR* (1967):152–53.

An interesting question which arises from Dorigen's quick agreement that the rocks have disappeared, even though Chaucer tells us that they have not but only seem to be away, is why Dorigen does not seem to question Aurelius's statement at all or even check its truth. Perhaps Chaucer is here showing us that not only do we deceive ourselves but that we actually want to be deceived. Perhaps human beings cannot bear too much reality. This action, which seems so ill-conceived, leads, however, to generosity of spirit. Harriet Hawkins writes about the dilemmas of truth and falsehood in Chaucer, Milton, Shakespeare, and other great English literary figures. As she puts it: "To be totally deceived 'by the best of this kind,' which are but shadows, may be madness. Yet not to be deceived at all seems madness too. It is like falling in love."[8]

The three main characters of The Franklin's Tale contrast very vividly with the three from The Merchant's Tale. Aurelius, Dorigen, and Averagus are in sharp opposition to Damian, May, and January. On the one hand, we have a noble triangle; on the other, an ignoble one.[9] If The Franklin's Tale is indeed an answer to the marriage group, this contrast does say something.

What we have then are three noble people and a clerk thrown into a dilemma in which generosity of spirit wins out. This victory makes us feel fine, and no one would ever accuse this tale of leaving a bitter taste in the mouth. Yet in spite of its heart-lifting and heart-warming people and story, the tale does end, as it began, on a question, a question not on marriage but one asking for a comparison of the generous behavior of the three main characters. The question seems almost irrelevant.

As I see it, this tale is not as satisfactory as The Merchant's Tale because the final question does not seem to be on the same level of importance as the question about God's providence and purposes raised by the rocks or the prayerful request to Apollo. This tale, unlike The Merchant's Tale, does not transgress limits—in fact, it stays within them in a remarkably consistent way[10]—but it raises a serious question within close limits and then rather peters out at the end.

[8] Poetic Freedom and Poetic Truth, Chaucer, Shakespeare, Marlowe, Milton (Oxford: Clarendon Press, 1976), p. xiii.

[9] "...it is difficult not to see in the Franklin's Tale a calculated antithesis to the Merchant's Tale." Robert Kaske, "Chaucer and Medieval Allegory," ELH 30 (1963):175–92.

[10] Except perhaps for the speech to God by Dorigen.

The two major questions—those of the rocks and of generosity—differ not merely in profundity but even more seriously in their structural role. The second, at the end, is a metaquestion and occurs on the author or persona level and is directed at the other pilgrims or at the audience. The question Aurelius raises, his request to Apollo, does not raise moral and philosophical issues and seems ill-placed.

This split of the last question from the narrative line separates us at the end of the tale from the protagonists and the actions and asks us to judge their actions from another perspective. These characters are, as we have seen, pagans living under natural law. We are already separated from them by religion, but we see that they are good people and recognize that a man's troth is important and that true love is incompatible with force. It may even be, as Daniel M. Murtaugh puts it, that "*because* Averagus and Dorigen free themselves from the patristic view of womanly virtue [a matter of preserving the flesh intact], *therefore* Aurelius frees himself from the courtly, adulterous view of love."[11] Yet a doubt arises, for certainly no Catholic would ever have accepted the notion that the patristic view of female virtue is purely fleshly and probably few medieval men would have had a purely adulterous view of courtly love.

Although *The Franklin's Tale* is no *Troilus and Criseyde*, we do get a sense of distance and a feeling of separation in the tale. At least twice we have references to the old books the author is following (lines 813 and 1243). Good does come out of evil. The rocks led to a notable display of human generosity, and, as Donaldson says,[12] it is in the dead of winter that the Orleans clerk starts his magic performance which is to lead to the apparent removal of the rocks—out of darkness comes light, out of despair comes hope. Yet the total feeling is of disharmony and disproportion. As William Henry Schofield wrote almost seventy years ago, "The *Franklin's Tale* is not, it is evident, an entirely harmonious whole."[13]

Yet in spite of its clashes and inharmonies, the tale gives its readers an extraordinary sense of happiness and fulfillment. If Dorigen had

[11] See his "Women and Geoffrey Chaucer," *ELH* 38 (1971):491.

[12] E. Talbot Donaldson, *Chaucer's Poetry: An Anthology for the Modern Reader*, 2d ed. (New York: Ronald Press, 1975), p. 1089.

[13] William Henry Schofield, "Chaucer's *Franklin's Tale*," *PMLA* 16 (1901):446.

been forced to grant her favors to Aurelius out of a foolish word made because of her love for her husband, we would have felt that the world is too horrible to contemplate. It cannot be so. Although we do not see how Dorigen is going to get out of her dilemma, at the same time we do anticipate a happy ending. We know that in some way "it may be wel, paraventure, yet today" (line 1473). Arveragus's hope, we feel, must be realized. The world simply could not be that cruel.

We are not then really surprised at the extraordinary generosity of the young squire. Some unusual act of grace or mercy we had expected – the only question was what one. Compared with his act, the generosity of the Knight and the Clerk was unimportant in the economy of the story. They smoothed things for the supreme act of kindness by Aurelius. It is his generosity which solves the problem of a rash vow and teaches the heroine a supreme lesson: our natural questions about the justice of the arrangements of the world should not lead us into ridiculous requests and dishonest promises.

The persistent feeling that Chaucer himself is speaking in the tale – as in the theories that Chaucer is proposing in it his own answer to the marriage-group question (who should have the sovereignty in marriage?) – is interesting in itself. I am here concerned not with the basic issue whether there is a marriage group of *The Canterbury Tales* or whether this is indeed Chaucer's answer (both may be so) but rather with the attribution to Chaucer's own mind and thought of the fundamentally optimistic view of the world that *The Franklin's Tale* reveals.[14]

Wordplay is a protest by opposition to the fact that verbal signs and their referents do not agree. It is an attempt to correct language and its supposed deficiencies by making signs indicate in some way their rationality. We do not want to accept a world in which the relation between words and things is purely arbitrary. To avoid this unpleasant conclusion, we create puns, double entendres, verbal repetitions,

---

[14] I certainly do not agree with the arguments of James L. Hodge, "The Marriage Group: Precarious Equilibrium," *ES* 46 (1965):296, that "the Franklin has quite unknowingly told a tale which subtly denies the ideals he hopes to support." The basic difficulty with this interpretation of the tale as "a subtler and more damaging indictment of marriage and courtly love than the Merchant has presented" (p. 298) is simply that it strongly conflicts with our sense of the tale and Chaucer's plain words.

rhymes, alliteration, and so on. We also do not want to accept a meaningless world. Frank Kermode has written, "A plot satisfied a need for
causality, a peripeteia our sense that ends are predictable absolutely
but not contingently."[15] So too paranomasia attempts to satisfy our
need for meaning.

The plot of *The Franklin's Tale* satisfies our need for order in a rock-
strewn world, for decency in a world dominated by sin and self-
interest, and at the same time it reminds us by its questions that there
are no simple answers. It is, in Robert M. Adams's[16] terms, "a closed
novel." There is no major irresolution of themes or plot. The question
with which it ends seems to leave the tale open, but that is really not
the case. Part of the great pleasure of the tale comes from the satisfactory resolution of its plot elements, as well as from its happy ending.
Our only problem is which of three noble acts is the noblest. That is
not much of a problem, and the mere fact that the tale ends on such a
question is the best testimony to the satisfaction it affords. We are not
told that Averagus and Dorigen lived happily ever after. Such would
have been too tame an ending for their joy or our joy. Instead we are
asked to speculate upon a most pleasant question. We are left with
happy thoughts indeed. It is a question which is finally not very
troubling. We shall lose no sleep over it.

In fact, it may not be a question at all. It may merely be a method of
indicating that human nature under certain circumstances may rise to
generous heights and overcome the pride and pomp of this world.
Chaucer may wish to convey to us the depth of human decency when
faced with difficult dilemmas.

In this light the earlier question about the rocks, which is certainly a
very troubling question, takes on a different appearance. This question
which led to an elaborate plot which teetered on the edge of the tragic
finally leads to happiness. The rocks which objectified Dorigen's fears
for her husband and led to a serious probing of God's purposes in
creating a universe somehow or other fade out as the nobility of the in-

---

[15] "The University and the Literary Public," in Thomas B. Stroup, ed., *The Humanities and the
Understanding of Reality* (Lexington, Ky., 1966), p. 71.

[16] See his *Strains of Discord: Studies in Literary Openness* (Ithaca, N.Y., 1958). As the title
shows, Adams is more interested in the "open" than in the "closed" work of art.

volved human being is revealed. As an act of generosity saves Dorigen, so God's act of generosity will save us.

The final weakness of this tale is that it is set afoot by too mighty a vehicle for its rather tame ending. The clash between the fundamental quality of the first question it raises with the rather pat answer it seems to give and the folkloristic final question which seeks to bring the audience into the story is never resolved. The first question is at variance with the happiness of the tale. There is none of the "tension between the ethos of contemplation and the pathos of experience"[17] which could have arisen and given this tale the majesty it lacks.

There is charm and gaiety in the tale, but it ill consorts with the un-answerable questions about human destiny it raises. It leaves us on reflection with a curious feeling of dissatisfaction in the general happi-ness of the ending. In spite of the opinion of some, it does not leave a completely satisfying taste in the mouth.[18] It does, however, "reaffirm, more directly than other *Tales*, some of the moral values most worth cherishing."[19]

[17] Renato Paggioli, "Tragedy or Romance? A Reading of the Paolo and Francesca Episode in Dante's *Inferno*," *PMLA* 72 (1957). Some see the characters of *The Franklin's Tale* as limited, tasteless, and insensitive, even cruel (e.g., Chauncey Wood, *Chaucer and the Country of the Stars: Poetic Uses of Astrological Imagery* [Princeton, N.J.: Princeton University Press, 1970], pp. 259–71 and Russell A. Peck, "Sovereignty and the Two Worlds of the *Franklin's Tale*," *ChauR* [1967]:253–27, ["cupidinous"]), reflecting their teller's (the Franklin's) limitations of vision. Although there is a curious dissatisfaction which arises from reading the tale, I definitely do not attribute it to the deficiencies of the characters or of the teller. I do not believe "that there is something foolish and misdirected in the behavior of the Franklin and his heroine," as Robert B. Burlin writes in "The Art of Chaucer's Franklin," *Neophil* 51 (1967):72.

[18] See Nevill Coghill, *The Poet Chaucer*, Home University Library, vol. 185 (London: Oxford University Press, 1949), p. 170.

[19] Trevor Whittock, *A Reading of the Canterbury Tales* (Cambridge: Cambridge University Press, 1968), p. 177.

Part Six   THE SOCIAL CONTEXT

Margery Kempe in Jerusalem:
Hysterica Compassio in the Late Middle Ages

HOPE PHYLLIS WEISSMAN
Wesleyan University

URING THE 1430s the middle-class Englishwoman Margery Kempe narrated her spiritual biography to two successive male amanuenses.[1] The product of their collaboration, in which the precise contribution of each participant must remain conjectural, has come down to us in a single manuscript now known as *The Book of Margery Kempe*. The heroine of the *Book*, a sensation in her own time, has been regarded as a curiosity by modern medievalists, many of whom share the inability of her contemporaries to credit her "mystical" dreams. Some scholars, like R. W. Chambers, have relegated the narrative to anecdotal history, while others, like Dom Vandenbrouke, have recommended its heroine to the Viennese couch.[2]

Throughout much otherwise diverse commentary, one version of the latter strategy has persisted; Margery's story has been shown to resemble significantly the case histories of hysterical women analyzed by Freud in his early career. Yet to diagnose Margery's case as "hysteria" need not be to trivialize her significance or reduce her *Book*'s

---

[1] *Caveat lector*: Margery Kempe's life story defies the compression to which this essay perforce has subjected it. I hope in subsequent essays to treat fully issues which are only alluded to here, such as the question of authorship, the religious-political context, and Margery's personal relationships (especially with her husband and with Christ). The present essay, which had ever before it the example of E. Talbot Donaldson—endowed by nature with the grace to say a lot in little space—was helped on its way by the valuable suggestions of Robert Hanning, Mary Carruthers, and James Marrow.

[2] See R. W. Chambers, introduction to *The Book of Margery Kempe: A Modern Version by W. Butler-Bowden* (New York: Devon-Adair, 1944), pp. xv–xxvi; and François Vandenbrouke, in Jean Leclerq, François Vandenbrouke, and Louis Boyer, eds., *The Spirituality of the Middle Ages* (1960; trans. London: Burns and Oats, 1968), part 2, p. 426.

value as cultural testimony. On the contrary, social historians have become increasingly aware that the pervasive hysteria of nineteenth-century women cannot be regarded merely as a symptom of individual maladjustments; it was also symptomatic of repressive social and sexual attitudes and of rigidly defined sex roles.[3] In the same spirit, we can recognize that the case of Margery Kempe, whose hysterical devotionalism was remarkable but by no means unique in her time, can provide an invaluable witness to similar social and sexual repression in the later medieval world.

That world, as revealed in *The Book of Margery Kempe*, remains for all its quotidian detail a predominantly ecclesiastical one. It is, as well, a predominantly patriarchal world in which Margery's encounters with women authorities—the anchoress Julian of Norwich, the traveler Lady Margaret Florentine—occur as decided exceptions. Before the world of the patriarchal Church, Margery Kempe, mayor's daughter of Lynn, stands in a posture of confrontation. The recurring tests of faith to which she is subjected, tests ranging from catechization in bishops' courts to arrest on suspicion of Lollardy, can be recognized as metaphors for a still more fundamental interrogation. Margery Kempe, a secular woman of the common estate, is being summoned to justify her very nature before the Church whose ideology continues to dominate her world.

Despite its increasing involvement in secular administration, the later medieval Church did not significantly relax its traditionally rigorous positions on sexuality and gender roles. The most careful recent studies of ecclesiastical materials have shown that, at most, the Church responded favorably to the expansionist spirit of the central Middle Ages by showing increased toleration of procreative desire within marriage. By the same token, however, during the period of socioeconomic contraction which followed, even this limited concession was expressed more circumspectly, while in some quarters it was never admitted or else was effectively withdrawn.[4] The reactionary

---

[3] See Carroll Smith-Rosenberg, "The Hysterical Woman: Sex Roles and Role Conflict in 19th-Century America," *Social Research* 39 (1972):652–78; see also Howard M. Wolowitz, "Hysterical Character and Feminine Identity," in Judith M. Bardwick, ed., *Readings on the Psychology of Women* (New York: Harper and Row, 1972), pp. 307–14.

[4] See John T. Noonan, *Contraception: A History of Its Treatment by Catholic Theologians and Canonists* (Cambridge, Mass.: Harvard University Press, 1965), esp. pp. 141–300; Thomas N.

ideology of the fourteenth- and fifteenth-century Church is particularly
evident in its failure adequately to support new images of women
which were genuinely responsive to the needs of its lay population.
The governing paradigm continued to be the ancient antithesis between carnal Eve, whose lust for sex and knowledge resulted in her
subjugation to wedlock and childbearing, and the Virgin Mary, whose
perfect purity released her soul and body from earthly bonds. Only in
appearance was this antithesis modified by the three-tiered rating
system which had been derived exegetically from the Matthean sower
parable (Matt. 13.8). Virginity, widowhood, and lastly wedlock: Alisoun of Bath bore Chaucer's witness to the damaging effect of this formula, which insisted that the laywoman's status was necessarily a
lesser one even as social pressures, together with her own internal impulses, encouraged her to define herself in terms of the lesser state.[5]

Margery Kempe, responding to the same frustrating situation, shares
the Wife of Bath's confrontation strategy of formally accepting conventional images while actually coopting them. She differs significantly
from Alisoun, however, in the structure of her cooptation as well as in
its final aim. Alisoun does not challenge the essential distinction between virginity and wedlock but instead undermines its hierarchicali-
zation by insisting on the reality of sexual pleasure. Margery, acqui-
escing in the hierarchy and the sexual guilt thereby imputed, on the
other hand denies the humiliating exclusions of the distinctions themselves. The story of Margery's life thus becomes an extended argument that carnal Eve can assimilate not merely to chaste Anna but to
the Virgin herself. *The Book of Margery Kempe*, taken as a whole,
records the difficulty of making such an argument, with its structure of

Tentler, *Sin and Confession on the Eve of the Reformation* (Princeton, N.J.: Princeton University Press, 1977), esp. pp. 162–232; and for the English vernacular tradition, E. Talbot Donaldson, "Medieval Poetry and Medieval Sin," in *Speaking of Chaucer* (New York: W. W. Norton, 1970), pp. 164–74. For a more positive but still qualified view, see Henry Ansgar Kelly, *Love and Marriage in the Age of Chaucer* (Ithaca, N.Y.: Cornell University Press, 1975), pp. 245–334.

[5] For material on Eve-Mary, see Ernst Guldan, *Eva und Maria: Eine Antithese als Bildmotiv* (Graz-Köln: Hermann Böhlaus, 1966). Currently there exists no comprehensive and systematic study of later-medieval gender expectations comparable to those on sexual attitudes, but a number of recent specialized studies are suggesting a considerable revision of former optimistic assessments. In light of these it no longer seems adequate to discuss the "cultivation" of Mary's maternity or Saint Anne's without scrutinizing particular images carefully and inquiring into their patronage, diffusion, and reception.

insistent repetitions, false starts, falser stops. The first part of the *Book*, however, registers Margery's conviction that her argument in-deed could triumph, her assimilation be achieved. The structure of this section, accordingly, is constituted as an integral life journey, one which begins with Margery's conversion at Lynn, centers in her "hys-terical" weeping at Jerusalem, and concludes with her mystical mar-riage to the Lord at Rome. Embodying her deepest conflicts as well as her highest aspirations, this journey presents the clearest expression of the forces motivating its heroine, and as such it merits the close atten-tion of those who would understand her case. The following interpre-tation of the journey will combine the perspectives of typology and psychohistory in an effort to contribute toward that end: "'&, for-as-mech as þu art a mayden in þi sowle, I xal take þe be þe on hand in Hevyn & my Modyr be þe oþer hand, & so xalt þu dawnsyn in Hevyn wyth oþer holy maydens & virgynes.'"[6]

I

In accordance with its twofold intention of glorifying God and Margery, the *Book* recasts its heroine's life after the approved model of the saint's vita. Like the lives of the early Christian confessors, it rehearses a tale of persecutions and triumphs, of visions and even some minor miracles, which testify to its heroine's special status as a bride elected by God.[7] In awareness, however, of the peculiar difficulties of sanctifying a middle-class married woman, the *Book* also manipulates its model to serve untraditional purposes. Its most signifiant manipula-tion occurs at the very beginning, when the narrative bypasses the birth and childhood episodes characteristic of the vita format. It opens instead with Margery's marriage to John Kempe and the pregnancy which immediately followed; she must have been about twenty-one,

---

[6] See *The Book of Margery Kempe*, ed. Sanford Brown Meech and Hope Emily Allen, EETS, o.s., 212 (London: Oxford University Press, 1940), p. 52. All subsequent citations are from this text.

[7] The influence upon the *Book* of more recent lives is an important question which needs fur-ther research. Allen's copious citations from the lives of the German mystics, as she admits, can be regarded only as suggestive parallels. The second, priestly amanuensis mentions having read the lives of Mary of Oignies and Elizabeth of Hungary in order to credit Margery's (pp. 152–54). But Margery herself acknowledges the influence only of Saint Birgitta—aristocratic, widowed, and recently canonized (pp. 39, 47, 95, 143).

the year about 1394. Margery describes a difficult pregnancy and pain-ful labor in childbirth. After delivery, despairing of her life, she sent for her confessor, intending finally to unburden herself of an old and hid-den sin. Yet at the point of revelation, her narrative states:

> . . . hir confessowr was a lytyl to hastye & gan scharply to vndyrnemyn hir er þan sche had fully seyd hir entent, & so sche wold no mor seyn for nowt he mygth do. And a-noon, for dreed sche had of dampnacyon on þe to syde & hys scharp repreuyng on þat oþer syde, þis creatur went owt of hir mende & was wondyrlye vexid & labowryed wyth spyritys half ȝer viij wekys & odde days. (p. 7)

During this period of hard labor, a period significantly equal to that of her pregnancy, Margery is tormented by devils who tempt her to forsake God and abjure Christianity. Finally, however, on a day when her husband and keepers are absent, Christ appears to Margery as a beautiful young man in a purple mantle. Sitting at her bedside, he calls to her softly: "'Dowtyr, why hast þow forsakyn me, and I forsoke neuyr þe?'" (p. 8).

Christ's visitation stabilizes Margery in her wits, but in fact her pro-cess of conversion has only just begun. The next period of her life is marked by a series of relapses and heavenly rescues concerning always the related problems of social pride and sexual temptation. These events culminate in a particularly mortifying relapse, involving a male acquaintance who leads Margery into temptation only to turn on her with self-righteous words of reproach, and finally in the decisive rescue, on a Friday before Christmas, as Margery kneels weeping in Saint Margaret's Church. Christ now appears to Margery to proclaim her final triumph over despair. He announces permanent forgiveness of her sins, guarantees her admission to heaven, advises her nevertheless to continue receiving the sacraments – and, above all, Christ defines Margery's future earthly life as a vita of perpetual tears: "'Dowtyr, . . . I grawnt þe contrysyon in-to þi lyues ende. . . . And, dowtyr, þu hast an hayr vp-on þi bakke. I wyl þu do it a-way, & I schal ȝiue þe an hayr in þin hert þat schal lyke me mych bettyr þan alle þe hayres in þe world'" (pp. 16–17).

These initiating events of Margery's career form a unified though not conclusive episode. If regarded from a psychohistorical perspective, they can become a dramatic revelation of the institutional and spiritual limitations of the Church in the century preceding Luther. The events clearly illustrate the counterproductivity of a rigorist official ideology, for they show how its direct application in particular cases could actually vitiate the process of grace. In so doing, the events serve to justify Luther's equation of Church law with the Old Law of Romans, but, more important, they confirm his identification of the institutional vehicle which was responsible for the equation. This vehicle was the confessional, seen as the transactional and symbolic center of the penitential sacrament.

The sacrament of lay penance as experienced by Margery had been developed in response to the socioreligious unrest of the late twelfth and early thirteenth centuries. The contemporary Church, guided by the politically astute Innocent III, recognized in penance a means of extending its hegemony, and thus, in the Fourth Lateran Council, it promulgated legislation requiring periodic confession of all souls. The penitential manuals disseminated in the wake of this legislation sought to increase the authority of the confessor by a twofold process: by emphasizing his instrumentality in dispensing forgiveness and by establishing him as a scientist of the soul. In consequence of the second aim, the manuals elaborated a rhetoric of sin and censure; intended to instruct, the rhetoric could also be deployed by individual confessors to constrict the spirits in their care.[8] Margery's own experience demonstrates vividly what could happen when an overzealous clergyman wielded the club of official righteousness. Accepting her confessor's reproval as the voice of divine authority, Margery believed that she had been denied her hope of salvation. Her inability to perceive alternatives at this stage of her spiritual development resulted in her period of madness, a psychic split.

Although Margery, with Christ's aid, recovered from her actual madness, she never fully resolved the trauma of the confessional. Her continuing anxiety expressed itself in the violent, compulsive weeping which her narrative renders in a formulaic expression—"plentyuows terys and boystows sobbyngys, lowde cryingys and schille schryk-

---

[8] For a useful history of penance, see the articles by E. Amann and A. Michel, s.v. "Pénitence," in *Dictionnaire de théologie catholique* (Paris, 1909–50), v. 12, cols. 722–1050. The most thorough study of the penitentials is Tentler's *Sin and Confession*.

yngys"—and which can be recognized as "hysteria" in the lay and psychoanalytic senses of the term.[9] In the context of Margery's narra' tive, however, one purpose of the formula is to associate Margery's symptom with the later medieval Compassion. By assimilating Mar' gery's weeping to a sanctioned form of extravagant grief, the formula argues that her behavior confirms Margery's superior piety. In so doing, the formula becomes an instrument not merely of revelation but of Margery's self-cure. This instrument and its manipulation have been the center of much modern controversy, and the discussion has been useful at least in focusing on the issue of interpretation—an issue which was crucial to the heroine herself. One must nevertheless question whether the problem of weeping adequately reveals the heart of Mar' gery's argument; its inner springs are better inferred from a passage ex' plicitly addressed to them, Christ's pivotal absolution speech.

The function of Christ's speech is to encapsulate the process of Mar' gery's self-cure by identifying a series of alternatives to the confessor who had denied her. Most immediately important, Christ presents himself as an alternative confessor and in fact provides Margery with far more than an alternative sacramental absolution by guaranteeing absolutely her future bliss. Second, however, Christ circumvents the potentially heretical implications of his gesture by instructing Margery to undertake two acts designed to secure her official acceptance: she is to receive the sacrament every Sunday and confess to the respected anchorite affiliated with the Dominicans of Lynn. These particular obligations recognize the continuing importance to Margery of achiev' ing formal validation; Christ's final instruction, on the other hand, demonstrates her ability to transcend external recognition in her quest for renewed self-esteem. Christ not only authorizes Margery's con' tinued weeping but also significantly extends its meaning when he represents it as a hair shirt in the heart. By invoking this conventional image of penance,[10] Christ invites the reinterpretation of Margery's

[9] In the Freudian vocabulary Margery can be diagnosed as a conversion hysteric who theatri' calizes her symptom to elicit secondary gains. See especially Freud's cogent remarks in two papers of 1908, "Hysterical Phantasies and Their Relation to Bisexuality" and "Some General Remarks on Hysterical Attacks," translated in *The Standard Edition of the Complete Psychological Works of Sigmund Freud* (London: Hogarth Press, 1955), 9.159–66, 229–34.

[10] One important Scriptural source was Psalm 68 (Vulgate), v. 12: "Et posui vestimentum meum cilicium / Et factus sum illis in parabolam."

hysteria as a concrete demonstration of her striving for purification. Implicit in this reinterpretation, since her guilt evidently has been sexual, is the further idea that Margery's way of tears ultimately will perfect itself as the way of virginity. Margery, in effect, is instructed to undergo a passion of contrition and compassion designed to earn and to validate publicly her recovery of prelapsarian purity. She is instructed to achieve a mystical reversal of the effects of Original Sin which—the Church had induced her to believe—stemmed not merely from sexual excess but from female sexuality itself.

Christ's use of the hair-shirt image to identify weeping with purification thus reveals the deepest motivation of Margery's quest; equally important, it illustrates a characteristic mode of procedure. In technique as well as in aim, Margery's journey is a re-creative one; the narrative appropriates and reworks traditional paradigms in serving its heroine's concerns. Regarded in this light, the narrative technique itself can be recognized as an instrument of healing. It is used by Margery to articulate a complex new relationship to authority, one which mediates between her desire for formal validation and her awareness that such validation might finally be withheld. If the initiating events of Margery's journey are now briefly reviewed from a more explicitly typological perspective, it will be possible to identify more precisely the language which achieves this mediation—and which, in so doing, moves its heroine from a position of subjection to tradition toward one of incipient control.

In the psychohistorical interpretation above it was emphasized that Margery's life story differs from the typical saint's vita in beginning not with her birth but with the complications of childbirth which led to her aborted confession of sin. This significant difference can here be attributed to the strategic alignment of Margery's life with a model of still greater authority. Margery's life story in fact begins at the genesis of sacred history: Margery's old sin within her life is the Original Sin within Eve's, and it is Eve's curse, the pains of childbirth, which compels Margery's acknowledgment of the sin which is woman's eternal reproach. Once this initial identification is recognized, it becomes possible to read the ensuing events—recounting the frustrated confession, the period of relapses and rescues—as analogies to the Scriptural Expulsion and the Wandering in the Wilderness. Christ's appearance to Margery on the Friday before Christmas to deliver his absolution represents, finally, the giving of the new dispensation; it is at once an Annunciation and a Nativity marking the birth of Christ in Margery's soul.

As in the Scriptures, the moment of birth defines and adumbrates the redemption–for Margery, her recovery through tears of virginal purity, the redemption through Mary of Eve–but redemption can be realized only in a still more arduous quest. Christ's absolution speech, consequently, is supplemented in a second vision by instructions which reaffirm the meaning of the quest and direct Margery on her way. Christ orders Margery to undertake a pilgrimage to Jerusalem so that she can participate in the Lord's suffering, and he instructs her simultaneously to assume the white robe of his virgin bride. Margery's attempts to fulfill Christ's second commandment are not sanctioned, however, by Church authority; Bishop Repingdon of Lincoln defers her investiture until after she proves herself at Jerusalem. Unwittingly, the bishop thereby enables Margery to perfect her self-alignment with the sacred paradigm: to Jerusalem, in suffering, becomes Margery's way to Rome.[11]

II

The narrative of Margery's suffering at Jerusalem employs a strategy similar to the one which is used in describing her conversion. The *Book* again aligns her activities with established Scriptural and extra-Scriptural models. Thereby it argues not merely for the toleration of Margery's hysteria but for its validation and admiring approval. Validation of her weeping in principle is argued by invoking the *Quis dabit* text of Jeremiah, a text frequently associated with the Virgin's Compassion but in the *Book* still more frequently with Margery's.[12] Validation of her weeping in practice is argued by interpreting her behavior in terms of the familiar devotional triad–contrition, Compassion, and Passion. Weeping, that is, is represented as a sign that Margery has performed an effective penance, has identified with the

[11] Another crucial prerequisite of Margery's pilgrimage, to be discussed in a separate essay, is her husband's agreement to release her from the physical bonds of wedlock. The scene occurs on the Feast of Saint John Baptist and is rich in eucharistic symbolism (pp. 23–25).

[12] The *Quis dabit* is explicitly referred to on pp. 81/19, 99/23, 141/20 (emending Allen's note on p. 299), and 249/1.

Virgin in her love and purity, and, finally, has associated her personal suffering with that of the persecuted Christ.[13]

In the Jerusalem narrative, however, as in the conversion story, it is not the mere presence of conventional elements but their unconventional manipulation which finally secures the unqualified approval aspired to by the heroine. An obvious, strategically candid example of such manipulation occurs in a speech delivered by the Virgin in an appearance at her place of burial. The Virgin, in effect, redefines the traditional understanding of her persecution as Christ's Mother in order to justify the scorn elicited by Margery's extravaganzas of compassion:

"& þerfore, my derworthy dowtyr, be not aschamyd of hym þat is þi God, þi Lord, & þi lofe, no mor þan I was whan I saw hym hangyn on þe Cros, my swete Sone, Ihesu, for to cryen & to wepyn for þe peyn of my swete Sone, Ihesu Crist; ne Mary Mawdelyn was not aschamyd to cryen & wepyn for my Sonys lofe. And þerfor, dowtyr, ȝyf þu wylt be partabyl in owyr joye, þu must be partabil in owyr sorwe." (p. 73)

By suggesting that her mourning and that of the Magdalene were subjected to the same kind of censure, the Virgin invites the inference that Margery's hysteria is the truest realization of the *imitatio Mariae* – the self-subjection, through sorrow, to shame.[14]

A less obvious and far more profound manipulation of conventions can be discerned in the sections of the Jerusalem narrative devoted specifically to Margery's weeping on Calvary. In these two descriptions Margery's identification with the Virgin moves through and

---

[13] Although the specifically Christological parallels cannot be discussed here, one is particularly relevant because of its cooperation with the virginity-purification theme. On the way to Jerusalem, Margery's fellow pilgrims exile her to the foot of the table, enjoin silence upon her, and invest her with "a whyte canwas in manner of a sekkyn gelle, for sche xuld ben holdyn a fool" (p. 62). This apparently autobiographical incident is also a realization of Passion Psalm 68.10–13, with the hair cloth changed to the *veste alba* worn by the mocked Christ in Luke 23.11.

[14] For the more traditional conception of the Virgin's persecution, see the description of Longinus's scorn in the *Meditationes vitae Christi*, caput 80, in *Sancti Bonaventurae opera omnia*, ed. A. C. Peltier (Paris, 1868), 12.608. For a more elaborate but still essentially conventional treatment, see John Gower's description of the Virgin's suffering at Christ's trial in his *Mirour de l'Omme*, esp. lines 28933–56, in *The Complete Works of John Gower*, ed. G. C. Macaulay, Vol. I: *The French Works* (Oxford: Oxford University Press, 1899; reprint, 1968). The theological background is summarized by Giovanni Miegge in *The Virgin Mary: The Roman Catholic Marian Doctrine*, trans. Waldo Smith (Philadelphia: Westminster Press, 1955), pp. 133–77.

beyond the shameful Compassion to achieve a participation, both existential and metaphysical, in the act of the Virgin Birth. Through her
participation in this quintessentially Marian experience, Margery
fulfills the deepest motivation of her vita, the recovery of a virginal
purity lost in the sexual exercises of her womanhood. And through its
articulation of this experience, Margery's *Book* develops an interpretation of its protagonist's hysteria which does not merely detail its symptoms; it penetrates to hysteria's etymological, and culturally deter-
mined, source.

The key passage, for the purposes of this interpretation, occurs in
the second, and somewhat fuller, description of Margery's behavior on
Calvary: "Þan sche fel down & cryed wyth lowde voys, wondyrfully
turnyng & wrestyng hir body on euery syde, spredyng hir armys
a-brode as ȝyf sche xulde a deyd, & not cowde kepyn hir fro crying"
(p. 70). From a typological perspective it can immediately be recognized that the passage consists largely of iconographic motifs adapted
from Scripture and devotional tradition with the intention of associating Margery's actions with those of both Christ and the Virgin. The
outspread arms are clearly an imitation of Christ's posture in the
Crucifixion; in the view of Hope Emily Allen the loud crying also is
Christological, an echo of the cry from the cross.[15] Yet the alternative,
Mariological interpretation seems even more clearly indicated by the
verbal context. For the entire clause, "Þan sche fel down & cryed with
lowde voys," in fact is a narrative formula, one frequently encountered
in later medieval devotional writings, which was derived ultimately
from the Virgin's histrionics in the Eastern redaction of the apocryphal
Gesta Pilati.[16] Finally, the extreme physical violence of Margery's grief,
although extravagant even within later medieval tradition, also is
derivative of the Marian Compassion. Its violence is anticipated, for
example, by the Virgin's performance in an early-fourteenth-century
paraphrase of Pseudo-Bonaventura's *Meditationes vitae Christi* by
Robert Manning of Brunne.[17]

[15] See Allen's note to lines 68/12ff., *Book*, p. 290.

[16] These histrionics occur in the second Greek recension of the *Gesta Pilati*, for which see
Evangelia Apocrypha, ed. Constantinus von Tischendorf (Leipzig: Hermann Mendelssohn, 1876),
pp. 287–332.

[17] See Robert Manning, *Meditations on the Supper of Our Lord, and the Hours of the Passion*, ed.
J. Meadows Cowper, EETS, o.s., 60 (London: N. Trübner, 1875), e.g., lines 783–86: "For whan

As in the conversion story and the shameful Compassion, however, a fully adequate understanding of the *Book*'s purposes here can be achieved only by distinguishing more precisely between the mere presence of conventional elements and the unconventional emphasis and manipulation which characterizes Margery's narrative. Its departure from the main-line tradition of Compassion narratives is marked by the phrase "wondyrfully turnyng & wrestyng," a phrase not found in the seminal works above mentioned, the *Gesta Pilati* and the *Meditationes vitae Christi*, not even in Manning's lively paraphrase. The phrase, indeed the entire iconographic complex, has obvious erotic overtones which it shares with many other late-medieval Passion meditations; it shares too an intellectual derivation from Simeon's prophecy, in which the Virgin is transfixed by sorrow's sword. More significant in the present context, however, is that the phrase "wondyrfully wrestyng" also is highly suggestive of a woman laboring with child.

Other passages in the vita which describe Margery's compassionate weeping lend support to this interpretation. The first association of her weeping with writhing, though not yet with the loud cries, occurs in a chapter preceding the Jerusalem narrative which recounts Margery's visit to Norwich. Margery is instructed by Christ to seek out the sympathetic vicar of Saint Stephen's and reveal to him her visionary experiences, which the narrative thus summarizes: "Her dalyawns was so swet, so holy, & so devowt þat þis creatur myt not oftyn-tymes beryn it but fel down & wrestyd wyth hir body & mad wondyrful cher & contenawns wyth boystows sobbyngys & gret plente of terys, sumtyme seyng 'Ihesu, mercy,' sum-tyme 'I dey'" (p. 40). What makes the description particularly significant is its larger context; Margery's journey to Norwich had begun in childbirth and with her deliverance from the labor of bearing child: "On a day long befor þis tyme, whyl thys creatur was beryng chylder & sche was newly delyueryd of a chyld, owyr Lord Cryst Ihesu seyd to hir sche xuld no more chyldren beryn, & þerfor he bad hyr gon to Norwych" (p. 38). The appearance of the language of labor at this moment of Margery's life story suggests that her compassionate weeping is being conceived as an alternative,

---

she say hym drawe to ende, / Y leue she wax oute of here mynde; / She swouned, she pyned, she wax half dede, / She fylle to þe grounde, and beete here hede."

spiritual childbirth. This conception is made explicit in a transitional passage between the two accounts of Margery's weeping on Calvary which describes her customary practice of the Compassion. Margery, the narrative relates, was aware of the criticism elicited by her weep-ing, now combined with the loud cries:

And þerfor, whan sche knew þat sche xulde cryen, sche kept it in as long as sche mygth & dede al þat sche cowde to withstond it er ellys to put it a-wey til sche wex as blo as any leed, & euyr it xuld labowryn in hir mende mor and mor in-to þe tyme þat it broke owte. &, whan þe body myth ne lengar en-duryn þe gostly labowr but was ouyrcome wyth þe vnspekabyl lofe þat wrowt so feruently in þe sowle, þan fel sche down & cryed wondyr lowde. & þe mor þat sche wolde laborwyn to kepe it in er to put it a-wey, much þe mor xulde sche cryen & þe mor lowder. (pp. 69–70)

Once established, this representation of Margery's Compassion becomes paradigmatic. The same iconographic complex – weeping, writhing, loud cries, exclamations of "I die" – recurs in the description of Margery's Compassion at Rome, immediately following her return from Jerusalem, and again some years later at Lynn.[18]

The interpretation of Margery's Compassion as a spiritual childbirth is, then, remarkable for its consistency and intensity, the latter indeed to the point of scandal. Nevertheless, despite these features, and despite the fact that it is not characteristic of main-line Compassion narratives, the interpretation of Margery's *Book* once again must be considered distinctive rather than devotionally or doctrinally aberrant. A clue to its orthodox meaning can be recognized in the Compassion narrative of the *Mirour de l'Omme*; for although Gower does not actu-ally describe the Virgin's suffering in the language of childbirth labor, he does state the association in explicit terms (lines 29110–12):

> O tu virgine et mere seint,
> Le dolour de la femme enseinte
> A ta dolour n'est resemblant.

[O thou, Virgin and Holy Mother, the grief of a pregnant woman to your grief is not comparable.]

This devotional exclamation of Gower's meditator is rooted in estab-

[18] See *Book*, p. 98/10–17, and pp. 98/27–99/3 (at Rome) and p. 140/11–29 (at Lynn).

lished doctrine, specifically, in the idea that the Virgin suffered at Christ's Passion the pains not suffered at his birth. The doctrinal idea, perhaps most familiar to the later Middle Ages from the Eastertide hymn "Stabat iuxta crucem Christi,"[19] in its turn is derived from the conception of Mary as the antitype of the laboring woman in Old Testament prophecy. Its most favorable prophetic context, the one most amenable to association with the Virgin, is provided by Micah's identification of the woman as the suffering daughter of Jerusalem (Micah 4.10):

> Dole et satage, filia Sion, quasi parturiens,
> Quia nunc egredieris de civitate,
> Et habitabis in regione,
> Et venies usque ad Babylonem.
> Ibi liberaberis,
> Ibi redimet te Dominus de manu inimicorum tuorum.

[Be in pain and labour, O daughter of Sion, as a woman that bringeth forth: for now shalt thou go out of the city, and shalt dwell in the country, and shalt come even to Babylon, there thou shalt be delivered: there the Lord will redeem thee out of the hand of thy enemies.][20]

The existence of this group of devotional and doctrinal materials can explain the otherwise casual-seeming allusions one occasionally finds in descriptions of the ritual lamentation practiced by saintly women and pilgrims to Jerusalem. In the life of Saint Mary of Oignies, for example, a life certainly known to the priestly amanuensis if not also to Margery, Jacques de Vitry writes of the saint's confession that she "more parturientis cogebatur proclamare"—or, as the Middle English translation states even more explicitly, she was "constreyned to crye loude in maner of a womman trauelynge of childe."[21] Similarly, in the pilgrimage

[19] The idea is most concisely stated in stanza 6 of variant 58bC of the hymn in *Analecta Hymnica Medii Aevi, VIII: Sequentae Ineditae. Liturgische Prosen des Mittelalters*, ed. Guido Maria Dreves (Leipzig: Fue's Verlag, 1890): "Nunc extorquet cum usura / Gemitus, quos paritura / Natura detinuit."

[20] The Latin is cited from *Biblia Sacra iuxta Vulgatem Clementinam, nova editio*, ed. Alberto Colunga, O.P., and Laurentio Turrado (Madrid: Biblioteca de Autores Cristianos, 1965), and the translation from the Douay-Rheims version in the 1971 Tan reprint.

[21] Cited by Allen, p. 323, from the *Vita* as printed in the *Acta Sanctorum*, June 23, p. 551E. For the priest's reading of Saint Mary's life, see again his account on pp. 152–54.

narrative of Margery's contemporary Felix Fabri, the traveler, in the course of describing the grief expressed by his companions in the Holy City, remarks: "Super omnes autem mulieres peregrinae sociae nostrae et sorores quasi parturientes clamabant, ullulabant et flebant" ("Above all, however, our fellow pilgrims the wives and sisters, as if giving birth, cried out, wailed and wept").[22]

The effect of these allusions by Fabri and Jacques de Vitry is to associate the laments of their female subjects with the maternal agony of the Virgin; these women are thus represented as experiencing a realization of the Marian Compassion which is similar in devotional principle to the realization of Margery Kempe. The fact remains, however, that the allusions of the pilgrim's diary and saint's life are local ones whereas the allusions to childbirth labor in Margery's *Book* have a system and complexity which renders them qualitatively distinct. If, therefore, our typological analysis of the Jerusalem sequence can conclude with an identification of the devotional topos, psychohistorical analysis must search further to discover its inner rationale. The motives of Saint Mary Oignies and Fabri's pilgrims must remain forever hidden from us, but in the case of Margery Kempe the evidence seems clear. At Jerusalem Margery is reenacting her own harsh labor of childbirth, the labor unto madness, and almost unto death, with which her vita begins. By reexperiencing the pains of labor at the scene of Christ's Passion, Margery confesses to and atones for the "great sin against her Lord," the sin of female sexuality, which labor in childbirth punishes. Simultaneously, however, Margery cancels both the sin and the legacy of shame. For by reexperiencing her labor pains at the scene of the Virgin's Compassion, Margery demonstrates her passage beyond Eve's biological maternity to achieve a maternity suprasexual and faultlessly pure.

On Margery's arrival in Rome from Jerusalem, she attempts to symbolize her passage from Eve's state to Mary's by assuming the white mantle of virginity "as sche was comawndyd for to do ȝerys be-forn in her sowle be reuelacyon, & now it was fulfilt in effect" (p. 80). The consequence of Margery's self-investiture is that the redefinition of her

---

[22] The Latin text is cited from Fratris Felicis Fabri, *Evagatorum in Terrae Sanctae, Arabiae et Egypti Peregrinationem*, ed. Conrad D. Hassler (Stuttgart: Bibliothek des Literarischen Vereins, 2, 1843), 1.239 (my translation).

womanly nature can no longer be dismissed as a private fantasy; it becomes a direct challenge to the ecclesiastical and secular ideologies of her world. For what Margery is claiming as a common married woman is the right to choose freely her mode of existence and to choose from among options ordinarily denied to those of her estate. Her assertion of autonomy might have found easier acceptance had she limited her choice to chaste marriage, an effective widowhood. But Margery here insists on her right to attain absolute perfection at the expense of violating the established categories of her time. And, as the self-created oxymoron of a married virgin, she becomes a thorn in the contemporary flesh. Speaking for the ecclesiastical establishment, an English priest stirs up her countrymen against her on the grounds that "sche weryd white clothyng mor þan oþer dedyn whech wer holyar & bettyr þan euyr was sche" (p. 84). He persuades her confessor, a German priest, to command her to disrobe and resume the customary black clothing, whereupon, for her presumption, she "suffyrd...many scornys of wyfys of Rome. Þei askyd hir ȝyf malendrynes [highwaymen] had robbyd hir, & sche seyd, 'Nay, madame'" (p. 85).

The gathering of Roman wives into a scornful circle around the heroine is a pictorial image with multiple implications. It evokes, once again, the Mocking of Christ and the Virgin; it testifies, like the priest's censure, to the world's resistance to the violation of its categories; but it also justifies Margery's action in a way that the priest's criticism cannot do. For the gathering of Roman wives is a gathering of women held in subjection. Their scorn expresses the resentment of colluders in the system at another's attempt to escape the bonds with which they have been bound. Like all other such colluders, the scorning wives have secured the support of established authority, but they have purchased external authority only by sacrificing their own. The content of the wives's scorn bespeaks a profound and unwitting self-degradation: not only does it consign secular women to a perpetual fleshly service; it reveals, through the imperceptivity of its judgment, that the wives are themselves confined mentally to the fleshly realm. In rejecting Margery for her assertion of freedom from wedlock and childbearing, the wives fail to heed the darker warning in Christ's speech to the Daughters of Jerusalem. But Margery Kempe, mayor's daughter of Lynn, has not failed to heed this warning, and she has responded from within her resources to its implication. Arrayed in black, Margery patiently endures the wives' mockery, and thereby she transforms the function of the old reproach of barrenness. It now becomes the basis of her claim to a New Testamental fame: "'For behold, the days are coming in which they will say: "Blessed are the barren, and the wombs that never bore, and the breasts that never gave suck"'" (Luke 23.29).

In the Apostle's Church at Rome, in 1414, on the feast day of Saint John Lateran, Margery the spouse of Jesus was married privately to the Godhead. Following the ceremony Margery was commanded to resume the virginal mantle, and finally her German confessor agreed to authorize her inward command: "& so weryd sche white clothys euyr aftyr" (p. 92).[23] Margery Kempe, in this consummation, reveals that she did not escape the system which had molded her; yet in a special sense, she was a woman who triumphed in her destiny. By affronting the authority of the patriarchal establishment with her hysteria – her woman's disease of womb-suffering – Margery transcended its cure.

---

[23] The narrative contradicts the finality of this statement, however, since Margery's actual procurement of white clothing does not occur until after her arrival in England (p. 104). Her garb continues to provoke criticism and, during the tense period 1415-17, to invite suspicion of Lollardy (see esp. p. 116).

"Ore pur parler del array de une graunt mangerye": The Culture of the "Newe Get," Circa 1285

CONSTANCE B. HIEATT
University of Western Ontario

Tell me what you eat: I will tell you what you are.
—Brillat-Savarin

N ENGLAND by the end of the thirteenth century a distinctively English culture had emerged, one common to native
speakers of both English and Anglo-Norman French and independent of Continental French culture. One area in
which this can be seen to be true is a vital one of domestic customs.
Food, its methods of preparation and manner of serving, is, as readers
of Lévi-Strauss[1] will realize, a basic clue to culture. It is true that the
French component in early English culinary terms is obvious, and indeed many medieval English recipes read like slightly elaborated translations of Continental French examples,[2] but if one compares the large
collections of such recipes from the fourteenth and fifteenth centuries,
it is immediately obvious that more than half of the most frequently

---

[1] See, e.g., Claude Lévi-Strauss, Le Cru et le cuit (Paris, 1964).

[2] French recipes of the fourteenth century can be found in Le Viandier de Guillaume Tirel dit
Taillevent, ed. Jérôme Pichon and George Vicaire (Paris, 1892); and Le Ménagier de Paris, composé
vers 1393 par un Bourgeois Parisien, ed. Jérôme Pichon (Paris, 1896; the menus and recipes are in
vol. 2); and, in part, Eileen Power, trans., The Goodman of Paris (London, 1928; contains fewer
than half of the recipes). The most readily accessible collection of English material is in Two
Fifteenth-Century Cookery-Books, ed. Thomas Austin, EETS, o.s., 91 (London, 1888, reprint,
1964). Two rarer (and much older) volumes contain a selection of fourteenth-century recipes: The
Forme of Cury, ed. Samuel Pegge (London, 1780), and Antiquitates Culinariae: Tracts on Culinary
Affairs of the Old English, ed. Richard Warner (London, 1791; reprints Pegge's recipes and some
from an earlier volume published by the Society of Antiquaries, reproducing all the errors of the
books reprinted and introducing some new ones). An edition of fourteenth-century English
recipes, including those previously printed and many never before edited, is in preparation by
Constance B. Hieatt and Sharon Butler, and will soon be published by the EETS.

repeated recipes are in fact peculiar to one country or the other.[3] It is possible that part of this observable divergence is simply a gap in documentation and that further research may bring to light French versions of some "English" specialties, but menus of the period are well represented from both countries, and these present evidence of strong differences between French and English practice.

That this difference goes back into the thirteenth century and originates in Anglo-Norman circles can be seen in a work of early English literature much better known to students of Anglo-Norman than to Middle English specialists, the "Treatise of Walter of Bibbesworth," or, as it is described in one of the manuscripts, "la treytez ke moun sire Gauter de Bibelesworth fist."[4] Written toward the end of the thirteenth century,[5] this work is a sort of cross between a *nominale* (a word list giving equivalents in the other language of common vocabulary) and a courtesy book: the introductory remarks which appear at the beginning of a few of the manuscripts state that it was intended to give instruction in French terminology for young people. The fuller versions consist of over 1,100 lines of Anglo-Norman verse, discussing such matters as the parts of the body, items of clothing, household objects, and so forth, with hints on proper etiquette. Some interlinear and marginal Middle English glosses appear in many of the manuscripts, and in one, which gives only the last part of the *Treatise*, the Anglo-Norman couplets alternate with a Middle English prose translation. Fortunately, this section is the one we are concerned with here, the description of a feast.

The *Treatise* has, of course, considerable philological interest to stu-

---

[3] The extent of the difference was first pointed out to me by Brenda Thaon, who translated *Pleyn Delit: Medieval Cookery for Modern Cooks*, by Constance B. Hieatt and Sharon Butler (Toronto, 1976) into French (*Pain, vin et veneison: un livre de cuisine médiévale*, Montreal, 1977). We had assumed that Thaon could find French equivalents in the *Viandier* and the *Ménagier* to substitute for most of the Middle English recipes printed in the original book, but that turned out not to be the case; surprisingly few of the English recipes correspond to anything in either French collection.

[4] The name of the author is variously spelled in the manuscripts: in Cambridge University Library MS Gg.1.1., for example, it appears as Gauter de Bitheswey. For the identification with Bibbysworth, Kimpton, Herts., see W. Aldis Wright, *Notes & Queries*, 4th ser. (1877), p. 64.

[5] According to the headnote referred to above, for the lady Dionysia de Munchensi, who died in 1304; this and other evidence point to a date for the *Treatise* between 1280 and 1290.

dents both of Anglo-Norman and of Middle English, whose fields here are interdependent – that is, sometimes the Middle English scholar can provide the vital clue to the meaning of the Anglo-Norman, and vice versa. A point which may not be as clear is the cultural information to be gleaned here, for that depends on comparison with French and later English sources of information. One important aspect is that the order of a formal banquet in medieval England differed from that usual in France throughout the period for which sufficient evidence is available, which means from the late thirteenth century on. The distinctively "English" order was already fixed in the thirteenth century, for there is absolutely no difference between the order to be found in the *Treatise* and that to be observed in such later sources as menus of banquets of the courts of Richard II and Henry IV[6] and literary descriptions such as that of the feast near the beginning of the alliterative *Morte Arthure*.[7]

A primary distinction is that French medieval banquets characteristically started with small delicacies much like the modern hors d'oeuvres, but no particular type of food is characteristically to be found in one and only one course of the usual two to four courses.[8] In English menus, on the other hand, the first course invariably consists of simpler foods, such as plain boiled or roasted meats (beef, venison, pork, and so forth) with such basic "pottages" as pease pottage or frumenty. During the sequence of the following courses – almost invariably making a total of three – the English menu becomes progressively more complicated, ending with the sweetest and richest confections. Certain dishes, if they appear on an English menu at all, always appear in the same positions. Boars' heads are always brought on first, and after a boar's head one usually finds venison, invariably accompanied by frumenty; this combination almost never appears later on the menu, as it often did in France.[9] On the other hand, fritters and similar complicated dishes, which could make an appearance in the first course (or elsewhere) on a French menu, are found only in the last course of the English menu.

[6] See, e.g., *Two Fifteenth-Century Cookery Books*, pp. 57–59, 67–68.

[7] Lines 176–242 in the edition of Valerie Krishna (New York, 1976), pp. 45–47.

[8] For sample menus see *Le Ménagier de Paris*, 2.91–108; and *Le Viandier*, pp. 194–199.

[9] Note that in the *Ménagier*'s menu on p. 98, "la teste de senglier à l'entremès" appears in the last course, as does venison with frumenty in several menus, quite contrary to English custom.

The witness, then, of the thirteenth-century *Treatise* is valuable evidence of the early emergence and persistence of a peculiarly English culinary culture, however "French" the terms used may seem. Unfortunately, no edition of the *Treatise* published to date is complete or accurate enough to convey all this information clearly.[10] I therefore thought it appropriate to make a "mini-edition" of the relevant (last) portion, collating all the manuscripts known to me and including the Middle English translation to present this information as fully as possible to all who might be interested — perhaps, it might be hoped, to show some who might not think they were in that group to become so.

The "edition" which follows is based on nine manuscripts now in English libraries, all of which I have had an opportunity to examine. I have not seen a tenth manuscript that includes this section of the *Treatise*, which is in Paris, and it is, of course, possible that there are others which have not come to my attention. The nine manuscripts consulted, with the designations used in notes and commentary hereafter, are:

W   British Library Additional 46919
G   Cambridge University Library Gg. 1.1.
T   Trinity College, Cambridge o.2.21
A   Arundel 220
H   Harley 740
S   Sloane 809
O   All Souls (Oxford) 182
Se Selden Supra (Bodleian) 74
B   Trinity College, Cambridge B 14 40

The order listed above will be, generally, the order of references in the notes. Manuscript B is listed last because it is the unique manuscript giving a Middle English translation; this translation, which is given in a parallel-column format, logically comes after the Anglo-Norman texts.

---

[10] The most recent edition is that edited by Annie Owen, "Le traité de Walter de Bibbesworth sur la langue français" (Ph.D. diss., University of Paris, 1929; reprinted, Geneva, 1977); this gives variants from many manuscripts, but does not actually give all significant variants or all glosses and has, in the brief section I have checked carefully (that here presented), a number of errors in transcription and typographical errors. Less satisfactory, though perhaps more easily accessible in some areas, is the older edition (based on only three MSS) by Thomas Wright, in *A Volume of Vocabularies* (London, 1857), pp. 142–74.

The manuscripts which have been used as bases for the printed editions are G (Owen) and A (Wright). T is one of the earliest and probably represents a base for the largest related group, T A H Se, all of
which agree more often than not.[11]

I have, however, preferred as my own base W, the only manuscript
for which we can confidently give the name of the scribe as well as the
date in the first quarter of the fourteenth century. It is of unusual importance to students of both Anglo-Norman and Middle English literature of the early fourteenth century, for it is the famous collection
made under the supervision of, and partly in the hand of, William
Herebert of Hereford: the *Treatise* is the first entry in the manuscript
and is in the hand of William Herebert.[12] It is written in a two-column
format, with points at the end of almost every line (rather unhelpfully).
In presenting this text with modern punctuation, I have been forced to
make one rather illogical conjunction; but this problem is discussed
below in the commentary on line 12.

W	B
Ore pur parler del array de	
une graunt mangerye.	

Un vallet de la novelerie	A ȝoman of þe newe get
Qui vient de une graunt mangerie	Þat cometh fram a gret feste

N.B.: Dozens of spelling variants are omitted here because they would have taken up several
more pages.

    Rubric: **Ore...mangerye}** *underlined in MS* Ore le fraunceis pur un feste araer G   Ore
pur haute feste araier S   *om.* T A H O Se B

    1. **Un}** Dun Se   **vallet}** "ȝoman" O   **novelerie}** "newvay" O

    2. **Qui}** *om.* T A H O S Se   **vient de une}** vint her de un G T A H S Se B   hery vient
dun "ȝesterday come fro" O   **graunt}** *om.* G T A H Se

  [11] On the basis of the section here presented, I cannot quite agree with Owen's analysis of
manuscript "families" (pp. 34–37); in this passage, aside from the group mentioned above, there
seems to be a close correspondence between MSS W and B, with O almost as close. MSS G and
S are the two which seem to overlap groups, falling mainly with the T group but giving some
verses peculiar to the W group.

  [12] This manuscript, now B.L. Add. 46919, contains works of great importance in both Middle
English and Anglo-Norman, with a tantalizing "table of contents" of somewhat later date (that is,
late fourteenth-century) which includes some items not to be found in the manuscript today, including "Valerius ad Rufinum de uxore non ducenda." For fuller information on the manuscript
see B. Schofield, "The Manuscript of a Fourteenth Century Oxford Franciscan," *British Museum
Quarterly* 16 (1952):36–37; and Paul Meyer, "Notice et Extraits du ms. 8336 de la Bibliothèque
de Sir Thomas Phillips à Cheltenham," *Romania* 13 (1884):497–541.

& de la feste nous ad countee,   Of þe feste me haþ y-told,

Come lour service fust arraee.   As hare service was arayde.

Sanz pain & vin ou cervoyse   Withoute bred & withoute goud ale   5

Ne serra nuls a feste a eise.   Ne shal man at feste be wel at eze.

Mais au meins fait a saver   But of oðer þyng hyt ys to wyte

Du cours quil eurent a primer: Of þe cours þat was fyrst:
         "i-armed"

La teste du cengler armee   Þe heved of þe boor y-armed
         "Þe wrot ful of banieres"

& pus le groign plein baneree.   And þe groyn wel y-bannereth.   10
         "mid þe wheete"

Puis veneysoun oue le furmente   After vensoun wyþ furmente
         "sundrinesse"

Puis mainte autre diversete   An after oþer diversite

Assez parmy la mesoun

"of grece tyme and taken out of grece"

De grese & de enfermeysoun,
         "cranes pecokes swannes"

Des gruwes, poouns, & cynes,   Of cranes, pokokys, & swanes,   15

3. &} om. B   nous} moy B   ad countee} "has tolde" O

4. Come} E cum S   Coment T O   service} feste S add y O   arraee} "araied" O adreste Se

5. pain} "bred" O   &} om. G O Se   vin} "wyn" O   vin ou} sanz bon B   ou} e G A H S   cervoyse} "ale" O

6. Ne} om. Se   nuls a} nule Se   homme al B   feste} add ben B   a eise} "at ese" O
After line 6: All MSS except W B Se add a couplet, as follows: Mes tut treis mout en liz (multz elitz A H) / Il eveyent (en hurent G) nos ad diz G A H   Mes tous tres ny out ellyz "chosin" / Il aveyent mys a dyz T   Mes de ceo i avore a grante plente / Cum li vadlett nous ad countee S   Mes de ce ny "non" ad mestrer "mist or nede" / Grande matiere ad escuter "herken" O

7. Mais} om. S   au miens fait} dautre chose fet S B   de autre feste G   saver} parler G S B   Mais...saver} Eins vous dirrey du primour cours "firste cours" O   om. T A H Se

8. eurent} ont S   fent B   primer} manger G   aymer S   D...primer} Au primour fut aporte T A H Se   Dont homme servoit le grande senours O   *The symbol* ❡ *precedes this line and lines 19 and 27*

9. La} "a" A   Primes la G   teste} "hede" O   teste...cengler} "bores heved" T A S cengler} "bore" O   armee} en arme T H Se   ben arme G S O   "wel armed" O

10. pus} E au A H   om. G B   groign} "groyn" O   "þe snout" S   plein} ben B   le coler en T A H   les colets en Se   baneree} "wit baneres of floures" T A   "flowrede" O

11. Puis} E pus T A   om. S   veneysoun} "veneson" O   oue} od S Se   furmente} "furmonte" O

12. Pus mainte} Et puis B   mainte} vient O   Puis...diversete} om. T A H Se

13-14. Assez...enfermeysoun} *In MS these lines come after line 2 at the bottom of the left-hand column, with notations here and in the next column to insert them here*   om. G S O B

14. grese &} treste "taken of gres tyme" A   enfermeysoun} "take out of time" T fermysoun H

15. Des} om. G T A H S   gruwes} add e T

"kides" "pigges"	
Chevereaus, purceaus, & gelynes.	Kydes, pygges, & hennes.
Puis avoient conyns en gravee	After þey hadde conies in gravey
"bidrenkt"	
Trestout de zucre enfoundree	Ful wel in zeugre y-foundre.
& puis tout autre foisoun de rost,	After þey hadde oþer fusoun of rost,
"bisiden oþer"	
Cheascun de emis autre encost:	Every tuo in oþer side: 20
Feisaunz, ascyez, & perdriz	Fesantez, wodekockes, & perdryches,
"larken"	
Gryves, alouwes, & plovers rostis;	Felfares, larkes, & alle y-rostud;
Braoun, crespes, & fruture,	Brawon, crispis, & freturys,
"þe mienging"	
Oue zucre roset la temprure,	With zeugre roset in temprure,
Maces, quibebes, clougilofrez,	Macez, quibibz, & cloues gylofre, 25
& dautre espiecerye assez;	And of oþer spicez ynowȝ;

16. Chevereaus} Houhes rosers T   Owes, rosees "wilde ges" A   Oues roseus H
Owesrosers Se   purceaus} "grise" O S   gelynes} "hennes" G O

17. Puis} Au ters T A H Se   add cours A H Se   conyns} "conynges" O   gravee}
"gravy" O

18. Trestout} "al" O   de} en B   zucre} "sukre" O   Trestout . . . zucre} E viande
de cypre T A H Se   but see note below on couplet missing here   enfoundree} "ȝoten" O

After 18: Add Viaunde de Cypre e maumene / Vin vermaile e blaunc a plente G   maces
quybibes clowe gelofrees / E dautre espicerie assez S   De maces e kubibes e clous dorree / Vin
blaunke e vermayl a (od Se) grant plentee T A H Se

19. &} om. G S B   tout} y ont O   y ount B   tout . . . de} aveyent diversetes en T Se
autre foisoun} diversite A H   foisoun de rost} "plenty of rost" O

19-20. & . . . encost} *These lines are inserted between what are here lines 14 and 15 in*
T A H Se

20. Cheascun} Sys checun T A Se   Assys chescun H   "ilkon" O   de emis} de eus G
deus S O   deeux B   cours O   om. T A H Se   autre encost} autre de cost T H Se   dautre de
cost A   en autre cost B   "þe toþer side" O   encost} en couste G

21. Feisaunz} "fesantz" O   E T H Se   pus aveyent fesaunz T A H Se   add e T   ascyez}
dasciez B   om. Se   "wodecok" A O   "woddekoches" G   perdriz} "pertrikis" O

22. Gryves} add e T   "feldefare" G   grues "cranes" O   plovers} add ben T   toutz B
plovers rostiz} "plovers rosted" O

After line 22: Add: Merles, "osels" vis de coqs, "cock" & mauvys "thrustelles" / Et des altres
oiseux "briddes" que nomer "name" ne puis O

23. Braoun} E T A braun et T A H "braun" O   crespes} trespes "tripes" O
fruture} "frutours" O   crispis} cuspis B

24. Oue} od S ke A   zucre} "sucre" O   roset} add poudre T A H   la} en B
temprure} "tempered" O   Od . . . temprure} Pur fere lour amesure Se

25. Maces} De maces T A H Se   quibebes} add e G T B   clougilofrez} clous dorree
T A H S Se   *and note that this line comes after what is here line 18 in* T A H S Se, *as noted above*

25-26. Maces . . . assez} *This couplet appears after line 18 but before the indented couplet noted
above in* G; *in* O *its order is reversed with the next couplet (lines 27-28)*

26. dautre} autre G S   des aultres O B   assez} "ynoghe" O   & . . . assez} om.
T A H Se

Et quant la table fu oustee,	And whanne þe table was y-led.
Blaunche poudre oue la grosse dragee	Gret poudre wyþ goud dragge
& dautre nobleie a fuisoun.	And of oþer nobley was fuson.
Ensi vous finyst le sarmoun	And now y ende here my resoun. 30
Car de fraunzoys i a assez	
De mult de manere diversetez,	
Dont vous finyst, seygnours, en taunt:	
Au Fyz Dieu vous trestouz comaunk.	

   Explicit ut supra dictum est, & c.

---

27. table} "bord" O   fu} fuist B   fu oustee} "taken up" O   Et...oustee} Apres manger aveyent a [*om.* Se] grant plentee T A H Se

28. **Blaunche**} Grant B   **Blaunche poudre**} "white poudre" *add* ont O   **oue**} od S od la} en G   la} *om.* O   la grosse} bon B   grosse dragee} "grete dragge" O   Blaunche ...dragee} *last line of* T A H Se

29. dautre} *om.* O   a} fuist B   fuisoun} "plenty" O

30. finyst} "y endis" O   le} ceste G S O   sarmoun} "þis tale" O   Ensi... sarmoun} Et ore finie icy ma resoun B; *last line of* B

31. a} ad S

32. de} de *om.* O   E de meinte G

33. Dont} *add* le S   en} a O

34. Fyz..trestouz} Jhesu Crist toutz vois O   vous trestouz} trestuz vous G trestouz} *om.* S

    1.   The Middle English "newe get" ("latest fashion"; cf. Chaucer's Pardoner, who thought "he rood al of the newe jet") is, in this context, a more attractive gloss on *novelerie* than any I have seen noted in an OF dictionary.

    2–3.   MSS W, G, and O, unlike other MSS, include both the *qui* of line 2 and the *et* of line 3; for the sentence to make grammatical sense, one or the other must be dropped.

    5.   Wine "with" or, as in most of the MSS, "and" ale is probably the true meaning here. Records of the period make it clear that, while more ale than wine was consumed, both were invariably served in aris-tocratic households (see, e.g., the household records of Eleanor, Countess of Leicester, for the year 1265, in *Manners and Household Expenses of England in Thirteenth and Fifteenth Centuries* [London, 1841; Roxburghe Club, Vol. 57] and the household "Rules" attributed to Robert Grosseteste, Bishop of Lincoln [mid-thirteenth century] in Dorothy Oschinsky, ed., *Walter of Henley* [Oxford, 1971], p. 404). In MS W, as frequently elsewhere in A–N, *ou* is frequently used as equivalent to *od* ("with").

After line 6. Most versions of this couplet seem to be confused. The G reading of the first line makes good sense if we can consider *liz* to be a spelling of *lez* and translate "there was plenty of all three on the side," since that is where these items probably belonged. Bishop Grosse-teste's "Rules," for example, say (p. 404) that ale was to go under the table and wine on the side tables, except at the high table, where both ale and wine were to be set before the lord and/or lady. If, on the other hand, *elitz* ("chosen") is the correct reading, the constructions offer difficulties, but the meaning may be that there were plenty of "choice" examples.

7. G's "de autre feste" appears to be a misreading of something like the SB version; as it stands, it suggests that we are now going to hear about an entirely different feast, which scarcely seems sensible.

9. In Middle English recipes, "armed" means "larded"; for example, "Cranes and herouns shul be armed with lardes of swyne" (before roasting) (*The Forme of Cury*, no. 146 in the editions of Pegge and Warner).

10. The *puis* of W, O, and S is undesirable since the snout is part of the head, not something to be brought in afterward. The gloss in three MSS suggests, probably correctly—particularly considering the version in T A H Se, referring to a collared effect—that "bannered" means "garlanded with flowers," but the use of "banner" here probably explains the origin of the term "standard" used in later menus for a featured dish, usually described as a "standard." A boar's head, frequently the first dish on a feast menu, is often said to be "standard" for the first course on English menus. Continental French menus do not use the term *baneree*; when a boar's head is a featured dish, it is "la teste de senglier à l'entremès," *entremès* or *entremetz* being the word used to describe elaborate or spectacular dishes, including those that English sources call "subtleties" (*Le Ménagier de Paris*, p. 98; note, however, that a boar's head was not a popular dish in France; this is the only mention of it in the *Ménagier*, and there is no reference at all in the *Viandier*).

11. This line is another example of the use of *oue* in the sense of "with"; the gloss "mid" is certainly correct. Venison and furmety (also spelled *frumenty* etc.; as the gloss says, a dish of boiled wheat) are not alternatives but a traditional pair in French culinary directions and

menus as well as in English equivalents (see the *Ménagier*, p. 211n.; and *Viandier*, pp. 15–16).

12. This line is needed to complete a couplet in all MSS except those which have omitted line 7; W, however, is the only MS that includes the line which follows it with the couplet of lines 13–14, and in this context it is disruptive: *enfermeysoun* is the closed season for deer, and line 14 refers back to line 11, yet the *autre diversete* of line 12 points forward to lines 15–16. That lines 13–14 are out of place in the MS (see collations for these lines) may be evidence for Owen's view that this MS is mixing two separate types; however, the couplet could conceivably have coexisted with line 12 if the two couplets were exchanged in position, though a slight modification of line 11 would then be necessary. This would not be the only case where an introductory *puis* was not the right word in context.

13. That enough of this particular dish was provided to serve the entire household implies that such was not necessarily the case with all the later dishes. Choicer foods were often provided in quantities which would provide servings only for the head of the household and his (or her) most honored guests. Bishop Grosseteste's household rules for the Countess of Lincoln advise that the lady order her dish to be generously heaped with the more delicate foods so "that you may courteously give from your dish to right and left to all at high table and to whom else it pleases you that they have the same as you had in front of you" (pp. 404–405).

14. A's *treste* probably misrepresents an original *gresce*—an easy confusion in many hands of this period; cf., e.g., O's misreading of *crespes* in line 23. In any case, the glosses on this line must be confused: why would anyone have eaten illegal (and probably tough, because not "in grease") venison taken out of season? It is most likely that the true original meaning of this line is parallel to a similar line in the alliterative *Morte Arthure*, "flesch fluriste of fermysoun" (line 180 [p. 46]), "flesh fattened during closed season," i.e., taken in the proper season after it has had a chance to become fat. Perhaps the *&* has been intruded into the line in error.

16. The MS pointing in A suggests that *owes rosees* are two separate items, but the gloss "wilde ges" appears to gloss both. It is highly unlikely that the word *rosees* occurring in the midst of this line could

refer to the elaborate dish (or sauce) elsewhere so titled in medieval culinary records, and it is probable that the phrase, however spelled, simply represents a misreading of *chevereaus* somehow or other. Perhaps *rosees-rosers*, etc., was understood to mean something like "brown" or "russet" (OF *rosset*).

17. *Puis* seems preferable to a variant indicating this to be the third course, because there is no previous indication of where a second course started, and if we try to divide the dishes which precede this line into two courses and leave everything which follows for the third, the division is clearly disproportionate. English menus of the four-teenth and fifteenth centuries, which, if they were meat menus, more often than not started with boar's head and venison and frumenty, in-variably include other simple meats in the first course. The second course usually featured more elaborate stews, such as "Conies in gravey," and more spectacular roasts – primarily large fowl. The third course generally included roasted small game birds, as well as more elegant fried and baked dishes, sometimes with some sweeter foods. It will be noted that the menu here follows this general order, as does that in the alliterative *Morte Arthure*, which also fails to give us the "course" divisions, though it also labels the "first" course as such. Possibly thirteenth- and fourteenth-century menus were not always divided into courses in the same way as the recorded historical menus; that is, perhaps the food was brought out in a sort of continuous suc-cession, not in three large batches. The only other extensive descrip-tion of a thirteenth-century English feast I have seen, that of Bartholo-meus Anglicus, does not number courses. It reads (in part): "First knives, spoons, and salts be set on the board, and then bread and drink, and many divers messes [dishes containing portions of food to serve to two or more diners]; . . . now wine and now messes of meat be brought forth and departed [apportioned]. At the last cometh fruit and spices, and when they have eaten, board, cloths, and relief [leftovers] are borne away" (in the translation of Trevisa, in Robert Steele, ed., *Medieval Lore: an epitome of the science, geography, animal and plant folk-lore and myth of the Middle Ages, being classified gleanings from the encyclopedia of Bartholomew anglicus on the properties of things* [London, 1893], p. 51).

18. The *Forme of Cury* recipe for "Connynges in gravey" calls for

both sugar in the "gravy" and more sugar sprinkled on the top as a gar-nish, which makes this reading of the line rather more likely than the variant; no recipe for the sweet dish known as "Viande de Cipre" (lit-erally, "Sweet-meat," so called from the sugar – "of Cyprus" – included to an unusual degree) calls for it to be "covered with" anything. On the other hand, however, the MSS which follow line 18 with the lines specifying spices, here lines 25–26, and, in the case of T A H Se, wines, have some logic in connection with Viande de Cypre, for it usu-ally had all these spices and wine too. But no recipe calls for both white and red wine, and G's specification of all these spices in a "Conies in gravey" recipe is very dubious for the early period; some of the earliest rabbit-in-gravy recipes do not even include sugar. On balance, the lines about spices fit well enough where they appear in W, while those about wine seem no better than a rather unnecessary filler, wherever they are.

After line 18: "Maumene" – variously spelled, but so most often in the earliest MSS – is a very common dish in English menus and recipe collections from the early fourteenth century on, as is the dish it is teamed with in this line, Viande de Cypre. Neither is attested in any French source – unlike "conies in gravey," which is a commonplace in France as well as in England. Thus with these two dishes MS G is ap-parently isolating two of the most distinctive and celebrated Anglo-Norman, as against French, dishes. Mawmenny was a dish of finely minced poultry in a spiced and colored sauce of wine and ground almonds; what made it essentially different from other minced dishes in similar sauces is hard to determine now, but it may have been teased to fine shreds: Warner suggested a derivation from Fr. *malmener* (*Two Fifteenth-Century Cookery Books*, p. 136), but the similar name of an Arabic dish makes this dubious. Owen's *maumerie* is mistranscribed; while *n* and *r* are easily confused in some hands, that is not the case here. The gloss of "malavasier, malmsey" advanced by Gerhard Schel-lenberg ("Bermerkungen zum Traité des Walter von Bibbesworth [Ph.D. diss., University of Berlin, 1933]) is simply misguided. The sec-ond inserted line, that concerning wine, may be suspected of being something of a metrical filler which could be inserted almost anywhere a rhyming line was needed to fill out a couplet, for we have already been informed about the supply of wine in lines 5ff. in most MSS.

20. While it is conceivable that W's *emis* is a spelling of *amis* and that the line can be taken as meaning "each of the friends sat next to the other," it seems more likely that this is a miscopying of *eus* and that what were next to each other were the various roast fowls—perhaps to be thought of as served two to a platter, which is frequently the case in contemporary pictures of tables being served with cooked fowl.

22. The O reading of "Grues" ("cranes") is clearly confused; cf. line 15, above.

After line 22: The best reason for including this couplet is that it mentions blackbirds and "mavis" (song thrushes), which were indeed eaten in England and France in this period. There is, however, an obvious problem here: *visdecoq* is a Norman-French term for a woodcock, a bird which has just been mentioned by another name, one which is glossed as "woodcock" a number of times in the *Treatise*, including MS O, which now glosses *visdecoq* (wrongly) as "cock."

23. The initial *E* of MSS T A H is clearly preferable here, since what follows in this line is not more roasts but a selection of fried foods, considered to be in an entirely different class by all culinary writers of the medieval period—including the medical authorities, who, like the medical men of our own day, disapproved of fried delicacies. *Braoun* in this context must mean fried cakes of minced flesh; I have not seen a recipe so titled, but "braun frytes" appears in at least one fourteenth-century menu in exactly the same context. Generally, "brawn" means lean flesh-meat; while the French editors of the *Viandier de Taillevent* and the *Ménagier de Paris* argue for the meaning "organ meats," the evidence in the texts they print suggests this to be a dubious conclusion—it is difficult, for example, to believe that a "Blanc-mengier" for invalids was made with chicken *livers* rather than chicken meat of the more usual kind. One note in the *Viandier* suggests "white meat of chicken" (p. 8), but the editors apparently did not notice that such a meaning was also demanded in many other uses.

24. "Sugar mixed with rosewater" is a candied confection for which recipes are found in both English and French medieval sources; e.g., *Ménagier*, p. 274. An English recipe will be printed in the forthcoming volume by Hieatt and Butler.

25. Note that this line, as noted above, appears in an entirely different context in MSS T A H Se, where it may be equally well justi-

fied. But spices of this sort were also eaten candied, "in confit," at the end of a meal. *Clougilofrez* ("cloves") is probably preferable to *clous dor-ree* ("gilded cloves"), since "gilded generally meant "coated with a golden coating," which would be the case with cloves only when they were used to stud a roast, such as a roast tongue, finished with a "golden" batter of egg and other ingredients (e.g., Longe de Buf, no. 43 in the "Ancient Cookery" section of Pegge–and Warner).

25–26. The order of O, which places these lines after the next couplet, may be preferable, if we are to judge by the witness of the next century or two, because such spices, along with "blaunche poudre" (a mixture of sugar and ground spices) and dragees (sugared almonds and the like) were later served only after the table had been "voided" (cleared). See, e.g., the household ordinances of Edward IV: "...the boarde avoyded when wafers come with Ypocras, or with other swete wynes. The King never takes a voyd of comfittes and other spices but standing" (*A Collection of Ordinances and Regulations for the Government of the Royal Household, Made in Divers Reigns, from King Edward III to King William and Queen Mary* [London: Society of Antiquaries, 1790], p. 36). The *Ménagier* speaks of such comfits as *espices de chambre*, which suggests that in France, too, they were taken after rising from the dinner table (pp. 112, 122; cf. also the alliterative *Morte Arthure*, which says that spices were served, with sweet wines, after "þey wesche and went unto chambyre [line 231 (p. 47)]). On the other hand, the witness of Bartholomeus Anglicus (see above, note to line 17) suggests that in the thirteenth century the spices came before the table was "voided"; this does not, however, explain why the spices and the "blaunche poudre" and "grosse dragee" are separated here, which there is no reason for them to be if the line about spices belongs in this part of the poem.

29. *Nobleie*, according to Tobler-Lomatzsch and other OF dic-tionaries, occurs nowhere else where it can be assigned a meaning com-parable to that which has been assumed here ("noble things," or something of the sort). A tempting conjecture is that someone has mis-copied *ou* as *uo-no*, thus turning *oubleie* ("wafer") into *nobleie*. Almost all later menus, French or English, include wafers at this point; in the French menus these are often called *oubleies*. If this was the original reading, then the O reading, omitting *dautre*, would (as in some earlier

cases where O seems to be better) be preferable. All we are missing to conform to later accounts of aristocratic dining habits is the *Ypocras* (sweet spiced wine) which should accompany the spices and wafers.

30–33. These lines evidently refer to the entire treatise (*le sar-moun*), not just the description of the feast.

Following is a translation of the Anglo-Norman text, based on W but including passages there omitted and using preferred variants and minor rearrangements suggested in the commentary above:

A fashionable yeoman who came from a great banquet has told us about the feast, how their service was ordered. Without bread and wine and ale, no one at a feast will be at ease, but there was plenty of all three on the side (or, of choice varieties) he has told us. But it is worth knowing about the course which they had first: the head of a boar, larded, with the snout well gar-landed, and enough for the whole household of venison fattened during the closed season, served with frumenty. And then there was a great variety of cranes, peacocks, and swans; kids, pigs, and hens. Then they had rabbits in gravy all covered with sugar, Viaunde de Cypre and Mawmenny, red and white wine in great plenty; and then quite a different multitude of roasts, each of them set next to another: pheasants, woodcocks, and partridges; fieldfares, larks, and roasted plovers; blackbirds and song-thrushes, and other birds I cannot name; and fried meat, crisps, and fritters, with sugar mixed with rosewater. And when the table was taken away, sweet spice powder with the large dragee, maces, cubebs, cloves, and enough other spicery and plenty of wafers. Now you have finished my discourse, for here in French there are enough of many diverse matters, which you have completely finished, gentlemen: I commend you all to the Son of God.[13]

---

[13] I am grateful to Brenda Thaon and Wolfgang van Emden for advice on various points in this essay, and especially to Robin Jones, who read the entire draft typescript. None of them, of course, is to be blamed for any blemishes in the final version.

Part Seven COURTLY LOVE

Chaucer, Love Poetry, and Romantic Love[1]

GEORGE KANE
University of North Carolina at Chapel Hill

Y CHAUCER'S LOVE POETRY I mean the dramatic love lyrics embedded in his narrative works and such of the narratives themselves as are concerned with emotional as well as physical arousal in the relation of the sexes, therefore love poetry objectively understood.

The immediate and obviously primary factor in the shaping of that love poetry is what a fairly recent book tells us to swallow our historical scruples and go on calling "courtly love." This it describes as "a comprehensive cultural phenomenon: a literary movement, an ideology, an ethical system, a style of life, and an expression of the play element in culture."[2] The description is too broad to be serviceable, too miscellaneous and too positive. I will offer another: what Chaucer once called "fyn lovynge,"[3] and what in the Auchinleck *Floris and Blauncheflor* is called "fin amour" (establishing the expression as Middle English),[4] was a shifting nexus of forms of thought and expression, associatively linked and reciprocally evocative in particular sets of ways, developed to express a fairly narrow class of emotions in the

[1] This venture into alien literary history is a gesture of gratitude to E. Talbot Donaldson for his "Myth of Courtly Love" (*Ventures* 5[1965]:16–23), which shocked me out of slothful acquiescence in the received opinions about the subject and set me trying to find out for myself.

[2] Roger Boase, *The Origin and Meaning of Courtly Love: A Critical Study of European Scholarship* (Manchester: Manchester University Press, 1977), pp. 129, 130.

[3] *LGWP* F 544, G 534. Chaucer references are to *The Works of Geoffrey Chaucer*, ed. F. N. Robinson, 2d ed. (Boston: Houghton Mifflin Co., 1957).

[4] Fol. 102*b*, col. *b*, line 37. The passage is printed in J. A. W. Bennett and G. Smithers, *Early Middle English Verse and Prose*, 2d ed. (Oxford: Clarendon Press, reprint ed., 1974), p. 50, line 268. And see *MED* s.v. *amour* n.(1)(c). This use takes away some of the force of Jean Frappier's argument in *Amour courtois et table ronde* (Geneva: Droz, 1973), p. 96, that we should reserve *fine amor* "à la sacralisation que l'on sait d'un amour en principe adultère." The marriage of Floris and Blauncheflor was made, it could be said, in heaven.

relation of the speaker of a poem with a woman or of lovers in a narrative; the forms of thought and expression being first found in any density in the twelfth-century lyrics called Provençal; having the appearance of conventionally established rhetorical and stylistic correlatives;
but in the poetry first of Provence, and then the imitating cultures,
represented as accepted values in the milieu where the relationship
was set.

Chaucer was interested in the manifestations of this phenomenon
transmitted to him and represented himself as puzzled by the lack of
definition in his understanding of it. "In nouncerteyn," says Troilus
(TC 1.337–38), jibing at lovers to keep his countenance, "ben alle
youre observaunces, But it a sely fewe pointes be" ("Your rites and
observances are all matters of uncertainty except, maybe, a few trifling
particulars"). Chaucer seems to have sensed that the phenomenon had
a history: the language of love changes with time and place, his narrator suggests near the beginning of Troilus, book 2 "for to wynnen
love in sondry ages, In sondry londes, sondry ben usages" (lines
27–28). He was familiar with the commonplaces about the perplexing
character of love. To match Bernart de Ventadorn's "Ai las! tan
cuidava saber / d'amor, et tan petit en sai,"[5] or Walther von der
Vogelweide's "Saget mir ieman, waz ist minne?"[6] there is the question
in his third Compleynt of Mars, "To what fyn made the God that sit so
hye, / Benethen him, love other companye?" "What was God's lofty
purpose in creating upon earth love or the relation of the sexes" when
they have no power to confer lasting happiness (lines 218–19)? His
locus classicus will have been Jean de Meun's long list of paradoxes
lifted from or imitating Alanus: love is a hateful peace, a security set in
anxiety, despairing hope, wise madness a joy full of misery, bitter
sweetness, and so on.[7] He knew the clichés: the power of love, the
folly of resisting it, how it improves the lover.[8] He could have resolved
the paradoxes philosophically or dismissed them by theological means.

[5] Can vei la lauzeta mover, lines 9, 10, in Moshé Lazar, ed., Bernard de Ventadour... Chansons
d'Amour (Paris: Klincksieck, 1966), p. 180.

[6] Poets of the Minnesang, ed. Olive Sayce (Oxford: Clarendon Press, 1967), p. 95. For a translation of the poem see Walther von der Vogelweide, Sprüche, Lieder, der Leich, ed. P. Stapf
(Wiesbaden: Vollmer, n.d.), pp. 306–11.

[7] RR 4703ff.

[8] TC 1.232–59.

That he chose rather to make literary capital of them and their contexts of convention—for which we must give thanks—bespeaks his interest not just naturally in the human experience to which fin amour
relates but also in its serviceability to the literary artist, and probably
also in its relation to actuality, observed experience.

The lack of definition in Chaucer's understanding of fin amour is not
surprising. First, total ambiguity, pretense, was a feature of the phenomenon from the outset. Second, acknowledgment of that ambiguity,
explicit in the work of the last generation of troubadours who wrote in
the *langue d'oc*, resulted in a profound change of attitudes in the poet-
speaker to the lady he addressed. Then presently the conventions
were subjected to successive modifications, whether actual or by selection and redistributed emphasis, by the French and Anglo-Norman
trouvères, by Chrétien de Troyes and his successors,[9] by the Italian
poets, by Guillaume de Lorris, and ultimately by Guillaume de
Machaut and Jean Froissart.

It is not impossible—one should go no farther—that Chaucer saw
poetry from all these phases. Collections of Provençal poetry, *chanson-
niers*, existed by his time.[10] He would have learned to read the
language, "A maner Latyn corrupt," easily enough, and Anglo-Norman
imitators of the troubadours left texts about.[11] He knew the *Roman*
(both parts, evidently) well enough, had read about Beatrice in *The
Divine Comedy*, had seen at least one sonnet of Petrarch's.[12] The more
extensive his reading, the greater his sense of a confused situation is
likely to have been. Today, even with the advantage of historical
perspective, students of medieval love poetry find the variety, the apparent inconsistency, the chronological and regional diversities of fin

[9] See for example, Frappier, *Amour courtois et table ronde*, pp. 13, 15, 21, 22, 29, 30, and
especially 93, 94. Frappier's essays seem to me the most authoritative writing on the subject.

[10] Many of these were actually copied in Italy. See J. H. Marshall, *The Transmission of Troubadour Poetry*, Inaugural Lecture Delivered at Westfield College (University of London), 1975, p. 5.
There is a traditional opinion that Chaucer is unlikely to have known Provençal; for a contrary
view see Robert M. Estrich, "A Possible Provençal Source for Chaucer's *Hous of Fame*,
300-310," *MLN* 55 (1940):342-49.

[11] See P. Meyer, "Mélanges de poésie Anglo-Normande," *Romania* 4 (1875):374-80; and M.
Dominica Legge, *Anglo-Norman Literature and Its Background* (Oxford: Clarendon Press, 1963),
pp. 33-61.

[12] See Patricia Thomson, "The 'Canticus Troili': Chaucer and Petrarch," *CL* 11 (1959):
318-28.

amour disconcerting (witness Boase's uncritical omnibus definition) and long for clear, positive factuality: there ought to be a code, something definitive to get one's teeth into.

Of course, there was never anything of the kind. The most striking feature of Provençal love poetry is the deliberately cultivated, flamboyant individualism of its composers, self-conscious performers striking attitudes, one of which was to pretend to entire sincerity, making their own rules, and essentially serious only about their virtuosity, of poetic technique, of linguistic and conceptual resource, and of music.

To coterie audiences such poets represented themselves personally and exceptionally as in a state of sexual tension, deliberately stimulated and carefully maintained, expressed in wittily extravagant language to a woman whose identity they made a show of concealing. She was "the best"; to be desiring her was preferable to actually possessing some other woman: "Mais vuolh de vos lo deman / Que autra tener baisan."[13] At the same time in the classic period of Provençal composition there was little if any spiritualization of her: whether directly or indirectly the poetic speaker registers his eroticism. The one I quoted has just said of the same woman, "par a la veguda / La fassa bo tener nuda" ("it's easy to see what a pleasure it would be to have hold of her naked") (lines 49–50). "Saber ben domnejar," being an adept at expressing that class of specialized arousal and uncomfortable euphoria, called for technical expertise but, even more, for facility in witty novelty of concept and expression, ingenuity in making one's own set of rules within the outside limits. The consequence is a greater diversity of attitudes in the poetry as a whole than the generalized themes of fin amour if abstracted (as, for instance, in The Allegory of Love) would lead one to expect.

To compound this variety, there is the circumstance that awareness of the preposterous and essentially self-contradictory nature of fin amour was registered by the poets from the earliest period. It is behind the calculatedly obscene verse of Guillaume de Poitiers, the first recorded troubadour.[14] It expresses itself in open moral criticism from

[13] Bertran de Born, Domna, puois de me no·us chal, lines 67, 68, in Albert Stimming, ed., Bertran von Born: Sein Leben und seine Werke (Geneva: Slatkine Reprints, 1975), p. 120.

[14] Here is the answer to the question put by Giraut de Bornelh nearly a century after Guillaume in a poem of regret for the decay, as he saw it, of an ideal courtly world: "Don es lo

his near contemporary, Marcabru. Moreover, common sense keeps creeping in. Here is Bernart de Ventadorn, most exquisite of the love poets: "Whoever heard of doing penance before the sin? The more I beg her the harder she is to me." "Mas si'n breu tems no·s melhura / vengut er al partimen" ("but if she does not soon become more agreeable it will have come to separation").[15] And in the early thirteenth century there is Peire Cardenal's scathing poem, *Ar me puesc ieu lauzar d'amors*, built of and ridiculing most of the clichés of the poetry of fin amour.[16]

The thirteenth century also saw an increase of sublimation in troubadour love poetry, the tendency which was to characterize its Italian derivatives. At the same time the deep cynicism inherent in Provençal *fin amour* from the outset became wholly explicit, as in this passage from a poem by Daude de Pradas:

I have now some pleasure from all the benefits that there are in love. For I have set all my hope, my thought and my application upon loving a gracious and beautiful lady; and I am loved by a young girl; and when I find a lively whore I take my pleasure with her. And I am not the less considerate of love if I divide it in three.

It is Love's wish that I should love my lady with appropriate fervour so as to become of greater worth. And I love the young girl so as to keep her loving me. And above that, for my pleasure, I arrange to sleep one or two nights from month to month with some girl who is good in bed, not jaded, and discreet, to pay my dues to love.

The man who wishes to possess his lady entirely knows nothing at all about

---

tortz issitz / D'elas malrazonar / No sai. – De cals, d'elas o dels amans?" ("Where the crime of speaking ill of ladies has come from I do not know. From whom, themselves or the lovers?") *Per solatz revelhar*, lines 37–39, in Adolf Kolsen, ed., *Sämtliche Lieder des Trobadors Giraut de Bornelh* (Halle: Niemeyer, 1910), 1.416. It was, so to speak, an original sin of the cult.

[15] "Qui vid anc mais penedensa / faire denan lo pechat? / On plus la prec, plus m'es dura; / mas si'n breu tems no·s melhura, / vengut er al partimen." *Lo tems vai e ven e vire*, lines 31–35, in Lazar, *Chansons d'amour*, pp. 233–34. Compare Walther, *Poets of the Minnesang*, p. 96, lines 15–19: "Frowe, ich trage ein teil ze swære: / wellest du mir helfen, sō hilf an der zīt. / sī aber ich dir gar unmære, / daz sprich endelīche; sō lāz ich den strīt, / unde wirde ein ledic man." ("Lady, the share I am carrying is too heavy. If you are willing to help me, help in good time. But if I mean nothing at all to you, say that once and for all. Then I shall give up the effort, and become a free man.")

[16] *Poésies complètes du troubadour Peire Cardenal (1180–1278)*, ed. René Lavaud (Toulouse: Privat, 1957), pp. 2–5.

the service of love. It is not loving service (*dompnei*) when the desire for full possession is realized.

> Non sap de dompnei pauc ni pro
> qui del tot vol se donz aver.
> Non es dompneis, pois torn'a ver.[17]

As I interpret this poem it is not an expression of the decadence of Provençal *fin amor* but rather one of total candor about it. The pretense inherent in the cult from the outset is exposed: devotion to the lady is of a very limited and special kind, calling for little self-denial: libido is satisifed elsewhere. Think of the possibilities of misrepresentation in quoting those last three lines.[18]

I turn my back on the temptation to speculate about any resemblance between Daude's three kinds of women and those in Saint Bernard's sermon on Canticles 1.3, *Introduxit me rex in cellaria sua*, namely, *regina, adolescentula* and *concubina*,[19] to look at subsequent developments of fin amour, which, by the differences they exhibit, would, on the one hand, intrigue and perplex Chaucer to the extent that he saw them as discrepancies in a whole and, on the other, make generalizations in our own time perilous.

The first development is one of transplantation. It is notably instanced in France by the poetry of the *trouvères* of the twelfth and thir-

---

[17] "De totz los bens qu'en amor so, / ai ieu ara calque plazer, / car ieu ai mes tot mon esper, / mon penssar e m'entencio / en amar dompna coind'e bella, / e soi amatz d'una piucella, / e quan trob soudadeira gaia, / deporte mi cossi que·m plaia; / e par tant non son meins cortes / ad amor si la part en tres. / Amors vol ben que per razo / eu am mi donz per mais valer, / et am piucella per tener; / e sobre tot qe·m sia bo / s'ab toseta de prima sella, / qand es frescheta e novella, / don no·m cal temer que ja·m traia, / m'aizine tant que ab lieis jaia / un ser o dos de mes en mes, / per pagar ad Amor lo ces." *Amors m'envida e·m somo*, lines 11–33, in A. H. Schutz, ed., *Poésies de Daude de Pradas* (Toulouse: Privat, 1933), pp. 70–71. De Pradas is rarely anthologized or discussed. I first came upon this poem in the Estrich article referred to above (note 10). Schutz grouped it with "Chansons Plaisantes ou Satiriques," and John Newton, in "Clio and Venus: An Historical View of Medieval Love," called it a "humorous song." F. X. Newman, ed., *The Meaning of Courtly Love* (Albany, N.Y.: SUNY Press, 1968), p. 33. But a fairly recent history of Provençal literature does not credit de Pradas with a sense of humor: "Son expression amoureuse est d'une simplicité, d'une banalité qui n'engagent jamis l'homme." R. Lafont and C. Anatole, *Nouvelle Histoire de la Littérature Occitane* (Paris: Presses Universitaires de France, 1970), 1.137.

[18] They were quoted out of context by A. J. Denomy, *The Heresy of Courtly Love* (Gloucester, Mass.: Peter Smith, 1947; reprint ed., 1965), p. 24.

[19] Jean Leclercq et al., eds., *Sermones super Cantica Canticorum 1–35, S. Bernardi Opera* (Rome: Editiones Cistercienses, 1957), 1.144.

teenth century[20] and in England, on the one hand, by a small number of anonymous Anglo-Norman love lyrics[21] and, on the other, by some Middle English verse of the late thirteenth or early fourteenth century.[22] The striking feature of this situation is that, in at least one particular, their occasional open, even blasphemous eroticism, the Middle English lyrics are closer to the Provençal than are the French:

> He myhte sayen þat Crist hym seȝe
> Þat myhte nyhtes neh hyre leȝe,
> heuene he heuede here.

"The man who was able to spend the night with her could say that Christ was looking on him with favour; it would be heaven in this world."[23] The imitations by the French *trouvères*, while sometimes very close to specific Provençal lyrics, were selective. Most of the *trouvère* lyrics we have seem more abstract, more melancholy and "romantic" than the Provençal types to which they formally correspond.[24] There are too few Anglo-Norman lyrics to generalize about them: they are mainly important in suggesting that there were others. There is no doubt that Chaucer saw at least Anglo-Norman and English representatives of this phase. But the attitudes they represent, though restricted and therefore differentiated as a compound of conventions, are commonplaces of fin amour.

The essential differences come with the adaptation of fin amour as an ethos of narrative, in the twelfth- and thirteenth-century French

---

[20] See John Fox, *A Literary History of France: The Middle Ages* (London: Benn, 1974), pp. 121–28, 180–83.

[21] See note 11 above. C. B. West, in *Courtoisie in Anglo-Norman Literature* (Oxford: Blackwell, 1938), pp. 123–29, allowed the possibility but discounted the likelihood of much direct Provençal influence in England in favor of Northern France. By whichever channel, Gower's *Cinkante Balades* (ibid., p. 123) in all particulars of content as distinct from form and organization read like an early-thirteenth-century period piece.

[22] See Theo Stemmler, *Die Englischen Liebesgedichte des MS. Harley 2253* (Bonn: Universitätsbibliothek, 1962). This remarkable dissertation seems a conclusive demonstration of Chaytor's proposal of direct Provençal influence on the early English lyric. H. J. Chaytor, *The Troubadours and England* (Cambridge: Cambridge University Press, 1923), passim.

[23] *The Fair Maid of Ribblesdale*, lines 83–85, in G. L. Brook, *The Harley Lyrics* (Manchester: Manchester University Press, 1948), p. 39. Chaytor (*The Troubadours and England*, pp. 115–16) quotes this passage with Provençal analogues.

[24] Compare Frappier, *Amour courtois et table ronde*, p. 95; Fox, *A Literary History of France*, pp. 123, 124.

romances: these are the main Northern French contributions to the phenomenon. The adaptations are so radical as to amount to a major transformation.[25] The first has to do with the ennobling force of love. In Provençal poetry such improvement was not related to the trouba-dour's military performance. In the romances, by contrast, a direct con-nection between excellence as a lover and performance in battle was posited; to quote Jean Frappier, their theme was "armes et amour, encore et toujours."[26] The second is an assumption, taken for granted in the romances after Chrétien, that romantic, exalted love could exist between the partners of a marriage. This sentimentalization of mar-riage in literature set up a radical difference, and a complicated one. It was socially problematic because of the actual women's subjection to their husbands in the law; it differed from actuality to the extent that marriages of the landowning classes were arranged by parents from considerations of property rather than the feelings of the young per-sons concerned. And it was morally sensitive in terms of the doctrine "Omnis ardentior amator propriae uxoris adulter est": excessive affec-tion in marriage was sinful.[27] Speculation about the reasons for this development is intriguing. There is the social one that societies at cer-tain stages tend to restabilize themselves, or anyway to react against tendencies of instability; that might apply to the extent that fin amour reflected actual sexual mores. Another is simply that the religiosity of Northern French poets and their audiences (many of the romance writ-ers were clerks)[28] was greater than that of the southerners, who had a name for irreligion. The development then appears as a moral rectifica-tion.[29] Yet another might be that the fabliau, having preempted adultery as a principal theme, socially devalued it and made it seem un-

---

[25] Compare Frappier, *Amour courtois et table ronde*, p. 93: "On n'interprète Jaufré Rudel ou Ber-nard de Ventadour en dissertant sur Guillaume de Machaut, sur Chaucer ou sur Charles d'Orléans, comme si du XIIe siècle à la fin du Moyen Age il s'agissait toujours du même 'amour courtois.' A l'intérieur de ce concept global et trop flottant, il faut savoir discerner d'assez nom-breuses variétés." Frappier's discussion of Andreas (pp. 81–87) is a much-needed corrective of earlier opinions, especially that of C. S. Lewis, about the importance of *De amore*.

[26] See, e.g., ibid., pp. 15, 28–30.

[27] Ibid., pp. 13, 14, 94.

[28] Ibid., pp. 17–19, 21.

[29] Ibid., pp. 13, 14, 81.

fashionable as a component of polite or idealized narrative.[30] The likeliest reason, to my mind, is no more than a matter of literary practi- cality raised by the adoption of fin amour as a narrative ethos. In that genre, in a love story, marriage affords the ideal terminal objective. A lyric can fix a moment in an emotional career: outcome is not of conse- quence. But in the account of a drawn-out illicit love affair, the two possible endings are the decay of love and death. So the "immortal" lovers Tristan and Lancelot are paradoxically immortal lovers because they die in constancy of affection, their stories meanwhile having dragged on. One recalls that Chrétien did not finish his *Lancelot*, and how subsequent writers felt the need to endow the end of the affair with dignity and moment by associating it with the downfall of a kingdom. By contrast, in *Cligés*, with a freer hand, Chrétien could, after the sexual intrigue had begun to wear out its interest, bring all to a close and sanction the lovers' union in an ideal marriage. There is a third difference, less obviously radical, in the treatment of love in the thirteenth-century French romances. A marked interest appears in the mentality of lovers, as if the analyses of their disturbances of personal- ity vied in interest with the events they were involved in.[31]

The analytic tendency is pronounced in the *Roman de la Rose*, which marks the next phase in the development of fin amour. Guillaume's gracefully erudite first part extends the analysis of the male lover's psychology and develops a blueprint of this; magnifies Ovid's Amor into a cult figure, a lord of terrible aspect; formulates his command- ments; and, unexpectedly, raises the consideration of how the lady should behave. As for Jean de Meun, by deferring his declaration of authorship for some 6,000 lines after he has taken over,[32] he reaffirms in fin amour an ambiguity even more extreme than that of its Provençal phase. For by that deferment the ostensible sweet elegiac idealization of the first part is set in a situation of imperative contrast, exposed to critical assay, weighed against rational, cynical, satirical disillusion-

---

[30] A stage in such a devaluation might be the "satirical romance." See the discussion of *De Guillaume au Faucon* and *Flamenca* by S. N. Brody: "The Comic Rejection of Courtly Love," in *In Pursuit of Perfection: Courtly Love in Medieval Literature*, ed. Joan M. Ferrante and George D. Economou (Port Washington, N.Y.: Kennikat Press, 1975), pp. 238–46.

[31] Frappier, *Amour courtois et table ronde*, pp. 13, 16–18, 21, 22.

[32] The revelation comes at line 10535. Guillaume de Lorris et Jean de Meun, *Le Roman de la Rose*, ed. Félix Lecoy (Paris: Champion, 1970), 2.71.

ment. The elegant courtship turns without warning in a deliberately prurient burlesque of, meanwhile, unmistakable philosophic implica-tion. Such paradigm of play and reality is thenceforward a feature of fin amour. Whether or not Jean designed his continuation to form a unity with Guillaume's beginning, the text in Chaucer's day will have been read as a whole, the discrepancies of tone and literal sense deeply registered before the twofold authorship is discovered. As if that were not enough the *Roman* reaffirms the incompatibility of love and mar-riage. This poem was in Chaucer's blood.

The Italian version of fin amour he encountered in its extreme form in *The Divine Comedy*, a spiritualization of the woman addressed to the point where it might seem immaterial whether she had a flesh-and-blood existence. In the Provençal lyric, we recall, she was for looks and manners and sometimes disposition "the best," but also a physical ob-ject; the poet wanted to touch her, and in his language, *lo plus* ("the rest"). The Italian situation implied an unmistakable dichotomy, be-tween a poetry professedly about love, characterized by great abstrac-tion and intellectual toughness, and one of simple eroticism. A good in-stance is from Cavalcanti: in one poem he writes how love "Ven da veduta forma che s'intende" ("derives from a form seen and under-stood, which assumes, in the intelligence competent to receive it, a location and a place of stay as in a subject country")—a far cry from the heart-piercing *lanza* of love in Provençal—and in another poem, *In un boschetto trova' pasturella*, represents (albeit exquisitely) the most elementary sexual fantasy.[33] He and the other Florentines who wrote in this manner were not court poets playing a game before a coterie but highly cerebral artists writing to satisfy themselves and to impress other poets of corresponding ability and cultivation. If Chaucer saw any of their work, as was chronologically and geographically possible, he may well have found it difficult through unfamiliarity with many of its concepts and references. Petrarch's love poetry might have seemed by comparison easier and, albeit spiritualized, much closer to his other experience of love poetry.

One more phase of fin amour relevant to Chaucer's love poetry, and at a further remove from the Provençal, is its manifestation in

---

[33] *Donna me prega, perch'eo voglio dire*, lines 21ff., in Guido Favati, ed., *Guido Cavalcanti: Le Rime* (Milan: Ricciardi, 1957), p. 214; ibid., p. 305.

fourteenth-century France, most notably in the verse of Machaut, who was poetically active from the 1320s to 1377. Machaut's fin amour derives not from the imitators of the troubadours[34] but from Guillaume de Lorris.[35] What distinguishes it is Machaut's own involvement through his phenomenal prominence as court poet, an entertainer writing superb music and technically polished, if to some tastes insipid, verse for great magnates, a King of Bohemia, a King of Navarre, a Duc de Berry. The function of his poetry in that role, however disguised, would be to compliment the patron and his court, above all the ladies. There is an implication of subservience in his situation[36] which might be obscured by Machaut's eminence as a composer of music, and the urbanity of tone in much of his verse suggests that he was not embarrassed to make capital of his position. But one feature of it evidently struck Chaucer: a court poet had to appear knowledgeable about love, and only a man with experience of love could write truthfully about it: "Qui de sentement ne fait, — / Son dit & son chant contrefait."[37] The court poet had necessarily to be himself in love. A good half at least of Machaut's considerable output purports to be about his emotional experiences, fanciful or actual, whether represented in lyrics, in allegorical narrative, or, in his last work, Le Voir Dit, the true story, as avowed autobiography. Moreover, Machaut was a cleric: at one time he held three canonries and a perpetual chaplaincy. That may for his French public have added spice to the interpretation of his allegorically recorded emotional life; it will certainly have endowed his account of the affair between the aging and decrepit priestly poet and a girl of under twenty with a certain sort of interest.[38] The story is further

[34] Conon de Béthune, the last of the conscious imitators of the troubadours, died about 1220; and the most notable thirteenth-century practitioner of fin amour poetry, Thibaut de Champagne, in 1253.

[35] Daniel Poirion, Le Poète et Le Prince: L'évolution du lyrisme courtois de Guillaume de Machaut à Charles d'Orléans (Paris: Presses Universitaires de France, 1965), p. 192.

[36] Ibid., pp. 195ff., argues in extenuation that Machaut wrote relatively little complimentary verse to his patrons. But the subservience is implicit in his having written the kind of poetry they and their ladies wanted in the times he lived in.

[37] Guillaume de Machaut, Le Livre du Voir Dit, ed. P. Paris (Geneva: Slatkine; reprint ed., 1969), p. 61. On the court poet as a lover see, e.g., Normand Cartier, "Le Bleu Chevalier de Froissart et Le Livre de la Duchesse de Chaucer," Romania 88 (1967):241–42.

[38] Poirion, Le Poète et Le Prince, pp. 199–205, in a both judicious and sympathetic discussion of Le Voir Dit, is hard put to it to bring Machaut out of the matter well. His perorations on pp. 200

remarkable as a work of fin amour, where the secrecy of the affair and the good name of the mistress are paramount, and having regard to the degree of intimacy it reports, in that it gives the girl's name, in an anagram to be sure, but an easy one accompanied by directions for its solution.

Those various phases of fin amour, which we can see as historically related extensions of a single cultural phenomenon, would not have been discernible as such to Chaucer for all their greater proximity in time. He would see individual pieces, and might interpret evident differences of convention between them as discrepancies, anyway of poetic practice. But by their differences they would promote eclecticism, a practical and pragmatic treatment; so his selective use of fin amour concepts and terminology and his identification of its more broadly interesting themes appear. He could certainly write most effectively in the high mode, as in Antigone's love hymn in *Troilus* 2, or in the lines of Prologue F to *The Legend of Good Women* beginning "She is the clernesse and the verray lyght," which read like a personal love poem. But I nowhere find him appearing committed to the cult. He is mocking it already in *The House of Fame*; *The Parliament of Fowls* exposes it to cold philosophical and realistic examination; *Troilus* studies it in opposed terms of sexually generated illusion and moral actuality; above all it is represented in the Prologue to the *Legend* as a pretty game to be discreetly played. Alcestis, it will be recalled, is commended by the God of Love for having taught not merely "al the craft of fyn lovynge" but also "in particular how a wife should conduct herself," "namely of wyfhod the lyvynge," and in a line which tends not to be noticed or quoted, "al the boundes that she oghte kepe"[39] ("all the limits which she ought to observe").

His detachment invites speculation, and it is not enough merely to assert what is quite true – that fin amour was not something an intelligent person, even if a court poet, could take seriously in the second half of the fourteenth century in England. Detachment would develop for more particular reasons.

---

and 205 are more ingenious than convincing, and, as far as Chaucer's reading of *Le Voir Dit* goes, are totally anachronistic.

[39] *LGW* F 546, G 536. In G, incidentally, Alceste is not *kalender . . . To any woman that wol lover bee* (lines 542–43) but *calendier . . . Of goodnesse* (lines 533–34).

One such might be an increasingly critical view of his own situation as a court poet, expected to write for the diversion of patrons of inferior intelligence and cultivation. Striking the pose of devotee of the God of Love and servant of his servants had been part of his initial undertaking to import and naturalize contemporary French poetic modes. But with the ease of his mastery of these and the experience of Italian culture, the pose would become increasingly irksome. And if, as is possible, he came upon Machaut's *Voir Dit*, he is as likely as not to have read it as a crass exhibition of sexual boasting and indiscretion or as a paradigm of the ludicrous figure *senex amans*: it is only recently, after all, that Romance scholars have attempted to interpret the work as designed by Machaut to be ironically critical of fin amour.[40] What is not in doubt is that the mature Chaucer, in contrast to his earlier readiness to borrow from or imitate Machaut, pointedly adopts attitudes directly opposed to those of Machaut in *Le Voir Dit*.[41] He will not write any more love poetry like a court poet.

The conventions of fin amour were a main shaping influence on Chaucer's love poetry because of their intrinsic serviceability to him as a developing poet, because of their social vogue, and because, characterizing his first models, they equipped him with radical propositions that provoked examination of a primary human circumstance in terms of common sense and observed experience. But there was also an abundance of love poetry in the three languages Chaucer early commanded which had little to do with fin amour or which flouted it. This extended the range of masculine sensibility. For instance, into bitterness: a woman has kept her lover waiting too long before relenting; now she is no longer desirable, and he tells her so.[42] Or into fantasy: the poet

---

[40] Here is Gustave Cohen in a 1951 broadcast on Radio Française: "Le *Voir Dit* a, comme son nom l'indique, l'accent même de la vérité, le son passionné et un peu triste de la dernière aventure d'un barbon amoureux d'une audacieuse. *La Poèsie en France au Moyen-Age* (Paris: Richard-Masse, 1952), p. 100.

[41] See Alfred David, "Literary Satire in the *House of Fame*," PMLA 75 (1960):335. The most notable particular is Chaucer's profession of unaptness for or inexperience in love. See HF 612–40, PF 157–68, and especially TC 2.13 and 3.43, 44, where he uses the actual term *sentement* of Machaut's *Qui de sentement ne fait* (see note 37). In LGWP Alcestis represents the Dreamer as not wanting to be a lover (F 490, G 480). The profession of inexperience seems to have amused Chaucer; note how the Squire, that "lovyere"..."fressh as is the month of May," deploys it as a *recusatio* in his tale (F 278–82).

[42] *Les Chansons de Conon de Béthune*, ed. A. Wallensköld (Paris: Champion, 1921), pp. 17–18.

meets a golden girl whose father is the nightingale and whose mother the siren, or he meets the daughter of the king of legendarily splendid Tudela; may God give him happines, for he will never get her out of his head and heart.[43] In the pastorale Chaucer would find moral and social criticism of sexual selfishness and arrogance and pretense, or ridicule of the condescension of the gentleman who fancies he is conferring a favor on a shepherdess by propositioning her and is seen off by her peasant lover or her brothers or her dog. There he would be shown the woman's point of view in poetry.[44] This is dominant in the strain of French poetry that goes back (whether directly or by archaization) beyond the Provençal ascendancy to the popular lyric common to the romance cultures. These poems are about women, mainly unhappy in love: elegant ladies with antique names swooning for lovers who have been long away and then ride past their window,[45] young girls married to ill-natured or repulsive husbands,[46] girls whose lovers are away at or about to go on the crusade,[47] even a girl not yet fifteen, and lovely too, who feel sexual stirrings, *Je sens les doz maus desoz ma ceinturete*, and curses those who made her a nun.[48] It is because of necessarily assumed loss not possible to judge to what extent the variety of feeling suggested in such poetry was reproduced in Middle English counter-parts. But Middle English poets do seem to have extended the range in one particular: there is a lyric representing the foolish infatuation of a girl with the priest who seduced her, and there are others in which the speaker is a girl seduced and then left pregnant.[49]

To what extent Chaucer was aware of how Ovid's multifaceted rep-resentation of the relation of the sexes underlay the Continental love poetry of his experience seems indeterminable. Two things, however, seem not in doubt. One is its presence: Ovid the profligate is behind *fin*

---

[43] Pierre Bec, *La Lyrique française au Moyen Âge (XIIᶜ–XIIIᶜ siècles)*, vol. 2 (Paris: Picard, 1978), 2.60–61, 63–64.

[44] Ibid., vol. 1 (Paris: Picard, 1977), pp. 122–23.

[45] Collected in Karl Bartsch, ed., *Romances et pastourelles françaises des XIIᶜ et XIIIᶜ siècles* (Leipzig, 1870; reprint ed., Wissenschaftliche Buchgesellschaft, 1975), vol. 1, *Romanzen*, pp. 3ff.

[46] Specimens are to be found in Bec, *La Lyrique française*, 2.13–20.

[47] Collected in J. Bédier and P. Aubry, *Les Chansons de Croisade* (Paris: Champion, 1909; reprint ed., New York, 1971).

[48] There are two very different specimens in Bec, *La Lyrique française*, 2.20–22.

[49] See R. H. Robbins, ed., *Secular Lyrics of the XIVth and XVth Centuries* (Oxford: Clarendon Press, 1952), pp. 18–25.

amour; Ovid the student of his own and others' sexual psychology informs the *Roman de la Rose*; Ovid the mythographer furnishes always
sensational, variously pathetic or ludicrous instances of the consequences of overpowering love; Ovid the man sensitive to the feminine
predicament demonstrates a poetic register in *Heroides*. The other is
that to the extent that Chaucer actually discerned Ovid's protean influence his awareness would have compounded confusion, if only
because of the insistent moralization of his work by the French and
Latin exegetes.[50]

Even an imperfect and ill-proportioned sketch of the multiplicity and
variety of poetic concepts and matrices, of forms of thought, language
and feeling for the composition of love poetry available to Chaucer
must show how little likelihood there is of finding him in any unqualified alignment toward them. It is as if almost every intellectually
or artistically attractive position in respect of this subject were
matched by an equally attractive opposed or contradictory one. That
literary situation alone must have amounted for Chaucer to an imperative to the exercise of judgment.

The shaping force of Chaucer's constantly enlarging poetic experience was, in the second and ultimately decisive instance, the accumu-
lated and interactive structures of the philosophical and the pragmati-
cally satirical and the canonical moral thinking of his time about the
emotional and physical relationship of men and women. Elements of
those structures are what the student of Chaucer encounters piece-
meal in Robinson's notes or as selections in compilations of "sources
and backgrounds." They stand there prominent and isolated, as often
as not in apparent conflict. And indeed in the historically accidental
sum of the fourteenth-century cultural fabric they were no more likely
to have been harmonized than are the many discrepant concepts and
attitudes in a modern person's world. As unresolved elements in an
individual awareness they might qualify one another, interact and express the complexity of situations. In the fourteenth century, however,
if the interaction went beyond that stage, it would likely end not in a
harmonization but in the dominance of one element.

---

[50] The scholarship of Chaucer still lacks an informed, disinterested and synoptic study of his
relation to Ovid.

There is a case in point in *Troilus and Criseyde* 1.232ff., where the narrator addresses the wise, proud, and eminent among his audience in a cautionary commendation of love. Love, he tells them, can quickly reduce their liberty of heart to serfdom; love will in all times and places turn out to be that which "alle thing may bynde," love which has the power (and here the dictionary offers a wide choice) to join securely or fetter or ensnare or make subservient or unite harmoniously[51] all things, "For may no man fordon the lawe of kynde," no man has the power to frustrate or annul the law of—does *kynde* mean just "nature"? There is nothing in books, he goes on, about there being anyone more intelligent than those who were captured by love, or stronger or braver or more exalted. And this is as it should be, for the wisest of all have been gratified by love. In the dramatic situation the argument appears strong: that the law of nature cannot be frustrated seems incontrovertible, and no one in the audience is likely to think himself secure from love because more intelligent than Socrates or Aristotle or stronger than Samson or wiser than Solomon and so on. The point of interest is that, while in this context of sexually induced irrationality[52] Love must obviously mean Eros, in conjunction with *bynde* it signifies another order of love, that conceived of in neoplatonic thinking as the governing principle of the universe: "al this accordaunce of thynges is bounde with love, that governeth erthe and see, and hath also comandement to the hevene."[53] And transcendingly *love* can mean the principle of the Great Commandment, the Pauline *caritas*. So the polysemy of *bynde* is unmistakable and necessarily significant. As for the rhyme word *kynde*, its usual meanings in the expression "lawe of kynde," either "law of nature" or "natural moral law,"[54] are not at once evidently appropriate, and we look for others. If for instance *kynde* here means *natura naturans*, the creative principle,[55] then the law

[51] *MED* s.v. *binden*, v., 3, 4, 5, 11.

[52] For the notion that the operation of the intellect is disturbed by love see, e.g., *On the Properties of Things: John Trevisa's translation of Bartholomæus Anglicus De Proprietatibus Rerum I* (Oxford: Clarendon Press, 1975), pp. 101, 102.

[53] *Bo* 2, m. 8, lines 13–16, translating "Hanc rerum seriem ligat / Terras ac pelagus regens / Et caelo imperitans amor (*Boethius...The Consolation of Philosophy, with an English Translation by S. J. Tester* (Cambridge, Mass.: Loeb Classical Library, new ed., 1973), p. 226, lines 12–15).

[54] *MED* s.vv. *kinde*, n., 5b; *laue*, n., 2, 3.

[55] *MED* s.v. *kinde*, n. 8 (a): "Nature as a source of living things...often personified." The Trevisa quotations are especially good instances of that meaning.

which no man can annul or frustrate is the sexual impulse with which species were endowed to ensure their continuation. And of course since 1370 or thereabouts *kynde*, from Langland's use of it, could also mean God the Creator.[56] As for the most intelligent and strongest and wisest men having been unable to resist love, the argument is a clerical commonplace: it evokes Socrates ruefully drying his head, or the 700 wives and 300 concubines who turned Solomon's heart from the Lord, or Aristotle, saddled and cavorting about the garden, ridden "De cheli que il voloit a ami, / Qui en le fin couvent ne li tint mie,"[57] the girl he wanted, who in the end, broke her word to him; that is, it recalls antifeminism.[58]

In that passage Chaucer has made fine capital of a number of conceptual schemes of greater or lesser order available in his cultural situation: as we identify them, they both invite and appear to defy resolution. We have recourse to the now quasi-formulaic explanation that he is writing ironically here; that is correct but inadequate. For irony, whether as a figure or as a mode of meaning, is also a symptom, and so here. The lines I looked at begin the preparation for the reordering of love with which *Troilus and Criseyde* ends.

But I find more than just the reordering of love in Chaucer's poetry about the relation of sexes, and I wonder — to go further is not safe — whether there was not some circumstance in his own time and country which led to concern about sexual morality. Certainly the good Bishop Brinton was so concerned: of Luxury he said, "This sin has reigned so scandalously among the magnates that I can invoke from the Psalms, as an applicable quotation, *contaminata est terra in operibus eorum.* As for adultery [he goes on, and these exact words he has used elsewhere] there is not a nation under heaven so disgraced by adultery as the English nation."[59]

---

[56] *MED* s.v. 8(c).

[57] *Adan, mout fu Aristotes sachans*, lines 5–6, in A. Långfors et al., eds., *Recueil général des jeux-partis français*, SATF (Paris: Champion, 1926), 2.63.

[58] See R. W. King, "A note on 'Sir Gawain the the Green Knight," 2414ff.," *MLR* 29 (1934): 435, 436.

[59] Thomas Brinton, *The Sermons of Thomas Brinton, Bishop of Rochester (1373–1389)*, ed. Sister Mary Aquinas Devlin (London: Camden, 3d ser., no. 86, 1954), vol. 2, sermon 69, p. 318; sermon 54, p. 245: ". . . non est nacio sub celo ita de adulterio diffamata sicut nacio Anglicana." Compare what Alcestis says to the Dreamer in the Prologue to the *Legend* about men who "do nat but

One knows the need to discount the repetitiousness and overstatement of the zealous preacher. Chaucer's concern I find expressed not in the strident tone of an anxious director of pastoral care but in studies large and small of the effects of sexuality. An obvious one which he examines extensively and intensively is the capacity of sexual selfishness to injure, to cause unhappiness: the first study is of Dido in *The House of Fame*, where significantly he adopts the pathetic Ovidian presentation. He reveals two sharp but contrasting insights into sex as a violation, an indignity, in the accounts of Constance's wedding night (*MLT* B′ 709–14) and January's apology to May, "Allas! I moot trespace / To yow, my spouse and yow greetly offende" (*MerT* E 1828–29), as if reading Peter Lombard's "foeda est et poena peccati" in those two radically different contexts. He conducts two set-piece studies of the extreme opposite of libertinism, namely virginity, one in a pagan ethos of the utmost rigor,[60] the other in the strictest Christian terms, where what a court poet would call "love paramours" is seen as love "in vileynye," and sexuality is expressely "vileynye."[61] He recognizes in Emelye the feeling of unawakened girls not ready for marriage (*KnT* A 2295ff.). He inserts a remarkably gratuitous injunction of moral responsibility to those who have the care of young girls in *The Physician's Tale* (C 72ff.). How selfish and inconsiderate sexuality both deludes and destroys human dignity he represents in Sir January of *The Merchant's Tale*, one of the cruelest miniatures of satire in English literature; it is not impossible that he meant us to see the Wife of Bath – welcome the sixth! – in something like the same light. Then there is the Manciple's assertion of the humbug of fin amour: there is no difference between a gentlewoman and a maidservant who are unchaste except that in the one instance we use ameliorative language (*ManT* H 212–22). As to the effect of sexual selfishness upon integrity, "trouthe" in his language, he offers you May's histrionic, high-pitched speech just before she goes up the tree to her lover (*MerT* E 2187–2202) or the totally cynical monk and wife in *The Shipman's Tale*.

---

assayen / How many women they may doon a shame; / For in youre world that is now holde a game" (F 487–89, G 477–79).

[60] *The Physician's Tale*, of course.

[61] *SNT* 8.156, 231.

What conclusions a full and systematic examination of the kind I have just sketched might produce it is hazardous to forecast. One approaches studies like this with a presumption that they relate to soluble problems, but that may be a false presumption. It comprises too many others to feel secure, such as that an artist's career will develop along a uniform course; that if he accepts the absolute validity of the moral code in force in his time, he will always conform to it; that the literary works he produces will always perfectly represent his intellectual and moral position, to name only the obvious ones. But it is not easy to keep the implied cautions always in mind.

"Paradis Stood Formed in Hire Yën": Courtly Love and Chaucer's Re-Vision of Dante

ELIZABETH D. KIRK
Brown University

> Swich fyn hath, lo, this Troilus for love!
> Swich fyn hath al his grete worthynesse!
> Swich fyn hath his estat real above,
> Swich fyn his lust, swich fyn hath his noblesse!
> Swich fyn hath false worldes brotelnesse!

N THESE LINES (*TC* 5.1828–32)[1] the narrator of Troilus and Criseyde summarizes the story he has finally brought to a conclusion, inextricably mixing Troilus's best qualities and the world's worst in common responsibility for what has befallen him. This passage, however, carries implications that are absent from the Boccaccio stanza it translates. Chaucer gives Troilus, as it were, two ends, by superimposing on the unhappy ending of the *Filostrato* to which Boccaccio's stanza referred a second and apparently contradictory one taken from a different Boccaccio poem altogether. On the one hand, Troilus is betrayed and dies; on the other, he alone, of all those involved in his story, enters Paradise. Neither of these conclusions offers him the happy ending pictured by Criseyde before she was exchanged for Antenor (4.788–91):

> For though in erthe ytwynned be we tweyne,
> Yet in the feld of pite, out of peyne,
> That highte Elisos, shal we ben yfere,
> As Orpheus with Erudice, his fere.

Yet it fulfills the highest hopes voiced by the narrator as he began his story: that Love may bring ill-fated lovers "soone owt of this world"

---

[1] All Chaucer quotations follow F. N. Robinson, ed., *The Works of Geoffrey Chaucer*, 2d ed. (Boston: Houghton Mifflin Co., 1957).

and lead them "in hevene to solas" (1.41, 31). Why does he not feel about it as he tells us his hero did, who "held al vanite / To respect of the pleyn felicite / That is in hevene above" (5.1817–19)? Surely he ought to find that Troilus's heavenly reward has transformed "litel myn tragedie" into the very comedy he hoped one day to write.[2] Does Chaucer's double ending reflect his inability to resolve the issues raised by the story,[3] or is it, precisely, his means of doing so?

Behind all modern discussion of the problems raised by this conclu-sion lies E. Talbot Donaldson's distinction between the narrator who voices it and the poet who devised the structure: "Chaucer discovered in the medieval modesty topos a way of poetic life. . . . [The narrator] and *ars poetica* are, to be sure, on parallel roads, moving in the same direction; but the roads are a long way apart and are destined to meet, perhaps, not even in infinity." Out of the resulting dialectic between *Troilus* and its ostensible teller, he argued, a meaning emerges that can be formulated only in paradox.[4] The hero's translation affirms his value and therefore the values embodied in his life.[5] Yet the overt language of the ending appears to contradict this; it is so expressive of contempt for the experiences that have been central to Troilus's life that it seems to demand the jettisoning of the entire poem that precedes it. And, as Donaldson's analysis of the rhetorical shifts makes clear, this paradox-ical juxtaposition of contradictory elements is no accident but an effect intensified by every structural and stylistic means available.

One can see, as Donaldson does, the differentiation between speaker and poet as the conscious device of the omniscient poet; or it can be seen as an extrapolation of the real problems the subject imposes on its teller, implications so fundamental to the material that they must have been a factor in Chaucer's choosing this subject to write about (I am

[2] Monica McAlpine, *The Genre of Troilus and Criseyde* (Ithaca, N.Y.: Cornell University Press, 1978).

[3] See, for example, Elizabeth Salter, "*Troilus and Criseyde*: a Reconsideration," in John Lawlor, ed., *Patterns of Love and Courtesy: Essays in Memory of C. S. Lewis* (London: Edward Arnold, 1966), pp. 86–106.

[4] E. Talbot Donaldson, "The Ending of Chaucer's *Troilus*" (1963), reprinted in E. Talbot Donaldson, *Speaking of Chaucer* (New York: W. W. Norton, 1970), pp. 84–100.

[5] For recent reassertions that the heaven is not Christian or that, even if it is, the apotheosis is not meant to constitute an evaluation of Troilus's life, see John W. Conlee, "The Meaning of Troilus's Ascension to the Eighth Sphere," *ChauR* 7 (1972):27, 36; and Joseph E. Gallagher, "Theology and Intention in Chaucer's *Troilus*," *ChauR* 7 (1972):44–66.

not sure that these positions are so opposed as they at first appear). In any case, differentiating the speaker from the poem does not resolve the problems of the poem's structure unless we make two further distinctions. One is between the narrator's point of view and that of Troilus, or, rather, between the views we see the living pagan character express and those attributed to him after his death. The other is between the narrator's religious position and the Christian orthodoxy he is trying so hard to articulate. His language is explicitly Christian; but has he understood the implications of the doctrines he invokes any better than he understands love or history? Behind the passage in Boccaccio's *Tesseida* which Chaucer introduces, causing so major an apparent dislocation in the structure, lies a crucial scene in Dante's *Paradiso*.[6] If we look at *Troilus* in the light of Dante, Chaucer's reasons for building the poem as he did become clearer, and the "epilogue," so far from reflecting a lack of resolution in the poem, reveals itself as the culmination of a pattern that has been in evidence all along.

We certainly receive no help in relating the two parts of the poem from the narrator's own language in the epilogue, which mirrors the very conflict it seeks to explain.[7] Hatred for the finite world which Troilus has found so costly is only part of what he tries to communicate. He lurches awkwardly between the language of *contemptus mundi* and words which caress the reality they ostensibly reject, denying with their own compassion and sweetness that finite duration is evidence of ultimate worthlessness. He addresses his cautionary "moralitee" to youth "In which that love up groweth with youre age" as if there were continuity as well as contradiction between the loves appropriate to the different stages of life. He calls the finite world he denigrates one that "passeth soone as floures faire" (5.1835–36, 41). This richness of compassion contrasts harshly with his bitter recommendation, as of a jilted lover on the rebound, that we should love God primarily because "he nyl falsen no wight, dar I seye" (5.1845). Nor is Troilus himself any more helpful. He does not appear to see any connection between his life and his heavenly reward. The laugh with which he greets "the wo / Of hem that wepten for his deth so faste"

---

[6] Jeffrey Helterman, in "The Masks of Love in *Troilus and Criseyde*," *CL* 26 (1974):14–31, has some cogent comments on *Troilus* as a "secular analogue" of *The Divine Comedy*.

[7] Donaldson, "The Ending of Chaucer's *Troilus*," pp. 97–99.

(5.1821–22) shows no more respect for the experience of lovers than the laugh with which we saw him respond to their vulnerability and suffering in book 1, before he had any reason to understand it. He is as ready to classify the major experience of his life under "blinde lust" as is the narrator himself. The result is a conflicting pattern of overt evaluations of Troilus's experience which has evoked equally conflicting critical opinion. Rigorists find it too soft on sin (Gallagher calls it "a complex reflection of its author's attempt to evade the strict terms of medieval religion").[8] Others find it too harsh and regard the epilogue's religious language as an ultimately superficial evasion of Chaucer's deeper insight into his material; Alfred David observes that Chaucer "failed in his didactic purpose, because he understood, perhaps subconsciously, that such a limited goal had never been his purpose in the first place."[9]

Too much attention to the individual value judgments expressed in the epilogue, however, may blind us to the more fundamental challenge it offers. Both the ostensibly a-Christian love story and the *contemptus mundi* language of the close are called into question by the addition of Chaucer's "second ending": a pagan lover who refused to withdraw his commitment to a secular love finds himself in heaven. Furthermore, this heaven is based on the Christian heaven of the *Paradiso* and is presented by the narrator as of a piece with the explicit Christian theology to which he reverts as he returns from ancient Troy to his own Christian present in fourteenth-century England.[10] This heaven is, as Donaldson put it, "physically pagan but theologically Christian."[11]

[8] Gallagher, "Theology and Intention in Chaucer's *Troilus*," p. 66.

[9] Alfred David, *The Strumpet Muse: Art and Morals in Chaucer's Poetry* (Bloomington: Indiana University Press, 1976), p. 36.

[10] Two essays arguing that Troilus's heaven is not Christian call useful attention to how drastic the implications of such an apotheosis are: Murray F. Markland, "*Troilus and Criseyde*: the Inviolability of the Ending," *MLQ* 31 (1970):155–56, 158; and Peter Heidtmann, "Sex and Salvation in *Troilus and Criseyde*" *ChauR* 2 (1968):248–49. Various versions of the apotheosis and the heavenly journey are differentiated by John Steadman, *Disembodied Laughter: Troilus and the Apotheosis Tradition: A Re-Examination of Narrative and Thematic Contexts* (Berkeley: University of California Press, 1972). Gertrude C. Drake gives a useful summary of the debate over which sphere Troilus is in: "The Moon and Venus: Troilus's Havens in Eternity," *Papers in Language and Literature* 11 (1975):3–17. I continue to believe that Chaucer clearly means Troilus to have his vision where Dante and Arcite had theirs, though he may not remain there.

[11] E. Talbot Donaldson, *Chaucer's Poetry: An Anthology for the Modern Reader* (New York: Ronald Press, 1958), p. 979.

The problem about this is not primarily the obvious one of why a pagan should be in heaven. The pagan translated to an explicitly Christian paradise is a recognized medieval *topos*. The tears of Bishop Erkenwald release a pagan judge from his tomb in the foundations of Saint Paul's Cathedral.[12] Langland portrays the emperor Trajan as saved not, as in earlier legend, by a pope's miraculous intervention but by his own intrinsic qualities: "Nouȝt þoruȝ priere of a pope but for his pure truþe."[13] Dante's Cato is not debarred by a suicide permissible in his own moral code from being the guardian of Purgatory shore. Dante places in Paradise not only the traditional figure of Trajan but also the Trojan Rhipeus; and Rhipeus is not merely rescued by grace but honored and celebrated by Faith, Hope, and Charity (*Par.* 20.118–23, 127–29):[14]

The other [Rhipeus], through grace which wells from so deep a fountain that no creature ever thrust his eye to its primal spring, set all his love on righteousness; therefore from grace to grace God opened his eyes to our coming redemption. . . . Those three ladies whom thou sawest by the right wheel [of Beatrice's car] stood for baptism to him more than a thousand years before baptism.

But none of these analogies justifies the salvation of Troilus. In each case the pagan in question demonstrates an evident continuity between Christianity and the life of a particular exceptional individual that marks him as already living Christianity in spite of historical ignorance. What Troilus has done that singles him out in a comparable way is anything but clear. Nor do the narrator's comments about the end to which love has brought him suggest continuity between a pagan love affair and the harmony of the spheres.

The main thing that Troilus has done that is relevant is a sin by the standards usually associated with the narrator's religious language.[15]

[12] Henry L. Savage, ed., *St. Erkenwald* (New Haven, Conn.: Yale University Press, 1928).

[13] William Langland, *Piers Plowman; The B Version,* ed. George Kane and E. Talbot Donaldson (London: Athlone Press 1975).

[14] Quotations from *The Divine Comedy* follow the edition and translation of John D. Sinclair (1939); reprint ed., Galaxy Books (New York: Oxford University Press, 1961).

[15] See D. W. Robertson, Jr., *A Preface to Chaucer* (Princeton, N.J.: Princeton University Press, 1962), pp. 472–79; A. J. Denomy, "The Two Moralities of Chaucer's *Troilus and Criseyde*" (1950); reprinted in R. J. Schoeck and J. Taylor, eds., *Chaucer Criticism* (Notre Dame, Ind.: Notre Dame University Press, 1968), 2:147–48, 158–59.

This may not be as much of an obstacle as pulpit language suggests. It is a mistake to read Reformation (to say nothing of Victorian) over-emphasis on the seriousness of sexual sins, as opposed to sins of violence and fraud, back into the Middle Ages. Dante himself stands as a warning against assuming that sexual sins are any more of an obstacle to salvation than anything else or that the presence of illicit elements in sexuality altogether obscures the analogy between erotic and divine love which is so fundamental to his anthropology. Paolo and Francesca may drift on a black wind and Brunetto Latini may be in Hell for a love so solipsistic that it has left him a shriveled and barely recognizable version of himself. But at the top of Mount Purgatory repentant lovers, homosexual and heterosexual, run in opposite directions around the mountain, embracing as they meet, in a flame that expresses not only their voluntarily embraced penance but the reestablished splendour of loving itself. In the Heaven of Venus, the notorious Cunnizza "gaily" forgives herself, and the harlot Rahab sparkles like a sunbeam in clear water (*Par.* 9.32–35, 113–17). No one in *The Divine Comedy* is rewarded or punished for what he or she did but for the transformation of the self effected by the attitude each took to having done it. Even so, why is Troilus, distinguished primarily for a disastrous love affair, the only actor in the story who can cross the line between the pagan world of Troy, where Christian ethics and metaphysics are ostensibly suspended, to the perspective of medieval England, where experiential knowledge will have to be reconciled with doctrinal and historical necessity if the implications of the story are to be dealt with?

The answer comes in Troilus's final summation of his experience within the story proper, when he is confronted with what even he must acknowledge is uncontrovertible evidence that Criseyde has betrayed him. Fully grasping the implications of his new knowledge, he speaks in terms that are completely antithetical to those of the narrator (5.1695–98):

> ...I se that clene out of youre mynde
> Ye han me cast; and I ne kan ne may,
> For al this world, withinne myn herte finde
> To unloven yow a quarter of a day!

His attitude is far from stoic or detached. He speaks as if he almost resists his own constancy (5.1699–1701, 1722):

> In corsed tyme I born was, weilaway,
> That yow, that doon me al this wo endure,
> Yet love I best of any creature. . . .
> That ye thus doon, I have it nat deserved.

But this bitter articulation of his pain serves only to underline the reality of a love that literally cannot be withdrawn, whatever revelations about its object experience may bring forth.

Troilus's consistency, as his name suggests, has been his central characteristic all through the poem, with a concomitant inability to make his experience of love anything but embarrassingly total. Criseyde, a far more perceptive judge of character than he, bases her ultimate decision to love him not on the myriad considerations that ran through her mind when she first caught sight of him from her window but on a sense that she can trust him like "a wal / Of stiel" (3.479–80) because of his "moral vertu, grounded upon trouthe" (4.1672). The process by which Troilus falls in love, which Chaucer carefully divides into two stages, demonstrates this quality from the start. The first stage, like Criseyde's "Who yaf me drynk?" is anything but voluntary. When Troilus first sees "this in black" in the temple, her impact on him is so total and intense as to supersede choice, as the narrator indicates by superimposing on his realistic vignette the traditional image of the God of Love's arrow and his own comments on determinism. There is, however, a second part to the process. Troilus goes home to his palace and when he is alone makes "a mirour of his mynde, / In which he saugh al holly hire figure" (1.365–66), finds it "a right good aventure / To love swich oon," (1.368–69), and, finally, resolves to make what was initially involuntary a fully considered choice (1.391–92):[16]

> For with good hope he gan fully assente
> Criseyde for to love, and nought repente.

"Fully assente . . . and nought repente": this promise is almost as drastic as the one Dorigen made her husband that "nevere sholde ther be defaute in here" (FranT F 790). Yet Troilus actually keeps it.

The complexity of this commitment is underlined by the elusiveness of its object. What makes Criseyde "so feyr and goodly to devise"

---

[16] The crucial lines are not in Boccaccio.

(1.277) can be described, after a series of negatives, only as a suggestion implicit in a movement (1.285-87):[17]

> ...the pure wise of hire mevynge
> Shewed wel that men myght in hire gesse
> Honour, estat, and wommanly noblesse.

Troilus's story is the story of a man who went home and guessed. Did
he guess right? Yes, in the sense that he actually had the experience
such a person would make possible. No, in the sense that she ultimately acted like quite another kind of creature when her qualities
were proved by time and change, remorseless diagnosticians of human
worth. Was Troilus's experience illusion or reality? His story is not so
much a love story per se—if there is such a thing—as an inquiry into
the factitious character of human experience in time. What kind of
reality pertains to experiences that are partly the creations of those
who take part in them? *Troilus and Criseyde* is a story about a man (the
narrator) creating a poem about a man (Pandarus) creating a love affair
for a man (Troilus) who is creating the woman who makes it possible.
Yet she is what seems most real in the poem, to them and to us. And
the man who refuses to consider his commitment invalidated by the
rest of the truth about her is the only one who transcends the finite to
discover what the "reality" of the finite itself may be. His consciousness alone can expand to the point where he can see that the experience both was and was not what it appeared to be, that it was
both real and unreal, and that it epitomizes the relationship of finite
and infinite. In a profoundly ironic sense Troilus was not wrong to
think that he saw in Criseyde the vehicle of heavenly perfection.

In this perspective we see why Chaucer superimposed on his source
so much material from *The Divine Comedy*.[18] By doing so, he makes the
poem not simply a love story but an analysis of the tradition of "courtly
love" in the sense in which it had been central to the development of
medieval poetry, whatever it may have had to do with real life. *The
Divine Comedy* and *Troilus* are the two great retrospective analyses of

---

[17] E. Talbot Donaldson, "The Masculine Narrator and Four Women of Style," in *Speaking of
Chaucer*, pp. 53-59.

[18] The extent of borrowings large and small is clear in the notes to *The Book of Troilus and
Criseyde*, ed. Robert Kilburn Root (Princeton, N.J.: Princeton University Press, 1926).

"courtly love" and its meaning in the larger universe of Christian revelation, and the second is a commentary on the first. Both in their different ways set fin amour in the biblical tradition of man's love affair with
God, consummated in the workings of human history.

However diverse this tradition was and however problematically related to medieval sociology,[19] the tradition of fin amour or "honeste
love" celebrates not sexual desire itself but the idea that the experience
to which desire leads differs qualitatively according to the kind of person one becomes. Erotic experience may take on an almost unlimited
range of qualities and meanings depending on the attributes with
which the lovers invest it and on those they elicit from themselves in
response to it. Poetry in this tradition was written on occasion by
women, and at the outset of narrative treatment of it we find *Érec et
Énide*, one of the few works before Chaucer to view the courtly experience as one which happens to the woman as well as the man in the
sense of requiring her development as well as his. In general, however,
the tradition portrays a masculine experience, or the dream of one, in
which a man sees in the excellence of a woman a revelation of what he
is not but can become, and must become to be admitted to her world.
She is the occasion of his acquiring qualities hitherto outside his experience because it is of the essence of the dream that she is free to choose
whether or not to love and that the love he seeks from her is voluntary, compelled neither by duty nor by force. She plays this role for
him precisely because she stands outside the necessities and experiences in which a man's excellence is measured in the "real" world.
Desire itself becomes, qualitatively speaking, what the man himself
becomes: "Amore e 'l cor gentile sono una cosa" (*Vita nuova* 20). What
Dante called the poetry of *venus* or *amoris accensio*, Singleton points
out, shares a boundary with the poetry of *virtus* or *directio voluntatis*,
so that Dante classified his own work, which had begun as the culmination of love poetry in the first sense, in the second instead.[20]

Needless to say, this had nothing to do with what women's lives
really were. Rather, it portrays a man thinking of himself as receiving

---

[19] See Roger Boase, *The Origin and Meaning of Courtly Love: A Critical Study of European
Scholarship* (Manchester: Manchester University Press, 1977).

[20] Charles Singleton, "Dante: Within Courtly Love and Beyond," in F. X. Newman, ed., *The
Meaning of Courtly Love* (Albany: State University of New York Press, 1968), pp. 43–54.

from a woman a revelation which depends not so much on what she actually is as on her difference from himself. He sees something in her
that both is and is not there, something which becomes real in its effect
on him whether or not it was ever real in her. The courtly lady is
always in some sense, like the Beatrice of the *Vita nuova*, "la gloriosa
donna de la mia mente." It is no surprise that this tradition began in the
lyric; this feeling can be expressed in a lyric and other feelings about
erotic experience in other lyrics, without its being necessary to corre-
late them. As soon as one begins to tell a story about the lover's experience, however, questions arise about the meaning and the value of
the experience and the self it seems to create, vis à vis other selves,
realities, responsibilities.[21]

The story will also raise questions about the lady herself. What connection is there between what she reveals to her lover and what she is
in herself? Either she really is the source of what is happening to him
or she is not. If she is, the plot leads to deification of the lady with
which the presence of an actual woman subject to human necessity
and as much in need of qualitative development as her lover interferes.
If she is not, the plot moves toward disillusionment or irony. The lady
may continue to be revelation by ceasing to exist, or she may continue
to exist by ceasing to be revelation. Both Dante's and Chaucer's syn-
theses depend on removing the lady. The death of Beatrice is so central to her role for Dante that it makes its first and deepest impact
before it happens, when in the *Vita nuova* it is merely dreamed and en-
visaged in poetry. In *Troilus* the lady removes herself. Although
Troilus and Criseyde seem to have had a central experience in common, it was not an experience of the same thing. After all, until each
becomes to the other a real body in a real bed, each has encountered
primarily the version of the other mediated by Pandarus. As soon as
exterior events break in again on the world of love, the differentness of
their experience reemerges. "Courtly love" necessarily involves some
form of this problem. Inherent in the dream of a truly voluntary relationship is the necessity of creating a special world in which a kind of
free will can exist for the lady which the roles of women in actual life
precluded. The discipline of secrecy brought into being a reality as

[21] See Robert W. Hanning, *The Individual in Twelfth-Century Romance* (New Haven, Conn.:
Yale University Press, 1977).

266

special as that of Chrétien's "Joy of the Court," the garden whose fruits and herbs nourish and heal but cannot be taken out through the garden wall, even though it is only a wall of air. If an experience is made possible only by creating an alternative reality that can accommodate it, is its value in any way transferable to the rest of existence? Thus the courtly affair is ultimately more than a subject for works of art that offer an attractive alternative to present life. In the hands of an artist interested in assessing the nature and reality of man's experience and knowledge, its implications are ultimately epistemological and metaphysical. Is reality what befalls – happens upon – men and women? Or is it what they create, what they make of what befalls, what would not have existed without their cooperation, their artifice?

Human experience is by its very nature linear, sequential. Its shape is a shape in time, a shape that comes into perceptibility with the loss of one experience and the emergence of another. No human experience can be fully known except in retrospect. The courtly affair, even one that ends as happily as it can, in the eventual death of the parties, has, like Aristotle's plot, a beginning, middle, and end. It has built into it the perspective that art seeks to give to life, and its end is implicitly present in consciousness wherever there is awareness of the mystery of beginning. Most courtly romances show their awareness of time by concentrating on the inception and establishment of a love affair rather than on its conclusion. Time conflicts often, as in *Yvain*, mark the tension between the different roles of the characters within and without the world of love. But *Troilus* carries through the entire cycle; the perspective which death gives to life is provided by the unfaithfulness of Criseyde, which is presented less as malice or villainy (as later writers were to do) than as epitomizing the unsubstantialness of life itself. The reality of this experience must be decided by the narrator who is writing about it as a fact of history, by the go-between who managed it into existence, and by the lover who suffered it. Only the one of the three who refused to "unlove" Criseyde, to take dissolution as a judgment of value, can ultimately transcend it.[22]

In *The Divine Comedy* continuity, potential or actual, between all levels of experience is basic to the poem. It is reflected in the pattern of

[22] McAlpine, *The Genre of Troilus and Criseyde*, p. 162ff.; see comments on the dissenting view of Alfred David.

echo and response that binds the three *cantiche* together, especially in the presence of two characters who cross the structural boundaries of the poem: Virgil, who can reach man at the lowest point to which he has sunk, and Beatrice, who sent him and who brings the revelation of God. Each is eventually superseded, Virgil by Beatrice and Beatrice by the direct experience to which Saint Bernard and the Virgin Mary raise Dante. As Beatrice tells Dante, "Not in my eyes only is Paradise" (*Par.* 18.20–21). But it *is* in her eyes, and it *is* elsewhere. In his final vision Dante sees the eternal light subsuming all other realities, not by denying their autonomy in their own spheres nor by attributing abso-luteness to them: "In its depth I saw that it contained, bound by love in one volume, that which is scattered in leaves throughout the uni-verse" (*Par.* 33.84–93). "The love that moves the sun and the other stars" is "painted with our likeness" (*Par.* 33.145, 131). At the very point where Dante the Pilgrim, like the Troilus of the epilogue, looks down through the circling spheres at the little "threshing floor" of the earth, he can affirm that "all things whose bite can make the heart turn to God have wrought together in my charity," bringing him from the "sea of perverse love" to the "shore of the love that is just."[23] It is im-mediately after this affirmation that Beatrice tells Dante: "Open thy eyes and look on me as I am; thou has seen such things that thou has gained strength to bear my smile" (*Par.* 23.46–48).

We can see why it was this precise part of the *Comedy* which Chau-cer, like Boccaccio before him, chose as the place for Troilus's vision; presumably Chaucer turned from one Boccaccio poem to the other at this point for that very reason. For Dante the tinyness of the earth in heavenly perspective gives it a *vil sembiante* at which he smiles, but the eyes of Beatrice to whom he turns affirm the continuity from first love to last and make Dante's smile something far more complex than a re-jection. In *Troilus* the little threshing floor holds no Virgil, only Pan-darus; no one sees anyone "as I am"; there is no Beatrice, only Criseyde; and Criseyde has been left behind. Dante's smile marks the point at which he becomes able to bear the smile of Beatrice; Troilus's bitter laughter affirms no such continuity. Once, indeed, the beauty of Criseyde seemed to be revelation (1.102–105):

---

[23] "Perverse" is *torto*; "just," *diretto*.

> So aungelik was hir natif beaute,
> That lik a thing inmortal semed she,
> As doth an hevenyssh perfit creature
> That doun were sent in scornynge of nature.

Even God himself was not so unworldly as that, the Second Nun reminds us, paraphrasing Dante (*SNT* G 41–42).[24]

> . . .no desdeyn the Makere hadde of kynde
> His Sone in blood and flessh to clothe and wynde.

Yet even as revelation Criseyde never brought the divine into immanence in the way the young Beatrice did (*Vita nuova* 11):[25]

Whenever and wherever she appeared, in anticipation of her marvellous greeting, I held no man my enemy, and the flame of charity burned brightly within me, a flame that consumed all past offenses; and during this time if anyone had asked me about anything, I could only have answered "Love," with a countenance clothed in humility.

And certainly by the end of *Troilus*, Criseyde's numinousness has gone. The narrator who was once so sure about her "aungelik beaute" can only say in wistful reliance on his old books (5.816–17):

> Lo, trewely, they writen that hire syen,
> That Paradis stood formed in hire yën. . . .

Did it? No one can know. Yet it is clear that her eyes are not in Paradise; divine reality brings no reunion. The "scorning of nature" that once seemed embodied in Troilus's angel is now Troilus's own: he "fully gan despise / This wrecched world" (5.1817–19). Dante says of those that mourn the dead, "Who so laments that we die here to live above has not seen there the refreshment from the eternal showers." But those who weep for Troilus's death are only objects for his laughter. The lover who did not love Beatrice in the body affirms the body's inclusion in the community of divine love (*Par.* 14.43–54, 56–58):

---

[24] Her words are based on the same prayer of Saint Bernard to the Virgin as Troilus's final plea to Criseyde (3.1254–74; cf. *Par.* 33.1–39).

[25] As quoted in Dorothy L. Sayers, *The Comedy of Dante Alighieri: Hell* (Harmondsworth, Middlesex: Penguin Books, 1949), p. 28.

When the flesh, glorified and holy [*gloriosa e santa*], shall be put on again, our person will be more acceptable for being all complete. . . . this effulgence which now surrounds us will be surpassed in brightness by the flesh which the earth still covers.

The lover who loved in the body cannot. Yet something in Troilus's experience must have been akin to the "hevenyssh melodie" of the "erratik sterres" or why is he among them?

There is much in the epilogue that directs us not to take the narrator's evaluations of Troilus's experience as the most adequate expression of the light shed on it by the theology the narrator invokes. Does God see the little spot of earth as the narrator tells us Troilus did? Rhetoric of this kind is common enough in the Middle Ages (and since) and can be illustrated from speakers as diverse as Chaucer's virtuous parson and his simultaneously prurient and moralistic Reeve. But Chaucer's contemporary Julian of Norwich spoke for many when she used imagery closely related to Dante's and Chaucer's picture of the tiny earth to portray the world in a very different light from that described by the *Troilus* narrator. God showed her, she tells us,

a little thing, the quantity of an hazelnut in the palm of my hand, and it was round as a ball. I looked thereon with the eye of my understanding and thought: *What may this be?* And it was answered generally thus: *It is all that is made*: I marvelled how it might last, for me thought how it might suddenly have fallen to nought for little[ness]. And I was answered in my understanding: *It lasteth and ever shall [last] for that God loveth it.* And so all thing hath being by the love of God.[26]

For her, shortness of duration and smallness of size do not settle questions of value, nor, as her dialogues with the crucified Christ repeatedly insist, does the suffering incurred because of an experience negate its worth.

Does God "despise" this world and "laugh at the woe" of those who mourn the death of the body and the death of hope? As the crucial tenets of Christianity invoked by the narrator himself make clear, God does nothing of the kind (5.1842–44):

[26] Julian of Norwich, *Revelations of Divine Love*, ed. Grace Warrack (London, 1901), p. 8.

>...loveth hym, the which that right for love
>Upon a crois, oure soules for to beye,
>First starf, and roos, and sit in hevene above.

God's response when we "falsen" him is not to seek a more reliable lover, as Pandarus advised Troilus, and as the narrator advises the "yonge, fresshe folkes, he or she"—as, indeed, God himself did earlier when he sent a Flood and replaced most of the world's population. For the narrator a comparison of divine and human love means a comparison between objects of love: Criseyde, the "feynede love," and Christ, who "nyl falsen no wight." But there is a more fundamental comparison to be made, not between objects of love but between ways of loving, that of Troilus and that of the suffering God incarnate. Here, in spite of so much ironic contrast, we find not unlikeness but likeness. To paraphrase Etienne Gilson's remark about Abélard and Héloïse, God loves not as Criseyde loved Troilus but as Troilus loved Criseyde.[27] So it is that Troilus, of all the characters, enters heaven.

At first sight an analogy between God and the poem's least dynamic, least gripping, least effectual character is difficult to accept. But there is a reason for Chaucer's paradoxical choice of a vehicle. *Troilus* is full of Boethius because, like *The Consolation of Philosophy*, it is about the problem of suffering and injustice. This is the perennial problem of monotheism, which has no one but God to be responsible for a universe in which suffering is a central reality. God's deliberate noninterference with the autonomy of his creatures bears a disturbing affinity with the inexplicable passivity of Troilus which has made him so unsatisfactory a courtly or tragic hero to many readers. Langland's Reason, when his Dreamer brings up this disturbing subject, confirms his worst suspicions: "Who suffre[þ] more than god?...no gome, as I leve. / He myȝte amend in a minute while al þat mysstandeth" (B 12.371–72). God, as the narrator reminded us earlier in an even more disturbing comparison with Criseyde, did not even avenge his own death: "What God foryaf his deth, and she also / Foryaf" (3.1577–78).

Troilus's imitation of Christ is as clumsy, as partial, as flawed as the narrator's attempts to achieve *ars poetica*. He would unlove a quarter

---

[27] See Drake, "The Moon and Venus," p. 5; Helterman, "The Masks of Love in *Troilus and Criseyde*," p. 30; and Stephen A. Barney, "Troilus Bound," *Speculum* 47 (1972):458.

of a day if he possibly could; he simply cannot. His central quality may be disinterestedness, but it emerges gradually from a tangle of solipsism, possessiveness, self-pity. He has, as Pandarus puts it, a "mouse's heart" and an almost complete inability to deal with the real world, at least *qua* lover, once his familiar assumptions have been thrown into disarray by a new ideal. Although, without Pandarus, he might never have acted at all, we must note that thoughts of how to "arten" Criseyde to love were in his mind from the start, so that, when Pandarus elicits and develops them, he is not proposing something unthinkable to Troilus himself. Certainly Troilus bears ultimate responsibility for the stratagems and chicanery, the moral blackmail, devised by Pandarus. He even produces an elaborate lie of his very own to preface the consummation of his love, reflecting, however sadly, that "for the lasse harm, he moste feyne" (3.1158). It is true that his refusal to make Criseyde's mind up for her in book 4, even when Pandarus assures him that she would probably prefer it, epitomizes disinterested love and faithfulness to the terms Criseyde laid down for him in book 3 (lines 169–71):

> "But natheles, this warne I yow," quod she,
> "A kinges sone although ye be, ywys,
> Ye shal namore han sovereignete
> Of me in love, than right in that cas is."

But the courtship as a whole is, ethically speaking, a far more complex matter. Throughout, elaborate maneuvers present Criseyde at every point with a fait accompli rather than with a choice, a situation which she cannot refuse, for which she need not be held accountable, and which everyone promises will have no consequences. This strategy bears no little responsibility for her ultimate inability to sustain "corage" and "trouthe" when she has to deal directly with reality. For some readers this duplicity is so central a feature of the courtship as to render her eventual guilt almost inevitable and to make any moral judgment of her meaningless. Certainly Farnham is right that book 5 marks a major turning point in the poem not because there duplicity and betrayal first enter its world but because for the first time it is Criseyde who is the chief deceiver.[28]

Still Troilus's attempts to keep faith with his original vision and commitment, and to respect Criseyde's autonomy and integrity, ultimately emerge as his central quality. As Monica McAlpine comments, "The aspect of Troilus's courtly love that draws Chaucer's criticism is not its passionate sexuality but its passionate fantasizing," which is "a solipsism that can be corrected by human love itself."[29] In Troilus's case it brings the lover by degrees to such respect for the beloved's independent reality that he will defend it at any cost: "The 'fyn' of his love for Criseyde is not his loss or her infidelity; it is instead this critical moment of decision, in which the honorable and manly qualities of his love are displayed." This and his refusal to "unlove" remain acts of absolute moral stature, however they may remain mixed with what McAlpine calls "stagey idolatry," "sensuality," "eruptions of aspects of his earlier infatuation and...symptoms of his present distress."[30]

The sense of the painfully incomplete extent to which even the most committed character can incarnate his vision, or the most decisive motives remain unmixed, is of a piece with the way the poem renders everything problematical. Troilus finds it no easier to be a courtly or a tragic hero than the narrator finds it to write a poetic history, and harder than Pandarus finds it to decide whether or not he is a pander, a point he never resolves. All that is clear, vivid, and sparkling in Boccaccio has become obscure and problematical in Chaucer, as if a sponge had been wiped across the clear lines of the *Filostrato*. The reader must grope his way through the characters's experience as he does through his own. The conflict between story and "epilogue," between divine and human values, is only the last and most overt of the conflicts that run through the entire poem. Every aspect of the story is presented so as to render as devastating as possible the conflict of good with good, motive with motive, reality with reality, and, above all, love with love. Chaucer has written the only kind of divine comedy he can in a world

---

[28] Anthony E. Farnham, "Chaucerian Irony and the Ending of Chaucer's Troilus," *ChauR* 1 (1967):209; and Robert P. apRoberts, "Criseyde's Infidelity and the Moral of the *Troilus*," *Speculum* 44 (1969):383–402.

[29] McAlpine, *The Genre of Troilus and Criseyde*, p. 56 and n.2.

[30] Ibid., p. 162; see Helterman, "The Masks of Love in *Troilus and Criseyde*," p. 30.

into which he cannot put a Virgil, in which Beatrice will not be waiting even among the fixed stars. If the world Dante creates is still the world of Saint Thomas Aquinas, that of *Troilus* is the world that was left after William of Ockham had carried to a radical point the critique of Saint Thomas that had begun almost before his synthesis was accepted.

In such a world the connections and continuities between phenomena, and between the created order and any underlying absolutes, have fallen away.[31] The chasm that separates the reality of God from that of man is unbridgeable except by flashes of apparently arbitrary revelation: "Finiti et infiniti nulla proportio." The same lack of connection exists between language and experience. The gap between the word and the thing to which it refers, recognized by Saint Thomas but without calling the validity of language into question, has opened into another chasm. Language becomes more and more a closed world of its own, cut off from the reality to which it ostensibly refers; the only statements that can be made with absolute truth are hypothetical. It is unclear whether we can even use the word "good"—at least as it has meaning for human beings—of God. We cannot extrapolate from what we know of good to his nature. Ethics too have lost their connection with perceived good. For Thomas, God's ethical demands are "organic" to the creature for whom the demands are made. They require of the creature behavior that will most nearly completely fulfill the potentials, aptitudes, possibilities, and wholeness of that creature. In the world William of Ockham delineates, God's demands are arbitrary expressions of his will as such. In his *potentia absoluta* he might as easily have commanded us to murder and blaspheme as the reverse, though in his *potentia ordinata* he has bound himself otherwise; and if he had, murder and blasphemy would be virtuous.[32] It no longer seems possible for man to know his own experience clearly, to communicate it clearly to others, or to extrapolate from what we perceive as good in one area

[31] Extremely useful summary comments are found in Heiko Oberman, "Some Notes on the Theology of Nominalism," *HTR* 53 (1960):47–76; and Armand A. Maurer, "Some Aspects of Fourteenth-Century Philosophy," *M&H*, n.s. 7 (1976):175–88.

[32] Heiko Oberman, *The Harvest of Medieval Theology: Gabriel Biel and Late Medieval Nominalism* (1962; rev. ed., Grand Rapids, Mich.: William B. Eerdmans Co., 1967), especially pp. 36–40, 96–103.

to the good as it reveals itself in another. Neither by analyzing our own finite experience nor by jettisoning it in favor of a concern with absolutes can we hope to reach an inclusive vision. We call upon a God whose unconditioned being sets the limits to our finitude: "Thow oon, and two, and thre, eterne on lyve, / That regnest ay in thre, and two, and oon, / Uncircumscript, and al maist circumscrive" (5.1863–66). But we cannot see how all can be bound into one reality, and we feel God's surrounding presence as limitation rather than delineation. We can only hope to be defended from "visible and invisible foon" (5.1886). God's absoluteness is no longer a comfort and is not, as in Dante's final vision, marked with our likeness. We can only cling to the fact not of his transcendence but of his immanence, his birth through a woman, his death for love at a place and time in history, his willingness to love at utmost cost under the very conditions within which man's loving, too, must take place (5.1868–69):

> So make us, Jesus, for thi mercy digne,
> For love of mayde and moder thyn benigne. Amen.

Even for God himself the movement of redemption is, in Donaldson's words, "towards heaven, indeed, but towards heaven through human experience."[33]

What "fyn," then, has this Troilus for love? Chaucer's double ending is not a symptom of something fundamentally unresolved in the poem. He cannot merely jettison one perspective for another, nor can he soften the contrast between them. Most resolutions we might envisage would err in one of these directions. Critics often speak as if the narrator makes heavy weather of his task only because he is exceptionally stupid or exceptionally naïve. But this is a story that is exceptionally difficult to tell, at least for any teller who is really trying to understand it. The overt clumsiness of the narrator is an extrapolation of the difficulties inherent in his creator's very enterprise: the attempt to show that divine love and human love are far more different than Dante saw and yet that in the very loving in which the unlikeness of God and man is most clearly displayed we see also the one point of convergence between them. How is a poet to show an experience both

---

[33] Donaldson, "The Ending of Chaucer's *Troilus*," p. 101.

as it is perceived and defined in time and as it is known beyond time? Chaucer's strategy for the ending is the very one he has used all along, that of juxtaposing multiple versions of the same event. What he achieves in The Canterbury Tales by superimposing multiple narrators he achieves in Troilus by multiple representations and evaluations (the disparate pictures and the separate stages of Troilus's falling in love are a simple example). The story is tragic and comic, sinful and sacred. Troilus guessed wrong and guessed right. Criseyde was worth loving, and she was not. Troilus's love reflected every limitation of his character, his society, and his myth of love, and it transcended them. Chaucer's portrayal reflects the sense of dislocation that William of Ockham analyzed at the philosophical level, but it shows him trying to say how the pieces come together in the only way there seems to be for saying it. The truth is not one or another perception of an event, or something that can be abstracted from them all, but something that can be said only by saying each of them in succession. The poem cannot be reduced to a statement like "The flawed and fallible Troilus imitates Christ." Chaucer's meaning is ultimately religious, but his only way of conveying it has been to quarantine his story, as it were, by historical distance, from the Christian values he ultimately hopes it will illuminate. He keeps the story ostensibly isolated in a pagan era long enough that the issues it raises are thrown into relief, before they are prematurely assimilated to familiar and simplistic versions of dogma and morality. Perhaps he had to do so, not only for his reader but for himself.

Yet the poem ultimately brings us, by virtue of this very strategy, to the point where two seemingly autonomous perceptions of reality must converge. The city of Troy merges with the little threshing floor of the planet earth itself, in the physical perspective of the circling spheres and in the theological perspective of biblical history. The point is not whether the "real" poet emerges from behind his narrator in these final stanzas. What is essential is that the world familiar and real to the reader replaces that of ancient Troy. The speaker is now the friend of real, known people, Gower and Strode, moralist and philosopher. He offers them not a hypothetical translation of "myn auctor Lollius" but the imperfect and actual manuscript of the very Troilus we have been reading. The world of the poem converges on that of its audience, demanding simultaneously the assent and the judgments we accord to literature and to life itself. Conceptually, the problems of reconciling divine and human values here become too agonizing for rational solution. Yet in that very process the God "uncircumscript" who all may "circumscrive," whom we can only know as he works in history, stands in elusive but definite authority behind Troilus's love and what it reveals about human nature. In the world not of Troy but of the historical present Troilus's commitment to his own experience and that of another being, however flawed and fragmentary, brings us as close to the absolute revealed in God as finite vision can reach.

Part Eight GENRE AND CONVENTION

Troilus and Criseyde:
Poet and Narrator

ELIZABETH SALTER
University of York

T WAS E. TALBOT DONALDSON who first accurately diagnosed the literary symptoms of "a kind of nervous breakdown"[1] toward the end of *Troilus and Criseyde*. Where
others had ignored or explained away the uncomfortable
signs of distress—distracted skirmishes, rapid changes of mood and
direction—he treated the situation as one of crisis. His analysis of the
last eighteen stanzas of the poem was precise and subtle. And more
than this: his affirmation of serious disturbance in a key area of
Chaucer's poetry not only was startling but raised questions of far-
reaching importance about the process which went to the making of
this most distinguished and, in many ways, most enigmatic of
Chaucer's works.

The authoritative account offered by Donaldson of the "shifts and
turns" in the business of ending *Troilus and Criseyde* defined, as no
earlier study had done, the reader's difficulties with this section of the
poem. It left us sensitized to the inconsistencies, the oddities even, in
Chaucer's handling of the denouement of his "tragedye." The defense
which was also offered, based upon the argument that we have here a
brilliantly dramatic demonstration of the poet-narrator relationship—
"Chaucer has manipulated a narrator capable of only a simple view of
reality in such a way as to achieve the poetic expression of an extraordinarily complex one" (p. 43)—was itself a brilliant demonstration of
problem solving. It effectively located tension in the narrator, not in
the poet, and sought to prove that the "emotional storm-centre" of the
narrator's trouble with his story is made to generate energy for the
"great complexity of the poem's ultimate meaning" (p. 34). But for some

[1] E. Talbot Donaldson, "The Ending of Chaucer's *Troilus*," in A. Brown and P. Foote, eds., *Early English and Norse Studies Presented to Hugh Smith* (London, 1963), p. 34.

of us it was the convincing nature of the analysis of the narrator's "trouble" which encouraged an uneasiness about the attractive neat-ness of the solution.

The theory of the "fallible first-person singular," with its corollary of an interesting ambiguity of relationship between the author and his narrator, has been richly applied to medieval narrative fiction. Devel-oped out of "the conventions of the dream-vision, and extending to other fourteenth century poetry narrated in the first person,"[2] it seems to have given both Chaucer and Langland a controlled range of ap-proach to their subject matter; "the poet behind the narrator"[3] manipulates a series of situations which encourage, resist, and chal-lenge the hopeful reader. And the same theory has had an even more fruitful application to postmedieval narrative fiction, in which the pres-ence of "seriously flawed narrators"[4] has the authority of the authors themselves: if we are forced to deduce the working of the theory from the poetry of Chaucer and Langland, we can find it discussed in the notebooks of Henry James. There can be no question that author-narrator dualism is skillfully exploited by Chaucer in his early dream poems and again in *The General Prologue* to *The Canterbury Tales*. But the operation of this "dualism" in *Troilus and Criseyde* seems to me more difficult to accept—at least, without doing some damage to the poet's deep involvement with his poem. Indeed, the discovery of unreliable narrators in medieval fictional narratives could already have become more convenient than true; just such a state of affairs was reached in twentieth-century criticism of the novel, where overreaction to "ex-treme unreliability" in a whole series of famous witnesses provoked statements from authors: "If he means the narrator, then it is me."[5]

We do not have to imagine Chaucer putting his case in quite those words if we say that there may still be room for debate about the modes of narration in *Troilus and Criseyde*. The debate must focus largely upon the extent to which the "quandaries," so persuasively described for us by Donaldson, can be said to be engineered by the

---

[2] George Kane, "The Autobiographical Fallacy in Chaucer and Langland Studies," *Chambers Memorial Lecture* (London, 1965), p. 16.

[3] Donaldson, "The Ending of Chaucer's *Troilus*," p. 36.

[4] Wayne Booth, *The Rhetoric of Fiction* (Chicago: University of Chicago Press, 1961), p. 346.

[5] Henry Miller, quoted by Booth, ibid., p. 367.

poet for his narrator, in the service of a higher and all-embracing inte. pretation of the story. One of the alternatives is to persist in attribut- ing most of the quandaries to the poet himself, as he makes his difficult way through a major recasting of his Italian source and "annotates," both for his contemporaries and for posterity, his progress. There are many different modes of address in *Troilus and Criseyde*, suggesting that Chaucer anticipated many different readings of his poem—atten- tive and inattentive, courtly and learned. But one mode of address is, surely, that of the poet to his art; one important reading concerns his dealings with older European narratives of the *Troilus* story and the gradual evolution of his "myght to shewe in som manere" what he could offer, uniquely, to that European tradition.

To observe that even the most privileged members of Chaucer's public could not have assessed the exact nature and quality of his con- tribution does not, of course, deny that his anticipated public was in- fluential at certain levels of his artistic calculations. And clearly it was responsible for some of his most careful commentary upon the develop- ing narrative. Those of his listeners or readers who were unacquainted with any particular literary version of the Troy story would have had the firmest of views about the unalterable sequence of events consti- tuting the "double sorwe of Troilus"; any substantial variation, however temporary in effect, would have required some explanatory glossing, some authorial reassurance. Later readers, with their more comprehensive knowledge of Chaucer's materials and their different historical perspective upon his methods of procedure, may find a number of those glosses and reassurances curious rather than crucial. But what remains of permanent interest is the way in which all readers are given some access, from the very beginning of the poem, to the inner drama of its growth. We should, indeed, be cautious about con- cluding that we can identify the voice which speaks to us throughout the work as that of a simple narrator, used dramatically by an inven- tive poet, or that we can easily recognize a division of the narrational voice between poet and narrator.[6]

[6] As, for example, the division proposed by G. T. Shepherd between the voice of the *narratio* and that of the *argumentum*. See "Troilus and Criseyde," in Derek S. Brewer, ed., *Chaucer and Chaucerians* (London, 1966).

The careful arrangement of *Troilus and Criseyde* into five books, reminiscent of classical precedent and a departure from the more varied canto structure of the *Filostrato*, inadequately disguises a work which evolves gradually, according to decisions taken during the act of composition. Chaucer's changing purposes, or, to put it more positively, his capacity for change, give the poem some of its most remarkable characteristics.[7] But this is a matter of authorial responsibility, and we miss the creative excitement at the heart of the matter if we continue to think in terms of a poet-narrator arbitration as the over-all controlling and justifying device. For here may be the first time in English literature when the poet goes some way toward an acknowledgment, both to himself and to his public, of the controversial and troublesome part he finds himself bound to play in the handling of his received "matere." We are allowed, even encouraged, to speculate upon "workshop activity." And, if, indeed, the poem makes any use of narrator as distinct from author, it does so at the same time as it engages in a process of transformation: the medieval fiction of "naïve narrator," already given a particular Chaucerian likeness in his earlier poems, is made to cope with the pressing problems of the poet himself, as he presents a freshly thoughtful version of a narrative familiar to all in general outline if not in literary detail. In *Troilus and Criseyde* (to imitate a famous aphorism of C. S. Lewis) the narrator died into reality, enabling the poet to speak out with a kind of freedom hitherto denied to him.

This "death" was not immediate, however, and we hear, from time to time, that voice from *The Book of the Duchess* or *The Parliament of Fowls*, protesting mock-humble attitudes; what is there in the proem to book 1 (lines 15–16):

> For I . . . / Ne dar to love, for my unliklynesse[8]

comes again in the proem to book 2 (lines 19–21):

> Ek though I speke of love unfelyngly, No wonder is, . . .
> A blynd man kan nat juggen wel in hewis.

---

[7] Elizabeth Salter, "*Troilus and Criseyde*: A Reconsideration," in J. Lawlor, ed., *Patterns of Love and Courtesy* (London, 1966).

[8] *The Book of Troilus and Criseyde*, ed. R. K. Root (Princeton, N.J.: Princeton University Press, 1945), 1.15–16.

And in book 3 (lines 1408–10), even after the assured treatment of the "blisful nyght, of hem so longe isouht":

> For myne wordes, . . .
> I speke hem alle under correccioun
> Of yow that felyng han in loves art. . . .

The lingering usefulness of such protestations may be more closely related to contemporary social circumstance than we have recently been asked to believe. But it is significant that by book 3 they do not appear in the cruder forms of books 1 and 2;[9] even the lines quoted above from book 3 are prefaced by a confident statement about the way in which the source material may, "at loves reverence," have been "eched for the beste" (lines 1405–1407)–that is, "expanded and improved." It is an author's piece of self-advertisement, and not in the sáme world as that of the polite disclaimer which follows. The poet, not the narrator, is in the ascendant; if he is a learner, he is clerk to no sublunary court of love but to the goddess herself, as the strong proem to book 3 makes very clear (lines 39–42):

> Now lady bryght, for thi benignite,
> . . . .
> Whos clerk I am, so techeth me devyse
> Som joye of that is felt in thy servyse.

The problems to which this clerk addresses himself are those of art, not of experience, and at such points his humility is proper in a high creative context, rather than in that of medieval rhetorical convention or medieval courtly society. This is confirmed by the end of the poem, when Chaucer places his work in an antique literary tradition and defines his "modesty" as a dignified act of obeisance to "the storied past" (5.1786, 1790–92):

> Go litel book, go, litel my tragedye,
> . . . .
> But subgit be to alle poesie,
> And kiss the steppes, where as thow seest pace
> Virgile, Ovide, Omer, Lucan and Stace

[9] See, for instance, the examples at 3.1319–20 and 4.801–805.

It is important, therefore, that in our search to identify the "fallible narrator," concerned and confused about the way in which events are turning out, we do not fail to recognize what may be the poet, making his own statements, tentative as they may sometimes be, about the problematic background to his artistic decisions and procedures. We cannot miss the significance of the signal at the end of book 3, when we are given direct information about the poet's changes in the original Boccaccian sequence division (3.1818):

> My thridde book now ende ich in this wyse....

But we could miss, by attributing the stanzas to a reluctant and incon- sistent narrator, the significance of the proem to book 4, when we are certainly introduced to a poet's sense of dilemma — a prescribed "matere" now seriously at variance with the situation and characters as he has chosen to develop them (4.15–21):

> For how Criseyde Troilus forsook,
> Or at the leeste how that she was unkynde,
> Moot hennes forth ben matere of my book.
> As writen folk thorugh which it is in mynde.
> Allas! that they sholde evere cause fynde
> To speke hire harm! and if they on hire lye,
> I wis, hem self sholde han the vilanye.

This could be read as the narrator's willful, inexplicable refusal to face what the omniscient poet must arrange to happen. But it could just as easily be understood as the poet's own lament for the inevitable tarnishing of a lady whose special brightness had been his deliberate creation. It could also be the poet's bid to his readers, or listeners, for a more reflective attitude to coming events than was traditionally accorded — "as writen folk thorugh which it is in mynde" — to the narra- tive of Criseyde's betrayal of Troilus. The poet, in fact, may be sharing with them, and with us, his mixed feelings about the largely unequivo- cal materials with which he must henceforth work and preparing us, by unexpectedly raising the questions of their veracity — "and if they on hire lye" — for the possibility, at the very least, of an opinion about, rather than a simple judgment upon, Criseyde's perfidy. And this is what book 4 goes about to demonstrate. Much of Chaucer's energy is here devoted to the crossing and recrossing of the plain story line with invitations to reflect upon the complex relationship between Criseyde's motives and her actions (4.1415–21):

> And treweliche, as writen wel I fynde,
> That al this thyng was seyd of good entente;
> And that hire herte trewe was and kynde
> Towardes hym, and spak right as she mente
> . . . .
> And was in purpos evere to be trewe,
> Thus writen they that of hir werkes knewe.

Here he refers to authorities other than Boccaccio, and, indeed, some of his boldest departures from the Italian text in this book serve to delay as long as possible the moment of our final disillusionment with Criseyde. The transference to her of the speech "'For trusteth wel, that youre estat roial / Ne veyn delit. . . / This made, aboven every creature / That I was youre, and shal, whil I may dure'" (4.1667–82), which was originally given to Troilus in the Italian,[10] is a move in keeping with his assurance of her "good entente"—it contains some of his best and warmest writing (lines 1672–73):

> "But moral vertu, grounded upon trouthe,
> That was the cause I first hadde on yow routhe."

And here, although it may be objected that there is some inaccuracy in Criseyde's memory of the first occasion when she "had pity" upon Troilus, there is no inaccuracy in the poet's recollection of his labor—and some would say his almost perverse labor—over the preceding books, to make her into the kind of woman who might meditate so tenderly upon the long days of falling in love.

There are other places in the poem where we may be in danger of mistaking poet for overanxious narrator: the comment, for instance, in book 2 about the "suddenness" of Criseyde's attraction to Troilus (2.666–68):

> Now myghte som envious jangle thus:
> "This was a sodeyn love; how myghte it be
> That she so lightly loved Troilus. . .?

---

[10] Canto 4, stanzas 164–66: "Non mi sospinse ad amarti bellezza," *Filostrato*, ed. M. Marti, *Giovanni Boccaccio: Opere minori in volgare* (Milano, 1970).

The comment is not only redundant but reductive, for nothing could be further from a proper description of the slow process by which Pandarus and circumstance bring her to love than the word "lightly." What anxiety is displayed here, however, belongs to the poet, not the narrator, who has worked to transform the "light loving" of his Italian heroine into something more hardly won. It is, no doubt, the poet who remembers Boccaccio's Criseida, "already...stricken by love," ("trafitta gia," *Fil.* 2, stanza 66), even as Pandarus puts the suit of Troilus to her: Boccaccio's Criseida, standing invitingly at one of her windows, "suddenly taken" with the sight of the young man, "so that she desired him beyond any other good" ("E si subitamente presa fue, / che sopra ogni altro bene lui disia," *Fil.* 2 stanza 83).

The stanzas in question (lines 666–79) offer a surface record of the deeper troubles encountered by the poet as he wrought decisive changes in his source.[11] No apology was needed, in reality, for the newly delicate account of Criseyde's first step toward capitulation— we accept the naturalness of "Who yaf me drynke?" because we have been prepared so well. But Chaucer's own loss of confidence is both real and understandable; he labors a point already made, partly because he still has in mind the Italian source, and partly because he is only too conscious of the difficult task he has set himself—that of asking his readers to take a more generous view of Criseyde. The lines permit us to assess just how much effort he is expending, in this crucial book, upon the conversion, not just the translation, of the *Filostrato*.

It is in this light that we must view that later loss of confidence—the "nervous breakdown" of the approach to the ending of the poem. Nothing in book 5, as it goes about its stern and often patently distasteful business of charting the ruin of all that Troilus believed in, could lead us to doubt that we are meant to understand ourselves in the hands of the poet from start to finish. The only "fallible voice" within this book, as, indeed, within all the preceding books, is that of Pandarus, whose narrow involvement with the buildup and breakdown of the affair does truly give us a commentary from a "seriously

---

[11] The transposition of Criseyde's somewhat calculating thoughts, so that they follow her sight of Troilus from the window rather than, as in the Italian, precede it, is just such a "decisive change," which helps win her a moment of grace, however temporary.

flawed" viewpoint. But in book 5 the authorial voice is strong and purposeful throughout; in no other part of the work are we so constantly
kept in touch with the assembly of materials and the craft of the poet
as he deploys them.[12] And it is interesting that these references corre-
late with Chaucer's increasing use of other versions of the Troy story
to augment the Italian. It is to Benoît de Sainte-Maure that he often
turns to "flesh out" the otherwise psychologically bare account of Criseyde's treachery; his borrowings, which begin in book 4 but become
more frequent and significant in book 5, serve to stress both the intolerable pressures upon her in the Greek camp and the shocking realities
of her behavior, once she has taken "a purpos for tabyde" (5.770).

We are again encouraged, in book 5, to consider the internal workings of the poem and the problems faced by the poet as he attempts to
make sense—and, more accurately, all kinds of sense—out of his authorities. The magnitude of those problems can be gauged by the various-
ness of the commentary, which not only reminds us of the presence of
"olde bokes" behind the English text but also reveals to us a good deal
of the mind of Chaucer, questioning, assessing, synthesizing, and interpreting what those books contained. Thus Benoît's lines describing
Criseyde's "compassionate" surrender to Diomede are put into a
freshly ambiguous context by the addition of "I not" (5.1049-50):[13]

> And for to hele hym of his sorwes smerte,
> Men seyn, I not, that she yaf hym hire herte.

The indication, in the *Roman de Troie*, that two years elapsed before
that surrender was complete, is used to suggest some slight mitigation
of her guilt (5.1091-92):

> For though that he bigan to wowe hire soone,
> Or he hire wan, yit was there more to doone.

Most striking, however, is an unusually direct passage which introduces the possibility of modifying what "the storye wol devyse" by a
sense of pity for Criseyde (5.109-94, 1097-99):

---

[12] See, for instance, lines 19, 272, 799, 834, 1037, 1044, 1050, 1051, 1088, 1089, 1094, 1562,
1758, 1765, 1777, 1786-99.
[13] *Roman de Troie*, ed. L. Constans (SATF, 1907; reprint ed., 1968), lines 20208-209.

> Ne me ne list this sely womman chyde,
> Forther than the storye wol devyse.
> . . . .
>
> And if I might excuse hire any wise,
> For she so sory was for hire untrouthe,
> I wis, I wolde excuse hire yit for routhe.

Even at this late stage of harsh certainty, a desire to refer fact to opinion persists; speculation is invited in the most hopeless contexts: the second, empty letter of Criseyde to Troilus, for example—was it prompted by some stirring of her easy compassion? The parenthetical phrase seems to suspend the decision (5.187–88):

> For which Criseyde upon a day, for routhe—
> I take it so. . . .

But none of this can, I think, be relegated to a sentimental narrator. The commentary in *Troilus and Criseyde* carries the burden of authorial doubt and assurance, thought and afterthought. It records the poet's busy—and sometimes not entirely happy—engagement with his medieval materials, with his medieval public. It records also the poet's struggle to express something of what he dimly understood about the new kind of life he had given to his characters. This is particularly relevant to Criseyde, whose gradual transformation from the shallow girl of Boccaccio's poem to the intriguing and baffling woman of the English work was such an expensive though triumphant experiment for Chaucer. For, ironically enough, in the process of rewriting an old story, he made the near discovery of a way of viewing and presenting human beings which led, logically, to the abandonment of commentary altogether, whether by poet or by narrator. There are long stretches of *Troilus and Criseyde* in which the narrating voice is virtually eliminated and the characters act out their parts uninterrupted by anyone whose function is to "stand in the gaps to teach you / The stages of the story."[14] This direct exposure of scene and dialogue is essentially dramatic in method; it is often highly successful, especially when the relationships in question admit some degree of enigma. Thus passages of dialogue between Criseyde and Pandarus in book 2 and between

[14] *Pericles* 4.4.8–9.

Criseyde and Troilus in book 4 stand independent, evoking rather than dictating our responses and, as in drama, allowing obscurities to exist without comment: "...the unfocussed aspects of character work within the minds of those who encounter them, like yeast in bread."[15]

The potential of such a discovery could not, of course, be fully realized within the bounds of a medieval narrative form—especially one which was to present itself as a "tragedye." The necessity of meeting obligations to a clearly prescribed story sequence and of providing some interim as well as final statements which could lighten obscurities, resolve all problems, was absolute. It was this necessity, to make all clear, in a description and a reading of life inevitably at odds with his subtler perceptions of the "breeding of causes"[16] in human nature, which precipitated Chaucer's "nervous breakdown" as he came to the ending of his poem. After some desperate manoeuvers he turned to the conclusion of another of Boccaccio's works, the *Teseida*, to achieve that clarity of judgment alien to his poetic (and dramatic) imagination. It is his own "Ode to Duty," his dismissal of the "uncharted freedom" which had withheld nothing from him in this poem except repose.

[15] M. S. Bradbrook, *English Dramatic Form* (London, 1965), p. 13.
[16] See 5.1027-28.

A Note on Gower's Persona

PAUL STROHM
Indiana University

NE OF JOHN GOWER's problems with modern literary critics is undoubtedly his tendency to describe in somewhat laborious fashion his artistic goals and his proposed means of accomplishing them. Yet historians of literary theory, at any rate, can be grateful to him for spelling out many matters which are taken for granted in the works of his contemporaries. In his creation and use of a persona, for example, he explains assumptions which remain tacit in the works of Deschamps, Machaut, Chaucer, and others.

The idea that a version of the author might be projected as a persona into his or her work received little support from most classical and postclassical literary theorists. As far as they are concerned, the audience of a literary work encounters an *auctor* who speaks in his or her own voice, a persona in the sense of a created character who is wholly separate from the *auctor*, or a combination of the two modes. This system of classification was influentially set forth by the fourth-century grammarian Diomedes in his *Artis grammaticae*. He recognized the narrative mode of the *Georgics* or certain songs in which the poet does all the talking ("in quo poeta ipse loquitur sine ullius personae interlocutione"), the dramatic mode of tragedy or comedy in which the personae do all the talking ("in quo personae agunt solae sine ullius poetae interlocutione"), and the mixed mode of the *Iliad* and the *Odyssey*, in which both poet and characters speak ("in quo poeta ipse loquitur et personae loquentes introducuntur").[1] While our modern ideas of self-presentation might incline us to dispute these categories and to argue that the "I" of the *Georgics* is indeed an authorial persona, Diomedes (and such followers as Bede) felt no inclination to make such a point.

With the rise of new and distinctively medieval literary genres – par-

---

[1] Diomedes, "Artis Grammaticae," lib. 3, in *Grammatici Latini*, ed. H. Keil (Hildesheim: Georg Olms, 1961), p. 482.

ticularly the Latin *visiones* of the twelfth century and the vernacular visions of the thirteenth and fourteenth centuries—we encounter an increasingly ambitious use of an "I" who not only tells a story but is projected as a protagonist into a wide variety of visionary or hypo-thetical situations. In Latin *visiones* we are likely to encounter Spitzer's "visionary I," whose field of awareness and insight is potentially far wider than that of the author and who retains certain of the author's experience.[2] In vernacular love visions we are likely to encounter a hapless lover whose capacities and attainments are manifestly less than those of the author. Whether the perspective of this "I" is broader or narrower than that of the author, the "I" has moved beyond a simple narrative voice to become a separate character and participant in the events of the poem.

New forms of practice are bound to result in new theory, and one new aspect of theory appears in John Gower's *Confessio Amantis*. When Gower decided in this work to project an imagined version of himself, bearing his name and some of his characteristics but equipped with the universal experience of those who have grown old in the ser-vice of love, he characteristically had something to say on the matter. With his authorial Prologue behind him and this imagined self at the point of introduction, he notes in his marginal gloss, "Here, as if in the persona of others whom love binds, the author, imagining himself to be a Lover, intends to write about their different passions individually in the different sections of this book" ("Hic quasi in persona aliorum, quos amor alligat, fingens se auctor esse Amantem, varias eorum passiones variis huius libri distinccionibus per singula scribere proponit").[3] This short gloss contains several clues to Gower's understanding of the role of the author-as-persona. The most obvious is that the author imagines for himself the role of Lover—the persona is fashioned or imagined, rather than simply formed through exaggeration of existing traits or worked out in performance. Furthermore, the persona illustrates the tendencies not just of a plausible other person but *aliorum*—the

[2] Leo Spitzer, "Note on the Poetic and the Empirical 'I' in Medieval Authors," *Traditio* 4 (1946):417–18.

[3] John Gower, *Works*, ed. G. C. Macaulay, vols. 2, 3 (Oxford: Clarendon Press, 1901), gloss to 1.61.

presumably universal traits of a plural number of other persons. This strong push toward universality may be one of the reasons why modern readers find Gower's persona less various and less exciting than Chaucer's, but some degree of universality of outlook is common to all the fourteenth-century personae, Chaucer's included.

The best framework for understanding Gower's persona in action remains the threefold scheme which E. Talbot Donaldson first described in "Chaucer the Pilgrim."[4] Just as Donaldson has made us aware of the interaction in Chaucer's poetry between and among Chaucer the Pilgrim, Chaucer the Poet, and the historical Chaucer, so is our enjoyment of *Confessio Amantis* sharpened by the interplay of Gower as Amans, Gower as Poet or *auctor* of the *presens libellus*, and the historical John Gower.

Gower's three persons can be distinguished with some confidence – the more so because the *Confessio* is explicitly designed to be circulated as a *written* work, with such relevant attachments as a dedicatory prologue and epilogue, verses of Latin commentary, and additional dedication, marginal glosses, and (in some cases) a Latin history of Gower's literary production.

Gower's persona is called "Sone" and "this man" by Venus and Genius and is identified as Amans in the glosses and title of the poem. The exemplary nature of his experience is emphasized throughout, and Gower the Poet tells us at the beginning that he will describe his meeting with love in order that "the world ensample fette / Mai after this" (1.86–87). This persona holds many traits in common with the narrator-protagonists of the French love visions, and also with those of Chaucer's *Book of the Duchess* and *Parliament of Fowls*. Like many of them he is so narrowed in his interests and capacities that he requires outside education and guidance – in this case he is immobilized by a predominance of will over reason and a consequent addling of the wits: "...my wittes ben so blinde, / That I ne can miselven teche" (1.228–29). He has long served love but has achieved few favors of which to boast or confess (1.2435–36). He is punctilious, fearful, prone to "wanhope," but singlemindedly persevering.

---

[4] E. Talbot Donaldson, *Speaking of Chaucer* (New York: W. W. Norton, 1972), pp. 1–12.

Gower the Poet is the creater of this work which the glosses call the *presens libellus*. These same glosses designate him as *auctor*, and his movement away from self-deprecation and toward authorial pride may be seen in a revised gloss in which he eliminates an earlier description of himself as "compiler" in favor of "composer" (gloss to Prologue, line 22). The glosses in fact have a crucial role in reminding us of the presence of Gower the Poet as distinct from the obviously limited viewpoint of Amans. This presence is further underscored in the Prologue and some parts of the Epilogue, in which Gower as Poet tells us how the book came to be written, of the "middel weie" he intends to pursue (Prologue, line 17), and of his own aspiration to sing in the voice of Orion, whose harp brought all into "good acord" (Prologue, lines 1053–69). Having carefully drawn a distinction between himself and his persona, Gower the Poet seems interested throughout most of the book in keeping the distinction sharp. Unlike such predecessors as Guillaume de Lorris (in his sections of the *Roman de la Rose*) and Boccaccio (in the Prologue to the *Decameron*), he shows no interest in alluding, however playfully, to a real or imagined love life outside the work; the follies of Amans in pursuit of his lady are his follies alone.

The historical Gower is more visible to readers of a complete manuscript or edition of the *Confessio* than is the historical Chaucer to a reader of *The Canterbury Tales*. The activities of a historical Chaucer may be inferred from such biographical and historical convergences as his loss of preferment during the eclipse of the royal faction between 1386 and 1389 and the possibility that he began writing *The Canterbury Tales* during this period. Yet Chaucer confines such matters as direct dedication, appeals for favor, and advice to princes to *The Complaint to His Purse* and other short, occasional poems. Gower, in contrast, shows no hesitation in incorporating such matters directly into his longest English poem, not only in dedicatory verses (to Henry of Derby) but in the body of the poem—in his direct dedications and appeals to Richard II (in the Prologue and Epilogue to the first version) and then to Henry (in the Prologue to the final version). While Gower's passionate concern with politics is one aspect of his poetical stance, his shifting dedications inevitably remind us of "extrapoetical" considerations.

Donaldson reminds us that Chaucer's three persons "frequently got together in the same body."[5] This interpenetration occurs less often with Gower, undoubtedly to his artistic loss. But it does occur—crucially and also movingly—in the closing stages of the *Confessio*.

The end of the *Confessio* chronicles the return of Amans from obsession to self-awareness, from willfulness to reason. Amans, becoming aware that he can neither succeed in love nor relinquish love, turns to Genius for final advice. Genius speaks to Amans in the voice of a priest as well as a servant of Venus, and counsels him to withdraw from an earthly to a more perfect love. Upon Amans's final supplication to Venus, she appears and asks him his name, which is given for the first time as John Gower. The substitution of John Gower for "Sone" and Amans in turn marks a station on the way to lucidity and reunion of Amans with the broader perspective of the Poet—just as, according to Spitzer's perception about the *Commedia*, Dante is addressed by his name only in canto 30 of the *Purgatorio*, when he is about to become "a true Christian personality."[6] Venus's counsel is for a "beau retret" (8.2416), and she instructs Cupid to remove his fiery lance. At this point she holds before Amans a "wonder Mirour" (line 2821) of self-knowledge, in which the would-be Lover sees himself dwindle to the physical person of the aged Poet, with dimming eyes and thinning cheeks and wrinkling countenance and graying hair. Likening the course of life to the passing of the seasons, he knows that his time of love is over (lines 2853–56):

> The Wynter wol no Somer knowe,
> The grene lef is overthrowe,
> The clothed erthe is thanne bare,
> Despuiled is the Somerfare. . . .

Returning home, the Poet now prays in his own voice for the state of the realm (lines 2971–3105). And, in final recapitulation, he addresses his readership in all three interpenetrating voices: as Poet ("Y undirtok / In englesch forto make a book," lines 3107–3108), as historical John Gower ("So preye y to my lordis alle / Now in myn age, how so befalle, / That y mot stonden in here grace," lines 3129–31), and as

[5] Ibid., p. 1.
[6] Spitzer, "Note on the Poetic and the Empirical 'I' in Medieval Authors," p. 417.

awakened or educated Amans ("my final leve / I take... / Of love and of his dedly hele," lines 3152–55).

While Gower at other times lumbers a little, he closes out the Con-fessio with dignity and skill. His success is due in part to his own under-valued talents and in part to the support of a narrative tradition— shared with Chaucer and others—which enabled a poet without fear of misunderstanding to involve himself or herself as a character in a poem. As Gower's gloss on the subject indicates, his manipulation of his per-sona within the boundaries of this tradition was highly conscious. His explicit comments on the use of his persona reinforce Donaldson's analysis of Chaucer's own practice, even as Donaldson's discussion of Chaucer's three entities illuminates Gower's artistic technique.

Morwe of May:
A Season of Feminine Ambiguity

ELEANOR WINSOR LEACH
Indiana University

OME YEARS AGO I had the pleasure of investigating under E. Talbot Donaldson's guidance the nature, if not the existence, of good women – the Chaucerian kind of course. Among the complexities masked by simplicity that Donaldson has taught readers of Chaucer to perceive, the polymorphous ambiguity of women must take a high place. His ability to persuade even a woman in this matter would outrank any other triumph of scholarly style did he not always find such infallible support in his poet. Even so, he is scarcely to blame for my construction of an argument which sought more credit for my scholarly pretensions than for my sex: that not even rhetoric could create a good woman, since he, with the true courtliness of an efficient graduate director, maintained that a woman who finished her dissertation was good enough for the moment. Reacquaintance with Donaldson has, however, complicated this issue by the introduction of that troublesome Chaucerian question of "trothe"; a genuinely good woman might have demonstrated her fidelity to poet and director alike by a published dissertation. Useless to plead that Chaucer himself would not frown upon my long years of dalliance with those Roman Diomedes – Vergil, Ovid, Horace, and their like – and it is therefore my pleasure to present these few observations by way of penance.

A graduate student seeking to demonstrate the complexity of Chaucer's *Legend of Good Women* may surely be forgiven for having given more attention to the respectably ponderous questions of sources and rhetoric[1] than to the May month of the Prologue over whose sparkling skies still hung – at least in 1962 – the cloud of an embarrassing simplic-

---

[1] Eleanor Jane Winsor, "A Study of the Sources and Rhetoric of Chaucer's *Legend of Good Women* and Ovid's *Heroides*" (Ph.D. diss., Yale University, 1963).

ity, no matter if the first paragraph of Robinson's introduction declared that the "simplicity was not naïve."[2] But Donaldson's essay "The Masculine Narrator and Four Women of Style" offers not merely a locus for his career-long argument that Chaucer's poetry is less simple than he tells us[3] but also the implicit suggestion that Chaucerian May Days might also be less than simple. At the same time that he persuades us that the substance or insubstantiality of Emelye or "faire, fresshe May" cannot be separated from the shaping visions of their narrators, one notices the consistency with which these visions have resort to certain tangible or affective characteristics of the May month itself. The month supplies, in Donaldson's words, the imagery by which the Knight introduces an Emelye scarcely separate from the garden in which she walks:

> May, May, May, May; lily, stalk, flowers, garden, flowers, garland; green, rose, yellow, white red; morning, day sunrise: all the best of nature in the Spring . . . not only an embodiment of all pretty young girls in the Spring, but a proof that the Spring of pretty young girls is a permanent thing, and that May in their persons will always warm the masculine heart as May warms their hearts and sends them out among the flowers.[4]

The chivalrous restraint of the Knight's vision gives the gentlest accommodation to the erotic element in this permanence and discovers even a structure within which the young lovers can accommodate it, though with less paternal detachment, in the rapidly successive stages of their passion: two sudden and physically experienced wounds whose pain is distanced by the recognition of a rivalry that reaches its culmination in Arcite's theoretical distinction between two versions of love (KnT 1158–59):

> Thyn is affeccioun of hoolynesse,
> And myn is love, as to a creature; . . . .

Although Emelye, as Donaldson says, deceives her lovers by a passiv-

---

[2] *The Works of Geoffrey Chaucer*, ed. F. N. Robinson, 2d ed. (Cambridge, Mass.: Riverside Press, 1957). All quotations used in this paper follow this text.

[3] E. Talbot Donaldson, "The Masculine Narrator and Four Women of Style," in *Speaking of Chaucer* (New York: W. W. Norton, 1970), pp. 46–65.

[4] Ibid., p. 49.

ity more appropriate to a symbol than to a woman,[5] such deception is preferable to that exercised by the other Maylike beauty who is set before our eyes in a condition equally passive, equally unshaped by experience, yet tinted by the prejudice of an embittered narrator's eye that hints at her potential to be other than ideal. Words fail, we are told, to articulate the specifics of her beauty save by its own self-limiting names of beauty and May lest they should look beneath surface passivity to discover some stirring seeds of a character.[6] Different, then, as the two ladies may be by virtue of the ideas their narrators impose upon them, something, nonetheless, makes them similar within the May metaphor: nothing other than its appropriateness to a moment of first meeting with all its present visual satisfaction that suspends future promise, either ominous or benign.

If Emelye is insubstantial, the May metaphors of her first portrait become less so when we place them within the larger context of a narrative whose three most critical actions occur within this very month however many years apart. Given the long stretches of intermediary time that pass by in this narrative with a few words, it can only appear characteristic of the particular order human vision imposes upon a random world[7] that it should be another May morning when Palamon breaks loose from his imprisonment to encounter the prospering Arcite-Philostrate. Like the lady of his worship, Arcite is caught a-Maying, but the season works rather more vigorously upon his masculine nature (lines 1500–1503):

> And for to doon his observaunce to May,
> Remembrynge on the poynt of his desir,
> He on a courser, startlynge as the fir,
> Is riden into the feeldes hym to pleye, ...

Where Emelye gathered flowers, Arcite chooses his garland of leaves (lines 1510–12):

> "May, with alle thy floures and thy grene,
> Welcome be thou, faire, fresshe May,
> In hope that I som grene gete may."

[5] Ibid., pp. 48–50.

[6] Ibid., pp. 52–53.

[7] The general concept is owing to E. Talbot Donaldson, *Chaucer's Poetry: An Anthology for the Modern Reader* (New York: Ronald Press, 1958), p. 904.

Since greens in their literally accessible form are scarcely sparse enough on May mornings to be an object of mere hope, the tenor of Arcite's modest wish is clear enough. He senses the appropriateness of the season to the furtherance of his desire. Nor is it any less the interaction of season and desire that spurs the young men into combat once they have recognized each other's identity within that territory beyond prison where Emelye, for all practical purposes, is as much a woman as a vision. The high formalities of their challenge and courtesy of their arming give a brittle shape of ceremony to the clash of animal spirits which the narrator, in his sifting out of heroic metaphors, aptly typifies by hitting upon one that conjures up an unembellished mating battle in the woods: "That foughten breme, as it were bores two."

Nor again, when Duke Theseus in his civilized wisdom and sense of his sister's dignity and indivisibility decrees a rechanneling of the mating drive into the more appropriately chivalric form of a tournament, can we be surprised at his placing the event a year hence, and thus in May. The orderly patterns of *The Knight's Tale* have much to do with the social restraints that modify the elemental forces in man's nature.[8] But in the other tale where social forms are exemplified in the justifications and ceremony of January's marriage are undertaken to permit the release of such forces, it is appropriate that the action does not remain caught within a decorously recurrent May but marches straight on into lusty June for January to gain the ironic fruition of his desired "paradys." The larger force that governs *The Merchant's Tale* and nourishes its characters is that amoral energy that turns spring months into summer and makes planted gardens achieve a life of their own; it is a force whose action within human nature is echoed by the supernatural as Pluto and Persephone make their playground within January's stonewalled garden, not to influence but to universalize the tale. January's error of calculation is that he can at once surrender himself to this force for his pleasure and contain it within the boundaries of his will.

In both these tales, then, May visions begin with the multiple possibilities of lovely women and expand to the greater multiplicities of

[8] My generalization is based upon the remarks of Charles Muscatine in "Form, Texture and Meaning in Chaucer's *Knight's Tale*," in Edward Wagenknecht, ed., *Chaucer: Modern Essays in Criticism* (New York: Oxford University Press, 1959), pp. 71–81.

love. In the vitality of its greenness May is an atmosphere full of promise, preserving innocence short of fruition and yet offering a present
sensuousness in the luxuriance of its flowers. Within this context the
expectations raised by our two ladies are two sides of a potential that
will be discriminated only in the future when the chaff becomes separate from the corn.

Lest this contrast appear too neat for a pair of tales not written for
such juxtaposition, one may consider how aspects of May's potential
figure in other poems. Emphasis falls upon rebirth on the day of Pandarus's mission to Criseyde whose dawning opens the second book of
Troilus with a May carol (2.50–55):

> In May, that moder is of monthes glade,
> That fresshe floures, blew and white and rede,
> Ben quicke agayn, that wynter dede made,
> And ful of bawme is fletyng every mede;
> Whan Phebus doth his bryghte bemes sprede,
> Right in the white Bole....

Along with the spirituality of quick and dead goes the sensual intermingling of balm and sunshine. As the mother of succeeding months of
fulfillment, May is an anticipation of the direction love will follow. The
season is not only atmospherically and emotionally appropriate to Pandarus's errand but, by his calculation, astrologically appropriate as
well. It would be scarcely an ambiguous beginning save as all joy in
Troilus is ambivalent. In the garden of *The Parliament of Fowls* there is
almost too much of "grene and lusty May" for the sensibilities of the
bookish dreamer entering into Cupid's lush paradise from the disciplined cosmology of the *Somnium Scipionis*. He witnesses a moment in
which, as a critic has recently put it, "the separation of man from
nature is at its sharpest when all the birds choose their mates for the
coming year."[9] But the harmonies of bird song that conclude this vision
reecho within the natural meadow of the F Prologue of *The Legend of
Good Women*, which blooms with a May Day luxuriance more overwhelming, perhaps, than any other in Chaucer, submerging us in
flowers, greenness, and sweet breezes. In spite of its power to lure the
poet, like a schoolboy, from his study, this May seems at first glance

---

[9] John M. Fyler, *Chaucer and Ovid* (New Haven, Conn.: Yale University Press, 1979), p. 92.

the chastest of seasons, prompting no lusts either open or secret but rather stately formulas of floral adulation composed by a narrator whose professed lack of experience implies a lifelong innocence of love. All the same, as the *Legend* is related to Chaucer's other poems, both past and future, so its May, I believe, is related both in spirit and in elusive substance to other Chaucerian Mays whether feminine or at-mospheric, for it hides complexity beneath its simple surface in a man-ner that tells us something about the poem itself.

One facet of the *Legend* that has come to command enough critical attention to need no further proof is its self-consciousness about the theory and craft of poetry. No longer does one have to argue for Chau-cer's artistic commitment to the piece or for its holding a significant place among his works. In their recent studies R. W. Frank and R. O. Payne have defined this position as that of a transitional *ars poetica* summarizing the poet's career by a combination of allusion and direct reference and charting new directions for new poems. With this one point in common the two interpretations still differ as fully as previous readings of the *Legend*. For Payne its significance lies in the poet's crystallization of his own fictional-autobiographical persona as specta-tor of love,[10] while Frank sees, rather, a major turning point for his work in the expression of a desire to break free of the "garden" of tradi-tional courtly love poetry and move, as it were, into broader fields.[11] While Payne concerns himself almost entirely with the Prologue as a self-contained unit, Frank continues beyond it to discuss the legends as the experimental embodiment of a new phase of Chaucerian develop-ment that squarely confronts the demands of narrative composition along with the lusty—as opposed to courtly—realities of love in the histories of vigorous and amorous pagan women. In his opinion the achievement of these stories lies in their "amazing" and "unexpected dedication to story, to narrative as such, to the simple 'and then, and then' of E. M. Forster's simple narrative." "The variety and extent of narrative in the *Legend*," he observes, "are remarkable in themselves and doubly remarkable in a narrator who had moved most often slowly

[10] R. O. Payne, "Making His Own Myth: The Prologue to Chaucer's *Legend of Good Women*," *ChauR* 9 (1974–75):197–211.

[11] R. W. Frank, Jr., *Chaucer and The Legend of Good Women* (Cambridge, Mass.: Harvard University Press, 1972), p. 36.

and deliberately, devoted to elaboration of a situation rather than multiplication of incident."[12] Only by mastering his techniques in this new workshop, Payne argues, could the poet prepare himself to spin the more complex and flexible narratives of The Canterbury Tales.

Although this explanation makes supreme sense of the poem's apparent ironies of literary discussion, it does not, to my mind, increase the palatability of the legends, whose difficulty, for a Chaucerian, lies precisely in their multiplication of incident at the expense of those subtle exploratory meanderings into description, philosophy, and speculation that provide at once the poetic and psychological complexity of Chaucer's previous and later works. Writing some years ago, I argued that the legends are poetically shaped, or—to be more honest than I was then—poetically disfigured, by their narrator's rigorous application of the principles of abbreviation and expansion laid down as his compositional guidelines by the Cupid of his dream.[13] Hardly new to the texture of Chaucerian poetry, these are principles of flawless medieval literary pedigree and seemingly most considerate of a reader's time and attention span but of most dubious consequences both for the complexity of narrative and for the kind of "trothe" that poetry promises to deliver. Recent attention to this problem of truth in the legends' distortion of their sources relieves me of the burden of rehearsing the detailed proofs of my argument.[14] Suffice it to say, with a phrase borrowed from John Fyler, that the "Procrustean bed" of rhetoric succeeds in transforming women of most questionable morality into saints of love in a manner that convinces no one of their virtue. Beneath my argument lay the perilous admission that our narrator never intends to convince us of the existence of "good women," but a more attractively devious course lay in evading that issue in favor of the contention that the poem was not seriously about women or love at all but merely the

[12] Ibid., p. 185. In spite of this appreciation of the narrative experiment, Frank comments (pp. 169–87) appropriately upon some of the weaknesses of story, the omissions and ambiguities created by Chaucer's practice of abbreviation, but tends to excuse these as virtually endemic to the kind of efficient, short narrative he undertakes.

[13] Winsor, "A Study of the Sources and Rhetoric," pp. 42–96.

[14] Fyler, Chaucer and Ovid, pp. 99–115. In the second part of this chapter, which examines the consequences of Chaucer's attempt to find truth where none exists (pp. 115–23), Fyler takes a subject scarcely treated in my dissertation: the paradoxical aspects of the Legend's "religion of love."

artificiality of rhetorical systems: a liberal-minded Chaucerian exposure
of the inherent fallibility of "auctoritee" to bring us out of the chill
rigors of a medieval spring into the warmer, more humanistic May Day
of the early Renaissance.

At this point I scarcely want to disavow that argument if only
because others have made their way through its labyrinthine verbal in-
vestigations and accepted it, but I am no longer ready to insist that an
exposure of rhetoric is the total substance of the poem.[15] For a poem
neither about love nor about women, the *Legend* places a remarkably
strong emphasis upon women and love. As always in Chaucer, these
two topics are closely bound up with men's ability to judge women,
which brings me back to May as the season in which their judgments
are most likely to be blurred by the fullness of promise. In the Prologue
the narrator reveals exceptionally faulty judgment, not only because of
his professed want of experience but also in his attitudes toward that
experience he chooses to relate. Although recognizably the Chaucerian
narrator with his familiar, befuddled approach to love, he does not, as
in other dream poems, dwell upon his distance from this elusive emotion but rather contents himself with the deflection of his energies
toward the daisy whom he celebrates with romantic formulas that
sound, by some odd accident, very like phrases for love (F 50–57):

> That blisful sighte softneth al my sorwe,
> So glad am I, whan that I have presence
> Of it, to doon it alle reverence,
> As she that is of alle floures flour,
> Fulfilled of al vertu and honour,
> And evere ilyke faire, and fressh of hewe;
> And I love it, and ever ylike newe,
> And evere shal, til that myn herte dye.

Such sentiments are appropriate enough within the thinly veiled referential idiom of French courtly poetry from whose repertoire the marguerite is drawn, yet their literal flavor makes Chaucer's reader

---

[15] Pat Trefzger Overbeck, "Chaucer's Good Women," *ChauR* 2 (1967):75–97, provides a new
and very different interpretation in discussing Chaucer's women, both individually and collec-
tively as "women free from the strictures of convention...a human being who is free and willing
to choose between alternative courses of action," but her evaluation does not concern itself with
the interrelationship between the narratives and the subtleties of the Prologue.

suspect a mix-up, as if the new daisy poet had somehow lost sight of the meaning in his sources and indeed believed that daisies should be the normal recipients of masculine affection: May innocence in the extreme![16] This literal touch is a creation of context, for the emotional eloquence poured over the daisy is part and parcel of a total sensuous surrender to the breath and breezes of May (F 116–22):

> And, as I koude, this fresshe flour I grette,
> Knelyng alwey, til it unclosed was,
> Upon the smale, softe, swote gras,
> That was with floures swote embrouded al,
> Of swich sweetnesse and swich odour overal,
> That, for to speke of gomme, or herbe, or tree
> Comparisoun may noon ymaked bee.

It is an absolute May wallow, yet wholly free from the unsettling eroticism that colors the springtime images of the *Parliament*, and free also from the painful fears and expectations other Chaucerian lovers experience in this season. The courtly French marguerite elicits all love's accustomed energy in an idealization untroubled by conflict. Clearly she represents love as an idea, but as a poet's, not a lover's, idea abstracted from the compromise of fleshly incarnation (F 84–93):

> She is the clernesse and the verray lyght
> That in this derke world me wynt and ledeth.
> The hert in-with my sorwfull brest yow dredeth
> And loveth so sore that ye ben verrayly
> The maistresse of my wit, and nothing I.
> My word, my werk ys knyt so in youre bond
> That, as an harpe obeieth to the hond
> And maketh it soune after his fyngerynge,
> Ryght so mowe ye oute of myn herte bringe
> Swich vois, ryght as yow lyst, to laughe or pleyne.

Such a situation may abundantly satisfy a poet, but most lovers desire something more. Within the May meadow all the conflicting forces

---

[16] Frank, *Chaucer and The Legend of Good Women*, p. 21, puts this point more boldly in saying, "The daisy passages skirt dangerously close to the shores of parody," but to read them in this manner focuses our attention on the passages themselves instead of on their contribution to Chaucer's developing portrait of the naïve narrator.

previously recognized by Chaucer's love poetry seem to have achieved their effortless resolution. The poet has it all: recurrent resurrection, flower and leaf with no decision between them, amorous bird song with faithful, fruitful mating. The discomforting rumor of lust that came from the lower-class fowls of the *Parliament* is silenced by these birds' triumphant chorus, "The foweler we deffye, / and al his craft" (F 138–39). It is indeed the May morning of Emelye's garden stroll or May's wedding without question of future meaning or consequence.

All this intermingling of innocence and sensuousness might by its own nature prolong itself indefinitely were the narrator able to achieve his aim of a quiet night's rest on his luxuriant bed of garden flowers in preparation for tomorrow's renewed devotion, but the disturbing dream that re-creates the image of the meadow divides his harmonious. May season into two conflicting personifications: the solar Cupid and benign Alceste, an ill-assorted pair, green clad both, but with their symbolic statures clearly discriminated by the pearly white of Alceste's crown and the red flowers of Cupid's robe. Thus resolved into its ambivalent components of restraint and passion, the May Day of dream confronts the narrator with the almost incomprehensible charge that what he has written in bona fide dedication to love disqualifies him completely from the fellowship of love's servants and even from his own floral version of love. The dream, that is to say, breaks into an artificially perfected world of illusion with a reminder of the real world in which love poems deal with the unruly passions of men and women, not daisies, and where the poet has somehow unfolded the complexities instead of the simplicity of love (F 323–26):

> And of myn olde servauntes thou mysseyest,
> And hynderest hem with thy translacioun,
> And lettest folk from hire devocioun
> To serve me.

Although Cupid may not be the most perceptive of Chaucerian readers, he can scarcely be faulted for holding it intolerable that the realities of love, whether experienced or theoretical, should dissuade men from emotional commitment. The obtuseness of the god lies in his taking so limited a view of poems that are many-sided that he fails to recognize that such a situation is no more intolerable for lovers than for the poet writing about love. In keeping with such obtuseness is his compromising instruction to be efficient: to abbreviate the full circum-stances of his subjects' lives to facilitate the clarity and continuity of the legends. Nor is there any less poetic compromise in Alceste's in-structions about clarity which call for emphasis upon the fidelity of women at the expense of the failings of men. These are formulas in keeping with the ambiguities of a May morning, deceptively lucid in the abstract but leading to unpredictable effects in proof.

In the Prologue the Chaucerian narrator accepts a task that no other of his dream narrators has faced: to carry the precepts of his vision over into that world of reality where poets must wrestle with the meaning and effects of their words. As I mentioned before, the tech-niques of expansion and abbreviation are not new to Chaucer's poetry, but his previous use of them has provided that subtle and perceptive first-person intervention that informs his poems, and especially the *Troilus* with a sense of love's indefinable ambivalence.[17] Reduced to the bare bones of passion and disappointment, the legends exclude all that poetic wisdom and with it the humane sympathy with which Chaucer conveys many of his most difficult truths: that few mortal ex-periences can sustain for very long the perfection they have at their best; that the failings of lovers arise not from black intention but rather from the complex interaction of forces and circumstances beyond con-trol of the individual will. These are truths that Chaucer's authorities have demonstrated in their own ways and that any honest and sensi-tive poet must continue to demonstrate in spite of imperfect readers or partial audiences that might prefer him to spin illusions by rendering human experience with one bias or another. Few men indeed have been in heaven or hell; their need is for understanding of the mixed area of life between. What the legends then prove is that Chaucer could be a simpler poet if he put his mind to it but also that simpler poetry would do as scant justice to its subject as do the legends to their sources. In this respect the poem may at once make subtle mock-ery of the artifice of conventions and formulas, and indeed of "good women," but it also affirms the stated and unstated premises of his work; it is an *ars poetica* to be sure, but also an *ars legendi*. As I look at

---

[17] E. Talbot Donaldson, "The Ending of Chaucer's *Troilus*," in *Speaking of Chaucer*, pp. 90–101.

it with a Latinist's eye, I find its title transforming itself into an insistently repeated gerundive: *Implicit legenda; explicit legenda; legenda;
legenda,* until the reader's task ceases upon the brink of a moral that
needs no elaboration:

The tale is seyd for this conclusioun.

The Intangible and Its Image: Allegorical Discourse and the Cast of *Everyman*

CAROLYNN VAN DYKE
Lafayette College

EGINNING ACTORS must find the script of *Everyman* perplexing. They are likely to have been taught that the "imaginative ability to put [oneself] truly in the place of a fictitious
character in a meaningful way . . . provides the vitality of all
good acting."[1] They may have been encouraged to cultivate that ability through "a program of self-questioning: Who is this character? How
old is he? Where was he born? What were his parents like?"[2] It is
sobering to contemplate the heroic, if not blasphemous, labors of imagination by which students might apply that advice to such roles as
Death, God, Fellowship, and Knowledge. And if they sensibly abandon the attempt at empathetic projection, they face the equally difficult task of enlarging the definition of a dramatic role. Similar, if less
pressing, difficulties confront all readers and spectators who wish to
understand the "characters" of allegorical drama, personifications
which are also dramatis personae.

One apparently simple solution is provided by traditional definitions
of allegory. If "an allegory is but a translation of abstract notions into a
picture-language,"[3] then the allegorical dramatist employs his actors
only as porters for pieces of dogma. That definition is also, of course, a
negative judgment. In *English Religious Drama*, Katherine Lee Bates
opens her chapter "Moralities" with a charmingly devastating conces-

---

[1] Robert L. Benedetti, *The Actor at Work*, rev. and enl. ed. (Englewood Cliffs, N.J.: Prentice-
Hall, 1976), p. 2.

[2] John Dolman, Jr., *The Art of Acting* (1949; reprint ed., Westport, Conn.: Greenwood Press,
1970), p. 60.

[3] Samuel Taylor Coleridge, *The Statesman's Manual*, in *The Complete Works of Samuel Taylor
Coleridge*, ed. Shedd (New York: Harper and Brothers, 1856), 1.437.

sion: "The very word is like a yawn." In a more analytic vein she explains that "these old plays manage it to be so dry and tuneless...
because in these is committed the cardinal sin of literature, – the forsak-
ing of the concrete for the abstract."[4] That is, the "characters" of
morality plays are bogus people, abstractions in human disguise. Given
the prevalence of that idea, it is not surprising that morality plays were
not staged between the Middle Ages and the twentieth century.

In 1901, however, when William Poel defied the grim anticipation of
"those who knew their dramatic history" by producing *Everyman*,
Bates's judgment was challenged.[5] "In Poel's performance," according
to a recent study, "the 'lifeless abstractions' of the medieval text turned
out to be what they must always, invisibly, have been – not walking
categories, but realized figures, parts in a play."[6] There followed a
theatrical reclamation of *Everyman*, based on a new vision of the play's
cast. As Glynne Wickham writes, nearly seventy years after Poel,

Fellowship, Kindred and Cousin, Strength and Discretion may all be abstract
personification and, as such, contemptuously dismissed as shadows rather
than characters by some literary critics of mediaeval Morality Plays; but each
is characterized broadly and firmly enough for the imaginative actor to fill in
just enough detail to endow the character with a personality. The spectator
can then easily take the last step and equate this personality with a real-life
character of his own acquaintance.[7]

For Wickham the actors are not carriers of abstract ideas; on the contrary, each abstract name is a portmanteau for any number of personalities, one of which the actor must display. Thus we can witness, for instance, Fellowship with a North Country accent, Everyman in jeans
and a reefer jacket, and Death as a "Marine Commando."[8]

Wickham's approach has helped make *Everyman* playable, but it has
not been universally welcomed. As he anticipated, certain "literary

[4] Katherine Lee Bates, *English Religious Drama* (1893; reprint ed., Folcroft, Pa.: Folcroft Library Editions, 1977), pp. 201–202.

[5] Robert Potter, *The English Morality Play: Origins, History, and Influence of a Dramatic Tradition* (Boston: Routledge and Kegan Paul, 1975), p. 2.

[6] Ibid., p. 2.

[7] Glynne Wickham, *Shakespeare's Dramatic Heritage: Collected Studies in Mediaeval, Tudor, and Shakespearean Drama* (New York: Barnes and Noble, 1969), p. 33.

[8] Ibid., p. 33; Potter, *The English Morality Play*, p. 2.

critics of mediaeval Morality plays" have denounced the tendency toward deallegorization. Lawrence V. Ryan argues that "the impression made by this morality on modern audiences as pure drama has served to obscure its original doctrinal purpose."[9] Following Ryan, Joanne Spencer Kantrowitz defines the moral play as "a didactic, allegorical drama" whose personae are "simply a convenient means of representation."[10]

A predictable compromise between pure doctrine and pure drama has been articulated by Michael J. Warren. *Everyman* presents two kinds of meaning simultaneously, according to Warren: the "simple fiction" concerns an individual who must go to Jerusalem, while the "allegory of that plot" is about a representative human being preparing for death.[11] The actors particularize their roles, but the audience is led "to construct a series of conceptual syntactic formulations for what is presented in spatial terms" (p. 138). Unfortunately, however, the two-meanings theory leaves the director and critic with certain problems. The play contains many overtly doctrinal speeches which intrude on the "simple plot" about the journey to Jerusalem and baffle any attempt to conceptualize that plot, since they clearly do not need conceptualization. Warren tries to preserve two levels by conceptualizing the doctrinal discussions as the thoughts of a "representative soul." For instance, Everyman hears a lecture from Good Deeds and then one from Knowledge because his "unremitting concentration on the current worthlessness of his Good Deeds forces him to the recognition that they can be restored to value only by his use of his knowledge" (p. 140). As Warren concedes, however (pp. 138, 143), certain speeches are somewhat too long to be thoughts, some of them are addressed directly to the audience, and several are delivered while the representative soul is offstage, otherwise occupied. Should the diligent allegorizer decide that only actions, not speeches, are to be conceptualized, he must account for other anomalies: Death leaves Everyman alive and then fails to return as promised, even though Everyman does in fact

[9] Lawrence V. Ryan, "Doctrine and Dramatic Structure in *Everyman*," *Speculum* 32 (1957): 722–23.

[10] Joanne Spencer Kantrowitz, "Dramatic Allegory, or, Exploring the Moral Play," *Comparative Drama* 7 (1973):68, 72.

[11] Michael J. Warren, "*Everyman*: Knowledge Once More," *Dalhousie Review* 54 (1974):137.

die; Discretion, Strength, Beauty, and Five Wits are introduced to Everyman late in his life—long after, in fact, he has been said to possess one of them.[12] In short, if the playwright of *Everyman* was trying to parallel dialogue or action with allegorical meaning, he was a very poor geometrician.

Thus none of the obvious descriptions of the cast of *Everyman* seems adequate. The characters are not simply abstractions; they are not simply human beings; they are not human beings on one level and ideas on another. All those formulations are based on theories about the nature of drama or allegory or both. Discussions of allegory are usually theoretical, of course, for critics commonly assume that the real meanings of allegory are by definition not literal ones and thus cannot be discerned empirically. But if theoretical description has indeed failed, it may be best to approach the dramatis personae of *Everyman* through the text of the play.

A natural starting point is the protagonist. Everyman is on the one hand the most easily individualizable of the play's roles, for he easily becomes anyman—or, by an ironically surprising extension, any woman. Thus he confirms Wickham's sense of the cast as individuals with general names. On the other hand, Everyman does not begin as an individual. God's opening speech employs "everyman" as a collective pronoun (lines 40–41, 60–62):

> Euery man lyueth so after his owne pleasure,
> And yet of theyr lyfe they be nothynge sure.

> They be so combred with worldly ryches
> That nedes on them I must do iustyce,
> On euery man lyuynge without fere.

God shifts from "he" to "they" in referring to "euery man," as V. A. Kolve has noted,[13] providing divine confirmation for the suspicions of innumerable freshmen that the term may be technically singular but is ineluctably plural in spirit. Only after God's collective decree do we see the individual who bears the name Everyman. The entrance of that

---

[12] A. C. Cawley, ed. *Everyman* (Manchester: Manchester University Press, 1961), line 168. Subsequent references appear in the text.

[13] V. A. Kolve, "*Everyman* and the Parable of the Talents," in *The Medieval Drama*, ed. Sandro Sticca (Albany: State University of New York Press, 1972), pp. 82–83.

individual, blithely ignorant that he represents Death's generic victim, produces a powerful effect which might well be called dramatic, even though it has little to do with conflict among characters. The drama is the enactment of a metamorphosis. John C. Webster writes that, in referring both to all men and to a single character, *Everyman* "forces us to entertain *both* meanings, even though they are logically contradictory, and to do so simultaneously."[14] I would modify Webster's statement: we do indeed entertain both meanings simultaneously, but "contradictory" is an inaccurate description of the relationship between a category and its members. The collective "euery man" becomes the singular Everyman by a shift in perspective, an act of re-cognition. We cannot account for such effects if we see Everyman as an individual on one "level" and all mankind on another, for the drama of his appearance depends on the mutual convertibility of category and individual. The medium of exchange for that conversion is, of course, language. It appears, then, that the center of Everyman's composite identity is his name.

The audience's re-cognition of the categorical "euery man" as the individual Everyman is repeated, in reverse, by Everyman himself in his encounter with Death. Asked where he is going and whether he has forgotten his Maker, Everyman offers, as Webster puts it, the "extraordinarily non-plussed and (from our informed point of view) obtuse reply: 'Why askest thou? / Woldest thou wete?'"[15] Even when informed about Death's identity, he still responds as if to "a random encounter with an obnoxious stranger" who can perhaps be bribed (p. 362). The resulting humorous irony is not incidental. Webster explains that "we are...previewing a major theme of the play, that the logic of literal things is not the only logic in the universe, that being saved depends on one's ability to keep seeing double, to keep both the literal and figurative possibilities of language in mind at once" (p. 362). "Literal" and "figurative" are unfortunate terms here, since Everyman's "literal-mindedness" is his myopic focus on the figurative representative of death. But if we substitute "concrete" and "abstract" for those terms, Webster's point becomes clear. Everyman responds to the individual

---

[14] John C. Webster, "The Allegory of Contradiction in *Everyman* and *The Faerie Queene*," in David A. Richardson, ed., *Spenser and the Middle Ages* (1976), microfiche (Cleveland: Cleveland State University Press, 1976), p. 360.

[15] Ibid., p. 362, citing *Everyman*, lines 87–88.

agent and the particular encounter, not to the concept which they embody. He thus demonstrates for the first time what Thomas Van Laan calls a blindness to "any values higher than those of world and time."[16]

The kind of naïveté which Everyman displays toward Death is usually regarded as a chronic condition of allegorical personae. C. S. Lewis writes, ". . . to the characters participating in an allegory, nothing is allegorical,"[17] and Robert E. Wood cites "the essential condition of allegory, that the characters react to circumstances in their realistic rather than their allegorical significance."[18] That "essential condition" is violated with astonishing regularity in the major allegories, as it is here. If allegorical meanings were inaccessible to Everyman, we would have to find an allegorical correlative for his encounter with Death. The obvious allegorization is "Everyman has died," but of course he has not. Short of accusing the playwright of violating "allegorical logic," as does Webster (p. 365), we may as well accept the allegory literally — that is, according to the text. Everyman's meeting with Death is not his expiration but his encounter with death. In a particular sensual experience, a frightening conversation with a stranger, he confronts God's message about his own mortality. The play constitutes, in part, Everyman's education in allegorical vision, which is the recognition of the particular and timebound as the universal.

His education continues in the well-known scenes with Fellowship, Cousin, and Kindred. Warren points out that those characters "have a dual quality; at times they appear as Everyman's friends in their particularity, and at others in their abstract roles as representative figures and aspects of Everyman's thought. The first attendant problem, however, is that the separation is never exact."[19] That "problem" is not the playwright's lapse, but his point. Fellowship is a particular human friend, but, being that, he must obey the laws of friendship (lines 213–14):

> I wyll not forsake the to my lyues ende,
> In the waye of good company.

[16] Thomas Van Laan, "*Everyman*: A Structural Analysis," *PMLA* 78 (1963):466.

[17] C. S. Lewis, *Spenser's Images of Life*, ed. Alastair Fowler (Cambridge: Cambridge University Press, 1967), p. 29.

[18] Robert E. Wood, "Britomart at the House of Busyrane," *SAB* 43 (May, 1978):7.

[19] Warren, "*Everyman*: Knowledge Once More," p. 137.

Kindred generalizes about his loyalty (lines 325–26), but his unthinking reliance on clichés reveals him as only too typical. Cousin's pitiable claim to a particular exemption from Everyman's journey – "I haue the crampe in my to" (line 356) – confirms, ironically, his categorical frailty. The point is not that the characters are particularly weak friends and kinsmen; neither, however, is it simply that earthly friends and kindred cannot figure in anyone's final reckoning. What amuses and moves us is Everyman's enlargement of perspective, from the promises and eva-sions of his friends and kin to what he has always known about friend-ship and kinship.

After his human friends desert him, Everyman turns to Goods, who, like Death, is not a category but an abstraction. Goods is also like Death in being an actor, of course, and it is in the latter form that Everyman first responds to him. "Vp, let vs go thyder to-gyder," he urges (line 424), as if Goods were really a man. What he must learn is to take Goods's name literally (lines 394–97):

> I lye here in corners, trussed and pyled so hye,
> And in chestes I am locked so fast,
> Also sacked in bagges. Thou mayst se with thyn eye
> I can not styre; in packes, lowe I lye.

Goods is lying not just under bags, though the actor is sometimes rep-resented that way, but *in* bags; being Goods, he can "folowe no man one fote" (line 426). He resembles a human being only in his ability to expound his nature to anyone who will listen. His representation by an actor is not meaningless, however, for the illusion that Goods can ac-company Everyman is exactly the illusion of potency and loyalty often produced by material goods. Thus Goods, like Death, Fellowship, Kin-dred, and Cousin, teaches Everyman to understand particularities through the categories whose names they bear and whose laws they must obey.

Goods's amusing self-exposition evinces particularly clearly the func-tion of the actors in *Everyman*: they enact their roles, which are their names. The names designate individuals whom the text invites the actors to personalize, but they simultaneously designate categorical laws which define the individuals. Thus far, the play's peculiar power has arisen from the revelation of those laws to Everyman, to the audience, and to some of the characters themselves. After Goods the dramatis personae alter, for "good deeds," "knowledge," and "confession" do not denominate classes of people or even of material objects. The actors who play these more abstract roles will enact their names in a new way: instead of showing that particular phenomena manifest universal principles, they reveal the force and meaning of universals in the phenomenal world. The change begins with Good Deeds, and it constitutes Everyman's conversion.

Unlike his appeals to Fellowship, Kindred, Cousin, and Goods, Everyman's meeting with Good Deeds is not an experiment but an acceptance of instructions given him some time ago (lines 106–108):

> And loke thou be sure of thy rekenynge,
> For before God thou shalte answere, and shewe
> Thy many badde dedes, and good but a fewe. . . .

Everyman admits somewhat ruefully after his disappointment with Goods that he will "neuer spede / Tyll that I go to my Good Dede" (lines 480–81). In that context the appearance of an actor named Good Deeds is a sign of Everyman's spiritual progress. The actor is usually dismissed as a conventional equivalent for Everyman's good deeds, on the assumption that "the medieval imagination" could personify anything at all without considering "moral or metaphorical logic."[20] As such she is another instance of sloppy allegorical geometry, for Everyman's good deeds have already been represented – in the account book to which Death referred and which now lies "vnder the fete" (lines 503–505). Good Deeds will in fact emphasize her own redundance by saying to Everyman, "Than go you with your rekenynge & your Good Dedes togyder" (line 529). Taken as a code for "good deeds," Good Deeds also has produced an apparent doctrinal problem: Everyman's good deeds seem to play the decisive role in his salvation, implying a theology of "works" which Arnold Williams finds essentially unChristian and attributes to the plot's Buddhist origin.[21] But if we abandon the assumption that the actors are merely ciphers for ideas,

[20] The reference to indiscriminate personification is from Bernard Spivack, *Shakespeare and the Allegory of Evil: The History of a Metaphor in Relation to His Major Villains* (New York: Columbia University Press, 1958), p. 93.

[21] Arnold Williams, *The Drama of Medieval England* (East Lansing: Michigan State University Press, 1961), pp. 161–62.

we can see in Good Deeds's redundance a solution to the theological problem. Because Everyman's good deeds are recorded in his account book, their appearance also as a personification—an agent capable, after he has repented, of going with him to God and pleading on his behalf—is literally gratuitous. The actor is not simply good deeds but good deeds made manifest and potent by God's grace and Everyman's repentance.

Good Deeds's gratuitous personification is reinforced by the materialization of Knowledge. Knowledge is probably the most controversial personification in the play, having been identified with many and diverse kinds of knowledge. As Warren says, "there is no sound reason why Knowledge should not be accepted simply as knowledge since that is the name of the character."[22] Such acceptance will be easier, however, if we take seriously Knowledge's appearance as a character, in a particular context. Throughout the play Everyman has behaved as though ignorant of anything but empirical reality. Unlike the protagonists of other morality plays, however, he appears as an adult; Death asks him, "Hast thou thy Makere *forgete?*" (line 86; emphasis added), and God's opening speech makes clear that he has had ample opportunity to learn "my lawe that I shewed, whan I for them dyed" (line 29). His apparent ignorance of intangible truth is illusion, sinful blindness "of ghostly syght" (line 25). The first half of the play disillusions Everyman, forcing him to acknowledge what he knows. The appearance of Knowledge, following that of Good Deeds, confirms Everyman's disillusionment. Anyone who translates the encounter with Death as "Everyman is dead" will probably assume that the encounter with Knowledge means "Everyman has learned," but both readings are inaccurate. Everyman is in fact encountering knowledge, accepting knowledge as his guide and companion. Something with no obvious empirical manifestation is thereby externalized and personified as a more vocal and potent agent than Fellowship and Goods.

Knowledge convinces Everyman to seek confession, which accordingly materializes before him (lines 535–43). At this point Everyman accepts not only the reality of the intangible fact called confession but also the provisional nature of its tangible form; that is, he recognizes

---

[22] Warren, "*Everyman*: Knowledge Once More," p. 137. Warren summarizes on p. 136 the critical opinions about Knowledge.

the man called Confession as only one manifestation of his name.
Knowledge first calls Confession "that clensynge ryuere" (line 536);
Everyman then speaks of "that holy man, Confessyon" (line 539) and is
directed to the "hous of saluacyon" (line 540). When Confession materializes, presumably as a male actor, Everyman addresses him as "O
gloryous fountayne" and then, oddly enough, as "moder of saluacyon"
(lines 545, 552). The incompatible appositives are not careless aurea-
tion but a sign that Everyman has escaped the tyranny of particular
material forms. Even as he responds appropriately to the priestlike
agent who manifests confession to him, he also perceives the aspects of
confession designated by "river" and "mother." The alternative
metaphors bring him as close as earthly man can come to apprehending
confession itself.

Everyman has at last achieved spiritual sight, the recognition of the
spiritual as real and of the material as radically metaphorical. That
vision lets him understand Confession's shifting references to penance
—first as a "precyous iewell" and then, four lines later, as "that
scourge" (lines 557, 561). Everyman himself brings the metaphoric
epiphany to a climax in his reverent, rhapsodic *pronominatio* (lines
581–91):

> O eternall God / O heuenly fygure,
> O way of ryghtwysnes / O goodly vysyon,
> Whiche dyscended downe in a vyrgyn pure
> Bycause he wolde euery man redeme,
> Whiche Adam forfayted by his dysobedyence:
> O blessyd God-heed, electe and hye deuyne,
> Forgyue me my greuous offence!
> Here I crye the mercy in this presence.
> O ghostly treasure, O raunsomer and redemer,
> Of all the worlde hope and conduyter,
> Myrrour of ioye, foundatour of mercy. . . .

After his prayer Everyman "wade[s] the water" of penance on a dry
stage (line 617) and is given Contrition to wear (lines 638–50). Objects
appear here in response to their names, and visible actions depend on
invisible conditions. Everyman will shortly be directed to the proto-
type for such miraculous materialization: the sacrament in which a man
may "with v. wordes . . . [handle] his Maker bytwene his handes" (lines

737–39). The play itself is now virtually transubstantiated, its actors and dialogue translucent to spiritual reality.

Understandably, some directors and critics feel that the play should end at this point.[23] Like the allegories of Langland, Spenser, and Bunyan, however, *Everyman* continues past the moment of supreme vision into anticlimax. Indeed, the reference to transubstantiation just quoted opens a discussion of the intransigence of the material: Knowledge explains that Priesthood, which holds the power to manifest God, is itself subject to fleshly corruption (lines 750–63). Everyman has been directed to Priesthood as he was to Confession, but the encounter apparently occurs offstage while Knowledge and Five Wits converse. That Priesthood does not appear as an actor might be taken as a development of the allegorical vision achieved with Confession, an indication that actors are not needed now to manifest spiritual realities. On the contrary, however, the dialogue concerning Priesthood draws our attention to the problem of the inevitable embodiment of the spiritual reality. Spoken of as "they," "he," and "thou," Priesthood clearly has multiple forms, some of them perhaps present in the audience, and Knowledge raises the possibility that its spiritual power may depend on the purity of a particular materialization.[24] The play's intangible realities have not transcended their material basis, after all; Everyman is still alive.

That is why he must encounter a new and ambivalent set of agents. Discretion, Strength, Beauty, and Five Wits imitate both the reliable guides who have recently materialized and the would-be companions who deserted Everyman earlier. Everyman deliberately evokes them in obedience to Good Deeds's and Knowledge's instructions; the actors constitute another metamorphosis of truth. That is, Everyman is not receiving discretion, strength, beauty, and physical sensation but recognizing those qualities and capacities as companions and counselors "of grete myght" for his journey to death (lines 658, 663). That they will abandon him at the grave does not invalidate them. As Lawrence

[23] See especially John Wasson, "Interpolation in the Text of *Everyman*," *TN* 27 (1972):14–20.

[24] I refer to lines 750–68. Knowledge's suggestion is refuted by Five Wits's persistent trust in Priesthood and by the evident efficacy of Everyman's receipt of the Sacrament, but the problem of Priesthood's embodiment is raised seriously and helps direct our attention back to the imperfect world in which Everyman must live.

Ryan points out, their promises to Everyman are entirely honest: Strength "wyll by you stande in dystres, / Though thou wolde in batayle fyght on the grounde" (lines 684–85); Five Wits will remain "though it were thrugh the worlde rounde" (line 686); Beauty will not depart "vnto dethes houre" (line 688).[25] If beauty and the five senses often mislead the Christian, this Beauty and this Five Wits, respond-ing to the control of Good Deeds and Knowledge, faithfully superin-tend Everyman's charitable testament and his visit to Priesthood. Their materialization is part of his proper disposition of his life in preparation for death. Nonetheless, it is his life which Everyman is disposing, and the disposition can lead him up to the grave but not beyond it. At the grave Discretion, Strength, Beauty, and Five Wits drop their formerly ritualistic diction and turn as colloquial as villagers (lines 800–801, 816–25):

> I crosse out all this. / Adewe, by Saynt Iohan!
> I take my tappe in my lappe and am gone.
>
> Ye, I haue you ferre ynoughe conueyde.
> Ye be olde ynoughe, I vnderstande,
> Your pylgrymage to take on hande.
> . . . .
> Go thryst the in to the grounde.

Their earthiness completes their enactment of their names: capable of attaining spiritual status, they are of course fundamentally sensual. Beauty cannot "smoder" in the grave and "[i]n this worlde lyue no more," as Everyman would have her do (lines 796–98), for she is in-separable from life in the world. The "persones of grete myght" thus materialize twice—as effectual aids in Everyman's salvation and then as homely creatures, aids only for that part of his salvation which can be enacted in the world.

The colloquial curtain lines of Strength, Beauty, and the rest com-plete a pattern in the play's style of acting which is also the pattern of its meaning. Initially Everyman and his friends are as realistic as the most traditional director could wish. They are doubly realistic, in fact: they behave like familiar individuals, and they sustain the conviction that the world of individuality is the primary locus of reality. Thus

[25] Ryan, "Doctrine and Dramatic Structure," pp. 730–31.

when they later display categorical limitations, they demonstrate the subjection of all individual phenomena to the laws of a different reality. From that other reality come Everyman's new friends, beginning with Good Deeds. The actors who embody Good Deeds, Knowledge, Confession, Discretion, and so forth are clearly not autonomous creatures; their materialization is sacramental, and they accordingly speak and act ritualistically. Even at their most impersonal, however, the actors inevitably suggest personality: we imagine Good Deeds as sweet and gracious, Knowledge as more direct, and Confession as paternal and eloquent. If, as I have argued, those characters' material forms not only represent but also redefine their names, the suggestions of personality are doctrinally meaningful. At the same time, hints of personality are necessary consequences of the concepts' embodiment—concessions, in fact, to our sensual apprehension. Even in experiencing conversion, even in sensing God's presence, Everyman can approach the intangible only through images. As he nears death, the human images that have strengthened his spiritual vision reveal afresh their personalities, their inseparability from the material world. They have come full circle, back to the realism of Fellowship, Kindred, and Cousin. But Everyman does not complete the circle, and neither do we: as the play reverts to realism, we pass beyond the play.

Everyman ends with the actors' unmasking. First Everyman and Good Deeds violate the theatrical illusion called the "fourth wall" by addressing the audience directly. "Take example, all ye that this do here or se," Everyman begins (line 867). Then Knowledge, continuing the direct address, appears to drop her identity as a personification: "Now hath [Everyman] suffred that *we* all shall endure" (line 888; emphasis added). Finally a "Doctour" summarizes the action as if it had yet to occur, transforming Everyman back into every man and the other characters' names back into common nouns (lines 905–11):

> And remembre Beaute, V. Wyttes, Strength, & Discrecyon,
> They all at the last do Eueryman forsake,
> Saue his Good Dedes there dothe he take.
> But be-ware, for and they be small,
> Before God he hath no helpe at all:
> None excuse may be there for Eueryman.
> Alas, how shall he do than?

In those breaches of illusion the actors transfer their roles from the play's microcosm back to the wider reality of doctrine and universal experience. They thus reenact for us the lessons that Everyman has learned: that there is no permanent separation between individual action and universal reality, that all embodiments are vehicles of general truth, and that Everyman himself—that is, we ourselves—must dissolve as autonomous creatures to achieve our fullest identity.

The student of acting who fears that he cannot imaginatively realize the roles of *Everyman* is halfway toward understanding those roles. As categories and abstractions, they cannot be fully realized by any creature. By the same token, however, their embodiment in individual actors is not fictional representation, as in post-Renaissance theater; still less is it the arbitrary convention of a bogus dramatization. It is a function of the relationship between object and word, a relationship which *Everyman* dramatizes with unparalleled power. *Everyman*'s allegorical cast is in fact literal: its dramatis personae are words, realizable in many dimensions. In presenting those roles, the skillful actor must call upon the techniques of realistic characterization, upon the more impersonal tones and gestures of ritual, and, above all, upon his own allegorical vision of the metamorphoses of reality, the points at which, in Robert Potter's fine phrase, "the Truth comes true."[26]

---

[26] Potter, *The English Morality Play*, p. 16.

Part Nine   THE USES OF LITERATURE

More, Castiglione,
and the Humanist Choice of Utopias

RICHARD A. LANHAM
University of California, Los Angeles

ANTAYANA, in *Later Soliloquies*, offers two polar definitions of freedom: "the liberty of liberalism" and "German freedom." "German freedom," he tells us, "is like the freedom of the angels in heaven who see the face of God and cannot sin. It lies in such a deep love and understanding of what is actually established that you would not have it otherwise; you appropriate and bless it all and feel it to be the providential expression of your own spirit."[1] Against this Nixon team-player paradise he sets a liberty of liberalism which "consists in limiting the prescription of the law to a few points, for the most part negative, leaving it to the initiative and conscience of individuals to alter their life and conversation as they like, provided only they do not interfere with the same freedom in others."[2]

The modern liberal, especially in recent chiliastic moods, obviously feels the pull of "German freedom" too. He wants to enself the larger polity, inhabit a society whose interests he expresses spontaneously as his own. Modern liberalism might, in fact, be defined as the assumption that we can enjoy the advantages of both freedoms with the disadvantages of neither. The ups and downs of liberal democracies suggest that this homogenized heaven does not come easy. The two freedoms vary inversely, not concomitantly. In a state where "compulsory service" becomes "perfect freedom," it is the individual who withers away, not the state. The game they play is zero-sum.

More's *Utopia* has earned its sacred niche in the humanist pantheon

---

[1] George Santayana, "German Freedom," in *Soliloquies in England and Later Soliloquies*, introduction by Ralph Ross (Ann Arbor, Mich., 1967), pp. 169–73; the quotation is from p. 169.

[2] George Santayana, "Liberalism and Culture," in ibid., pp. 173–78; the quotation is from p. 174.

by camouflaging this unhappy fact. It fools us in exactly the way we want to be fooled. In both feelings and ills felt, *Utopia* foreshadows – perhaps we should say founds – the basic self-contradiction of modern humanism. More has had, of course, an immense stroke of luck. His martyrdom has made him not only a saint but a secular Socrates redivivus whom we tremendously *want* to believe. This numinous penumbra, as yet undissipated,[3] obscures how *Utopia* really works, how it manages to reconcile the mighty political opposites. More works this reconciliation by a scam, and since we are still building our vision of social paradise on the same trick, it may yet be useful to see how More brings it off.

Utopia works in two ways, through argument and through literary structure, and these two ways stand fundamentally opposed. The argument offers an either-or choice, not a reconciliation. About this choice, the historian J. H. Hexter has made the definitive statement:

Here, I think, lies the heart of the matter. Deep in the soul of the society of More's day, because it was deep in the soul of all men, was the monster Pride, distilling its terrible poison and dispatching it to all parts of the social body to corrupt, debilitate, and destroy them. . . .

The Utopian Discourse then is based on a diagnosis of the ills of sixteenth century Christendom; it ascribes those ills to sin, and primarily to Pride, and it prescribes remedies for that last most disastrous infection of man's soul designed to inhibit if not to eradicate it. For our understanding of the Utopian Discourse, it is of the utmost importance that we recognize this to be its theme.[4]

More originally embodied this theme in the island-paradise vision which, in the final *Utopia*, Raphael Hythlodaeus delivers as book 2. Later, however, according to Hexter's brilliantly convincing recon-struction of *Utopia*'s textual history, More added another section, most of the present book 1, as a broad social critique of European soci-ety. Thematically, if Pride is More's main target, book 2 follows natur-ally from book 1. We have in the first the diagnosis; in the second, the

---

[3] G. R. Elton has, however, taken a step in this direction with his brilliant "Thomas More, Councillor (1517-1529)," in R. S. Sylvester, ed., *St. Thomas More: Action and Contemplation* (New Haven, Conn., 1972), pp. 87–122.

[4] J. H. Hexter, *More's "Utopia": The Biography of an Idea* (New York: Harper Torchbooks, 1965), pp. 75–77.

cure. And the "Dialogue of Counsel," the section in book 1 where the usefulness of courtly service to a prince is debated, fits perfectly. The debate has two real sides, but the noes seem to carry the day. For More, as for Marx, conventional politics were doomed to inconse-quence just because man was dominated by Pride. If not, why had poli-tics not accomplished something before now, why allowed the present abuses? In its diagnosis of man's central ailment as Pride, *Utopia* becomes a homogeneous whole. It was, of course, to extirpate Pride that Plato, in *The Republic*, had invented the German idea of freedom in the first place.

But what, when you denounce Pride, do you really outlaw? We can profit here from a terminological revision. Pride is obviously a loaded word, a Christian vice, but the concept emerges from a deep Platonic paradox. *The Republic* argues for a hierarchical society but a frozen one. Ordinary folk were not to become self-conscious about social status and begin to look aloft. Hierarchy was necessary, but it had to be stable. Hierarchy, however, is unstable by nature. The bottom always wants to be the top. The naturally stable social form is equal-ity. *The Republic* unites the two by positing a hierarchy whose *ruling class* was egalitarian. More faced the same basic problem, but he could not adopt the same solution, however special a case he made for scholars. It smacked too much of pride, for one thing, and it too much resembled the Tudor status quo for another. What to do? He sepa-rated the hierarchical impulses into separate strands. The hierarchical elements conducive to peace and stability—the basic family structure, respect for old age, a modicum of political power—would be preserved, but the central offender, the as-we-now-know basic male primate urge for social status, would be banished. In Tudor terms this meant the chivalric cluster. More saw it clearly as the heart of the matter. So in Utopia no hunting, no knightly war, no courtly love (the courtship aspect of male status competition). More's satire here corresponds ex-actly to Thorstein Veblen's in *The Theory of the Leisure Class*. Every-thing that leads to invidious comparison must go in the name of plain purpose—food is for nourishment, marriage for children, housing for shelter, clothing for warmth. Plain purpose is the only kind of motive Utopia permits—except, of course, for the scholars. Now when you banish invidious comparison, you banish a great deal, as More and

Plato saw (Veblen, whose utopianism was the temperamental beatnik variety, did not). The arts must go. Since the only range of motive permitted is the plain purposes we are all supposed to share, individualism must go. As a consequence, with both you must banish *style*, the formal machinery by which we dramatize status. Play, too, must go. And —remember Utopian euthanasia and premarital sexual inspections— sentiment as well. And dramatic motive, our role-playing selves. And reality-maintenance behavior, all the activities which have as their end not plain purposes but only proving to ourselves that we are still alive, that the social-encounter group of life remains in session. All these add up to an enormous price to pay for social stability.

The term "Pride" disguises this price. We can have, for example, "justifiable" Pride, "real" status, "genuine" difference. The way More chooses to construct Utopia shows that he recognized what "Pride" disguised, how much would in fact have to be given up. Popes, he knew, were "proud" in the same way kings were. If More outgrew the confusions of the term, so should we. Let me substitute two less weighted ones. Let us call the behavior Utopia admits "purposive" and the behavior it excludes "stylistic." Of course, purposive behavior has its stylistic element, and stylistic behavior its own purposes, but it was just these overlaps that More was concerned to disentangle.

A rigorous and uncompromising choice, then. But the literary structure does not reflect or intensify this choice. It moves in the opposite direction. Michael Holquist has argued that the utopia, as a genre, lacks literary interest.[5] Precisely such interest More sought to supply in the revision. Hexter has so cogently reconstructed and accounted for this revision in historical and biographical terms that we tend to overlook the basic alteration in literary structure which the added material brought with it. This alteration serves, in little and large, to blur the conceptual choice between style and purpose.

To Hytholodaeus's utopian monologue in book 2, More prefaces the dialogue of book 1. Dialogue suggests a truth tentative and socially determined which counterbalances the absolutism both of Utopia itself and of Hythlodaeus's monologue about it. Yet since the section added in London details the abuses to which Utopia supplies satiric answers,

[5] Michael Holquist, "How to Play Utopia: Some Brief Notes on the Distinctiveness of Utopian Fiction," *YFS* 40–41 (1968):106–23.

book 2 seems to follow inevitably from book 1 rather than contrast with it. It is often remarked that book 1 offers dramatic characteriza-tion lacking in Utopia itself. True, but not really the main point. The *kind of* self book 1 depicts would not occur in Utopia, yet More, through his narrative structure, makes it seem otherwise. The intense self-consciousness of the humanist circle More takes such pains to depict would never develop in Utopia but seems to dwell there nevertheless.

So too with More's humanist Latin. Humanist Latin stands for the central Christian Humanist effort to save the world by a stylistic paideia. It enshrines all the stylistic virtues of a literary culture which, in the name of clarity and plain purpose, would most certainly have to be banished from a consistent utopia. It sneaks into Utopia by the back door precisely what More banishes from the front—style and all that it represents (I cannot pursue here a rhetorical analysis of More's style, relevant as it would be; Elizabeth McCutcheon's detailed analysis of litotes in *Utopia* shows how extensive such an analysis would have to be and the interesting results it would certainly yield).[6] More was obviously writing a self-consciously ornamented Latin. He was using the devices of literary style to urge upon us a utopia where such devices—like literature itself—could have no place.

The banishment of money works in a similarly oblique way. It is money which allows us to convert naïve purpose into stylistic behavior without anyone else's knowing it, including ourselves. Money repre-sents the perfect practical purpose. No one has to explain why he wants to get rich. Everyone thinks greed the most hardheaded of motives. And yet the rich man immediately begins to play. It is not the impersonality of money that muddles human relations, as a modern economist might argue, but the way it allows us to shift from one kind of motive to the other. More saw this clearly, and so money had to go.

Minor details often work in a subliminal way too. More tells us, for example, that Utopians have fools—the professional kind. If we pause to think about it, the Utopians have no more need for fools than for the comedy they represent, for both are generated by the stresses of an open society. But we do not pause to think about it. We accept it as a

6 Elizabeth McCutcheon, "Denying the Contrary: More's Use of Litotes in the *Utopia*," *Moreana* 31–32 (1971):107–21.

seemingly inconsequential detail and then *assume*, on the basis of it, that Utopia includes the social stresses that generate comedy and make it necessary, the stresses of an open society. In the same way, in a society like Utopia, those emeriti professors, when not playing king, would have no occasion to sit around pondering the nature of good-ness, evil, human happiness, and so on. These ruminations are rem-nants left over from the open society of a fallen world, but More needs them to effect his reconciliation of utopias. Like the fools, they imply that Utopia possesses the atmosphere and pleasures of the open soci-ety while at the same time remaining fully closed.

More drags in other details from the nonutopian world with a similar intent, to provide ligatures between the two worlds, air ducts which the reader will never notice. The character of Hythlodaeus, as an obvi-ous example, takes form in book 1. He is a man of peace, shrewdness, and goodwill. Thus when he comes to describe Utopia with such glow-ing approval, we assume it to be peaceful, shrewd, and kind too, else he would not have felt so at home there. And More had taken pains at the beginning of Utopia to introduce Hythlodaeus as a real person, one with whom he and Peter Giles shared that private world of Latin humanism to which the prefatory letters attest. The utopian island is a different kind of place yet in the same world, else Hythlodaeus could not have gone there. So, too, the Utopians not only read Sophocles but they read him in the edition with the small Aldine type. So, too, in the much-remarked political overlap with Christianity. Again we overlook the central significance: an unfallen world like Utopia would not need or understand a religion based on a Fall myth. But such an inconsis-tency does not matter. As long as we keep debating the doctrinal sig-nificance of this overlap, we will never notice—as the commentary proves—its literary significance, the opening of another duct to let open air into a closed society. So, too, with the banishment of lawyers, perhaps the most obvious of these dogs that do not bark. A lawyer class which would never have arisen must be banished to establish yet another presumption for a kind of atmosphere Utopia would never have permitted.

Thus the *Utopia*'s literary form does more than provide dramatic in-terest, draw the reader from his chimney corner. *Utopia*'s literary form allows More to suggest and get credit for an open society, to make us feel that he understands the values of one, without formally admitting such a society to his argument. The greatest artist of this con game is Plato, but More follows not far behind. Plato's rhetorical stratagem to hide totalitarian thinking was a central protagonist who bragged incessantly about his open-mindedness. More does something similar in inventing the fictional More in the *Utopia* who may not be the historical More and the Hythlodaeus who really may be. Modern commentators have vexed themselves about "What did More really think?" not unduly perhaps but in the wrong way. *Utopia*'s literary structure does indeed, as has often been noticed, make us read deep and hard, pose for us not More's answer but More's choice. But it also makes the commentators rehearse by their own disagreements the impediments More saw to the political stability of the open society. Making us ask, "What did *More* think?" is a rhetorical trick to make us realize that such an open society can never agree on where to go and so can never get there.

What More has done stands clear enough. His reconciliations between the two kinds of freedom, two kinds of society, are literary. Like the character of Hythlodaeus himself, they smuggle the stresses, virtues, and pleasures of an open society into a closed one which, logically, could not tolerate them. In the context of this over-all rhetorical strategy More's tone and wit begin to make sense. Hexter points out that whimsy and playfulness come not, as we would expect, in the Dialogue but in the Discourse,[7] not in book 1 but in book 2. They come, that is, in the context where they do not belong, a context which would never by itself have generated them. Hexter explains this difference as a *historical* one, but it is obviously formal too, and perhaps even more significant in its formal than in its historical aspect.

Utopia thus aims to reconcile Santayana's two humanisms, but it never makes a point of this reconciliation. Just the opposite: it makes a point of never making a point of it. The commentary of *Utopia* often makes it seem as if it *does not have* a literary form, as if it rings true to Holquist's type. But the opposite case prevails. *Utopia* offers us a literary reconciliation while posing an intellectual choice. Its style and structure, its literary form, aim to reconcile stylistic and purposive

---

[7] *Utopia: The Yale Edition of the Complete Works of St. Thomas More*, vol. 4, ed. Edward Surtz, S.J., and J. H. Hexter (New Haven, Conn., 1965), cxxii.

behavior. *Utopia* as a utopia insists, in the most uncompromising way — scholars excluded — that these two ranges of motive can *never* be reconciled and that, if we want peace and quiet, we must choose the purposive Utopia and banish the stylistic one. This choice is the only choice, and it an be posed in no other way. *Utopia* offers us this choice in the most tough-minded manner — and then implies, through its literary form, that finally we need not make it. It uses style to repudiate style. It assumes as constants all the desirable things stylistic behavior creates and gives to stylistic behavior only the destructive ones. It does, that is, what humanism has tried to do ever since. It offers the best of both possible worlds and the worst of neither. No wonder it has been so popular.

In *Utopia*, if not in Utopia, we can be equal and yet individual, preserve the pleasures of style *and* the pleasures of renouncing it, take no thought for the morrow yet harvest the deserved crop of forethought. David Bleich has argued that Utopia constituted a wish fulfillment for More: More really wanted to be king, thought he could invent a better England and rule it better than Henry VIII; Utopia resolved the inner stresses of his private life — his need to provide for a large family, serve God and Wolsey too, gain the sexual satisfaction Dame Alice failed to provide.[8] Bleich is probably right. Utopia seems an embarrasingly personal utopia. But *we* should be embarrassed too. The really significant wish fulfillment is ours, *Utopia*'s, not More's and Utopia's. "We" in two senses. As men of liberal goodwill, we have accepted *Utopia* as a utopia, a literary as a conceptual reconciliation. "We," in another sense. "We" scholars. For it was as a *scholar* that More fooled himself as well as the rest of us. In the scholarly arguments More caught himself off guard. The scholars are allowed true leisure. They are allowed to *play*, the *play* of the mind, and this (witness the humorlessness of Teutonic scholarship) will always stand at odds with German freedom and, if continued, always bring it down. The flinch here reenacts the basic scholarly self-delusion, a Utopia embarrassingly like the "Good-Guys U" we all daydream of. As scholars we are all natural conservatives. We want a surrounding society that stays still and lets us get on with our work. Bursts of religious zeal may overpower us, as the

[8] David Bleich, "More's *Utopia*: Confessional Modes," AI 28 (Spring, 1971):24–52.

campus disruptions of the 1960s proved, but they do not last. Our minds move naturally in the other direction. We want the German kind of freedom because it depends on Kultur (I am borrowing again from Santayana), and making and retailing Kultur constitutes our basic business. At the same time we value the free play of the mind, knowledge "for its own sake," stylistic behavior in its purest form. Such behavior, we are sure, will prove in the end the most *purposive* of all. We do not want to think through the inconsistencies of our position. That would interrupt our work and might prove too piercing. And thus we assume that what we want to be so is so, and when a document like *Utopia*, written by one of us, comes along to tell us we are right, we clutch it to our bosoms. And if, being good scholars, we ask it many questions, we make sure not to ask it the right ones.

But now we have got to. Our humanism cannot be based on this amiable self-delusion any longer. For it is just the failure to outgrow More's categories and diagnosis that has condemned modern humanism to its present aimless disarray and growing inconsequentiality. Because we have failed to find the true legitimating premises of humanism, we cling to More's sleight of hand. We cling especially to his *diagnosis* of social evil, to finding the *principia malorum* in Pride. What "Pride" includes, what More excludes from Utopia, amounts to nine-tenths of human behavior. We must abjure not only the status games we like to play but play itself. Hexter remarks that in Utopia "there are practically no adiophora, practically no things indifferent":[9] no loose ends, no goofy hobbies, nothing done for its own sake, no collectors because no objects to collect. No one wastes his time working around the house—how totally More has designed Utopia as a scholar's paradise—because the houses, all the same to begin with, get swapped every ten years anyway. No one can get interested in clothes either, since everyone goes around in Peking unismocks. Scholars seldom ask what Utopia would be like if you did *not* like to study. Not only forbidden to spend your leisure as you wish—no racetracks, card parlors, or bars—you would not, unless you were one of Utopia's professional graduate students, be allowed much real leisure anyway. No loafing allowed. Academics seldom feel that this is a problem—*Utopia* is, after

[9] *Utopia*, ed. Surtz and Hexter, p. cxv.

all, an *academic* paradise – but the lower orders would surely be hard-pressed for entertainment.

More's Utopia models perfectly the satiric simplification of human nature. The satirist plies his trade by singling out for scorn the non-purposive, playful, stylistic behavior mankind so likes. The premise is More's premise, the great unexamined one. The satirist assumes that man is fundamentally a purposive creature, that his behavior possesses, or should possess, a fixed purposive center. His whole conception of "reason" and of "reasonable" behavior exfoliates out from this fixed center. Satire depends on the Fall of Man myth that in Platonic or Christian form has dominated Western thinking from the beginning. The Fall myth establishes man as by nature unself-conscious and purposive. His stylistic motives, his ornamental impulses, are aberrations. This distinction inheres in our language; our terminology focuses human nature in this way. If we banish all ornament, for example, we cannot wholly repine because ornament and ornamental behavior – the very word tells us – do not really matter; they take us away from the center rather than toward it.

The satirist, like More, assumes that man possesses a fixed central self which society can influence but which it does not create. Thus the whole range of stylistic behavior – the social drama which allows us to reenact ourselves, to keep the self alive by social rehearsal – becomes frivolous and dispensable. Serious people need not bother with it. Utopia abolishes it.

In doing so, although we shrink from admitting it, Utopia also abolishes man. A cure indeed worse than the disease. The Western Eden has always left out nine-tenths of human behavior and human motive. Our continual fixation upon such a drastically simplified paradise poses one of the most interesting questions in Western intellectual history. Western man has always wanted to deny his essence, pretend to be a different creature from what his history and his common sense reveal him to be. Perhaps this is why we so like satire. The more it castigates us, the more it flatters us by its implication that we are, at heart, the purposeful, serious, unself-conscious, unplayful beings we would like to be and – in *Utopia* – become. If this delusion were only daydreaming, it would do little harm. But it does do harm. Utopias define for us, albeit often in an indirect way, where we are going, would like to go.

They define our essence. And Western man, by thinking that eliminating style takes him toward the center of experience rather than away from it, has systematically deluded himself about his motives. This delusion has made an enormous difference and continues to do so. We have refused to recognize – and hence make full use of – the principal means of social regulation which as a species we possess. Our fixation on our own purposefulness threatens perpetually to intensify the problems it seeks to correct.

That the humanities have accepted this purposive Eden must be more surprising still, since the humanities study precisely the stylistic behavior Utopia abolishes. To put More's Utopia at the center of our humanism means abolishing humanism. This did not bother More, just as it did not bother Plato, but it ought to bother us. What happens when we ignore it we are now finding out. We lose our sense of what we are about; our pedagogy for language teaching falls into disarray; we have a composition crisis; the humanities curriculum disintegrates into an intellectual A&P. And when we have to make the choice of choices, ask ourselves – about energy sources, the undergraduate curriculum, or anything else – what man really needs, we can return no useful discriminations at all, nothing intermediate between Strawberry Fields and a Ferrari in every garage.

The central problem remains More's central assumption, the satiric assumption that all stylistic behavior is "Pride," and all Pride, Sin. This equation is a Marxist equation as well as a Christian one, and until it is rejected, humanism will never stop trying to pull the rug from beneath its own feet. What happens if we do reject it? What happens if we accept as legitimate the stylistic behavior More would banish? Try to control human nature without abolishing it? Well, a post-Darwinian humanism of just this sort is even now emerging. It is coming from ethology, from sociobiology, from a drama-centered sociology and anthropology, from perception psychology, from neurochemistry – from everywhere, in fact, except the humanities.

This post-Darwinian humanism accepts man as having a central self that grows out of the social drama rather than coming into it from the outside. It accepts as legitimate the purposeless reality maintenance, the stylistic, ornamental behavior More would banish. It accepts men as essentially ornamental as well as serious, playful as well as pur-

posive. This new paradigm establishes, in fact, a totally different conception of "seriousness" from that upon which More's Edenic paradigm
is based.

The modern choice of utopias, then, goes beyond the either-or choice
posed by More. We can choose a post-Darwinian utopia. Such a choice
seems a more hopeful one because it is built on the *inclusion* of stylistic
behavior, built, that is, on the whole of man. When Renaissance
scholars continue to accept the Utopia paradigm uncritically, they
doom both More's vision and the teaching of Renaissance literature
and culture to inconsequentiality. For, after all, More's diagnosis of
human motive was as severe as that offered by the post-Darwinian
consensus. He saw the Europe of his own time as dominated, over-
whelmed, by stylistic motive, as predominantly playful and ornamental. Accepting his draconian cure—Utopia—as referential and then interpreting the age in its terms mean inevitably misinterpreting the age,
imposing an anachronistic purposive motive on it, repudiating More's
description of the age, and adopting his *cure* as the description. For the
most part, this is what has happened. We have taken a purposive view
of a stylistically motivated age.

We need not, however, depend on the post-Darwinian image of man.
More's own time was offered the same wider choice of utopias we face
today. It is, in fact, just this similarity that right now lends to Renaissance studies their particular relevance. It would require a longish
book to juxtapose the utopias which offer this choice—*The Prince, The
Book of the Courtier, Gargantua and Pantagruel*, for a start—and study
how each examines the proper nature and balance of human motive.
Among them they stake out the basic positions, from More's pure purpose to Rabelais's pure play. But one of them demands comment
because it provides a precise theoretical counterstatement to More's
Utopia, charts clearly the principal dynamics of what has become post-
Darwinian humanism: Castiglione's portrait of Urbino. It chooses the
opposite utopia from More's, puts style at the center of reality, not at
the periphery. It argues that social stability lies through style, not
around it. Society, Castiglione argues, must be self-consciously styl-
ized, literary as well as purposive, if it is to create a self-regulating
stability. *The Courtier* charts with the utmost clarity and grace precisely the utopia modern behavioral science tries to pace out with its

seven-league boots of sociologese. Thomas More felt that the two kinds of freedom could be reconciled only in a literary structure. Castiglione accepts this premise but philosophizes it, creates a *society* which has a literary structure and so permits a genuine reconciliation.

Castiglione seeks not to exclude stylistic motive but to found his society upon self-conscious manipulation of it. No starting-up or stability problems exist. Devising the perfect courtier starts as a game and gradually comes to include ordinary purpose within its boundaries. Castiglione starts from the impulse toward stylistic motive and works outward. The structure of *The Courtier*, unlike *Utopia*, does not enshrine an absolute choice between conventional politics (*Utopia*, book 1) and radical politics (book 2). Instead it moves gradually from a beginning in idle amusement to Bembo's soaring exaltation in book 4. In between, first one utopia is premised and then the other. All utopias are games, Holquist argues. The Urbino court plays "the best game that could possibly be played," the best because the most flattering, the most narcissistic, the most serious—the game about themselves, about their ultimate values and how they are held. More's rhetorical strategy minimizes our self-consciousness about his literary reconciliation of conceptual irreconcilables. Castiglione does the opposite, maximizes our self-consciousness about his dialogue's domain. It is both purposive and playful by turns, and it deals with a social reality created through a similar oscillation. Over and over it abjures the essentialist position that man has a simple, central, purposive nature and ought to have a single form of society to maximize this nature. As in the beginning of book 2, so throughout *The Courtier*; all things, defined by their opposites, find their real existence in ordinary behavior in time, not in an ideal pattern standing outside it. We see this most obviously, perhaps, in the famous doctrine of *sprezzatura*. *Sprezzatura* was a new word for a new conception of identity, that paradoxical natural unnaturalness, sense of effortless effort, of instinctive artifice, that in a static world like More's simply makes no sense. It can work only in a universe anchored in behavior and time, a world where a man can enself a pattern, make natural and spontaneous what was once laboriously learned. *Sprezzatura* stands at the center of Castiglione's conception of human identity, and the rest of Urbino develops out from it. A self based on *sprezzatura* means a self created within society, not preexistent to it, one created by stylistic behavior, behavior that takes place just to dramatize and sustain the self.

At every point Castiglione embraces the diversity More would banish. Diversity constitutes his system of social control. Utopia is a society dominated by rules. It aims, finally, to render interpretation otiose. No one need think how to apply the rules. *The Courtier* shows how to apply the rules, how to create in the citizen intuitive norms which transcend rules. The only ironclad rule is to avoid affectation, never act according to rule. Urbino promulgates no rules for acceptably purposive behavior. The only social corrective is the comic corrective of reproving laughter, and this depends on a judgment of style. *The Courtier* insists that the norm for human behavior, the potential stable balance, is created by a balance of the two kinds of motive, purposive and stylistic, and that these can be held together only by a self-conscious society, one which understands and allows both kinds of behavior.

If Castiglione is right, More is wrong. Suicidally wrong. Utopia destroys the social utility of play, the necessary countervailing force to a hypertropic purpose. It shuts down that random variation which, on the level of ideas, it is play's business to introduce.

Let us try, for a moment, to put the problem in evolutionary perspective. We are born with a pattern of plain needs and purposes. We are also born with a primate biogrammar which evolved to cope with needs and purposes we no longer have and which often conflict with our present ones. These biogrammatical urges make themselves known as play urges, as stylistic behavior. They are so strong that they continually threaten to swamp ordinary purpose. This More saw happening in his own day. A ceremonial chivalry was eating up the land with its obsessive ceremonial demands. If ever a purposive corrective has been needed, it was then. But More threw out the principle of regulation with the behavior which needed regulating. We have no reason to think Castiglione a man of less feeling than More or less aware of social abuses. But he did not reach for the jugular vein in a paroxysm of indignation and combative zeal. He argued that the mature, self-regulatory culture can, by a judicious use of play, both express and suppress the biogrammar. It will arrange the two kinds of motive and two kinds of behavior in a symbiotic oscillation, one in which purpose is galvanized into action by stylistic motive and stylistic motive displaced into play when it threatens to destroy purpose. Society, that is, will express for all who live in it the particular scholarly pleasure: thought pursued as play is applied to practical purposes, purposes which in turn generate further thinking for its own sake. Such a society seems closer to the genuine spirit of the university than Utopia, for all the special status scholars enjoy there.

But does this balance of motives promise as effective a control of "Pride" and the aggression that comes from it? Better, I think. It moves toward greater dramatic intensity and not away from it, as Utopia does, and the need for that intensity, an inadequate and inept public drama, generates wars. More says that wars do not just happen. Men choose them. He was righter than he knew. Castiglione suggests a more accurate explanation of why they choose them. He also offers a paideia which locates human reality maintenance in less pathological kinds of behavior than war. The choice of utopias comes down to this: more individualism or less, more self-consciousness or less, more style or less. We stand now in the case opposite to More's, at the end of a long Newtonian interlude of naïve purpose. Our threats, in the developed world at least, are more likely to come – as Gregory Bateson has made clear – from the hypertrophy of purpose, not from its opposite.[10]

We confront again the fundamental contradiction in More's Utopia and in our humanist admiration of it – and in the humanist position in general. Humanists, when they define and defend the humanities, argue that they are useless but essential. With Lear we cry out, "O reason not the need!" No one gives us an argument on the "useless," but we are often pressed on the "essential" and seldom make much sense of our defense. The business of humanists is stylistic behavior, nonpurposive behavior. We *feel* this, but we do not *know* this. We think that what we do explains much human behavior that otherwise will remain unexplained, but we do not know why. And we never will as long as we still proceed from a Utopian paradigm that thinks human behavior essentially purposive. By choosing More's Utopia, we cut the ground from beneath our own feet. No wonder our defense of the

[10] Gregory Bateson, "Conscious Purpose Versus Nature," *Steps to an Ecology of Mind* (New York, 1972), pp. 426–39.

humanities makes no sense. If society really accepted the full implications of More's Utopia, we would lose our jobs. There is no logical place for humanists in More's Utopia because he has abolished the dimension of behavior it is their job to study. And so More has to fudge the roles and create an exceptional status for scholars. His vision of society as an ideal humanistic community turns out to be just the opposite. It might logically support a technological institute or an agricultural school, but not humanistic learning. And yet we persist in our devotion to More's Edenic Utopia. This fondness has immediate and profound political implications. It is leading us now toward a polity very like Utopia's, but one in which we will really pay the price *Utopia* so cleverly disguises. Humanistic inquiry is beginning to do so even now. And more's the pity, there is no omnipotent author to grant us the special status More reserves for scholars in Utopia. We have yet to get straight what "need" and "purpose" and "use" really mean to man. We remain, in our analysis of motive, as naïve as Veblen and as merciless as More. We persist in thinking that the way to the center lies around style rather than through it. If the public drama is bad, we want to abolish it, return with More to naïve purpose, pure sincerity, "real" need. We plan our social policy on the basis of this naïve, simpleminded purposive conception of human motive and then wonder "why . . . achievements differ so widely from aspirations."[11] What seems required is a new kind of seriousness, one based on self-consciousness, on the post-Darwinian conception of man. Only by accepting the double range of human motive, accepting stylistic motive rather than repudiating it, can we maintain the self-corrective element More's Utopia destroys. The two kinds of motive correct one another cybernetically. This surely must be their evolutionary relationship. A genuinely modern, ironic humanism must be built on this evolutionary balancing principle. To abolish it throws away the only real behavioral instrument for social control, for peace, *Homo sapiens* finds in his evolutionary repertoire. It is a matter, then, of some moment that the humanists should cease their systematic self-deception and recognize the kind of behavior that constitutes their real object of study.

[11] Karl Popper, *The Open Society and Its Enemies* (Princeton, N.J., 1971); the quotation is from 2.95. Popper is a notable victim of the purposive delusion.

When humanists talk about what they are doing, the words "higher" and "lower" often occur. We are trying, we say, to defend the "high" culture against the pop culture, man's higher nature against his lower. More offers one definition of this distinction: High is purpose; low is pride. I've used Castiglione's brilliant social analysis to suggest that this distinction ought to be reversed. What "high" points to—from fashions to morals—is stylistically motivated, playful, not purposive, behavior. Until, as humanists, we see the high culture in these terms, as expressing this definition of man, as choosing this kind of utopia, we'll continue to misapprehend the basis of our endeavor. And, thus misapprehending, we will have no right to fuss when our students sense this confusion and leave us to go where the action is.

The Existential Mysteries
as Treated in Certain Passages
of Our Older Poets

JOHN C. POPE
Yale University

HE PHRASE "existential mysteries" has, for all I know, been used many times, but I happened upon it in an essay on children's books by Arthur Schlesinger, Jr., while I was trying to christen this rambling essay.[1] I had thought of putting "mutability" in the title, because it applies more or less exactly to most of the passages I discuss, but it is not quite inclusive enough. Perhaps no title short of a paragraph can describe these desultory reflections on themes of life, love, death, and the world as they are treated in the passages I have chosen.

I shall begin with two famous stanzas from the conclusion of Chaucer's *Troilus*, because they have cast their spell over me these many years, and were in fact the starting point of the reflections that follow (5.1835–48):[2]

> O yonge, fresshe folkes, he or she,
> In which that love up groweth with youre age,
> Repeyreth hom fro worldly vanyte,
> And of youre herte up casteth the visage
> To thilke God that after his ymage
> Yow made, and thynketh al nys but a faire
> This world, that passeth soone as floures faire.
>
> And loveth hym, the which that right for love
> Upon a crois, oure soules for to beye,
> First starf, and roos, and sit in hevene above;

---

[1] Arthur Schlesinger, Jr., "Advice from a Reader-Aloud-to-Children," *New York Times Book Review*, November 25, 1979, pp. 3, 94.

[2] *The Works of Geoffrey Chaucer*, ed. F. N. Robinson, 2d ed. (Boston, 1957), p. 479.

> For he nyl falsen no wight, dar I seye,
> That wol his herte al holly on hym leye.
> And syn he best to love is, and most meke,
> What nedeth feynede loves for to seke?

I will not dwell on the part these stanzas play in adjusting the perspective and righting the balances in a story that has been told with such absorbed attention to its own self-centered microcosm. In the conclusion Chaucer's impressionable narrator, who has persistently disclaimed responsibility for the story, struggles, in a sometimes comically bewildered way, to disentangle himself from the tragedy. His behavior as a part of Chaucer's well-calculated design has been capably accounted for by the man we are honoring.[3] Here I need only suggest that these two stanzas reflect in their tone and in their ostensibly wholehearted rejection of all worldly values something of the narrator's continuing distress at the conduct of his heroine. In his kindly and compassionate way he would save all those "yonge, fresshe folkes" from any such betrayal as befell Troilus and at the same time, perhaps, soften a little our censure of Criseyde by putting some of the blame on what he now wishes to regard as the typically "feynede" loves of this inconstant world.

What concerns me at the moment is not the strategy of Chaucer's conclusion but the imaginative felicity and the underlying equivocation of the two lines that close the first stanza, describing and outwardly disparaging the deceitful mutability of the world:

> . . .and thynketh al nys but a faire
> This world, that passeth soone as floures faire.

The word "vanyte" has occurred earlier in the stanza, but it is a far cry from this image of a fair to Bunyan's harsh vision of the world as Vanity Fair. The "rich" rhyme of noun and adjective helps accent the enjoyable aspect of fairs, and if we nevertheless think of them as including much that is coarse and ugly, as does the world, this not entirely pleasant complexity is finely balanced if not purged by the delicate fragility of the fair flowers. Donaldson has called attention to

---

[3] E. Talbot Donaldson, "The Ending of Chaucer's *Troilus*," in Arthur Brown and Peter Foote, eds., *Early English and Norse Studies Presented to Hugh Smith* (London, 1963), pp. 26–45; reprinted in E. Talbot Donaldson, *Speaking of Chaucer* (London, 1970), pp. 84–101.

the sweetness of tone that pervades the whole stanza and well says of these lines, "All the illusory loveliness of a world which is man's only reality is expressed in the very lines that reject that loveliness."[4] It is hard to think of anything to match the compression and subtlety of this emotionally equivocal disparagement of the world. A similar sweetness and a similar delicacy of feeling in a not altogether dissimilar context may be detected in Sidney's sonnet, "Leave me, O love, which reach- est but to dust," but not quite so obvious a backward glance at the at- traction of what is being rejected.

I am not sure in Chaucer's passage how much is included in the idea of the world and therefore how far-reaching is the charge of its treach- erous mutability. In many a passage of the *De contemptu mundi* tradi- tion, including the Bible, and perhaps here, the world (as its etymology suggests) is primarily or solely the world of man. In Chaucer's balade *Lak of Stedfastnesse* the meaning is clearly thus limited: mankind's failure to walk in the paths of truth, reason, and virtue is wholly responsible for the complaint that the world is no longer steadfast and stable. But of course the fact of human mortality is never far from any- one's mind. Even in our nonhuman environment nature's indifference to the individual qualifies her renewal of the species. And there is much to support a more general notion of a destructive mutability in what history tells us of the overthrow of kingdoms and what we see in the ruins of their citadels. What surpasses all such observable signs of dissolution is the expectation they can engender of the end of all things. In the Old English poem *The Wanderer* such an ultimate disso- lution is envisioned with great imaginative power.

The climactic passage in the poem moves from images of a vanished prosperity to the eventual nothingness of a loveless and lightless wasteland. It is a speech within a speech. The principal speaker, a homeless exile introduced as an *eardstapa* ("wanderer"), having set forth his personal sorrows in the first half of the poem, begins in the second half to brood over the world's decay, universalizing the essence of his own experience as he thinks of the ruins scattered over the earth, of the many hosts that once defended them when they were whole and have been destroyed in battle, as were his own lord and his

---

[4] Donaldson, *Speaking of Chaucer*, p. 98.

companions.[5] He has imagined how spectral the world will be when all its wealth lies waste. The creator of men, he decides, has harried the earth until the great cities, ancient work of giants (*eald enta geweorc*),[6] have stood empty and silent, lacking the noise of citizens. Now he conjures up a surrogate wiser than himself who, if he considers deeply this scene of desolation and this dark life, will recall from afar many a deadly combat and will speak these words:[7]

> Hwær cwom mearg? Hwær cwom mago? Hwær cwom maþþumgyfa?
> Hwær cwom symbla gesetu? Hwær sindon seledreamas?. . .

[Where is the horse? Where the young horseman? Where the giver of treasure? Where are the seats of banquets? Where are the joys of the hall? O bright cup! O mailed warrior! O chieftain's glory! How that time has departed, vanished under cover of night, as if it had never been. Now stands on the track of the beloved host a wall wondrously high, decorated with shapes of serpents.[8] Might of ashen spears destroyed the nobles, weapons greedy for slaughter, Wyrd the far-famed; and tempests batter these rocky cliffs, falling snow binds the earth, the terror of winter, when the dark nightshadow comes louring, sends from the north a fierce hailstorm in hostility to men. All earth's kingdom is full of hardship, the destined course of events changes the world under the heavens. Here wealth is fleeting, friend is fleeting, man is fleeting, woman is fleeting.[9] All this earthly frame will be empty at last!]

[5] I once argued that there were two speakers in the poem, the exiled wanderer and a wise man ("Dramatic Voices in *The Wanderer* and *The Seafarer*," in Jess B. Bessinger, Jr., and Robert P. Creed, eds., *Franciplegius: Medieval and Linguistic Studies in Honor of Francis Peabody Magoun, Jr.* [New York: New York University Press, 1965], pp. 164–93). But the prevailing view, that the wanderer speaks throughout, is more satisfactory in every way. The contrasts I pointed out between the two halves of the poem are undeniable, but so are some important connections.

[6] On possible implications of this much-used expression see P. J. Frankis, "The Thematic Significance of *enta geweorc* and Related Imagery in *The Wanderer*," ASE 2 (1973):253–69.

[7] *The Wanderer*, lines 92–93, as in G. P. Krapp and E. V. K. Dobbie, eds., *The Exter Book, The Anglo-Saxon Poetic Records* [hereafter ASPR] 3 (New York, 1936), p. 136; the translation includes lines 92–110.

[8] Tony Millns, "*The Wanderer* 98: 'weal wundrum heah wyrmlicum fah,'" RES, n.s. 28 (1977):431–38, gives persuasive evidence to show that the poet is referring to herringbone masonry in the shape of serpents such as can still be seen in the remains of Roman buildings in Britain and in some later imitations, and suggests that the reference to serpents may also have been taken as an appropriate memorial to those who died by the wall.

[9] In lines 108–109, "Her bið feoh læne, her bið freond læne, / her bið mon læne, her bið mæg læne," mæg can be taken as *mǣg*, m. ("kinsman") or *mæg*, f. ("woman," probably but not certainly with short vowel). Most editors, including the latest, have followed Thorpe (*Codex Exoniensis* [London, 1842], pp. 292–93) in choosing "kinsman," but I think *feoh* and *freond* (paralleled by *fé*

In its rhetoric and some of its ideas the poem has been influenced by Latin tradition, including perhaps not only biblical and patristic tradition but also that represented by the *Consolatio philosophiae* of Boethius;[10] but here, as throughout the second half of the poem, the poet has restricted his imagery to what an exiled survivor of a chieftain's comitatus would have experienced: the pleasures of the meadhall as well as the strife with human enemies and a hostile nature, and beyond this the sort of ruins a wanderer would have seen in the English countryside. There is no hint of the biblical prophecies of the last days and the judgment, though possibly the poet's imagination was stimulated by the belief that the sixth age (that of the Christian era) was the last and was like an aged man, a belief that is certainly reflected in lines 80–90 of *The Seafarer*. Earlier (at lines 62–63) the wanderer has said, "Swa þes middangeard / ealra dogra gehwam dreoseð ond fealleð" ("So every day this world decays and falls"). But the connection, if any, is a loose one and hardly necessary to account for the poet's transformation of the elements of a single man's bitter experience into a symbolic vision of the world's decline and fall.

There is equal independence in the poet's use of the *ubi sunt* formula. The elegiac note we associate with Villon's use of the formula in the refrain of his famous ballade was not the rule in the Middle Ages, which had inherited this rhetorical question from biblical and patristic sources.[11] In the Old Testament and in Saint Paul the formula is derisive, aimed at humbling the mighty and ridiculing the worldy-wise. This tone, though modified by the influence of such imaginative treatments of evanescence as are found in *Wisdom* (5.8–15), is still conspic-

---

and *frœndr* in the Old Norse *Hávamál* 77) make an effective pair as representing two things (property and friends) a man needs if he is to get along in the world, and the addition of "kinsman," besides being unnecessary in so cryptic a context, leaves us with an empty generality, *mon* ("man"), or a dubious interpretation of it as "liegeman" or "retainer." The interpretation of *mon* and *mæg* as "man" and "woman" appeared first, so far as I know, in Sir Israel Gollancz's edition (*The Exeter Book*, part 1, EETS, o.s. 104 [London, 1895], p. 293) and has since been chosen by several translators. I think it makes a far better complement to *feoh* and *freond*.

[10] See especially J. E. Cross, "On the Genre of *The Wanderer*," *Neophil* 45 (1961):63–75.

[11] See Étienne Gilson, "De la Bible à François Villon," in his *Les Idées et les lettres* (Paris, 1932), pp. 9–38. In his appendix, pp. 31–38, Gilson gives a list of *ubi sunt* passages that includes works in several different languages and some of comparatively recent date. The formula is still operative. The touch of humor that mingles with pathos in Villon becomes hilarious comedy in Cole Porter's song "Where Is the Life That Late I Led?" in *Kiss Me Kate*.

uous in the sometimes brilliantly rhetorical passages that use the formula in Old English sermons.[12] Here, on the contrary, the elegiac
tenderness belongs to the wanderer's own longing for his former satisfactions and to the native tradition of elegy as we encounter it in
Beowulf.

In *Beowulf* the dark side of mutability makes itself apparent from time
to time and spreads a gloom over the second part, where the mood of
elegy prevails and we are frequently reminded that life is *lǣne.* But formal elegy appears only in the rhetorically enclosed lamentation in the
midst of Hrothgar's report of Æschere's death and in the self-contained
lament of the sole survivor as he buries the treasure.[13] The poet's view
of worldly existence and worldly values is much more complicated
than that of the wanderer. Except for casual mention of Judgment
Day,[14] nothing is said about the future of the world, and not everyone
in the poem takes the same view of mutability.

The sole survivor's speech, except for a brief generalization at the
end, is strictly limited to his own situation and his personal sorrow. He
is grieving, says the poet, "an æfter eallum" ("alone for all").[15] The entire speech is like a spelling out of the first four or five lines of the *ubi
sunt* speech in *The Wanderer.* Both lament the passing of a typical
comitatus, the strenuous action, the fellowship, and the hall joys of a
company of warriors. The survivor's experience has been like that
which drove the wanderer into exile. But in the survivor's speech
there is not the philosophical detachment of the *ubi sunt* speech, and,
although the sorrow is more immediate and more exclusively personal,
there is no emotional outburst. Outwardly the speaker is composed,
almost matter-of-fact. He is taking a necessary course and explains his
reason: "Heald þu nu, hruse, nu hæleð ne moston, / eorla æhte!" The
earth must take charge of these noblemen's possessions because they,
being dead, can no longer do so. Good men formerly took the treasure
from the earth; it is time now to return it. All of this man's suppressed

---

[12] See J. E. Cross, "'Ubi Sunt' Passages in Old English—Sources and Relationships," VSLÅ,
1956, pp. 25–44.

[13] Lines 1323–29 and 2247–66, respectively.

[14] Explicitly in line 978, implicitly in line 2820, and less clearly elsewhere.

[15] Line 2268. Here and elsewhere my quotations are from the text of E. V. K. Dobbie, *Beowulf
and Judith,* ASPR 4 (New York, 1953). In these passages there are no substantive differences
from Klaeber's third edition.

emotion is concentrated in his outwardly rational comments on the precious objects, chiefly weapons and armor, that he is burying. There is no one to wear the sword or polish the precious cup or the richly ornamented, visored helmet. It will lose its gold plates. The half-personified coat of mail will disintegrate after its owner; its ringed steel can no longer go into battle by the side of its lord. Finally he imagines what is not present: the harp with its music, the hawk swinging through the hall, the swift horse beating the courtyard. Baleful death, he says, has sent forth many races of the living.[16] This is his only glance at calamities beyond his own.

The survivor has done all that the poet requires of him. What remains of his life is not relevant to the poem, and he is quickly dismissed with a gentle quietus. But the speech itself is central. It sets the tone for much that is to follow in the poem, and it finely prepares us for the decision of Beowulf's people to consign this same treasure once more to the earth. In their grief they cannot enjoy it, and in their dread of their enemies they cannot hope to hold it. So it still lives there, says the poet, as useless to men as it was before.[17]

Beowulf himself did not agree. He thought he had recovered something of great value to his people by his fatal encounter with the dragon. His attitude toward the future is not like that of his people, and his attitude toward the past is not like that of the sole survivor. To be sure, he remembers with regret the loved ones now dead: old Hrethel, who had brought him up, and Hygelac, whom he had served. He understands so fully the frustrated grief of Hrethel at the killing of one of his sons by another that he illustrates it with the wonderful simile of the old man grieving for his hanged son.[18] And he regrets the lack of an heir. Even so, as he dies, he is thinking hopefully of the future. Wiglaf shall succeed him. The treasure shall be used. He shall have his barrow on the headland, and men will remember him. Mutability has not shaken his faith in the value of earthly existence, which he counts in terms of achievement, the performance of *ellen*.

This attitude lends peculiar interest to the poet's description of the

---

[16] "Bealocwealm hafað / fela feorhcynna forð onsended!" (lines 2265b–66).
[17] Þær hit nu gen lifað / eldum swa unnyt swa h[it ær]or wæs" (lines 3167b–68).
[18] Lines 2444–62.

treasure[19] as Wiglaf enters the barrow to bring some of it out to his
dying king. The gold, as Wiglaf and we ourselves see it, is beautifully
and perhaps dangerously alive. The iron weapons are rusted and falling
apart, but the gold shines, and an eerie light from the golden banner
illumines the cave. In the midst of his description the poet exclaims,

> Sinc eaðe mæg,
> gold on grund{e}, gumcynnes gehwone
> oferhigian, hyde se ðe wylle!

I am inclined to take the unprefixed verb *higian* in the sense "hasten"
that it bears in later texts and so to interpret *oferhigian* as "outstrip" or
"overtake" rather than "overcome," as Klaeber and others would have
it. No matter who hides the gold, it will not die. It will outstrip, and
thus outlast, everyone; hiding it does not destroy it: "Treasure, gold in
the ground, can easily outstrip everyone of the race of men, hide it
who will." If we think of the curse on the gold, as very likely we
should, we may add a sinister touch to *oferhigian*, as we can in the
modern word "overtake," but I think there is reason to feel that its long
life, while it seems to oppose mutability as a universal principle, makes
us doubly conscious of the littleness of the human life span. Whether
or not I am right about *oferhigian*, it would seem that the poet had
thought of the long life of gold as significant, for he says that the sole
survivor expected to have only a short time to make use of the "long-
(lasting)" treasures: "...wende.../ þæt he lytle fæc longgestreona /
brucan moste."[20] Klaeber suggests that *long* means "long-accumulated,"
therefore "old," and even this would support my idea, but not quite as
obviously as "long-lasting," which seems the natural antithesis to *lytel*
fæc in the context.[21]

That Beowulf feels something of this long life of the treasure – and is
perhaps in some way reconciled by it to his own death – is suggested
by the passage just preceding Wiglaf's exploration of the barrow.
Beowulf, sorely wounded, makes his way to the entrance of the barrow and sits on a seat of some sort:

[19] Lines 2756–71.

[20] Lines 2239–41.

[21] Cf. also "þær hit nu gen lifað" (line 3167b), already quoted in note 17.

Đa se æðeling giong,
þæt he bi wealle   wishycgende
gesæt on sesse;   seah on enta geweorc,
hu ða stanbogan   stapulum fæste
ece eorðreced   innan healde.[22]

The main idea of this passage is fairly clear, but it is possible, as Eric Stanley pointed out in a very thorough study of its metrical and syntactical problems,[23] that two half lines have dropped out after *sesse* (half lines that would not materially have altered the sense but would have improved the meter by allowing *enta* rather than *seah* to alliterate), that *ece* ("eternal") is a scribal error for *ecne* (= *eacne*), accusative singular neuter weak of *eacen* ("huge"), and that present subjunctive *healde* is an error for preterite plural indicative *heoldon*. My point is only slightly affected by these possibilities, but I will assume that the readings Stanley seems to favor (though he is too cautious to insist upon them) are correct and translate accordingly: "Then the prince went and sat, meditating wisely, on a seat beside the wall;...he looked at the work of giants, and saw how the stone arches, set fast on pillars, held up the huge earth-house from within."

Beowulf, though dying, is concerned about more than the treasure. He is noticing how this ancient barrow is constructed. The description suggests to me the vaulting of Roman architecture or its imitation in such a crypt as Wilfred built at Hexham. At any rate it is a huge barrow, the work of giants, and the arches seem to catch Beowulf's thoughtful attention: the arches and the size and antiquity of the thing. (If the poet meant to call it *ece*, so much the better for my point, but its long life is evident anyway.) It is still, apparently, as firm and strong as ever, though it has held the treasure for at least three hundred and perhaps a thousand years.[24] As with the indestructible gold, here is something that seems to resist mutation, as Beowulf, tough though he

[22] Lines 2715b–19. The final *e* of *healde* had disappeared from the margin of the manuscript before Thorkelin made the second transcript. It is attested only by transcript A.

[23] E. G. Stanley, "Verbal Stress in Old English Verse," *Anglia* 93 (1975):307–34, esp. 308–21. I suggested the same interpretation of Beowulf's attitude, accepting the reading *ece eorðreced*, in "Beowulf's Old Age," in James L. Rosier, ed., *Philological Essays...in Honour of Herbert Dean Meritt* (The Hague: Mouton, 1970), p. 58.

[24] It is not clear how we are to resolve the apparent conflict between *þreo hund wintra* (2278b) and *þusend wintra* (3050a).

is, no longer can. As *wishycgende* suggests, Beowulf shares with the poet a wonder at something that pulls his mind away from his pain and his impending death, to admire the skill that made it and its power to endure. Instead of a lamentation over the mutability to which he himself is so painfully subject, we have admiration and awe at something time has not conquered.

Perhaps I am making too much of this short and almost enigmatic scene, but if I am right about its implications, it marks a halfway stage toward that surprising little poem *The Ruin*, one of the short pieces included toward the end of the Exeter Book.[25] Although the poem itself has been partly ruined by the firebrand (if such it was) that made an ugly hole in the middle of the leaf containing it, enough remains to indicate the direction of its thought as well as the poet's command of his medium. It is almost a reversal of the passage I have quoted from *The Wanderer*. The speaker tells us nothing about himself. He is looking with wonder and awe at the fragmented remnants of a large cluster of buildings. Their dilapidation is so extensive that, as if bewildered, he pours out at the beginning, after two broadly summarizing lines, an almost random series of thoughts and images:

> Wrætlic is þes wealstan, wyrde gebræcon;
> burgstede burston, brosnað enta geweorc.
> Hrofas sind gehrorene, hreorge torras,
> hrungeat berofen, hrim on lime,
> scearde scurbeorge scorene, gedrorene,
> ældo undereotone. Eorðgrap hafað
> waldend wyrhtan forweorone, geleorene,
> heardgripe hrusan, oþ hund cnea

---

[25] Exeter Cathedral, Dean and Chapter Library, MS. 3501. Text in Krapp and Dobbie, eds., *The Exeter Book*, ASPR 3 (New York, 1936), pp. 227–29. The best edition is by R. F. Leslie, in *Three Old English Elegies* (Manchester: Manchester University Press, 1961). For critical comment see especially S. B. Greenfield, "The Old English Elegies," in E. G. Stanley, ed., *Continuations and Beginnings* (London, 1966), pp. 142–75; on *The Ruin*, pp. 144–46; or, more briefly, his *Critical History of Old English Literature* (New York: New York University Press, 1965), pp. 214–15, where he gives extracts from one of Burton Raffel's happiest and freest verse translations (*Poems from the Old English*, 2d ed. [Lincoln: University of Nebraska Press, 1964], pp. 27–28). See also Karl P. Wentersdorf, "Observations on *The Ruin*," *MÆ* 46 (1977):171–80, for an intelligent treatment of certain literary analogues having to do with Roman ruins and some helpful comments on several difficult architectural terms in the poem.

werþeoda gewitan. Oft þæs wag gebad
ræghar ond readfah rice æfter oþrum,
ofstonden under stormum; steap geap gedreas.

Rare terms seemingly precise but no longer clear to us are mingled with impressionistic verbal trickery, rhymes and assonances in addition to alliteration binding the parts of speech in counterlogical coherence, em-phasizing, as it were, the common desolation of what was once differ-entiated in a significant order. The following fairly literal rendering misses, of course, the lyrical jugglery:[26]

Wondrous is this wall-stone — the fates destroyed it; the city's foundations have burst, the work of giants moulders away. Roofs are fallen, ruinous are the towers, the barred gate is broken. There is frost on the lime. The bul-warks against storms are shattered, cut away, decayed, undermined by age. The grasp of the earth, stout grip of the ground, holds the master-builders, who have perished and gone, till now a hundred generations of men have passed away.[27] Often this wall, gray with lichen and stained with red, has survived kingdom after kingdom, unmoved under storms; high-arched,[28] it has crumbled.

So far, except for the sharp observation of certain details, we might take this for a conventional lament on mutability. But as the poem pro-ceeds, the elegiac mood alternates with an excited wonder at what the speaker's imagination is able to reconstruct. He begins to recognize a

[26] I have modified only slightly my direct borrowings from the translations of R. K. Gordon, *Anglo-Saxon Poetry*, Everyman's Library, no. 794 (London, 1926; rev. ed., 1954), p. 84; and W. S. Mackie, *The Exeter Book*, part 2, EETS, o.s., 194 (London, 1934), p. 199.

[27] Leslie takes *gewitan* as a present infinitive with the auxiliary *sculan* understood and would translate, "Until a hundred generations of men shall pass away." But the older editors and trans-lators took *gewitan* as a preterite with short *i*, which in fact is required by ordinary metrical prac-tice (Sievers's type E with resolution). It seems possible that the poet's round number (which amounts to about three thousand years by the usual reckoning of generations) was influenced by recollection of the prototypical destruction of Babylon, as suggested by Hugh T. Keenan, "The *Ruin* as Babylon," *TSL* 11 (1966):109–17; and by James F. Doubleday, "The *Ruin*: Structure and Theme," *JEGP* 71 (1972):369–81. I do not agree with their views of the poem. Better treatments of the possible literary backgrounds of the poem are provided by Anne Thompson Lee, "The *Ruin*: Bath or Babylon? A Non-Archaeological Investigation," *NM* 74 (1973):443–55; and especially by Wentersdorf, "Observations on *The Ruin*," pp. 171–80.

[28] Mackie and Leslie are probably right in taking *geap* as an adjective, either "broad" (Mackie) or "curved," hence "arched" or "rounded," as in the walls of towers (Leslie). I have taken a chance on "arched" and combined the two adjectives.

design in the architectural remains, signs of extraordinary skill in work-manship and the mind's swift purpose ("mod...myne swiftne gebrægd"). Having observed hot springs, he detects the outlines of a circular pool and notes how it apparently served as a reservoir to feed hot water into the baths – "þæt wæs hyðelic," a convenient arrange-ment. He has already pictured to himself the men who must anciently have lived there, powerful, rich, and fond of pleasure – "wlonc ond wingal" ("proud and flushed with wine") – until there came, he sup-poses, days of pestilence (*woldagas*), and all were destroyed. He neither moralizes over the fate that has befallen these proud worldlings he has conjured up nor bewails it. The contrast he paints between then and now is almost staggering in its extremity, but at the same time he is fascinated by what those master builders had been able to accomplish. The fragmentary remnants of the conclusion of the poem contain what seems a note of pure admiration: "þæt is cynelic þing" ("that is a kingly thing"). The center of interest has shifted from pres-ent desolation to past magnificence. Yes, "Sic transit gloria mundi," but in its day the glory was not a contemptible thing, still less the skill and energy of mind that had made it possible.

The reason for this unusual attitude in a literature we think of as dominated by contempt of earthly achievement is not far to seek. The poet clearly has his eye on an actual ruin, and curiosity has led him to inspect it carefully, so that ultimately he has almost succeeded in re-creating it in his imagination. I agree, of course, with those who believe that this poet has been contemplating the ruins of the Roman city of Bath. We still think of it as a "cynelic þing," and we may remember that Benedict Biscop, Wilfrid, and Aldhelm were all builders of elabo-rate structures long before the builders of the great cathedrals. Aldhelm described some of these structures in his Latin verses. The poet's imaginative reconstruction may have been stimulated by literary treatments of other ruins, but the focus of his attention is on a specific ruin that he has studied in detail at first hand.

Even preachers did not always insist on the negative aspect of muta-bility. The cyclical renewals of nature can seem beneficent. Ever since Saint Paul's First Epistle to the Corinthians[29] the rebirth of the sup-

---

[29] I Cor. 15.36ff. See also John 12.24.

posedly dead grain of wheat has been taken as an analogy in support of the resurrection of the dead into life eternal. In one of Saint Augustine's sermons the analogy is introduced with a rhetorical variation on the *ubi sunt* formula:

Unde [*read* ubi *or* quo?] abeunt, unde redeunt frondes arboribus? in quæ secreta discedunt, de quibus secretis adveniunt? Hiems est, certe nunc arbores arentibus similes verno tempore virescunt. Nunc primum factum est, an et præterito anno ita fuit? Imo et præterito sic fuit. Interceptum est ab autumno in hieme, redit per vernum in æstate. Ergo annus redit in tempore, et homines, facti ad imaginem Dei, cum mortui fuerint interibunt?[30]

I think this passage helped Ælfric develop his largely original elaboration of the idea in a passage added to his sermon for the first Sunday after Easter in his first series of *Catholic Homilies*. I quote only the first few of his rhythmical lines:

> Hwær beoð wyrta blostman on winterlicre tide?
> Hwær beoð ealle ofætu of eallum treowcynne?
> Hwær beoð hi gesewene on winterlicum cyle
> on ænigum beame, þe ealle eft cuciað,
> on wyrtum and on treowum, þurh þone ecan wyrhtan,
> se ðe ða deadan ban of þam duste arærð
> eal swa eaðelice swa he hi ær geworhte?

Where are the blossoms of plants in the wintertime? Where are all fruits of every kind of tree? Where are they seen in the winter's chill on any bough, they that all come to life again, in plants and in trees, through the eternal creator, who raises up the dead bones from the dust just as easily as he made them before?

The passage proceeds with other analogies—flies and birds, hibernating beasts, silkworms, the phoenix, and the seven sleepers of Ephesus —before it ends with a well-calculated exhortation.[31]

Our faith in such analogies has been weakened by the knowledge

---

[30] Sermo 361, cap. 10 (Migne, *PL* 39, col. 1604).

[31] See the summary, with partial quotations, by Milton M. Gatch, *Preaching and Theology in Anglo-Saxon England: Ælfric and Wulfstan* (Toronto, 1977), pp. 86–88. In my review of this book (*Speculum* 54 [1979]:134) I quoted the passage from Augustine. A complete text of Ælfric's addition will be included in the new edition of Ælfric's *Catholic Homilies, First Series*, by P. A. M. Clemoes, to be published by the Early English Text Society.

that the seeds we sow are not dead, that silkworms come to life from tiny eggs, not mere dust, and by the persistent refusal of the sole Arabian bird to verify his existence. But nature's renewal of human as well as other species, sometimes with an increment, offers a valid argument for some sort of continuity through change, a continuity of which dwellers in temperate zones are constantly reminded by the cycle of the seasons. This relatively cheerful aspect of mutability is incorporated and carefully weighed against the darker aspect in what is perhaps the greatest of Spenser's mythological inventions, the posthumously published "Cantos of Mutabilitie." These cantos include nearly everything that can be said or thought about mutability as we encounter it in our experience of the world. They are far too long and complicated to be dealt with *in extenso* here, even if they had not had their due long since from critics and appreciative readers. But I hope I may be allowed to touch briefly on what is most relevant to the present exploration.

Spenser's very complicated attitude toward life in this world as conditioned by time and change unfolds gradually with the unfolding of his story. Our own attitudes as readers are manipulated by the action itself and by a deeply concerned and somewhat perplexed narrator who at first takes a wholly negative view of the protagonist Mutabilitie, the rebellious Titaness whose supremacy on earth has encouraged her to invade the heavens and challenge the Olympians, here treated as gods of the planetary spheres. As first presented to us, Mutabilitie is blamed for her "cruell sports, to many mens decay,"[32] including her responsibility for man's fall and the administration of its unhappy consequences. But when she confronts an angry Jove, he is suddenly disarmed by her beauty, an attribute the narrator had not previously mentioned, and when she so far relents as to agree to a trial of her claim before "great dame Nature," we are prepared to modify our original impression of her character. In the presence of Nature (a grandly-mysterious being who serves as a discreet substitute for God as ruler of the physical universe) her arrogance evaporates. She bows humbly before the judge and resorts to legal debate instead of war. We are

[32] *FQ* 7.6.1. All quotations are from *The Faerie Queene, Books VI and VII*, vol. 6 in *The Works of Edmund Spenser: A Variorum Edition* (Baltimore, 1938), except that I have modernized the use of i, j, u, and v.

thus prepared for the great pageant of times and seasons that she calls for as a major witness to her claim against the Olympians. That the witness is summoned by Nature's sergeant Order forewarns us that its testimony may be of doubtful value to the plaintiff. In fact this celebrated pageant, described by a narrator who is now in a mood to respond to all it can suggest of this world's worth and beauty, is at once a preparation for Nature's final decision and one of Spenser's most persuasively optimistic visions of our changeable but still orderly world. The pageant displays both the dark and the bright aspects of a partly ordered change, but the balance is tipped toward the bright. Thus three of the four seasons are described with stress on their pleasures and fruitful labors. A threat of war in the spring, of oppressive heat in summer, of remembered hunger in autumn serve only as an undertone to the prevailing cheer. Winter alone, poetically delightful as a caricature, presents no redeeming satisfactions (7.7.21):

> Lastly, came *Winter* cloathed all in frize,
>   Chattering his teeth for cold that did him chill,
>   Whil'st on his hoary beard his breath did freese;
>   And the dull drops that from his purpled bill
>   As from a limbeck did adown distill.
>   In his right hand a tipped staffe he held,
>   With which his feeble steps he stayed still:
>   For, he was faint with cold, and weak with eld;
> That scarce his loosed limbes he hable was to weld.

The procession of the months, in which weather, the mythological signs of the zodiac, and the seasonal human activities are half-playfully intermingled, conveys on the whole a mood of robust acceptance. Even the winter months are partly redeemed, December by the Christmas festivities, January and February by the provident countryman's preparations for spring. When Life and Death bring up the rear of the procession, it is obvioius that the narrator is doing his best to soften the dread fact of mortality (7.7.46):

> And after all came *Life*, and lastly *Death*;
>   *Death* with most grim and griesly visage seene,
>   Yet is he nought but parting of the breath;
>   Ne ought to see, but like a shade to weene,
>   Unbodied, unsoul'd, unheard, unseene.

But *Life* was like a faire young lusty boy,
Such as they faine *Dan Cupid* to have beene,
Full of delightful health and lively joy,
Deckt all with flowres, and wings of gold fit to employ.

More than any other part of Mutabilitie's long argument and Jove's rejoinders, this wonderful pageant prepares us for the two stanzas in which Nature, after long silence, delivers her verdict, and the dramatic narrative is concluded (7.7.58, 59):

I well consider all that ye have sayd,
And find that all things stedfastnes doe hate
And changed be: yet being rightly wayd
They are not changed from their first estate;
But by their change their being doe dilate:
And turning to themselves at length againe,
Doe worke their owne perfection so by fate:
Then over them Change doth not rule and raigne;
But they raigne over change, and doe their states maintaine.

Cease therefore daughter further to aspire,
And thee content thus to be rul'd by me:
For thy decay thou seekst by thy desire;
But time shall come that all shall changed bee,
And from thenceforth, none no more change shall see.
So was the *Titaness* put downe and whist,
And *Jove* confirm'd in his imperiall see.
Then was that whole assembly quite dismist,
And *Natur's* selfe did vanish, whither no man wist.

Surely we ought to be satisfied. The world we inhabit is on the whole beneficent, and we ought to make the best of it. Nature preserves the species, ever allowing it to work its own perfection by "dilation" (the mysteries of which may be sought in the commentaries), though she sacrifices the individual. And she admits that eventually time and change will have a stop and something better may be in store. What more could we ask?

But the narrator, whose mask will now seem to many readers remarkably thin, virtually transparent, is not satisfied. The two retrospective stanzas that follow, assigned to the otherwise missing eighth canto, are full of the disquiet that the narrator conveyed at the beginning of the story and never quite overcame, even in the prevailingly optimistic description of the pageant. These extraordinarily moving stanzas force us to think twice about what Spenser, through his narrator and beyond him, is ultimately wanting us to understand and feel (7.8.1, 2):

> When I bethinke me on that speech whyleare,
> Of *Mutability*, and well it way:
> Me seemes, that though she all unworthy were
> Of the Heav'ns Rule; yet very sooth to say,
> In all things else she beares the greatest sway.
> Which makes me loath this state of life so tickle,
> And love of things so vaine to cast away;
> Whose flowring pride, so fading and so fickle,
> Short *Time* shall soon cut down with his consuming sickle.

> Then gin I thinke on that which Nature sayd,
> Of that same time when no more *Change* shall be,
> But stedfast rest of all things firmely stayd
> Upon the pillours of Eternity,
> That is contrayr to *Mutabilitee*:
> For, all that moveth, doth in *Change* delight:
> But thenceforth all shall rest eternally
> With Him that is the God of Sabbaoth hight:
> O! that great Sabbaoth God, grant me that Sabaoths sight.

One can accept every word of what the narrator so beautifully says and believe that it expresses a deeply considered conclusion of Spenser himself. Even so, we cannot forget that it is Spenser who has used all the resources of his genius to create the very vision of the world whose power to satisfy the human spirit he now denies. The imagery and the attitude of the last four lines of the first of these stanzas recall, along with other passages in Spenser's own work, the images of the fair and the fair flowers that I quoted from Chaucer at the beginning of this essay. Thus the wheel, though badly out of shape, has come full circle. Chaucer's ending of *Troilus* and Spenser's simpler and less extravagantly contradictory ending of these cantos have in common not only a similar attitude toward the world but a similar strategy. Tillyard, commenting on the Mutability Cantos and these last stanzas in particular, has said of Spenser, "It is through the poignancy of his regrets for earthly instability that he so wonderfully expresses his overmastering passion for order and the old double pull to relish the world and to despise it."[33] He might have said almost the same thing of Spenser's avowed master, the "well of English undefyled." As for the strategy of the two endings, it would seem that both poets knew how, by a deliberate use of equivocation, to present strongly contrary or seriously divergent views of the world, its values, and its mysteries, not so as to cancel out one or the other but so as to suggest a *tertium quid* that holds both in suspension and points to an inexpressible synthesis.

[33] E. M. W. Tillyard, *The Elizabethan World Picture* (New York, 1944), p. 14.

Part Ten E. TALBOT DONALDSON

Speaking of Donaldson

Compiled by Mary J. Carruthers
With the assistance of John C. Pope and Elizabeth D. Kirk

Contributors: Judith H. Anderson, Marie Borroff, Mary J. Carruthers,
Suzanne Greene, Annie Gregory, Edward B. Irving, Jr., George Kane,
Elizabeth D. Kirk, Kay Macnamara, Alice S. Miskimin, Dorothy Sipe
Mull, Thomas Noble, Derek Pearsall, John C. Pope, Carter Revard,
Ann C. Watts

Of Donaldson and of his worthynesse
To speken wol I fonde, therby texpresse
Somdeel oure joye and solas in this feste
Wherin we him honouren as us leste.
And thou, Dan Chaucer, gyde my speche, I preye,
Whyl I thy sones herynge seye.
  Now certeynly to tellen his renoun
It nedeth nat, for Fames clarioun
Hath souned longe and loude his maistrye
In al that toucheth olde poesye
Endyted faire in English longe agoon.
In al this worlde, I gesse, is nowher noon
That gloseth bet the rum-ram-ruf of Will,
Or bet divyneth al the thoght subtil
Of Geffrey, whan he countrefeteth chere
Of som unconning wight, or wol appere
So daswed by Criseyde his creature
That hir to blame he can unnethe endure.
  But if Adam scriveyn, or of his craft
Som other, hath miswriten and biraft
His auctour of his pleyn entencioun,
Therof no fors; this sage champioun
Shal knowe anonright by his heigh science
The verray forme of his auctours sentence,

Right as he wroot or thoughte it in his minde.
He and his felawe Kane, men seyn, conne binde
The spirits of men dede, and doon hem telle
The secrees of al materes textuelle.
Therof I noot, but this I woot aright:
He knoweth God the Wrighte is nat a wight!
  This gentil doctour of philosophye
Counteth his dignitee nat worth a flye.
Him liketh wel to teche and to scoleye,
And therby wol he gladly laughe and pleye,
And ofte sythes, hertes peyne to scape,
Wol esen inward smerte with ale and jape.
To yonge folk that lernen wol aright
He yeveth strengthe and counseil day and night.
Curteis he is and amiable with alle,
But if som wight wol clawe him on the galle.
Beth war, ye lerned men of heigh bobaunce,
That ye no folye by youre text avaunce!
So kene and persaunt is his wit, pardee,
That er ye fele the wounde it shal you slee.
  In Bethlehem, but soothly nat the toun
Of which the gospel maketh mencioun,
This man was born, and hath in shoure and sonne
Ful three score yeer and ten his cours yronne.
Now lat him pleye as ferforth as he can,
And flouren faire in somer Indian.

                                        J. C. P.

Although many laudatory things might be said about E. Talbot Donaldson, my own fondest recollections of him have to do with his con-
summate performance in the graduate Chaucer course at Yale. His
classes were triumphs, animated always by his wit, his considerable
dramatic abilities, and his almost Johnsonian impatience with cant.
"*Down* with that reading!" he would roar, eyes flashing and monkish
fringe of hair bobbing up and down as he demolished a benighted critic
or two. And he was equally spirited when savoring an especially felici-

tous Chaucerian turn of phrase. Rarely, I think, has a scholar been so perfectly matched with his subject.

When I was a first-year graduate student taking the Chaucer seminar at Yale, there was an articulate and learned, but also somewhat pretentious, young man in the class. His recitations were frequent and elaborate, and more than a little intimidating to the rest of us. One day this student was going on at length and, becoming self-conscious, turned to Donaldson and asked, "Is it all right if this turns into a disquisition?"

"Sure," replied Donaldson without missing a beat, "go ahead and disquisish!" I don't recall that this deft bit of verbal deflation had any effect on the victim, but it eased the atmosphere wonderfully.

In the spring of my first year at Yale, our Chaucer class was invited to Talbot's house in rural Woodbridge. On that May morning some of us strolled back through a blossoming yard toward the trees, with Donaldson and his small daughter Deirdre leading the way, to see what vision the setting might produce. What it produced was a duck, but not one dabbling on a pond. This duck came suddenly out of a large hole high in an oak tree: quick, silent, and brilliantly colored, it flashed away, zigzagging behind a nearby garage and out of sight. "Oh, that's our wood-duck," Donaldson said with delight and wonder. His classes could be like that.

Two constants of Donaldson's teaching and writing have been his conviction that poetry is about life or it is nothing, and his brief, modest way of seeming to discover the general conviction in the particular text. For example, at the end of a long class in which others had had their say about Griselda, he praised her loyalty and utter fidelity to the word of her promise, no matter what was going on around her or being done to her, and then said, "But you cannot live that way—or if you can, you are in despair." This same idea shapes his short essay on *The Clerk's Tale* in the rear of *Chaucer's Poetry*.

One sunny late afternoon in May, a graduate student in Talbot's Chaucer seminar, temporarily installed in the professorial seat, was presenting a long report on the final book of *Troilus* and, with rash sentimentality, coming down hard on Criseyde, canceling the virtue of her earlier acts in the vice of her final one. A growing restlessness became audible in the rear of the room, attracting student glances toward Donaldson, who was seated in the windowsill, his thin figure outlined against the flowering dogwood in the courtyard below. As the student finished, Donaldson unwound himself from his seat and, after recalling to the class Criseyde's earlier actions, declared simply and emphatically, "All of what is—*is*." His pronouncement was the profoundest statement of a critical principle that I have ever heard.

A student in the graduate Chaucer seminar was so injudicious as to complain when the final examination consisted solely of quotations to be commented upon in detail. Why was this trivial activity necessary? Talbot replied, "Because I am tired of people who have read everything except the text."

I remember asking Talbot why he decided to stop being director of graduate studies. He said: "When you first start to do that job, you are learning how, and do the best you can. Then you begin to develop an instinct for what people can and should do with themselves, and you are very good at it for awhile. Then the day comes when you start relying on that instinct and stop using your brain. Then you should quit before you become dangerous."

Talbot would get very run down during the time of year when he had to select the graduate students for the coming year. He did this entirely by himself, sitting on the floor in his office surrounded by piles of applications and records. The decisions were terribly difficult even then, and I remember his saying that really the only fair way would be to put them all in a hat and pick out eighteen. This process almost immediately resulted in, among other things, a rise in the percentage of women graduate students admitted to the Yale English Department, from about 10 percent, when Talbot became director in 1953, to 50 percent. When asked years later why he did this, he responded, "Because it was right."

Comment on an attractive, polite Harvard applicant who came for an interview: "He was a good man—looks almost human."

In my senior year at Yale I went to see Talbot about whether it was even worth my while applying to the Graduate School for admission. He rechecked my Yale College transcript, said it probably was, that I might even get in, but added, "You must remember that everybody else will be first-rate."

When I saw Talbot for my first conference as a graduate student, he looked up and down at the tongue-tied girl before him from a little Quaker college and growled, "I see you got married over the summer. Married women never make it. They are always typing their husbands' papers instead of their own." I was so taken aback and annoyed that I only realized much later when I knew him better that the entirely salutary effect of this remark was precisely the one he had intended.

As I waited to be summoned by my examining committee at Columbia on the morning of my orals, I found that I was unable to remember anything that was likely to be useful in the next few hours. Equally alarming was the discovery that my legs were paralyzed and that I was therefore unable to leave quickly and quietly by the nearest exit. By the time Donaldson arrived to escort me to the exam, the signs of panic must have been evident. He seized my arm and propelled me down the hall, intoning:

> Hige sceal þe heardra, heorte þe cenre,
> mod sceal þe mare, þe ure mægen lytlað.

Like many other students I badgered Donaldson for recommendations, but one of these was a recommendation for a wedding. A Friends Meeting required assurances, inner light and its principled silence not-withstanding. When I asked him whether the Quakers could write to him, he said yes in his customarily helpful way. Their letter came, and he called me in. "Are you good?" asked he. "I'm not used to vouching for details of students' moral behavior. They're asking me if you're good, and I'm going to say that you are." "Please do," I said, though I wasn't good. He did.

As a nineteen-year-old college senior I journeyed by train from Welles-ley to New Haven one iron-gray day in early November. I wanted to apply to the Yale Graduate School and had been assured by my dean that I must have a talk with her dear friend Talbot Donaldson. I walked into an empty Hall of Graduate Studies at five in the evening and down an ever-darkening hallway. One light showed from an open door, which I timidly approached. I was expected and welcomed, and my transcript was spread out on the desk. Donaldson had just stopped smoking (again) and was coping by eating quantities of caramel can-dies. I was offered one, which I of course accepted, and as my teeth became inevitably and (it seemed) permanently glued together, we studied my transcript. "No American literature." "Ungh." "No Roman-tic literature." "Ungh." "No Eighteenth-century, no Victorian"—the litany continued. "Well, I spent some of my time," I said with great dif-ficulty, "taking courses in creative writing." A pause—"Yes." Then a much longer pause—"Of course, we *kill* creativity here!"

Comment on a student in a letter of recommendation: "A cheerful, en-thusiastic student. Lacks, perhaps, basic potential."

Before the Medieval Academy meeting in 1977 a well-known pro-fessor with whom Talbot had had a long-standing debate on Chau-cerian matters was elected to their number by the Fellows of the Academy. At a gathering held for new Fellows, as Talbot himself recalls the event, he had a long, amiable chat with a gentleman whom he had not seen before. Shortly afterward he asked a friend, "I understand that Professor – – is here, but I don't recognize him. Where is he?" The friend replied, "You were just talking to him." Greatly embarrassed, Talbot returned to his earlier companion. The gentleman accepted his apology but seemed puzzled himself. "And who," he asked, "are you?"

My husband and I had noticed the long-legged gentleman with the "Mr. Punch" face for several weeks. His coat had a fur collar and always lay on one of the seats in the Fox and Hounds pub, where we went to drink beer on Saturday mornings. Its owner was always engaged in conversation with another man, and we watched and listened from across the room. The day came when his companion, departing earlier, left Talbot alone, and we began our friendship, continuing it whenever he came to England. That is over twenty years ago. I think Talbot's eminence in the academic world eludes us. We just love him and wait patiently for his visits.

I first met Talbot at the MLA Conference in Chicago in 1963. I had arranged to call on him in his hotel room and couldn't understand why the instant he saw me he exited for the elevator, with me in tow, down twenty-five floors—but did understand when we got to the basement and found there a liquor store where bourbon was cheap. Back up twenty-five floors, and a healthy space appearing in the top of the bottle, Talbot felt fit to face me and to castigate in characteristic terms ("pussy-footed" was the mildest expression I remember) my practices in an edition I had just published.

In a huge room, more than two-thirds filled, with fewer than the usual number of shopping interlopers in the rear, Donaldson mounted the speakers' platform at the 1970 MLA, and the audience reacted with pleasure at the sight of him. I overheard a mature professor remark querulously, "Who is this Donaldson, that everybody laughs even before he begins?" He was soon *envoluped* himself, laughing at sin, of all things.

The committee appointed to nominate the recipient of the Haskins Medal for 1978 unanimously agrees that the award be given jointly to George Kane... and to E. Talbot Donaldson...for their edition of the B Version of *Piers Plowman*.... This is a long-awaited major edition of a major poem.

Piers Plowman presents enormous problems for its editors. William Langland's masterpiece is first of all an intensely original, unpredictable, and brilliant poem of the kind that suffers most at the hands of unintelligent copyists. Furthermore, it survives in three distinct authorial versions, the B version being the middle one and the one most widely read in modern times. Popular from the start, *Piers Plowman* exists not only in these three versions but in many early manuscripts of confused relationship and widely varying dependability. Professor Kane's edition of the A (first and shortest) version appeared in 1960; since 1950 he and Professor Donaldson have been at work on the much more formidable complexities of the B text.

After alluding in the preface to their infinitely frustrating labors, the editors add: "Looking back we have a sense of great privilege from having been engaged in the restoration of such a noble and splendid work of art." Restoration is precisely the word. Readers familiar with *Piers* in W. W. Skeat's edition of almost one hundred years ago must now feel that they are seeing it and hearing it for the first time; the dulling film of scribal infelicities expertly dissolved away, the colors brightened, the alliterative meter at last in tune, the harsh and exhilarating voice of Langland more audible than it has ever been before.

To attain this impressive goal, the editors make a thorough analysis of the complex manuscript tradition, reasoning carefully, never grinding axes or insisting on solving the insoluble but never letting prudence become timidity. Finding no satisfactory account of Langland's alliterative practice at hand, they make an entirely new study of it that they then use as an important guide to textual decisions. At every point they patiently explain their procedures, furnish copious examples for the skeptics to study, and take full responsibility for the hypotheses they adopt; as they themselves put it, they aim to provide an edition that will be "open to its users."

The committee speaks for all lovers of English medieval literature when we congratulate Professors Kane and Donaldson on the service they have rendered by producing this magnificent edition.

Reprinted with permission from *Speculum*

When I had finished my dissertation on *Piers Plowman*, Talbot looked at me quizzically and said, "I like *parts* of this very much." Later, when I had completed the manuscript of my book, he went over it with me in detail and made a number of invaluable suggestions. At the end of the session I remember he sighed and said, "I have always known that if anyone explained to me what this poem was really about I wouldn't like it."

The year Talbot was on leave at Englefield Green, he and I used to look in at the Fox and Hounds for a pint or so on the way home from college. Generally nobody turned up until we were ready to go, so we used the darts scoreboard for our editorial diagrams and manuscript schemata. After several weeks of this the landlord, his curiosity peaked beyond his reserve, asked us if we were atomic scientists planning some bomb. One evening we stayed a bit later than usual, and some locals came in, intent upon a darts game. We hastily cleaned our stemma off the scoreboard. They spotted Talbot for an American and challenged him to a game. He put them off until it was not possible any longer; then he beat them roundly.

In a Middle English seminar in which he was explaining the process of editing *Piers Plowman*, Donaldson began with a detailed account of how to collect the variants from the manuscripts, in the course of which he recalled for us having spent an entire year doing nothing but that for the edition. "What a waste!" one student exclaimed. "Surely that is the sort of thing a computer could and should do for you." Talbot replied gently and a trifle ruefully, "It was necessary to the education of the editor."

When I was his secretary, and had just spent hours doing what seemed to me like pages of strange chemistry equations on *Piers Plowman*, I asked him, "How can you spend your time doing *that*?" He answered, "Because I love it. I have loads of fun doing it."

Experience, though noon auctoritee
Were in this world, is right ynogh for me
To speke of Talbot Donaldson, a man
That fro the time that he first bigan
To writen bookes, he loved chivalrye,
Trouthe and honour, fredom and curteisye.
Ful worthy is he in his bookes lore,
And therto hath he writen, no man more,
As well in Chauceres as in Langlandes dresse,
And evere honoured hem for hire worthenesse.
He hath bestowed the fruit of al his age
On Langlandes book, write in newe langage,
And Chauceres, thogh he can but lewedly
On metres and on riming craftily;
For he hath told of poetes up and down
Mo than Caxton made of mencioun,
In his articles that been ful olde.
What sholde I tellen hem, sin they ben tolde?
In youthe he made *The C Text and Its Poet*,
And sithen hath he spoke of othere yet,
Of *Beowulf* and *Chauceres Poetrye*,
Speaking of Chaucer and *Piers Plowman B*.
Ah, Lord Crist, whan it remembreth me
Upon his youthe and on his jolitee,
It tickleth me about my herte roote.
Unto this day it dooth myn herte boote,
That he hath had his worlde as in his time!
But age, alas, that al wol envenyme,
Hath him biraft som beautee and som pith.
Lat go, farewel, the devel go therwith!
The flour is goon, ther is namoor to telle:
Translaciouns, as he can, now most he selle
(For soothfastnesse is sorwe, I understonde).
And yit to be right merye wol he fonde.

A. S. M.

E. Talbot Donaldson

Curriculum Vitae

Born Bethlehem, Pennsylvania, March 18, 1910.

Educated Kent School, Kent, Connecticut; Harvard University (A.B., 1932, Greek and English), *cum laude*; Yale University (Ph.D., 1943: "The C-Text of *Piers Plowman*").

Teacher of English, French, Latin, and Greek, Kent School, 1932–38, 1939–40.

Fellow in General Studies, Yale University, 1938–39.

U.S. Army Air Force, 1943–46, Private to Captain.

Instructor of English, Yale University, 1942; Research Instructor, 1946–47; Assistant Professor, 1947–51; Associate Professor, 1951–56; Professor, 1956–66; George E. Bodman Professor of English, 1966–67, 1970–74; Director of Graduate Studies in English, 1953–57, 1958–63, 1967, 1973; Associate Chairman of the Department of English, 1970–71; Acting Master of Saybrook College, 1963–64. Professor of English, Columbia University, 1967–70; Adjunct Professor, 1964–65, 1970–71; Chairman, Committee on Graduate Studies, 1970–71. Visiting Professor, Yale University, 1967–68, 1969–70. Visiting Professor, University College, London, 1951–52; Visiting Professor, King's College, London, 1971–72; Visiting Professor, University of Michigan, 1973–74. Professor of English, Indiana University, 1974–76; Distinguished Professor of English, 1976–80; Emeritus, 1980 – .

Phi Beta Kappa (Hon.), Harvard, 1957.

Litt.D. (Hon.), Lehigh University, 1980.

Mary Flexner Lectures, Bryn Mawr College, 1981.

Fellowships: Fellow of the Medieval Academy of America, elected 1973; Corresponding Fellow of the British Academy, elected 1974; Fellow of the American Academy of Arts and Sciences, elected 1975; Guggenheim Fellow, 1951–52, 1977–78; Director of Summer Seminars, National Endowment for the Humanities, 1977, 1980, on the subjects of Chaucer and Shakespeare.

President, Connecticut Academy of Arts and Sciences, 1966–67;

President, the New Chaucer Society, 1978–80; Vice-President and President, the Medieval Academy, 1979–81.

The Haskins Medal of the Medieval Academy (with George Kane), 1978, for *Piers Plowman: The B Version*.

Publications

Books

Beowulf: A Translation. New York, 1966.

Beowulf: A Translation. In *Beowulf: A Norton Critical Anthology*. Edited by J. Tuso. New York, 1975. Also in *The Norton Anthology of English Literature*. Rev. ed., 1968; 3d ed., 1974; 4th ed., 1979.

Chaucer's Poetry: An Anthology for the Modern Reader. New York, 1958. 2d ed., enl., 1975.

Essays and Studies (editor). London, 1976.

Piers Plowman: The C-Text and Its Poet. New Haven, Conn., 1949. 2d ed., 1966.

Speaking of Chaucer. London, 1970, paperback, 1972. Containing four new and eight reprinted essays, the latter asterisked under "Articles" below.

(With George Kane) *Piers Plowman: The B Version*. London, 1975.

Articles

"Adventures with the Adversative Conjunction in the General Prologue to the *Canterbury Tales*; or, What's Before the But?" In M. Benskin and M. L. Samuels, eds. *So meny people longages and tonges*. Edinburgh, 1981. Pp. 355–66.

"Arcite's Injury." In E. G. Stanley and D. Gray, eds. *Festschrift for Norman Davis*. Oxford, 1982.

"A Biblical Allusion in *Troilus and Criseyde*." *MLN* 76 (1961):4–5.

"Briseis, Briseida, Criseyde, Cresseid, Cressid: Progress of a Heroine." In E. Vasta and Z. Thundy, eds. *Chaucerian Problems and Perspectives*. Notre Dame, Ind., 1979. Pp. 3–12.

*"Chaucer, *Canterbury Tales*, D117: A Critical Edition." *Speculum* 40 (1965):626–33.

"Chaucer and the Elusion of Clarity." *E&S* 25 (1972):23–44.

"Chaucer in the Twentieth Century." *Studies in the Age of Chaucer* 2 (1980):7–13.

*"Chaucer the Pilgrim." *PMLA* 69 (1954):928–36. Reprinted in C. Owen, ed. *Discussions of the Canterbury Tales.* Boston, 1961. Also in R. Schoeck and J. Taylor, eds. *Chaucer Criticism: The Canterbury Tales.* Notre Dame, Ind., 1960.

"Chaucer's Final -e." *PMLA* 63 (1948):1101–24; 64 (1949):609.

"Chaucer's *Miller's Tale,* A3583–6." *MLN* 69 (1954):310–14.

"Chaucer's Three 'P's': Pandarus, Pardoner, and Poet." *MQR* 14 (1975):282–301.

"Cressid False, Criseyde Untrue." In G. Lord and M. Mack, eds. *Poetical Traditions of the English Renaissance.* New Haven, Conn., 1982. Pp. 67–83.

"Designing a Camel; or, Generalizing the Middle Ages." *TSL* 22 (1977):1–16.

*"The Ending of Chaucer's *Troilus.*" In A. Brown and P. Foote, eds. *Early English and Norse Studies.* London, 1963. Pp. 26–45. Reprinted in S. Barney, ed. *Chaucer's Troilus.* Hamden, Conn., 1980.

Essay on *Troilus and Criseyde,* from *Chaucer's Poetry: An Anthology for the Modern Reader.* Reprinted in J. A. Burrow, ed. *Geoffrey Chaucer.* Baltimore, Md., 1969.

"Gallic Flies in Chaucer's English Wordweb." In Donald M. Rose, ed. *New Perspectives in Chaucer Criticism.* Norman, 1982. Pp. 193–202.

"The Grammar of Book's Speech in Piers Plowman." In *Studies in Language and Literature in Honor of Margaret Schlauch.* Warsaw, 1966. Pp. 103–109. Reprinted in R. J. Blanch, ed. *Style and Symbolism in Piers Plowman.* Knoxville, Tenn., 1969.

Headnote on *Sir Gawain and the Green Knight,* from *The Norton Anthology of English Literature.* Reprinted in D. Fox, ed. *Sir Gawain and the Green Knight.* Englewood Cliffs, N.J., 1968.

*"Idiom of Popular Poetry in the *Miller's Tale.*" In A. S. Downer, ed. *English Institute Essays, 1950.* New York, 1951. Pp. 116–40. Reprinted in W. K. Wimsatt, ed. *Explication as Criticism: Selected Papers from the English Institute, 1941–1952.* New York, 1963. Also in H. Newstead, ed. *Chaucer and His Contemporaries.* New York, 1968.

"Langland and Some Scriptural Quotations." In L. Benson and S.

Wenzel, eds. *The Wisdom of Poetry: Essays in Early English Literature in Honor of Morton Bloomfield.* Kalamazoo, Mich., 1982. Pp. 67–72.

"Langland to Spenser." In W. H. Auden and N. H. Pearson, eds. *Poets of the English Language.* New York, 1950. Vol. 1, texts and glossing.

"Malory and the Stanzaic Le Morte Arthur." *SP* 47 (1950):460–72.

"The Manuscripts of Chaucer's Work and Their Use." In Derek Brewer, ed. *Writers and Their Background: Geoffrey Chaucer.* London, 1975. Pp. 85–108.

"The Middle Ages." In *The Norton Anthology of English Literature.* Vol. 1. New York, 1962. Pp. 1–378. Rev. ed., 1968, pp. 1–378; 3d ed., 1974, pp. 1–473; 4th ed., 1979, pp. 1–416.

"Middle English Seint, Seinte." *SN* 21 (1949):222–30.

"MSS R and F in the B-Tradition of *Piers Plowman.*" *Transactions of the Connecticut Academy of Arts and Sciences* 39 (1955):177–212.

*"The Myth of Courtly Love." *Ventures* 5 (1965):16–23.

"The Ordering of the *Canterbury Tales.*" In J. Mandel and B. Rosenburg, eds. *Medieval Literature and Folklore Studies.* New Brunswick, N.J., 1970. Pp. 199–204.

"Oysters Forsooth: Two Readings in Pearl." *NM* 63 (1972):75–82.

*"Patristic Exegesis in the Criticism of Medieval Literature: The Opposition." In D. Bethurum, ed. *Critical Approaches of Medieval Literature: Selected Papers from the English Institute, 1958–59.* New York, 1960. Pp. 1–26. Reprinted in W. K. Wimsatt, ed. *Literary Criticism: Idea and Act.* Berkeley, Calif., 1974.

"*Piers Plowman*: Textual Comparison and the Question of Authorship." In A. Esch, ed. *Chaucer und Seine Zeit: Symposium für Walter F. Schirmer.* Tübingen, 1966. Pp. 241–47.

"The Poet: Biographical Material," from *Piers Plowman: The C-Text and Its Poet.* Reprinted in E. Vasta, ed. *Interpretations of* Piers Plowman. Notre Dame, Ind., 1968.

*"The Psychology of Editors of Middle English Texts." In I. Cellini and G. Melchiori, eds. *English Studies Today.* Vol. 4. Rome, 1966. Pp. 45–62.

"Sexual Frustration in Chaucer." *Florilegium* 3 (1981). Pp. 256–58.

"Some Readings in the *Canterbury Tales.*" In J. B. Bessinger and R.

Raymo, eds. *Medieval Studies in Honor of Lillian Herlands Horn-stein*. New York, 1976. Pp. 99–110.

"The Texts of *Piers Plowman*: Scribes and Poets." *MP* 50 (1953): 269–73.

"Venus and the Mother of Romulus: *The Parliament of Fowls* and the *Pervigilium Veneris*." *ChauR* 14 (1980):313–18.

"A Vision of Will." *Speculum* 56 (1981):707–9.

Reviews

Paull F. Baum. *Chaucer's Verse*. In *Speculum* 39 (1964):112–14.

J. A. W. Bennett. *Chaucer at Oxford and at Cambridge*. In *MLR* 71 (1976):626–27.

– – –. *Chaucer's Book of Fame: An Exposition of* The House of Fame. In *N&Q*, April, 1969, pp. 147–48.

– – –, ed., *Essays on Malory*; R. S. Loomis, *The Development of Arthurian Romance*; and William Matthews, *The Tragedy of Arthur: A Study of the Alliterative "Morte Arthure."* In *TLS*, November 21, 1963, p. 952.

David Bevington, ed. *The Macro Plays*. In *TLS*, May 16, 1975, p. 542.

Nevill Coghill. *Chaucer's* Canterbury Tales: *A New Translation*. In *YCGL* 2 (1953):78–81.

R. T. Davies, ed., *Sir Thomas Malory: King Arthur and His Knights*; William Matthews, *The Ill-framed Knight*; and Beram Saklatvala, *Arthur: Roman Britain's Last Champion*. In *TLS*, November 30, 1967, p. 1126.

Norman Davis and C. L. Wrenn, eds. *English and Medieval Studies Presented to J. R. R. Tolkien on the Occasion of His Seventieth Birthday*. In *N&Q*, October, 1963, pp. 388–89.

Sister Rose Bernard Donna. *Depair and Hope: A Study in Langland and Augustine*. In *MLN* 68 (1953):141–42.

John Gardner. *The Life and Times of Chaucer* and *The Poetry of Chaucer*. In *YR*, Autumn, 1977, pp. 100–106.

P. M. Kean. *Chaucer and the Making of English Poetry*. In *ELN* 12 (1974):126–28.

Charles Moorman. *Editing the Middle English Manuscript*. In *MP* 77 (1979):84–86.

Charles Muscatine. *Poetry and Crisis in the Age of Chaucer*. In CL 25 (1973):262–63.

Rossell H. Robbins, ed. *Historical Poems of the XIVth and XVth Centuries*. In MP 60 (1962):56–58.

Ian Robinson. *Chaucer and the English Tradition*. In MP 71 (1974): 513–15.

Beryl Rowland, ed. *Chaucer and Middle English Studies*. In TLS, February 28, 1975, p. 212.

A. C. Spearing. *Medieval Dream Poetry*. In *Speculum* 54 (1979): 191–93.

Ann Thompson. *Shakespeare's Chaucer*. In RenQ 33 (1980):284–86.

Index of Proper Names

Tabula Gratulatoria of Individuals

Judith Anderson
Morton Bloomfield
Marie Borroff
Mary Carruthers
Robert Hanning
Constance B. Hieatt
Edward B. Irving, Jr.
George Kane

Elizabeth Kirk
John C. Pope
George Russell
E. G. Stanley
Paul Strohm
Carolynn Van Dyke
Hope Weissman